INVENTING CHRISTIC JESUSES

Inventing Christic Jesuses

Rules and Warrants for Theology

VOLUME 1: METHOD

Charles A. Wilson

CASCADE *Books* · Eugene, Oregon

INVENTING CHRISTIC JESUSES
Rules and Warrants for Theology
Volume 1: Method

Copyright © 2017 Charles A. Wilson. All rights reserved. Except for brief quotations in critical publications or reviews, no part of this book may be reproduced in any manner without prior written permission from the publisher. Write: Permissions, Wipf and Stock Publishers, 199 W. 8th Ave., Suite 3, Eugene, OR 97401.

Cascade Books
An Imprint of Wipf and Stock Publishers
199 W. 8th Ave., Suite 3
Eugene, OR 97401

www.wipfandstock.com

PAPERBACK ISBN: 978-1-5326-3144-3
HARDCOVER ISBN: 978-1-5326-3146-7
EBOOK ISBN: 978-1-5326-3145-0

Cataloging-in-Publication data:

Names: Wilson, Charles A. (Charles Alan), 1947–, author.
Title: Inventing christic Jesuses : rules and warrants for theology, vol. 1: Method.
Description: Eugene, OR: Cascade Books | Includes bibliographical references.
Identifiers: ISBN: 978-1-5326-3144-3 (PAPERBACK) | ISBN: 978-1-5326-3146-7 (HARDCOVER) | ISBN: 978-1-5326-3145-0 (EBOOK).
Subjects: LCSH: Jesus Christ—Historicity | Bible. Gospels—Criticism, interpretation, etc. | Jesus Christ—Person and offices.
Classification: BT303.2 W55 2017 (print) | BT303.2 (ebook).

Manufactured in the U.S.A.   NOVEMBER 6, 2017

Contents

Preface | vii

1. Orientation to the Inquiry | 1

2. The Terms of the Conversation | 38

3. Warrants: Why Should Theology Care about Historical Jesuses? | 101

4. Retrojection | 149

5. Case Study in Retrojection: The Invention of Jesus-Sage | 204

Appendix: Rules and Warrants Summary | 261

Bibliography | 273

Preface

Perhaps it is foolish to bother with another book about Jesus. There have been so many. Each one travels over the same territory. Yet the book covers promise new discoveries, new methods, new sources that reveal the real Jesus for the first time. Today after a thirty-year burst of historical research on Jesus of Nazareth, we have dozens of new tomes about Jesus. Each spins the historical Jesus in a different way. What new things can historians find to say and how is it that they can say such different things about the same guy?

We outsiders to the guild of Jesus historians wonder what prompted the sudden interest in Jesus. If we read through a few volumes, we will be bewildered by the many different, even incommensurable, new images of Jesus presented by the historians. How should we make sense of the new Jesuses? Indeed, what theologies should we produce, what sermons should we preach, in light of the new research? Today, the *Third Quest* for the historical Jesus seems to be over and done: after all, the Jesus historians have written their big books, the critics have had time to complain, revise, and dismiss their proposals, and a mountain of popular works has tantalized lay people with new Jesuses. But surprisingly, so far, theologians have had little to say about contemporary Jesus research. Perhaps they, like me, have not known what to do with the thousands and thousands of pages of new studies.

This book, the first of two, aims to begin theology's conversation with Jesus research in an ordered, not reactive, way. It charts how theologians may deploy Jesus research in a revisionist christology. As it rehearses the theological issues at stake in Jesus research and steps through the maze of contemporary studies, it proposes a systematic way for theology to employ the threatening and encouraging signals from the historians of Jesus. As a work of revisionist theology, it addresses theologians interested in historical research, Bible scholars with theological interests, sermon-writing pastors, and curious lay people who may have heard of controversial proposals about the figure of Jesus. The book is a how-to manual for theologians and others who may wish to incorporate a quested component in their christological reflections.

I wish to thank many people for support in this long project. I see first the faces of my growing family (Barbara, Jessica, Gregor, Peter, Joshua, Kristin, Zachary, Eleanor, Liam, Brynn, and Emma) and then I think of all the students, old friends, and colleagues who have wondered what would become of my study of Jesus research. Most immediately, I thank my colleagues of the Theology and Ethics Colloquy—Terence J. Martin, Richard B. Miller, Douglas Ottati, and William Schweiker—for their years of trenchant criticism and good fun. I wish also to thank Barbara S. Wilson for her intense editorial work and Provost Marci Sortor of St. Olaf College for her generous financial support of the project.

1

Orientation to the Inquiry

A. Introduction

This meta-study attempts to make theological sense of the bewildering world of Jesus scholarship. It will offer a primer on the deployment of a historical Jesus[1] in christology. The anticipated audience is of theologians and other serious Christian interpreters who may not have patience for the explosion of big books on Jesus but who may want some signposts through the research. The book aims to describe the terrain theology might traverse if its christology were to take seriously historical research on Jesus of Nazareth. How shall it proceed? Why should it proceed at all? What protocol should it set, what rules and warrants for itself, so far as it were to draw upon the historians' work on Jesus? Specifically, the study will sketch the formal elements present in a christology that attends properly and critically to modern study of Jesus of Nazareth, done by professional historians. Materially, it will draw heavily upon contemporary Jesus research, the historical work of the last thirty years or so, often called the *Third Quest* for the historical Jesus.[2] This burst of intense research, now seemingly ended, proposes some sweeping methodological developments and a possible paradigm shift; indeed, the first order assessments of the accomplishments of this phase for

---

1. We will use the common term in the quest, *historical Jesus,* and mean by it what Leander Keck calls "the probable Jesus" or "the historically recovered Jesus." See: Keck, *Who Is Jesus?*, 20, 35. I often use the term "the historian's Jesus" to indicate the Jesus constructed by historians.

2. N. T. Wright's term in Neill and Wright, *The Interpretation of the New Testament*, 379–403, and Wright, "Quest for the Historical Jesus," 796–802. The term itself is controversial, but convenient for naming the phase of Jesus research beginning around 1979 with the important study of Meyer, *The Aims of Jesus.* I will use the term without judging what characteristics obtain in this phase of Jesus research.

history writing have already begun to appear. This study aims to go beyond the accomplishments and failures of the Third Quest to an assessment of the usefulness of contemporary Jesus research for theology: to what extent can such research contribute to a christology? Our main interest will be to employ contemporary Jesus research more generally to think through how theology can use historical research on Jesus.

How shall theology deploy contemporary Jesus research? How indeed? So far, when some theologians have begun to analyze the achievement of contemporary Jesus research, they have employed analogies to earlier paradigms in Jesus research: for instance, what is the theological consequence of the shift to the *liberal* Jesuses of the nineteenth century or of the subsequent shift to the *apocalyptic* Jesus of the twentieth century? To be sure, the current interest in the historical Jesus may prove to be short-lived and historically insignificant, and it is possible that it is much historical energy without christological usefulness at all. But it is equally possible that contemporary Jesus research is inventing Jesuses for a forthcoming new era of christology, rather in the way that Johannes Weiss and Albert Schweitzer formulated the twentieth-century apocalyptic prophet Jesus.[3] Of course, when they proposed their *new* Jesus at the end of the nineteenth century, that Jesus threatened established (liberal) christologies. Recall that Johannes Weiss figured out that the *real*, historical Jesus was a prophet of the end of time, but at the same time Weiss could not find anything about that prophet that was christologically interesting. After all, how could theology use a sack-cloth-and-ashes world-denier, whom history had refuted? Understandably, Weiss retreated dogmatically into a liberal christology.[4] And Schweitzer, thematizing the self-reflexive character of Jesus research for the first time,[5] could be confident that he had glimpsed the *real* Jesus only when he stood before the apocalyptic oddball.[6] In Schweitzer's vision, only the ever-alien prophet of the end of time resisted the domestication endemic to Jesus research.[7]

Indeed, Schweitzer made a virtue of necessity by hinting at a permanent christological opportunity: he was confident that he had found the real Jesus when he discovered the one who was so weird and otherworldly that

---

3. Schweitzer, *The Quest for the Historical Jesus*, 2001 edition, especially 330–47; Weiss, *Jesus' Proclamation*.

4. See ibid.,133–35.

5. See Schweitzer's famous words, *The Quest for the Historical Jesus*, 2001 edition, 478.

6. Schweitzer, *The Quest for the Historical Jesus*, 2001 edition, 480–87.

7. In this study we will interpret the domesticating character of Jesus research through a theory about the retrojection of contemporary value onto Jesus.

he could stubbornly resist being tamed by Jesus researchers' self-projects.[8] Schweitzer, in fact, imagined such an untamed Jesus could revitalize a decadent Europe.[9] Despite this final, (negatively) normative christological hint, Schweitzer did not pursue a christology in dialogue with the apocalyptic wild man. Instead he made a mystical turn, and theologically "retreated to Africa" and formulated an early, post-Christian theology. Like Weiss, he too could not discover anything christologically promising in an apocalyptic Jesus. The story might have ended there, had twentieth-century theologians not recognized a wealth of christological possibilities inspired by Schweitzer's discovery of the *alien criterion*.[10]

In a sense, by translating the apocalyptic into *an analogous, but universalizable, christic principle of critique*, twentieth-century theologians followed the formal lead of Schweitzer's christological hint, but without the material retreat of Weiss and Schweitzer. The prophet of endgame could be translated into a permanent critical cipher against legitimating self-aggrandizement, and the theologies of the century invented a host of critical tasks for a historical Jesus. One day he would be the prophet of crisis, or, again, the one who called people to existential decision; on a later day he would become the one who enacted proleptic hope, and the next he would author various projects of liberation, and so on. It was always the apocalyptic prophet behind those critical Christs. If one were to compare, say, Bultmann's kerygmatic Christ, suitably demythologized of Jesus' eschatology, with a typical liberationist's political Jesus, or with virtually any major twentieth-century Christ, the difference among them amounted to a difference in hermeneutical self-consciousness, not in their confidence that they had translated the real Jesus into an appropriately modern form. Some were hermeneutically less circumspect and some had a deeper sense of the interpreter's role in converting the apocalyptic prophet into something

---

8. Note how strange and elusive is Schweitzer's position. It asserts by way of making a negation, or, its affirmation is founded in the negative, as in the style of *classic apophatic theology*. The peculiarity of Schweitzer's christological hint will be a clue to the argument that lies ahead of us, namely, that in a proper christological deployment of Jesus research relatively little is possible by way of a direct assertion (the cataphatic approach), whereas the apophatic approach promises more. In Schweitzer's reading, every quest faces the final either/or: to see Jesus as a "thorough-going apocalypticist" or become skeptical about finding a historical Jesus (the "thorough-going skepticism" of Wrede). In contemporary research N. T. Wright poses the same choice: every Jesus historian must decide to walk with Schweitzer (Wright's choice) or with Wrede (as in many Jesus Seminar scholars): Wright, *Jesus and the Victory*, 20.

9. See Weaver, *The Historical Jesus*, 39.

10. The term I use to identify Schweitzer's discovery, that the real Jesus is the one so odd or offensive that it could not be the historian's invention.

christologically useful. But all focused on the apocalyptic figure with which they had to deal christologically.

Since the emergence of modern historical work on Jesus, the reigning Jesus paradigm has lived in dialogue with christologies of the era. The six or eight types of twentieth-century christologies, for instance, developed in direct or indirect dialogue with the apocalyptic paradigm: applications, extensions, modifications, even repudiations of the apocalyptic foundation. As such, these christologies can be termed christologies *of* the apocalyptic Jesus. For some the *of* is a possessive genitive, as if they were direct representations of Jesus' own self-consciousness and sense of mission; others took the preposition more as an objective genitive: namely, as the sort of Christs generated by an era in which the apocalyptic paradigm dominated historical research on Jesus. Interestingly, even twentieth-century christologies that claim to be christologically immune to or indifferent to historical research on Jesus seem to have in mind exactly the apocalyptic prophet over-against whom they would be indifferent or immune. Arguably, had historians *discovered* a more palatable Jesus in their historical work, theologians hostile to questing might have warmed up to the historical Jesus. Had historians discovered, for instance, a historical Jesus who matched the narratives of the gospels, or a supernaturalist one similar to that of popular piety, or to the metaphysical constructions of the creeds and councils (whatever this might mean historically), would so many theologians be hostile to questing? I suspect not. If this suspicion is true, it indicates the extent to which the reigning apocalyptic paradigm dominated twentieth-century christology, even where questing had been categorically rejected.

After a hundred years contemporary Jesus research seems to have moved away from the "eschatological consensus,"[11] that is, away from the certainty that Weiss and Schweitzer got it right about Jesus. Whether we are headed to a new paradigm, say, to a sapiential one, is unclear yet.[12] Some reject the older paradigm completely (i.e., Borg[13]), some reassert it (i.e., Meier[14]), while others save the apocalyptic but so attenuate the prophet's

---

11. Marcus J. Borg's phrase: *Jesus in Contemporary*, 1. For a summary of many of the difficulties conceiving of Jesus as an apocalyptic prophet, see Patterson, *The God of Jesus*, 164, and Mack, *The Lost Gospel*, 134–36. Patterson announces the end of theologies informed by the apocalyptic paradigm, ibid., 177.

12. Despite the announcement of a new paradigm by Borg, *Jesus in Contemporary*, 4; Mack, *The Lost Gospel*, 31; and others. Even a scholar like Ben Witherington III, who is a theological conservative, has turned to the sapiential paradigm: Witherington, *Jesus the Sage*.

13. Borg, *Jesus in Contemporary*, 13.

14. Meier, *A Marginal Jew*, II, 237.

eschatology that it is not clear Schweitzer would recognize it (i.e., Wright[15]). In any case, in this era of the quest, the new Jesus researchers have been relatively gun-shy about claiming christological consequences for their emerging Jesuses. Some explicitly reject interest in a theological discussion generated by their historical researches (i.e., Sanders[16]); others seem to embrace some theological applications, either of a negative[17] or positive[18] sort, even as they insist that their historical work cannot be colored by any theological agenda. Undoubtedly, one of the most characteristic features of the contemporary Jesus research is its degree of methodological self-consciousness: questers today know well the lesson of Schweitzer concerning self-retrojections onto the figure of Jesus and go to great pains to guard against theology parading as history.[19] Nonetheless, several important researchers do move from historical reconstructions of Jesus to christological suggestions (again, either negative or positive ones), as if they believe Jesus research can bear on christological construction. And further, the whole era of research on Jesus, collectively known as the Third Quest, seems to explode with tantalizing christological hints; these opportunities, whether foreseen or unforeseen by the researchers themselves, beg to be drawn out.

This book will consider the christological opportunities of this new historical research. So far, the christological possibilities of recent Jesus research have only been announced and then usually with an *accent on the negative impact of historical findings on traditional christology*. Indeed, as yet the discussions have mostly been expressions of attack and regret from the right end of the spectrum. Most of the action has been too-ready applications of historical insight unto traditional christologies, while most of the reflection has been theological hand-wringing from those who believe that questing altogether or the current kind of questing are inherently

---

15. Today the theologically conservative option usually metaphorizes the coming of the Kingdom away from a literal apocalypse, and it then scrambles to rescue a Jesus ethic from end time—surely Jesus said something of moral value for an enduring world! See the metaphorizing of the Kingdom theme in Wright, *Jesus and the Victory*, 96, 198–243. Here we do not need to ascertain whether Wright and others are right about apocalyptic. The fact that Wright works so hard to insist that apocalyptic is *not* about the end of time supports a developing argument here: most Jesus scholars today start with a view that apocalyptic is world-negating: see ibid., 45.

16. See Sanders, *The Historical Figure*, 8, for instance.

17. Robert M. Funk is the most pronounced example in recent scholarship: *Honest to Jesus*.

18. For example, Witherington, *The Christology of Jesus*.

19. John Dominic Crossan's famous quote: "It is impossible to avoid the suspicion that historical Jesus research is a very safe place to do theology and call it history, to do autobiography and call it biography": Crossan, *The Historical Jesus*, xxviii.

destructive of christology. Here we shall attempt to move away from this polarized theological climate and to avoid unmediated christological applications of historical insights. The goals are: 1. to avoid the one-for-one application of a Jesus fact (so to speak) to a Christ of faith; and 2. to identify points in the historical Jesuses that theology can take as warranted recommendations to be incorporated into a comprehensive christology. What would those warranted moments look like?

B. Methodological Prolegomena

To proceed in this exercise, we adopt the position that it is *possible* to link historical research on the figure of Jesus to Christian christological activity, that is, that christology can be informed by historical work on Jesus.[20] As such, the project fits within the tradition of revisionist christology (in Ogden's term).[21] Like earlier theological investments in the quest for the historical Jesus, this one joins the ranks of those who see in historical research on Jesus the possibility of revising traditional christology.[22] It aims to ask what a quested christology would look like, but without claiming to write such a christology, without claiming that quested christological reflections ever could substitute for a comprehensive christology,[23] and without claiming that quested christologies are the only Christian or even the best revisionist approaches to christology. Before we begin mapping how christology can use quested materials, we will consider positions denying categorically that a link or "connection"[24] is possible. We will analyze those

---

20. The full warrant for this assumption will appear gradually in the course of the entire argument.

21. See Schubert M. Ogden's statement of program for revisionist christologies in *The Point of Christology*. We are following Ogden in his concern to revise classical theology but will take the revision quite far from his construction.

22. We hope to avoid some of the theological naiveté that characterized early reflections on the quest and, thus, avoid some of the things that bother Ogden, who advocates revisionist christology but not quested christologies. See Ogden, ibid., 15, 66–67. This book is an attempt to sketch how a quested, revisionary christology might look; as such, it shares the revisionary project with Ogden and others, but will be critical both of those on the right wing of Jesus research (who use the methods of the quest essentially to restore or re-secure main moments of the classic christological traditions, i.e., Witherington, Wright, C. Stephen Evans, and so on), and of those on the left wing who imply their Jesuses are directly christic (i.e., Borg, Crossan).

23. Just as revisionists do not think all theology comes out of christology, so also not all christology comes out of Jesus.

24. Vincent Taylor sets up a "connection" between the earthly Jesus and the resurrected Jesus: see Taylor, *The Life and Ministry*, 45–48.

positions and offer a critique of them. A counter case will be signaled here but will be developed gradually in a later chapter on warrants for Christian theological interest in questing. We will identify what we can learn from the anti-quest criticism of questing. These *lessons from the critiques of the quest we will convert into cautions and critical checks that support the building of a quested christology.*

For now we need not settle on an exact relationship between christology and historical research, or even on a single possible relationship, but we do need to move beyond those views that out of hand reject any possible positive relationship between questing and christology. Views that *insulate* christology from historical research or ones that are hostile to it are problematic, not because they reject per se historical research on the figure of Jesus. After all, Christian christologies have worked just fine throughout most of Christian history without the quest for Jesus; in addition, there continue to be good Christian christologies that do not converse with historical research.[25] Consequently, it is certainly possible to do a quality christology without Jesus research. Nonetheless, we question the wisdom of academic theologies today which reject questing in an era when historically conscious scholarship is possible and, indeed, is a fact in our midst.[26] Indeed, we argue that the rejection of questing in some theologies is unwise[27] and too often represents problematic decisions about methods and warrants in theology more generally. Quested christologies, we suggest, offer some powerful advantages to theology, especially for certain of its audiences.

C. The Insulated Position: The Heritage of Herrmann and Kähler

We speak of *insulated* positions as theological views that react against the quest for the historical Jesus.[28] The true *insulated type is a theological position*, not a historical one. A historical objection to questing is simpler and does not risk much: it articulates the agnostic point that we do not have suitable sources for writing history about Jesus and that the quest consequently

---

25. See the section on realizing Jesus below.

26. It is difficult to understand a religion that, wishing to be taken seriously today, operates with a theology that rejects historical work on its founder figure.

27. Carlston notes that people are already making historical judgments about Jesus and the only question is whether they make good ones: Carlston, "Prologue," in Chilton and Evans, eds., *Studying the Historical*, 5.

28. The use of the "insulated" category presupposes the criticism we will set out below.

will fail.[29] But like every historical judgment about Jesus, the agnostic position usually gets messed up with theological views, since too often in the history of the quest, theological concerns have been hidden in historical judgments. More so, advocates of the agnostic position frequently claim to know more about Jesus than their position warrants.[30] *In its purity the theological position argues that faith does not need, does not want, should not crave to have, historians' knowledge about the figure of Jesus.* The position usually gets identified with the figure of Martin Kähler who gave it to theology, once he and Wilhelm Herrmann invented a type of reaction to the quests of the nineteenth century.

Herrmann gets less attention in the production of the insulated reaction to the quest for the historical Jesus, but he is a full ten years ahead of Kähler. His response to historical study of the life of Jesus sprawled within a comprehensive Ritschlian theology. We know that Herrmann generally valued the liberal attention to historical research on Christian origins but that he was suspicious of applying to faith relative historical claims about the life of Jesus, as if historical facts could establish (or derail) the truth of faith. Such facts do not persuade unbelievers, nor do they discourage (or encourage) the faithful, since faith has a different foundation, Herrmann claimed.[31] Faith is not ahistorical but it is founded on a particular and different foundation, on the experience of faith by the redeeming action of Jesus: when God lifts humans into communion.[32] The faithful enter a new inner life and, simultaneously, come to view scripture differently, as an effect of the personal life of Jesus in history. Such a view of scripture is rather far from that of the new historians' knowledge of Jesus.[33] The impact of that inner life is clear and indisputable, independent of the details, and is preserved in the picture of it saved permanently in the church's scripture.[34] Herrmann therefore can conclude that the real life of faith proceeds apart from historians' research.

---

29. Luke Johnson, *The Real Jesus*, 103. It is interesting that Johnson's theological objection to questing always leads with the historical agnostic point: see ibid., 167.

30. In the former mistake, scholars with disguised theological views express them in historical judgments; in the latter mistake, historians and theologians move from a descriptive don't-know position to a can't-know position (a metaphysical claim) or a view that agnosticism means that such and such is known not to be. Typically, agnosticism then becomes the historical denial of traditional christological positions and ends in a claim thereby to know quite a lot about Jesus.

31. Herrmann, *The Communion of the Christian*, 17.

32. Ibid., 42.

33. Ibid., 60.

34. Ibid., 73–75.

Martin Kähler also recognized that winds of historical judgment blow from a different source from those of faith, and if people forget the distinction, historical criticism could threaten faith and faith's christological foundations. He sought an "invulnerable area"[35] for faith against historicistic erosion in the biblical-critical era. Understandably, Kähler was impressed by the negative impact of historical research on christology and just as impressed with the failure of various early defenses against that impact. Consequently, Kähler sought a position, like that of Herrmann, which did not swing in the winds of historical research. He spoke of the object of faith as the "living Christ" and as the "real Christ" who is hidden by "the historical Jesus of modern authors."[36] The historical project of the quest is doomed to fail—the agnostic point—but, were it even to succeed as history writing, it would be useless, or worse, for the life of faith. Why? Because the analogical procedure of historical reasoning *completes* the dot-to-dot memories of Jesus in the gospel and draws him as a typicalized human. This Jesus is the construction of some historian whose methods produce an alleged *real* Jesus behind the picturing of the historic Christ in the gospels.

At this point Kähler expresses his deepest suspicions about the historian's project with Jesus: what motive would want to flatten Jesus into like-us?; why would we trust historians' reconstructions by modern scientific methods instead of the testimony of the church to the decisive influence of Jesus on his disciples?; why would faith honor a faulty vision of Jesus abstracted from the Easter experience?; etc. Instead, we should turn to the "biblical picture of Jesus which confronts us in the Bible": "Yet all the biblical portrayals evoke the undeniable impression of the fullest reality, so that one might venture to predict how he might have acted in this or that situation, indeed, even what he might have said. This is why to commune with Jesus one needs nothing more than the biblical presentation."[37] And that impression, "the biblical picture of the Christ," goes back to Jesus himself.[38]

D. The Critique of Insulation

In both of these positions we find reasons to be skeptical of questing, especially so far as anyone imagines a christological payoff from historical

---

35. See the Carl E. Braaten Introduction to Kähler, *The So-Called Historical Jesus*, 10. Elizabeth A. Johnson speaks of the Kählerian appeal to the biblical witness as a "storm-free region": "The Word Was Flesh," in Donnelly, ed., *Jesus*, 148.

36. Kähler, *The So-Called Historical Jesus*, 43.

37. Ibid., 78.

38. Ibid., 87.

research on Jesus. Undoubtedly, much of the opposition to questing was and is a function of the intensely negative results of many efforts in the quest.[39] We also learn of models of faith that are disposed not to be interested in questing. In this writing we are less interested in Kähler's and Herrmann's actual positions and more in their positions as a type of reaction to the quest. We focus on the *insulated type*, not simply to have a foil for an argument, but to underline a logical point: *theology crosses a threshold and steps into a protected room when it decides categorically that it will not entertain historian's insight about Jesus.*[40] So to close the door requires strength beyond the historical, strength that can only come from a meta-historical, metaphysical, or theological point of view.

When historians are properly modest in their claims, they make descriptive-analytical claims, not metaphysical ones, and certainly not theological ones. They rightly adopt a wait-and-see approach towards what is beyond their descriptive ken. By itself, on its own momentum, history writing about Jesus is no enemy of theology,[41] and even a historical agnosticism about the story of Jesus is not anti-christological, unless people are confusing apples and oranges. Closing the christological door to historical research (and opening that door, too) *can never emerge from a historical warrant.* When a theology closes the door to historical research, it stands on a theory of faith impervious to the work of historical research, one that rejects that faith can change under the press of historical research.[42] Because it judges any faith that changes to be wrong-headed, it closes itself within the room with a kind of methodological stubbornness.[43] *In that room only faith gives birth to faith, to faith's facts, to faith's texts, to faith's icons.*[44] All of those

---

39. One wonders if the anti-quest position would have had any power, had the quest been discovering all kinds of support for Christian claims. *If so, we have more evidence that the anti-quest position presupposes the quest.*

40. Perhaps we should say that theology *remains* in a protected room, given the fact that historical research on Jesus is a relatively new phenomenon. Yet, after the emergence of the quest, every thoughtful theological voice must now choose to step away from the quest.

41. See Meier's judgment that the Kählerian tradition makes an unwarranted apriori judgment that questing is an enemy of faith and theology: *A Marginal Jew*, I, 173.

42. See the early critique of Kähler's attempts to insulate Christian religion from historical criticism in Troeltsch, *Die Bedeutung der Geschichtlichkeit Jesus*, 34.

43. For instance, in a comprehensive critique of the modern Enlightenment hue of questing, Francis Watson recommends that the historical paradigm for knowing needs an "act of epistemic repentance" before it can get at the figure of Jesus: Watson, "*Veritas Christi*," in Gaventa and Hayes, *Seeking the Identity*, 100. See C. Stephen Evans, *The Historical Christ*, 184–202, 331–55, for a similar argument that historians have historical research wrong and that philosophers, theologians, and peoples of faith must correct it.

44. Do Christians really want to say that everything in the Jesus saga is a product

on the other side of the door join a family held together by a willingness to learn from historical research on Jesus, however different may be their choices within historical methodology. And to be sure, some in that historical room include stinging critics of some or all of the work of contemporary Jesus historians.⁴⁵

Today, there are academic followers of Kähler's lead who make many similar points against Third Quest researchers.⁴⁶ Of course, they have behind them another century of insight and new phases of hostility, indifference, and renewed enthusiasm for questing to draw upon. The Kählerian position did pick up a lot of steam through the impulses from the so-called no-quest period and through the controversial claims of some of the recent Third Questers.⁴⁷ How shall we assess the position? It is fairly easy to see the

---

of faith?; so Dunn's question to anti-questers: "Word Was Made Flesh," in Donnelly, ed., *Jesus*, 45. It is interesting to note that Dunn's critique of the anti-questing position comes from the conservative side of the questing spectrum.

45. One thinks of Keck, *A Future for the Historical Jesus*, an important critic of the questing of the New Quest period, and Keck's more recent critique of new Jesus research in *Who Is Jesus?* See also Craig A. Evans, *Fabricating Jesus*. These and related works are powerful exposés of the way that certain Jesus historians (usually on the left wing of the research) retroject value onto Jesus. But these same critics who ridicule some questers' reconstructions of Jesus turn around and construct a Jesus of their own, usually a more traditional or ecclesial one that supposedly avoids the value trap. We are not interested in whether their Jesuses are better than the ones they criticize, but only that they participate in the wider world of historical research on Jesus as it bears on christology. Strictly speaking, we judge them on the side of the questers, differing from other questers in internecine battles over methods and sources to produce a good historical Jesus.

46. One thinks of Luke Johnson, the Gaventa and Hays group, C. Stephen Evans, and others. Johnson brings scant methodological advances to the Herrmann-Kähler positions but a fair amount of insight into the media circus associated with the antics of certain left-wing questers and into the cultural context for some of the Third Quest: see Luke Johnson, *The Real Jesus*, 9, 55. Johnson tries to read contemporary Jesus research as an expression of American culture wars over modernity and, incredibly, he reduces all questing to a modern, secular "attempt to flee the scandal of the gospel" (ibid., 59–61, 166). Evans' book title (*The Historical Christ and the Jesus of Faith*) plays on Kähler's title and indicates something of the aim of his book, namely, to redefine the terms of historical research itself so that the claims of the Jesus saga are historically credible. If the Kählerian position defines faith away from the impact of modern historical study, Evans' reformed epistemological effort defines historical study away from the values of modernity to reclaim the reasonableness of the Jesus saga. The two approaches are flip sides of the same coin and both represent options rejected here. We are neither immunizing faith from the stings of historical research nor attenuating historical study to the point that the guild of historians would not recognize its logic.

47. The no-quest period should be identified as a period of *little* interest in questing, not no interest, since it was primarily scholars in the Bultmannian tradition who gave up on questing. Joachim Jeremias, for one, continued determined and important

virtues of the insulated position. It has, for instance, a deep appreciation for the limits of modern epistemology and for the failures of modern historical method. When questers claim to know more than they can know, when they get scientized and lose a sense for value, when they get into an attack mode and forget to be humble, when they lose their own relativity, historicity, and subjectivity under the fiction of objectivity, they open themselves to justified criticism. Moreover, the insulated position has a fulsome sense that faith must be grounded differently from that of knowledge, that is, in the highest values of the community. To be sure, faith must be defended in its (relative) autonomy against the winds of change and relativity.

How shall we judge the position's opposition to questing, particularly its theological critique? 1. Perhaps the first thing to note about the Kählerian position is that it presupposes the critical position it rejects. That is, the insulated position would never have emerged in theology had scholars not applied historical criticism to the figure of Jesus.[48] It is a negative position, a position of reaction, which, against the outcomes of the quest, rejects the *model of realizing Jesus* embedded in modern historical research. That is, *it realizes Jesus by, among other things, rejecting the realization of Jesus under the modern historical mode and, in reaction, by posing a new mode of realization that has internalized the negation of modernity's historical mode.* The complaint about questing is that scholars are inventing a new thing, the modern historical way of looking at Jesus, which they press onto faith. In reaction, the anti-questers position invents another, new way of realizing Jesus, based on a defensive reasserting of the adequacy of the New Testament pictures. Kähler uses the term *historic* to name its difference from what he and they regard as bare, scientific historical accounting. *The historic stands as different from the historical but only on the shoulders of the historical, since something can be declared historic only in its relation to the historical. Indeed, what is historical about the kerygma becomes historic when someone reacts against modern historical research.* Hence, the insulated position presupposes the very thing it criticizes and wishes to dispense with. Another way of putting the point is this: up front, Kähler rejects the notion that there can be any analogy to Jesus, since Jesus is the alien one who is different in kind and for whom the historian's analogy does not work. But the rejection of analogy presupposes that historians have been comparing Jesus to other founders and have explained him.[49]

---

questing during this same time: see Jeremias, *The Problem of the Historical*.

48. As Allison puts it, "Even the claim that theology and faith should be independent of historical research is itself a response to the challenges that modern historical criticism has bred": Allison, *The Historical Christ*, 15.

49. Barry Henaut judges Kähler's move to be anti-incarnational in theology and as a

We arrive at a new observation. *The historic never was historic until there was a reaction against the modern historical.* The historic is as much a modern invention as the modern patterns of historical research, and is parasitic of the modern-historical. In the case of the figure of Jesus, only under the challenges of the quest do the Kählerians thematize the church's faith as historic.[50] The position we will be developing counters the way of insulation by noting that insulation cannot logically escape modern historical research. More generally, it argues that insulation is not what it advertises: *not the ancient and permanent position of the church's theology, but rather an inverted expression of modernity.*[51] Gerald O'Collins reminds us of the way insulation presupposes the very conditions of the Enlightenment it seeks to flee. That is, it is *"inverse Lessingism,"*[52] in that it takes the Enlightenment's doctrine of reason and finds historical findings wanting because they are contingent and at best probable. And when historical research cannot deliver the necessary, the anti-questers walk away from the entire project into a supposedly safe haven.

2. Next, we note that the insulated position tends to fix on the negative-critical impact of historical study on traditional christological and theological positions. There are good reasons, of course, why this negative aspect of questing gets the notice. After all, many of the early and some recent questers have gleefully attacked the faith by applying their Jesuses directly to traditional christology. It has been as if the historians had found new Christs within the historical Jesuses, which they would happily substitute for the ecclesiastical Christs.[53] Many questers have advertised their historical Jesuses as negatively christic, that is, as having the direct power to undermine aspects of the ecclesiastical Christs. Naturally, critics of questing have noticed the destructive power of the new Jesuses and have not much

---

closing down of history as historiography, all under a christological apriori in: Henaut, "'Historical Jesus,'" in Arnal and Desjardins, eds., *Whose Historical*, 243–44.

50. In my reading, Johnson is quite right that we have in questing a genuine pattern typical of modernity. He calls it the *history challenging faith* pattern in his defense of the insulated position: Luke Johnson, *The Real Jesus*, 50–56. The term itself demonstrates my point, that the critics of the quest tend to fix on the negative-critical aspect of questing. For Johnson the quest always seems to represent a challenge, not an opportunity, for traditional christology.

51. A position informed by Hans W. Frei's notion of *realism* in Frei, *The Eclipse of Biblical Narrative*, 1–2, 18.

52. O'Collins, *Christology*, 9.

53. A category error, we will argue, but one that religiously conservative interpreters intuit in questers. Note, for instance, the way that Johnson (rightly) sees in Crossan's construction a "theological revisionism" that never intended to let Jesus dwell in the merely historical: Luke Johnson, *The Real Jesus*, 50.

appreciated the virtues, advantages and necessities of questing; often they ignore judicious, moderate, and theologically conservative voices among questers. Instead they counter with a position that walls off traditional christology from attack but use the very methodological assumption of the positions they criticize: namely, that the results of historical research have direct, christic application to the life of faith. After all, if faith truly *is* insulated from historical criticism, there would be no point in criticizing questing or defending faith against it.

The insulated position, typically, is alarmed by the extreme claims of certain questers who overplay their historical hands. Years ago, it was Reimarus, or Strauss, or Schweitzer who spooked the anti-questers. Today it is the likes of Robert Funk and some of the Jesus Seminar folks. When Robert Funk can declare that the purpose of the quest is "to liberate Jesus from the scriptural and creedal and experiential prisons in which we have incarcerated him," or that "It is a good thing that the true historical Jesus should overthrow the Christ of Christian orthodoxy, the Christ of the creeds,"[54] such a historian is making metaphysical and theological claims that far outstretch the bounds of history writing.[55] Consequently, we arrive at **(Quest) Rule 1:** *History as history cannot pose normative christological views (whether negative or positive) without falling into a category error.*[56] With good reason, the anti-quest party says no to such extremes. But, unfortunately, *a categorical rejection of questing does not match the problem it discerns.* Abandoning the quest altogether is as extreme as when questers overplay their hands. Logically, the proper reaction to an over-extended application of insight by method is not to abandon method entirely, but to rein it in and make it judicious.

3. The insulated position presupposes historical criticism.[57] To a large degree, so too it presupposes the agnostic historical position, namely, that

---

54. Funk, *Honest to Jesus*, 20, 300.

55. See Robert B. Stewart's caution to keep our categories clean: "[H]istorians must be certain to handle texts historically, not metaphysically or theologically . . .": Stewart, *The Quest of the Hermeneutical*, 128.

56. History lives in the world of knowledge and of probable cognitive judgments, even when it involves belief in the sense of Hume's doctrine of belief as reasoned, probable assent. Christology certainly is rational discourse, but it works upon existential things, things we trust in or things we take as promises. While in Christian faith, there is always a *faith-that* (fides quae) or objective element, and here a historical belief-that component, the largest scope of faith is a receptive moment, *faith-in* (fides qua).

57. James M. Robinson makes the corroborating point that the original quest ended, not because of Schweitzer's strenuous retrojection critique but because of new developments within New Testament criticism, particularly form criticism's atomistic vision: Robinson, *A New Quest*, 39.

historical research cannot get in the know about Jesus of Nazareth and hence that the quest must fail. The true insulated position, a theological claim, would have scarce persuasive power, were it not the case that informed people recognize how problematic are the sources for knowledge of Jesus and how byzantine and controversial are the methods. But upon inspection we realize that the insulated position actually is an abstraction, not derived from actual historical research, but from a meta-historical decision, since it claims more than a historian ever can know: it knows for certain that we cannot have serious historical knowledge of Jesus. So to close the door on historical knowledge of Jesus is to do so dogmatically from an apriori, abstract position of skepticism.[58] The extreme position of the no-quest period, say, in the form of the famous dictum of Rudolf Bultmann,[59] cannot be articulated as a *historical* judgment. The theological view (usually articulated via Schweitzer's retrojection thesis and the values[60] of the no-quest period) judges beforehand the results of historical research and then dismisses the entire questing project by countering the mistaken extremes of some questers with an inverse position shaped by the same methodological flaws. On the one side, that of the overstepping questers, the historian's Jesus is really the real Christ (against the ecclesiastical ones); on the other side, the one hostile to questing, the historian's Jesus can never touch the real Christ. In both cases people assume that a historian's Jesus can be directly christic (whether in a positive or negative mode).

Because the insulated position claims things historians cannot claim, we see that it is finally *a theory about faith, about the nature of faith*. In effect, it says that faith is of such a different order of generality that it does not intersect with historical reality, as the business of history writing is done by the guild of historians.[61] Of course, advocates can boldly claim that the guild

---

58. The claim that we cannot know about the history of Jesus is itself an apriori claim. As such, it is independent of actual historical work and is surprisingly quite arrogant, since the position presents itself as modest. True historical modesty, however, respects the limits of what we can know and not know: see Patterson, *The God of Jesus*, 261; Luke Johnson, *The Real Jesus*, 131.

59. "I do indeed think that we can now know almost nothing concerning the life and personality of Jesus, since the early Christian sources show no interest in either, are moreover fragmentary, and often legendary; and other sources about Jesus do not exist": Bultmann, *Jesus and the Word*, 8.

60. These include the influence of Kantian epistemology, Kierkegaardian notions of faith, certain existentialist, and other anti-metaphysical developments in philosophy, recovered senses of faith and Melanchthon's style of locating christology within soteriology from the Reformers, and the like.

61. See the views of Gerhard Ebeling, one of the architects of the model of faith presupposed by the no-quest era, and to some extend that of the New Quest: revelation is not a historical datum or a historical event, but an act of faith: Ebeling, *Problems of*

is all wrong about history, that the guild does not understand the nature of history and of history writing.⁶² A simpler response, however, proposes that *the model of faith in the insulated position is theologically problematic, since it defines faith so that incarnation in ordinary history is impossible.*⁶³ But more generally in a historically capable age, can theology really live well with a notion of faith that hides from historical research on Christian origins behind a curtain of protection?

4. As we know, critics of questing use suspicion to reduce the historians' Jesuses to the ideals and values of the researchers and their worlds. A historian's Jesus amounts to a self-reflection-via-Galilee. Not only can we not learn anything about the real Jesus from the historian's Jesus, we cannot escape the subjectivity of the historian. In order to justify their dismissal of questing, they are required to *close off the possibility of new and creative things happening in the writing of history.* Thus, in history writing about Jesus we learn, not about Jesus, but only about ourselves, if anything. In an apriori judgment, the anti-quester decides that the real Jesus cannot emerge from the historian's work on Jesus and thereby negatively manipulates historical results. Such a judgment does not arise finally from history writing but from an ahistorical value. Moreover, it assumes that all questing stands against faith. At this point, one wonders how the anti-questing position could handle the conservative wing of history writing on Jesus. When conservative Jesus scholars do historical work to secure Christian beliefs, the anti-quest position could only complain that they were undermining the privileged view of faith as a leap. To follow the logic here, the anti-quest scholars have to reject historians' support of Christian claims as readily as they do the critical work of Jesus research. Probably, anti-quest scholars would factually embrace supports, but not attacks, from the historical sector, but could not do so without endangering their fundamental value judgment tied to a notion of faith as risk.

5. Critics of questing seem not to have digested the full impact of the collapse of gospel-realism, the view that the outline of a life in the gospel narratives captures what we can say historically about Jesus of Nazareth.⁶⁴

Historicity, 72.

62. In effect, the position of C. Stephen Evans, *The Historical Christ,* 306.

63. Note that C. Stephen Evans's defense of the incarnation narrative as historical requires an abandonment of (faulty) notions of history on the part of the guild of historians and a very Calvinist notion of the work of the Spirit, among other epistemological changes, to transform how we see history. Our position in this book does not require the spiritualization of the work of historians for historical research on Jesus to be theologically useful, and thus is more dialectical and Lutheran in its spirit!

64. It is striking how confident Luke Johnson is in the sense that the four gospels

In the world of New Testament criticism, Wilhelm Wrede's discovery that theological motives shape the story of Mark's gospel meant the end of gospel-realism.⁶⁵ After Wrede, scholars could no longer assume that the main plotlines in the saga about Jesus have to do with history. In his famous 1953 speech, Käsemann declared the end of the good faith that the gospels are mostly reliable.⁶⁶ Of course, sometimes we do need to counter pyrrhonist skepticism about the Jesus saga and point out that there are some genuine historical memories under the theological shaping in the earliest gospel. But here, in the insulated position, we find a pre-Wredean confidence in the rough historicity of the New Testament pictures or of the kerygma. It is as if anti-questers refuse to hear what New Testament critics have been saying since Wrede (i.e., in the atomism of form criticism, in the tendencies of redaction criticism, etc.) about the genesis of the synoptic tradition. How do anti-questers know, but by received trust, that the impressions and pictures of Jesus go back to Jesus?⁶⁷ If the Kählerians are alarmed at what the historians are saying, we should be doubly alarmed by their unwillingness to engage the historians in serious conversation.

If the anti-quest position is unduly optimistic about the realism of the Jesus saga, its optimism is a function of its either/or mindset about method. In its reading, theology either submits to the "narrative control" embodied in the Jesus saga itself or opens to an anarchy of method and capricious result. For Luke Johnson there is no middle ground. The former is clear, unambiguous, ahistorical, descended from heaven, and free of ideological

---

tell basically the same story: that we can discover the basic story, that the basic story is "remarkably consistent," that differences are "superficial," etc.: Johnson, *The Real Jesus*, 107, 157, 166. See the optimism about the historical task in C. Stephen Evans, "Jesus' Sources," in Moser, ed., *Jesus and Philosophy*, 39. Evans takes the historical task to Jesus' self understanding, to Sonship, and to messianism.

65. Indeed, gospel-realism has taken many hits (i.e., the critique of supernaturalism among rationalist interpreters of the nineteenth century and the atomism of form criticism in the twentieth century). Wrede's discovery, among the most conspicuous and devastating, displaced the widely held liberal assumption that there was a historical core in the gospels, particularly in Mark, to be found under layers of accretion. See: Wrede, *The Messianic Secret*. Wrede is particularly important for the quest because of the way that Schweitzer sees his skepticism about gospel-realism (or the historical Jesus) as the only serious alternate to Schweitzer's own "thoroughgoing eschatology." The sense that Wrede represents the skeptical alternative reappears in Wright's contemporary study. It is significant that the conservative Wright remains haunted by Wrede and thinks his own opponents have gone over to the Wredebahn: *Jesus and the Victory*, 28.

66. Käsemann, "The Problem of the Historical Jesus."

67. In short, the insulated position has never faced David Friedrich Strauss' criticism of the effect-to-cause moves of Schleiermacher's christology: Strauss, *The Life of Jesus*, 768–77, especially 772.

definition. The latter is speculative, secular, dangerously modern-Enlightenment, and hostile to the gospel.[68] No wonder he is critical of the quest. But against that view, a critic asks, what grounds the either/or mindset? The technique to save the former is essentializing. Now, most modern critics of questing admit to the unevenness of the given pictures of Jesus in the gospel, an admission that presupposes biblical criticism. But instead of concluding that there are a plurality of different, even incompatible, Jesuses in the New Testament, as questers do, the anti-quest position retreats into the hopeful notion that there is an essential unity to the picturing of Jesus behind the differences.[69]

6. Critics of questing do not take seriously the way that historical methodology generally and methods in the study of Jesus specifically have evolved over the centuries.[70] Against the anti-quest position, we argue that there is no single, fixed historical method and certainly not one framed for all time in the positivist mode of early modernity. *The quest too is not monolithic.*[71] Historiography is ever adapting; it is learning from its mistakes and its trials; it draws back and self-corrects as it learns from critique and from changes in epistemology. Questing for the historical Jesus too has changed dramatically since the days of Reimarus, Strauss, and Schweitzer. Today it does its best to avoid flaws of the early researchers; more importantly, it has learned much from the Herrmann-Kähler tradition and from a generation of no-questers. To be sure, when one reads Robert Funk on Jesus, it is easy to see little progress from Reimarus's day. Still, the best practitioners anticipate the critics' concerns and move ahead with care. The best questers and the most self-reflective of theologians have already learned the risk-to-faith argument from theologians who are inalterably opposed to questing. *In this writing we join ranks with careful questers and revisionist theologians when they honor the insulated position by claiming its concerns as cautions and critical checks on the conduct of a quested christology.*

---

68. See Johnson, *The Real Jesus*, 166.

69. See this compromising position, similar to the old ecclesiastical harmonizing of the gospels, in Johnson, "The Jesus of the Gospels," in Moser, ed., *Jesus and Philosophy*, 70.

70. See the point in Stewart, *The Quest of the Hermeneutical*, 1, where Stewart notes that the newer Jesus research has taken a hermeneutical turn, as older methods of history writing recede.

71. See the problematic assumption that the historical critical paradigm is monolithic in Watson's critique of questing: Watson, "*Veritas Christi*," in Gaventa and Hayes, eds., *Seeking the Identity*, 101.

E. Approaching a Quested Christology: The Search for Historical Opportunities

Behind our approach is a dual insight, namely, that *both questers and anti-questers often overdraw their positions.* Questers cannot escape a "built-in theology,"[72] however much they hustle historical objectivity; and anti-questers cannot escape history and historical research, however much they pray to the Christ. Positively put, the position advocated here proposes **(Theological) Rule 2**, *that theology needs to be extremely suspicious of sweeping claims, both in defense of and in attack on christological claims, in the name of history.* After all, the great lesson of the first two centuries of questing teaches that history and theology are rather distinct enterprises.[73] But the lesson is hard to learn. Historians rarely can resist taking a feature of the historical Jesus as if it had direct christological significance; it is tempting for them to want to *"baptize our theology,"* in Allison's phrase.[74] Even historians who claim no interest in theology, even Jewish or agnostic historians, do not avoid the common trap of questing: the temptation to apply something in the historical Jesus directly to the Christ.[75] Often their applications are negative; but today they can just as easily be in a positive key. Because of the enigma and the charisma associated with Jesus, and because of the history of his effects in our culture, historians seemingly cannot touch him without setting off theological sparks. While that fact may cheer some, revisionist theologians must start with suspicion of all historical applications. **(Theological) Rule 3:** *To apply the results of historical research directly to a theological issue is a category error.* Consequently, theologians must guard against expecting direct christological applications from questing, even when a proposal seems to advance their cause. So too those hostile to Christian faith, like Joseph Hoffmann and G. A. Wells, cannot be allowed to take historical skepticism about a real Jesus into a falsification of Christianity.[76] Such a move overdraws a theological conclusion from historical research and is a category error. That is, *extreme skeptical positions agree*

---

72. Allison's happy phrase: Allison, *The Historical Christ*, 9.

73. The burden of the position here: an emphatic, relative difference which opposes too easy sliding from history to faith/theology and endorses the possibility of an indirect, not direct contribution of history to christology. In other words, *history is important to theology but is not directly christological.*

74. Allison, *The Historical Christ*, 9.

75. Perhaps the classic example is the conclusion of Geza Vermes in *The Religion of Jesus,* where the Jewish Jesus historian cannot resist making direct and reductive christological applications of what he has found about Jesus: Vermes, *The Religion of Jesus,* 208–15.

76. Hoffmann, *Sources of the Jesus Tradition,* 3.

with theological fideism but refuse to realize Jesus according to the pictures in the New Testament.[77]

The failure of the original quest, with its theological naiveté and the inability of subsequent quests to learn how to deal with retrojected value teach theology the following lesson: **(Quest) Rule 4:** *Historical research by itself can never yield a christology or a christological application.*[78] Today, historians usually understand the lesson generally. But still too many cannot resist making particular applications to a theological matter. Even when a historian proposes something about Jesus that begs christological expression, theology must still insist on a wall between a Jesus and a Christ. To be sure, revisionist theologians look for a permeable wall, but not no wall at all. So, when a historian finds something that is evocative, say, of Jesus' inclusive practice, he/she must resist the temptation to apply that practice directly to the Christ and to faith. The historian must resist sermonizing, because even a suggestive item is voiceless until it has been framed and received within a faith community and its discourse. *The mistake rests not simply with historians who stretch their insights into territory beyond the historical; it is also a theological mistake when theologians and others forget that the whole of the faith and practice of the believing community must reconfigure any historical result.* To say it simply, so-called inclusive practice in the ministry of Jesus does not necessarily mean what it means for contemporary faith.[79] Consequently, on the basis of the category concern, theologians should not be too eager to pounce on some tidbit of historical insight. Thus, neither the historian nor the theologian, who is partially dependent on the work of the historian, can be fundamentalistic about what the historians say Jesus said and did. **(Theological) Rule 5:** *Theologians and others must reject the historian's fundamentalism that would apply a fact about Jesus directly to theology or the life of faith.*

Nonetheless, theology and faith should not retreat into a protected kerygmatic christology. **(Theological) Rule 6:** *Theology must hold to a relative interest in questing and deploy the results of the quest in a critical and*

---

77. Typically Hoffmann and Wells argue that there was no one to realize named Jesus. Hoffmann, "On Not Finding," in Hoffmann, ed. *Sources of Tradition*, 4, and Wells, *The Historical Evidence*.

78. Even if some historians sometimes conduct themselves as if their historical results had direct application of some kind to the life of faith. Keck insists that what historians find in Jesus cannot be the content of christology and, thus, what the historians give us is not what we have before the faithful to believe: *Who Is Jesus?*, 38. Yes, but I would say, a Jesus can have a relationality to a Christ.

79. Even to call what Jesus does by the category of *inclusive practice* is to assume a commonality between what the historian sees in Jesus and what we value.

*relative way.*⁸⁰ The use of the word *relative* suggests that theology should not imagine that all of christology is quested or comes out of quested results; such would be the historian's fundamentalism.

Our project then seeks some middle ground between a christology impervious to historical research, on the one side, and a christology expecting christological applications (either negative or positive ones) directly from historical work itself, on the other side. That is, we cannot proceed with the assumption that historical research can prove that Jesus is the Christ, nor that elements of a historian's picture of Jesus can be directly applied to the Christ. The middle ground might be a range of positions which insist that historical research on Jesus can offer something to proper christological deliberations.⁸¹ We shall speak of these offerings as *recommendations* to distinguish them from those in the direct, fundamentalistic approach above.⁸²

In time, we will illustrate some of the recommendations. For now we need to emphasize the point as **(Theological) Rule 7:** *that historical results, including those things that promise recommendations to theology, need to be refounded within a christological environment for them to be christic.* Historical judgments founded in fact must be selected and valued as having christic signification. Their potential must be founded in faith, and actuated in language, symbol, and gesture. They must be received within a community

---

80. Nils Dahl puts the point in the negative: that theology is "relatively uninterested" in the quest: *The Crucified Messiah,* 79–80.

81. For instance, Elizabeth A. Johnson offers a "correlation" model in which history and faith partner in a both/and relationship. Historical facts do not ground faith but when they are received in faith, faith and history can be partners; indeed a historical research can change Christian imagination, transforming memory in a work of the Spirit: "The Word Was Flesh," in Donnelly, ed., *Jesus,* 149–50. I am in sympathy with Johnson's effort, but think *conversation* works better for her theological purpose than correlation. I wish Johnson would pin down the particulars of what is an attractive proposal.

82. At this point in our considerations and in the spirit of a pluralized theological approach, we may suppose that historical research on Jesus could offer useful recommendations in a number of different ways. For instance, in certain contexts some theologians may wish (1) to find *corroboration* in historical research for christological claims; others might seek (2) to *define the parameters* of christological claims through historical work; or others may seek in historical research (3) to establish some *continuity* between Jesus and the Christ, or (4) to *defend* christological claims against criticism, attack or misunderstanding, or (5) to *make an apology* for Christian faith to a certain audience. Still others may want to employ historical evidence negatively: (6) to *criticize* implausible or inappropriate christological formulations, or (7) to *sharpen or select* a viable Christ out of the plurality of historic Christs. Or more modestly, a theologian might employ historical judgments about Jesus (8) to *buttress* certain preconditions for christological claims or (9) to develop possible *entailments* of them. Finally, theologians may wish to work historical research (10) to structure *conditions of possibility* for the reception of christological claims.

of faith (however loosely or narrowly defined[83]) and located within a framed sense for the figure the community understands to be redemptive. Such a Redeemer requires a theory of salvation set into a comprehensive theology. So to draw out the recommending promise of a historical fact is to *realize Jesus* as a Christ. But this realization is possible only upon (**Theological) Rule 8:** *that nothing the historian gives theology is directly christic.*[84] No historical Jesus is christic per se; and no element of a historical Jesus is directly christic. Its christological use is not given but must be worked up, realized. The consequence of our position here is that we must *bypass the fashionable distinction, from the era of the New Quest, between implicit and explicit christology.* While Jesus possibly may have had a christology of some kind, whether of an explicit or implicit kind, neither is christological in the normative sense for Christians. And the turn to implicit christologies after the supposed failure of explicit ones does not avoid our point about direct application. *Even if Jesus does have a christology, such would not be normative for Christians.*

The words *worked up* or *worked over* are exactly chosen to express an in-between position. On the one hand, we want a role for historical results about Jesus in theological inquiry on the assumption that historical research on Jesus is important for faith and theology.[85] Yet on the other hand, we

---

83. For some time I have been suspecting that the community of faith needs to be reconsidered in vastly wider and more diffused terms than in most of our ecclesiastical communities.

84. A rich example of the direct application of elements of a Jesus to theology can be found in Crossan's little "Some Theological Conclusions." In applying Jesus materials directly to theology, Crossan defies the nuance of his own hermeneutic and returns to an older positivist frame for his historical insight. That is, once he has finished his historical work, he applies it by interpretation: to call Jesus the Christ is to take the best-shot facts and interpret them. The former is the historical task, while the latter is theological. Jesus is his history and Christ is interpretation. *Within that frame, everything christic is relationality put on fact.* While roughly there is much to admire in this approach, in fact, it proves to underplay both Crossan's hermeneutically rich historiography and the vision of christology we have been articulating here. The problem with Crossan's theological approach is that *he returns from hermeneutically rich history writing to a theology based on the old-fashioned fact/value split.* In other words, his historical method is more sophisticated than his theology, for it recognizes how much value enters all historical method, while his theology has no stake in particular fact. Crossan, "Some Theological Conclusions," 18.

85. See de Jonge, *Jesus*, vii, 26, 56, where de Jonge sets out a full theory of continuity dependent on the New Quest, which "asks back" from the Christian narratives to historical evidence about Jesus: see Fuchs, *Studies of the Historical Jesus*, 25, for the phrase. Hurtado builds an impressive case for a specific continuity based on the developing devotion to Jesus from the historical Jesus to the Risen Lord. See the articulation in Hurtado, *How on Earth*, 138. The position poses a descriptive-normative continuity from Jesus to the Christ; note that the position differs from a normative christological

are rejecting whole-hog importing of the historian's results into christology. Only when theologians receive evocative recommendations from a historian or find them in a historian's Jesus, and subsequently when they have worked them over within a fulsome theology can we then say we have found some kind of *relationality between a Jesus and a Christ*.[86] Here we are employing a version of the "principle of continuity," first articulated in the New Quest, but under considerable modifications. Recall that scholars of the New Quest, chastened by Schweitzer's critique of questing, argued that, in principle, it would nonetheless be desirable if a continuity could be found between the findings of historical research and christological claims for the Christ. Such a continuity ought to be sought by christologically interested researchers, should be welcomed if discovered, and ought to be of comfort to faith. At times New Questers seemed to endorse the notion that elements of a historically recoverable Jesus could establish a direct continuity that would confirm christological claims: one thinks particularly of their fixation on Jesus' own self-understanding.[87] We will be rejecting this position as too much of a direct sort of continuity, on the one hand, even as we will endorse that some relationality means that something like a "de facto Christ"[88] lies in every life of Jesus, on the other hand.

---

claim). See also Hurtado, "A Taxonomy of Recent Historical-Jesus Work," in Arnal and Desjardins, eds., *Whose Historical*, 280, 293.

Interestingly, Gerd Theissen thinks this era of Jesus research promises the most continuity between Jesus and the Christ because it is an era that has recovered the biblical and Jewish pattern of thinking: *Historical Jesus*, 11. Tom Holmen and others rightly speak of this approach to be a "continuum perspective" which "seeks to uncover a Jesus who is both fitting within his Jewish context and in a comprehensible relation to early Christian attitudes": Holmen, *Jesus from Judaism*, "Introduction," 1–2. It is an attempt to honor the reclaiming of a Jewish Jesus and yet to seek historical foundations for the Christian movement. In a contemporary articulation, fully in keeping with that of the New Quest, Wright writes: "Is it possible to proceed, by way of historical study, to a portrait of Jesus which is sufficient of itself to evoke, or at least legitimate, that worship which Christianity has traditionally offered to him?": Wright, *Jesus and the Victory*, 121. Whether we use the words *evoke*, or *legitimate*, or some others, the point is the possible relationality between a crafted Jesus and a Christian Christ. But the consequence of my position here is that we can no longer locate the historical Jesus in a categorically different (and maybe dangerous) room from that of the Christ. *There is only a relative difference between a Jesus and a Christ.*

86. Here we identify the notion of continuity formally, but will fill it out in our chapters on cataphatic and apophatic continuity in the second volume of this project.

87. See Robinson, *A New Quest*, 107–8, in the New Quest era or Meyer, *The Aims of Jesus*, 95, for an expression of continuity from one of the giants of contemporary Jesus research.

88. To use Henaut's phrase: "Historical Jesus," in Arnal and Desjardins, eds., *Whose Historical*, 241. We will argue that the de facto is *there*, as it were, structurally woven into each historical Jesus. But again, scholars do not need to play the hand as christological.

Here we will not pre-judge what relation historians and theologians will find, nor will we set standards of a theologically useful relation.[89] But we do need to add a couple of qualifications of the issue. First, the question of relationality looks for a middle ground, without determining what sort, between the two extremes, of a completely samed Jesus and of a categorically different figure. The former locates Jesus within some specific cultural nexus without surplus of meaning: Jesus the Jew becomes completely like the typical Jew of the first-century Palestine. We can debate how narrowly or typically it is possible to draw such a Jesus without distorting the evidence, of course, but the direction of this extreme heads toward that of Vermes, namely that there is no historical connection between Christianity and Second Temple Judaism.[90] The other extreme tends toward radical difference, the categorically alien one of Schweitzer. Both positions preclude relationship, to be sure, as both of them pack into their methods and criteria the values they seek. The former unifies and flattens the Judaism in relationship to which Jesus looks just like every Jew, what Tom Holmen notes is a counter-tendency to co-opt Jesus' apparent values for the Judaism of his world.[91] Arguably the serious judaizers, like Vermes and Sanders, head in this direction.[92] Every apparent religious development in Jesus is anticipated, or even common, within Judaism. The range of values and practices that Jesus activated in his life is entirely present within Judaism. The latter option we know better, where Jesus is kept in radical difference via the alien criterion so that he is different from Jews back then (and from us). The former subtly makes Judaism like Jesus (and like versions of Christian religion) and ends with a bland Jesus,[93] while the latter launches a Jesus beyond our ken. The one analogizes Judaism to Jesus in an effort to *same* Jesus, while the other effects a negative analogy to protect Jesus as distinctive but risks that he has any relevance.

---

89. Unlike Paul Barnet's efforts where successful continuity seems to require that the Resurrection be paired with a clear consciousness of messiahship on Jesus' part and that continuity means a causal relationship between the pre-resurrection Jesus and the worshipful belief of the earliest churches: Barnet, *Finding the Historical Christ*, 1, 7. John Meier argues that we should not prejudge what historians will find in continuity and discontinuity: *A Marginal Jew*, I, 173.

90. Vermes, *The Religion of Jesus*, 214.

91. Holmen, *Jesus from Judaism*, 182.

92. As an example of this technique notice the occasional efforts to show things in Jesus, like the Golden Rule and the Abba phrase, as typical of what Jews were doing.

93. See Jacob Neusner's criticism of Sander's Jesus as a liberal protestantizing of Jesus by making Judaism essentially uninterested in ritual and purity: Neusner, "Mr. Sander's Pharisees, and Mine," 143–69; see also Neusner, *A Rabbi Talks*, 182–83.

Interestingly, both extremes seem historically improbable and have been discredited in subsequent research. Of course, people holding these views charge their critics with wanting to protect a Christ with historical research. That charge may be true: the one puts the real Jewish world against the Christian Jesuses in order to recover the real Jesus, while the other abstracts Jesus from Judaisms (and from us) in order to preserve Jesus as christic, if alien. In both cases, a vision of the real Christ presses mistakes in reading the concrete social world. *Such moves are theological dominations of history and should be rejected.* But behind this issue is one that is of more interest to the theologian. Both extreme positions and the debate about them turn on negative or positive senses of continuity between Jesus and Christianity.

In our reading the model of continuity in the debate is defective, since the issue is framed whether there can be a *direct continuity* from Jesus to the Christ. One party says no, while the other says yes. But in both cases the notion of continuity presupposes what we are calling a *direct application of materials from history to theology and faith.* Such a direct application of a Jesus to a Christ amounts to a sophisticated version of the *historian's fundamentalism* and must be rejected. It fails on substantive grounds as well as methodological ones. First of all, the sameness and difference historians use to discern values in Jesus may carry their own values and be blind.[94] The sameness and difference may be apparent and no more than a homology. Second, the theme moves from historical claims to faith/theological claims without recognizing the difference. Instead, here we look for indirect support, recommendations that support certain christological claims, to assure the faithful and others that Christian claims for Jesus are appropriate. To say it bluntly: is the Christian excitement for the guy appropriate?[95] By *indirect* I mean both to reject the notion that historical judgments can prove christological claims (or be applied immediately), and to affirm that they

---

94. L. Gregory Bloomquist criticizes the obsession with the poor and dispossessed in Crossan and others on the left wing. They assume that the poverty language in Jesus' sayings and actions means what it does for us, but a more sophisticated theory of rhetoric reveals that Jesus was more interested in shaming the rich than in glorifying poverty: Bloomquist, "The Rhetoric of the Historical Jesus," in Arnal and Desjardins, eds., *Whose Historical*, 105–16. Whether Bloomquist is right or not, our point is the assumption of sameness could well be of a homology.

95. In a contemporary articulation, fully in keeping with that of the New Quest, Wright writes: "Is it possible to proceed, by way of historical study, to a portrait of Jesus which is sufficient of itself to evoke, or at least legitimate, that worship which Christianity has traditionally offered to him?": Wright, *Jesus and the Victory*, 121. Whether we use the words *evoke* or *legitimate* or some others, the point is the possible continuity between a crafted Jesus and a Christian Christ.

might support certain christological claims when they have been mediated through the life and thought of faith. By *appropriate* I mean that the faith's christological judgments about Jesus are on the right track when historical evidence suggests something factual or something plausible, or when a precondition for an event can be historically ascertained, and so on. The historical judgment that Jesus is a quality exorcist, for instance, counts for something theologically when that item can be connected to a mission and an identity for the Christ. We arrive at a corollary to the above rule, **(Theological) Rule 9:** *Theology should never seek a direct continuity between Jesus and the Christ.*[96] Rather, it should always expect to mediate what the historians construct through faith's life and practice. Theology must suspect the notion of a direct continuity as a problematic and maybe a dangerous claim for immediacy. It is, after all, unclear that humans can know immediacies at all, and more so, the claim to be in the presence of what is immediate can be blind, manipulative, and uncritical. *Theology must resist putting a historical Jesus or elements of a Jesus under a sacred canopy, which, by fiat, authorizes historical claims as christic.*

The consequence here is that we are embracing a notion of continuity without some of the theological and hermeneutical baggage of the category. The baggage arises in the era of the New Quest when scholars seemed to endorse a continuity between Jesus and the early Church which looked as if they were trying to prove articles of faith with historical research. It might be assumed, for instance, if Jesus could be shown to operate with a messianic self-consciousness, then that datum would go a long way toward legitimating Christian christological claims. More fashionable were expectations that in Jesus we could ascertain an implicit christology tied to his sense that he was at the center of God's plan for a kingdom. Today, there are a few scholars who argue for an explicit christology in Jesus, and even more for some kind of an implicit christology. We can discuss whether either position best matches the evidence—I still favor the implicit model, but the point here is *that our call for continuity does not depend on Jesus having an explicit or implicit christology*; indeed we are suspicious when discovered historical results in Jesus are taken and applied directly to theology's christological efforts. Even a Jesus who had an explicit christology would be of no direct use to theology's task, since, once again, all historical claims need to be reconfigured within a comprehensive theology for them to be christologically interesting. If Jesus were to operate with some kind of christology, then that

---

96. Consequently, we bypass the difference between Jesus studies that accent more continuity between Jesus and the Christ (i.e, Meier or Wright) and ones that are more discontinuous (i.e., Crossan, Mack, Vermes etc.). We want to be in the position where theology can both employ things supposedly continuous and things discontinuous.

datum could be of indirect use and, were it to be refurbished within faith's experience, it could grow into a christological recommendation. In other words, we are seeking to honor continuity, when we find it, without the fundamentalistic assumption that a historical datum must be immediately christologically interesting.[97]

All of this talk of continuity is rather abstract. Perhaps, a concrete example of our *principle of continuity* might be in order. Christian theologies, classic and modern, make claims for the moral life founded in or informed by christological claims. Often, especially in modern christologies, these moral claims are tied to the figure of Jesus as the one who advocates a principle and embodies its qualities in his person, usually to an intense or maximal degree. But if historical evidence were to show that Jesus does not instantiate the qualities, would we not have a setback for christology? If Jesus' conduct turns out historically to defy moral appreciation of any sort, then we probably have a problem for christology. Contrariwise, historical evidence that reveals something morally suggestive about Jesus of Nazareth might support, if indirectly, certain christological claims. More so, a continuity between what can be known and what is believed would be desirable, should it be discoverable, for with some continuity, Christians could be assured that their claims were an appropriate response to the historically known.[98]

F. Approaching a Quested Christology: Realizing a Jesus[99]

The above reflections identify a second principle that operates in this study of the Jesus studies. It is a theory about the reality of Jesus, that is, about

---

97. We are in sympathy with historical and theological attempts to locate continuity between Jesus and the earliest Christians and with the effort, say, of de Jonge to "*ask backward*" from the positions of the early Christians to the views of Jesus (de Jonge, *Servant*, 14) but only as a locator for items that could grow into christological recommendations. We make the point about recommendations from history writing independent of the question whether Jesus has an explicit, or an implicit, or no christology at all.

98. Though not necessarily the only response possible. The faith/history relationship here, informed by that of Wolfhart Pannenberg, poses that the realm of history is the present of the knowable past, the presencing of the past, while faith is a present anticipating of a future. Faith is like trust or hope, as Pannenberg argues with Reformation support: *Basic Questions*, vol. 1, 209–17, where Pannenberg distinguishes between analogy, proper to historical inquiry, and doxology, proper to faith's expressions.

99. We might say *actualizing Jesus* to emphasize that a historian takes by selection, in judgment, and by inchoate fragments and actualizes them into a coherent whole, a person in a world. That is, the thing becomes *realer* in the sense that the inchoate takes on form, frame, and meaning when the historian assembles an intelligible whole of the

the way in which a *Jesus is realized in representational activity*. In the past Jesus researchers have often brought christological intentions into questing: typically they have sought in historical research the *real* Jesus. The discovered, real Jesus, lying behind the pictures of the New Testament, would have normative value as the christic or, at least, as foundational for the christic.[100] Questers commonly operated with a model of the reality of Jesus that bypassed or rejected a range of traditional alternatives: for them the reality of Jesus did not rest in representing the kerygma of the church, nor in reproducing the creedal formulations or the New Testament pictures of Jesus as the Christ, nor in the (implicit) choosing of a particular christology, whether from the New Testament, from a classic theologian or confessional symbol, nor in a liturgical, iconic, or moral reenactment of his reality. Rather they would leap behind all of these christological candidates to a *realer* Jesus constructed by modern historical research.

As we well know, the typical approach of the quests for the historical Jesus has been decisively criticized. Theological critics immediately discern when a historian's Jesus acts like a Christ. Such direct application of historical work assumes a Jesus is christic. It is an overstepping of the historian's task, founded in a fundamentalistic naiveté about the results of historical research on Jesus. Rightly, many theologians object: how can the historian's constructed Jesus be real? How can it be *realer* than other (scriptural, theological, liturgical, artistic) representations? On what basis can it criticize other representations? For some, the category error undermines for all time the entire questing project, because, in their reading, the results of human history writing have become idols: finite, relative, secular constructions intruding upon a sacred province. In this volume we too are critical of overstretched historical claims but reject the conclusion as too sweeping. Instead, we will draw the critique of a direct christological interest into a critical caution that focuses on an indirect theological use. While we will reject the fundamentalistic use of historical insight, we will not flip into an abandonment of the quest.

The fact that the Kählerians complain so about questing is proof that they recognize Jesus being realized via a different mode from their kerygmatic one. Their critique actually rejects an alternate way of realizing Jesus among the questers; *thus, they are making a theological point in the*

---

incoherent fragments by putting them through a linguistic-symbolic grid. As Hegel notes, the sheer being of the thing is not in question but only that the thing becomes more actual (verwirklich) when it has been processed by consciousness (from the first dialectic onward): Hegel, *Phenomenology*, 139–45, where Reason realizes it cannot be satisfied with an abstract comprehension, but must be concretized.

100. And sometimes in a negatively christic way, too.

historian's arena. Therefore, the critique overplays its hand. The abandonment of the quest altogether does not follow from the critique. What follows from the critique is the resolve to keep historical claims properly modest and for theology to become circumspect. Revisionist theologians at least will be unable to circle other modes of realizing Jesus (scriptural-pictorial, kerygmatic, creedal, moral, doctrinal, liturgical, iconic) and protect them from historical criticism.[101] In fact, the more we know about the quest and hermeneutical suspicion, the more we intuit that the retrojection of value onto Jesus in modern historical portraits is no isolated phenomenon. It is a value objectification that is not restricted to history writing nor simply to modern cultural artifacts. The pictures of Jesus in scripture, doctrine, artistry, and liturgy are all rich with value, relative to the cultural setting, decodable into the experiences of creators, artists, thinkers. This insight of the rise of historical consciousness seems rather prosaic by now, but it has not been sufficiently drawn into historical research on Jesus and has been resisted by modern christologies. Surprisingly, Jesus research, fully a child of a historically conscious age, has been blind to the relativity of its own historical work. We may suppose this blindness arises because in its founding generations, the quest used history itself to clean up the dogmatic Christ. But the hostility to the quest, the attempt to insulate the Christ from the historian's Jesus, is itself a historically relative expression of value retrojected onto christology.[102]

Perhaps surprisingly, critical, self-conscious historical portraits of Jesus are nearly as susceptible to Schweitzer's critique of self-reflexion as are naive, popular Jesus pictures or hermeneutically unsophisticated historical treatments. It appears as if *Schweitzer wins in all Jesus picturing, for we can discern the self-project of the theologian or artist or historian in every picture of Jesus.* Apparently, too, learning to be a careful historian, and indeed, learning to be methodologically sophisticated and able to incorporate the lessons of Schweitzer guarantee no air-tight protection against putting onto Jesus one's own values. There seems to be no escaping the observation that any kind of picturing of Jesus, including historical picturing, entails widespread activity of self-portraiture. *Therefore, we have only a modest*

---

101. See Monica Hellwig's words: christology must be reformulated to be "consistent with what the [historical] research finds but also in continuity with the traditions of the faith": Hellwig, "Historical Jesus Research," 90.

102. Henaut makes the insightful retrojective move on the anti-quest position: his effort to protect the Christ by insisting Jesus is beyond analogy amounts to a picture of the nineteenth-century crisis for the Europeans, as they faced historicism and the presence of other cultures and religions. Henaut, "Historical Jesus," in Arnal and Desjardins, eds., *Whose Historical*, 247.

difference between historical and non-historical portraits of Jesus, and between positivistic historical portraits of Jesus and those more hermeneutically sophisticated, between the popular and the scholarly pictures, between the theological and the historical picturing of Jesus. In other words, any and all imaging of Jesus, under any mode of realizing Jesus, is open to the retrojection critique. Of course, theologians and people of faith can always escape suspicious critique by hiding under the cover of a sacred canopy. But even their points of withdrawal have a value significance evoked at certain points in the life of faith. Both suspicion and the halting of suspicion have a history and new masters of suspicion, more thorough than the critics of the quest, can decode that history.

Evidently, historical portraits *realize* Jesus just as easily as do the other, explicit modes of realization in the ecclesial tradition. That is, they make him into a meaning-producing reality among realizations. Crossan names the realization in his famous words of "performance." A historical Jesus is an enactment; it is an invention.[103] In his words, every Jesus is "a program to be enacted."[104] Recall that the quest began as an effort to discover the real Jesus behind the dogmatic Christ and it sought this Jesus with christological expectations; the procedure, of course, was defective, but not in the manner usually criticized. The historical reality of Jesus sought in questing was not as christologically innocent as the original questers assumed, and the dogmatic Christs they opposed were not as unreal and unhistorical as they imagined. The quest did indeed wrongly assume that it could offer the real Jesus against certain unreal Christs, but the conclusion on this mistake is not that all questing invents unreal Jesuses or that the Jesus of the quest is by definition of no use to faith. Rather, another approach is possible: we may read questing as a mode of realizing Jesus, and a particularly modern one, whereby a datum of history can grow into something christic, into something compelling of possibility. And, as Crossan reminds us, the production of a real Jesus is a task for every age.[105]

Discreet pictures of Jesus, including historical ones, realize Jesus, each in its own location. And each may grow stale as the time and location

---

103. Crossan, *Historical Jesus*, xxvi. Crossan is right here about historical Jesuses, but sometimes he separates the enactment that is a historical Jesus from the way that enactment is completed in a christology, as if the Jesus part were only facts and the Christ part were only interpretation. In other words, as a historian he steps back from his performative insight in: Crossan, *Raid on the Articulate*.

104. Ibid.

105. Crossan, *Historical Jesus*, 45. Here invention does not mean "making up" but producing or crafting in light of the evidence, methods, the history of Jesuses, and needs of the day and values of contemporary experience.

changes. In this reading the real Jesus is not to be found only in ecclesial expressions of faith, not because these are somehow unreal and devoid of christic possibility, but because they are largely frozen, representative enactments of the reality of Jesus for a particular, past time and place. Their putative christic possibility is not immediate, not a given. Indeed, *a historically realized Jesus is incompletely real by the standards of faith*. Faith under the eye of theology must pick up the historically realized Jesus and test it critically, reclaim it, and reconfigure it to completion within Christian experience. Revisionist theologians do not begin with the assumption that past cultural and ecclesial expressions are automatically christic, but they do suspect that a historical Jesus, thus a partially realized one, can be "a theologically significant Jesus,"[106] that is, one about whom we can begin to evaluate for support or for informing a christic possibility for a location. The suspicion here is that there may be many *historically realized* Jesuses, each enacted in the struggle to make sense of the Jesus saga. Every age realizes Jesus in representing the images of Jesus in the New Testament, the creeds and symbols, and the formulations of the greats in a particular cultural setting. Further, in a historically conscious age, realizing Jesus can include the contribution of the best, modern historical research on the figure of Jesus in the mix of factors that contribute to a presentation of the christic for a time and place.[107]

Realizing Jesus in the historical mode shares formal (imaginative-symbolic) features with other modes of realization, though it brings its own material elements. Typically, such realizing does not come with a sacred stamp, though it can be troubled by academic orthodoxies; it certainly does not operate in first-order language and gesture, but, as we have seen, a historical realization draws from first order expressions and must offer a low-keyed narrative. Often historians cannot resist making applications to the life of faith, whether negative or positive. Typically, the historical mode does not emphasize ritualized repetition or exacting technical formulas, though when it establishes its paradigms for interpreting Jesus, it emphasizes the re-presentative; the community of the historical mode is a gnostic group,

---

106. Watson's decent phrase: "*Veritas Christi*," in Gaventa and Hayes, eds., *Seeking the Identity*, 105.

107. The figure of Jesus, according to the witness of faith, is realized completely through Easter and through the continuing experience of faith. Whatever history can accomplish in making sense of Jesus and whatever theology can use christologically of that accomplishment is probably unfinished without faith's completion. The realization of Jesus and any other historical figure under the historical mode, by its own self-critical limitation, does not enter upon ultimacies with comfort. Therefore by faith's standards, its value is limited: not nothing, but not absolute either. Cf. Watson's analogous formulation: Watson, "*Veritas Christi*," in Gaventa and Hayes, eds., *Seeking the Identity*, 106.

smaller and more exclusive than any community of faith, less interested in aesthetic features, perhaps, but just as earnest about moral practice.

In the historian's model the historian grasps and molds evidence from the Jesus saga according to his/her expertise, experience, wisdom, intuition, values, and interests. The framing of a Jesus is not an act of fantasy, despite the reductive judgment of the Kählerians. When it is good, a historical Jesus emerges in an act of the productive imagination, done in conversation with historical evidence.[108] The evidence, of course, has a thereness to it, but the more we know it,[109] the more we realize that its sheer thereness is hardly real by itself and speaks with an extremely quiet voice. It requires the voices of historians to speak clearly and loudly. When they speak with the evidence, they appropriate it and make it their own; they invent something in the human spiritual capacity, a cultural artifact[110] we name a historical Jesus. So to produce a Jesus is to make an intelligible whole from the abstract and dead fragments of the past, to put together a person who now has a living voice and who poses a way of picturing and being in the world.

The historians' method to make Jesus real differs materially from the traditional ways in which people have lived in the spirit of Jesus, but formally it is no less representational: with mimetic figuration and symbolic gestures that make the past alive. Formally, the enlivening of Jesus compares with what the historians do with any past figure, except for two material qualifications: first, by world standards Jesus is less important than most people remembered from the ancient world: that there is any memory of him at all is remarkable; and yet second, his charisma overloads the circuits

---

108. When we move from the re-productive to the productive imagination, we are moving away from a model of mechanical picturing of Jesus within a closed system of one-to-one correspondence between image and reality to a view of the imagination producing new meaning. The home of this view is ultimately Kant, but after the turn to language, the turn to praxis and the hermeneutical turn in theology, the productive imagination designates the image-producing capacity of the human to create possible worlds into which we can place ourselves and live meaningfully. When we think of the quest through a productive model of imagination, we see in the quested Jesuses the launchings of images, dialogically formed in relation to resisting evidence and to our experience, which pose a world into which we are invited to live. In a sense, *historians are realizing Jesus as a project for human life and action.* They realize Jesus in a way different from the Jesuses locked into the past (frozen by a gospel writer, a church council, a doctrinal formulation, etc.) in an imaginative synthesis that goes beyond simple reproduction or copying. Even the most resisting of moments in the saga cannot be copied without the imaginative mind of the historian.

109. Evidence about Jesus, to be sure, but more generally all historical evidence, if not all knowing of the world.

110. The notion of the real and of realization here has been informed by Hegel, as is evident.

so that there is more memory of him than of many a major ancient figure and more impact than all but a couple of figures in history. The combination of these two points means that Jesus becomes mythicized intensely and early. His mythic wake disorients both the memory of him and the process of writing history about him. But, with these two qualifications in mind, we can see the historian takes a dead-and-gone one and retrieves him from scraps of memory with all the tools and finesse of a good historian. He is enlivened in an imaginative abstraction.[111] Such an imaginative act can be saved only in some kind of meta-historical or mythic language.[112]

A lively creation of the historians tempts historians and theologians both. Historians make their figure intelligible, maybe even interesting, as they pursue historical work on the figure of Jesus, just as on any other ancient figure. They may want to learn from him; they may have existential

---

111. The position here suggests that all models of realizing Jesus are modes of representation of resurrection, an insight oddly often recognized in an inverted way by the enemies of the quest. In the position of the Center for Theological Inquiry critics of the quest, the real Jesus is alive in the present Christian experience of the resurrection; the historian's Jesus, in the view of the critics, can treat Jesus only as unreal, that is, dead and therefore is of no important significance for faith and theology. In this book we are rejecting this view, for all the reasons to abandon the insulated position, but we are cheered to claim the indirect testimony that the real Jesus is alive to present consciousness and experience. If, in fact, good historical research never kills, then the critics of the quest are fundamentally wrong. Cf. Gaventa and Hays, eds., *Seeking the Identity*, 18.

112. The defining moment of historical myth is of a commending of a past stretched for our present and future history. Myth here turns to an authoritative origination, crafted in value and existential concern, for the sake of the present and the future. Consequently, theories of myth that are hostile to history, to cognitive work, to modernity, and to secular experience, or that locate myth exclusively in archaic experience, in the emotions, in pre-scientific explanation, or in the so-called *religious* life are of little interest to this project. The use of myth here wants to ground transhistorical value in a dialogue with things it can say are true about the past and it emphasizes the enduring mythopoeic capacity of humans, aimed at conceptual and moral leadership in the future. A new past has become futural, paradigmatic of further signification and further aspiration. It sweeps aside older ways of being in a discovery. Those taken by the model find their intuitions valorized and are inspired to construct themselves and their culture under its direction. Myth reveals to us new possible selves and new possible worlds: Lewis S. Mudge, "Preface," in Ricoeur, *Essays on Biblical*, 25. Again, in our culture, the community defined by a Jesus myth will have to be loosely defined; indeed, even most ecclesial communities are loosely defined these days. For an analysis of the interaction of myth and community, see Dolgin, "The Invisible Event," in Dolgin et al., eds., *Symbolic Anthropology*, 351. Jesuses are more than plenary constructions, therefore, as they commend Jesus as modeling a picture-policy for the regeneration of human life, and maybe some sense of what is ultimately worthwhile. That is what myth does. Only the mythic offers regeneration through the continual reinventing of its founding stories: ibid., 352; see also Ricoeur's notion that symbols of regeneration are the work of the productive imagination: Ricoeur, *Essays on Biblical*, 36.

questions they bring to bear on their research. It is difficult for many historians to eschew christological applications, even if only negative ones, since a well-crafted Jesus is pre-christological. Theologians, too, can be eager to play historical cards in a christological game, whether negatively or positively. Of course they must be cautioned to avoid the fundamentalistic use of the historical Jesus. The risk of collapsing a Jesus into a Christ is particularly strong among theologians with revisionist aspirations, that is, those not opposed to the mode in which the historians realize Jesus, those who think that the historians' Jesuses may be useful in the production of a revised christology. Where the Christ can be informed by a historical Jesus, there are at once christological expectations for historical research and, and at the same time, a risk of naive christological retrojection onto the figure of Jesus and too ready appropriation of the results of historical research. Theology, then, must hold on to its *suspicions of well-crafted, historical Jesuses, since they appear to be friends of theology*, and since their apparent friendship tempts theologians to slide into a direct christological application.

In this project we look for an in-between position, a christological orientation that is at once hopeful for historical work and yet cautious about historical and theological naïveté, at once avoiding the insulated position and the collapsed position. Our in-between intention requires us to make some fundamental choices. We must reject christological positions of insulation, yes, but we have to go further. We must reject the rejection of questing, whether motivated by historical or theological concerns. We will endorse the principle of historical questing and the possibility that there may be christological promise in the results of the quest, while yet we have to be suspicious of questing, and in particular, on guard against naïve historical retrojection of value onto Jesus. The language of christological promise denotes a limit on quested results. What historians offer as historical results can lead us to the proper holistic christological effort, but they do not substitute for it, since at best the quested aspect is only part of a larger christology.[113] Indeed, we need to be suspicious when historians and others make a part for whole mistake and assume that a historical Jesus is the sum of christology, just as we must be willing even to employ historical work that looks suspiciously anachronistic, for the sake of possible christological gains from the use of quested materials.

We need finally to say a word about the theory of realization here.[114] Realizing a past figure is making that one alive to the present. An analogue

---

113. See O'Collins, *Christology*, 48.

114. By realization, I mean to apprentice myself to an insight of Hegel, that the inchoate finds its reality, becomes "realer," so far as it undergoes a mediating externalization through picture-think (*Vorstellung*) and concept. As Ricoeur notes, this position

can be found in the way in which the newly dead are alive to the grieving. The dead one as dead is not dead to the grieving, but present to hand in an ecstatic form, that is, living in a fully externalized form. The *standing out* is an offering up of the person, simultaneously revealed and exported, to one who internalizes the picture of the person. The act of internalizing makes the dead one real, realizes the dead, brings the dead to life, in a way continuous with the way a living person can be remembered by another, but in a way more powerfully present, in principle, because the picture has been abstracted and heightened. Presumably, the ecstatic presence of the dead must be preserved against loss and will dim if the picture, itself a representation, cannot be re-presented ritually. Each representation in the history of the picturing crystallizes the representation of the dead one so as to create a new representation in a way, in a particular setting, from some vantage.

The reality of the living dead one, we can say, is captured in each monadic representation, but each is a part of a history that realizes the dead one.[115] My operative suspicion is that each mode of picturing of Jesus, whether done in piety, in doctrine, in theology, in historical research or in aesthetic or liturgical gestures, realizes Jesus in its own way. Presumably, we might set standards for better or worse picturing, but here we need only to note that no one way is privileged or final, and that, if we were to assess the reality of Jesus in a comprehensive way, we would have to scan the history of all the Jesus representations. But questing for the historical Jesus must be seen as a modern, historically-conscious subset of the larger representational project of Christians and others. Entering a hermeneutically savvy historian's Jesus is not quite the fiction-to-speak-the-truth move that metaphor advocates look for, but it is close in the sense that it represents entering the frame of an artificial, scholarly construction to effect a more truthful discernment and vocation.[116] The fiction point has to be modified for application of myth to historical memory, for a historical myth must be grounded in and indirectly related to historically resisting evidence. The Jesuses of historical research are more cultural artifacts than texts, though

goes against the sentiment of much interpretation theory, where entering the figurative (i.e., symbol or myth) is viewed as a loss of reality, where scholars are locked into a reproductive or copying notion of image production: Ricoeur, *Interpretation Theory*, 39–42. It is intriguing to think that the mythic aura of a Jesus is enhanced by the indirect and gnostic procedure of crafting a new Jesus out of byzantine circuits of method and source choice accessible only to first-century experts. The Jesuses crafted often appear in language and image startlingly new compared to the cadence of pictures in the Jesus saga. And the gnostic production of a historical Jesus, under the control of the historian-experts, seems to lend authority to the myth.

115. Ideas in this paragraph have been informed by McGill, *Death and Life*.
116. See Ricoeur, *Essays on Biblical*, 101–2.

they come to us in texts, and consequently, by analogy, they have the fixed independence Ricoeur finds in texts.[117] Doctrinally, we must evaluate the effort to produce characteristic representations of Jesus, whether naive, dogmatic, or historically conscious, to be an Easter activity. The term *resurrection* designates, at least, the ongoing representational activity in which the dead Jesus of Nazareth is discovered to be present and alive.

G. A New Avenue

Finally, we can anticipate the ideas we will gradually bring together. The historian's mode of realizing Jesus is a "new avenue" available to the modern world. It can offer christic insight to culture and communities by taking up a route to the christic that goes incognito, via a detour through an externalization, the historian's Jesus.[118] That is, revisionist theologians do not prejudge how faith can be triggered in an earthly sense. While the anti-quest privileges the kerygmatic way, there have always been other ways to realize Jesus. And today, revisionists do not pre-judge what earthly means may generate the trusting character of faith.[119] Many have seen how a historical Jesus can offer a start toward a fully realized Jesus. If we free ourselves from a correspondence notion of truth, the very model that dominated the positivist era and lingers yet both in questing and anti-quest circles, we can imagine a realization of Jesus as a truth happening as manifestation or disclosure. Such a thing happens and has happened for two hundred years as people work through a historical reconstruction of Jesus. Sometimes they react negatively with disclosures of an inverted truth, namely, a critique of

---

117. Ibid., 27.

118. As Ricoeur says of metaphor: "[I]t causes a new, hitherto unnoticed relation of meaning to spring up between the terms that previous systems of classification had ignored or not allowed" (Ricoeur, *Interpretation Theory*, 51). In the case of a mythic Jesus it is a newly invented Jesus over against the various ecclesial and popular Christs (and sometimes in relation to earlier historical Jesuses) which opens discernment and possibility. On a large scale, producing new, historically mythic Jesuses metaphorizes Jesus—Jesus against Jesus for a Christ—and thereby presses those for whom Jesus is a possible lively myth to create meaning. The result can be an explosion of christic insight. At times the potential seems camouflaged, not fully recognized. And sometimes Jesus scholars have no interest in playing the cards of the deal. But for those who do, the only way to play is by way of a mythically figured Jesus, since broadly understood, every Jesus realizes provisionally a performance with opportunities for full realization. For the performative insight of the myth and ritual tradition of myth studies has been save and recast here, see, for instance, S. H. Hooke, *The Labyrinth* (London: SPCK 1935), ix.

119. See the apt comments on the way that a historical picture of Jesus, among others, can evoke trust in: Keck, *Who Is Jesus?*, 180–81.

something problematic. But just as often people find in a historical Jesus electric positive possibilities being disclosed. Of course, theology needs to process these raw materials, make judgments about them, and even correct them. But their truth is undeniable.

Our willingness to set the historian's realization among other traditional and ecclesial modes of realizing Jesus is a first step;[120] it will come with a set of warrants for theology's investment in historical questing for Jesus. The warranted model of realizing Jesus will be yoked with changes in historiography and the abandonment of a portraiture model for imaging Jesus. To these changes we will add various insights sponsored by the retrojection critique (i.e., a critique of the historian's fundamentalism) and will reconstruct the notion of retrojection as an opportunity for revisionist christological reflection. The combination of these factors will generate a theological appreciation of research on the historical Jesus focused on points of continuity between a Jesus and a possible Christ. Henaut speaks of the historical Jesus as a "christological construct." We accept that insightful way of putting it, but with a couple of qualifications: first, the continuities we seek must be *indirect* recommendations, ones rather thinner on positive appellations and fuller on negative opportunities.[121] And second, the continuities will be *incomplete*, as history can only take theology so far and a full blown christology must pick up and reconfigure the historian's results.[122] But so far it must. This entire project aims to offer a set of guidelines for deploying historical research on Jesus in a revisionist christology.

---

120. James M. Robinson notes that, properly understood, the kerygmatic and the quested are alternate routes to the "same decision": Robinson, *A New Quest*, 85, 90, 94. Roughly, Robinson is right. But we add two qualifications: 1. there are likely more than just two avenues of realizing Jesus; and 2. there is nothing automatic about any route until faith actuates its realization.

121. Or we are fundamentalistic about historical research. One of the main arguments in this manuscript is that theologians cannot expect to get all christology *out of* Jesus, much less all theology. Robinson makes a point that corroborates this argument, namely that the earliest image of Jesus, in Q, does not address the major ethical issues of Jesus' day, much less our day: "It is clear that the 'teachings of Jesus' as reflected in Q do not present the 'political correctness' of an ethical idealism for today": Robinson, "The Image of Jesus," in Meyer and Hughes, eds., *Jesus Then and Now*, 9. Therefore, Q's Jesus does not support the ethical idealism that many want who are more fundamentalistic about the historical Jesus.

122. We have learned from liberation theology that realizing Jesus cannot remain in recognizing good ideas about the Christ, but in some sense requires completion by entering upon the practice of Jesus. See Allison, "The Embodiment of God's Will," in Gaventa and Hayes, *Seeking the Identity*, 132, for a notion that realizing Jesus requires following his ethic.

2

The Terms of the Conversation

A. Changes in Historical Method

The orientation to historical work on Jesus articulated in chapter 1 represents a change in thinking about the nature of history writing. Previously, the discussions of the question have set the historical project, reconstructing the historical Jesus, on one side, while the Christ of faith rested on the other side. The former was the realm of fact while the latter was the realm of value. In this study we are abandoning the fact/value divide under the influence of developments in historiography and hermeneutics. The epistemology of nineteenth-century, historical positivism sought to *explain* past events causally, under law-bound, causal derivation, as if history writing were a lab science.[1] Then historians attempted, as we know, genuine biographical lives of Jesus: "what really happened," in Ranke's famous words.[2]

But this sought-after objectivism insisted on a separation of fact and value that no longer seems tenable.[3] Here we endorse both long-standing and contemporary criticisms of objectivism in history writing.[4] Fact is not

---

1. As a reaction against various older, theologized and speculative meta-accounts of history. See Isaiah Berlin, "The Concept of Scientific History," in Marsak, ed., *The Nature of Historical*, 52–62.

2. Unlike the more typical constructions of episodes of a life in contemporary Jesus studies: Le Donne, *The Historiographical Jesus*, 3.

3. Starting with the Neo-Kantians, Dilthey, Collingwood, Dray, and others who emphasize that history writing is a human science of human free actions, where interpreters explain action not by invariable law but by identifying intentions and typicalities of human behavior; see White, *Foundations*, 6, 217.

4. After an epoch of enthusiasm for scientific history writing in the sense of a natural science, neo-Kantian scholars and others began to pull away from a scientized or positivist vision for history writing. One thinks of Dilthey first in the effort to reassert

simply over there, untouched by method, perspective, interest, and the hand of the historian, nor are values ahistorical and insubstantial. As it turns out, history writing that attempts to be crisply objective cannot escape subjective moments, for the simple reason that the good stuff of history tends to be expressions of human subjectivity, saved in human memory and reconstructed by humans.[5] **(Theological) Rule 10:** *Consequently, theologians have to live with bias, with prejudice, with speculation along subjective lines; in short, they have to live with "the historicity of historical work."*[6] We simply have to accept the notion that there is no value-free history.[7] The world of fact is not value-free and elements of what we once called subjectivity enter into the genesis of the factual. Indeed, all history writing is laden with value. Value is behind our interest in history; value helps us take the past as memorable and worthwhile;[8] value poses the questions to the past;[9] value discovers the past as coherent and meaningful; value contemporizes the past, since the past in historical memory and construction is always the present of the past.[10] Therefore, we conclude with a potentially shocking conclusion: **(Historical**

---

the notion that history is a *Geisteswissenschaft*. Here a more idealist vocation turned history toward valuing understanding that honored rationality and human agency, not explanation tied to empirical law. See White, *Foundations*, 217. R. G. Collingwood is arguably the most important figure in representing history as a human science: Collingwood, *The Idea of History*. The early critiques of objectivism turned on the epistemological difficulties of floating concepts of law and causality within the terrain of the past free actions and focused on the role of subjective elements in historical construction. More recent criticisms, from Malthus and Marx, up to various feminist, liberationist, and post-colonial perspectives, have focused much more on the social location of the historical enterprise: see Schüssler Fiorenza, *Jesus and the Politics*, 47, for instance. For a summary of the range of contemporary critiques of historical objectivity (i.e., the plurality of interpretations, the cultural relativity point, the Saussure-inspired, postmodern vision of the relation of language to the world, the collapse of correspondence theories of truth, the critique of meta-narratives, etc.), see McCullagh, *The Truth of History*, 5–6; in Jesus research see Wright, *Jesus and the Victory*, 117, and Le Donne, *The Historiographical Jesus*, 3; and for the ubiquity of the selection process at every step of the historian's work see Ben Meyer, *The Aims of Jesus*, 14.

5. John Reumann speaks of the end of the I–It relationship and of the "impartial spectator" model in history writing in "Introduction," in Jeremias, *The Problem of the Historical*, xiv. See also Patterson, *The God of Jesus*, 252, 258.

6. Keck, *Who Is Jesus?*, 24.

7. As recent scholarship informed by feminist, liberationist, and post-colonial sensitivities notes: a point Schüssler Fiorenza (*Jesus and the Politics*, 5) and Allison (*The Historical Christ*, 19) emphasize in Jesus research.

8. White, *Foundations*, 10; cf. Benedetto Croce, "[O]nly an interest in the life of the present can move one to investigate past fact," as quoted in Marsak, ed., *The Nature of Historical Inquiry*, 11.

9. Appleby et al., *Telling the Truth about History*, 271.

10. As Augustine understood.

and Theological) Rule 11: *The Jesus of history cannot be categorically, but only relatively, different from the value-rich Christ of faith.* The difference is less on the facts about the figure in question and more on the overlapping values and the construal and what an interpreter wishes to do with them.

If we reject the fact/value split of older positivist history writing, we certainly open the door to so-called subjective elements in all history writing: the interests of and the artistry of historians as thinkers. No two histories of the same will be the same. But so to admit into the history writing room need not prompt the extreme reaction of some post-modern voices. In these voices, as we know, history writing, the assertion of my subjectivity onto a blank slate, is entirely without objectivity. What is history is the ideological expression of those in power.[11] Indeed, there is no truth in history in the old sense. To be sure, if we let Schweitzer's critique run full-bore over the quest, the *position amounts to a post-modern reduction: namely, that the historical Jesus is nothing more than the historian's mirroring for self-validation and self-aggrandizement.*[12] But Schweitzer does not take the retrojection theory that far, and neither do we.

By now the critiques of extreme post-modernism in history writing seem persuasive.[13] The trend among historians is to find some middle

---

11. One can hear the voices of Nietzsche, Saussure, Kuhn, cultural relativists like Geertz, Derrida, Foucault, Lyotard, etc. in the post-modern position on history. See Novick, for instance, *That Noble Dream*, 6, for the idea that objectivity is an inspiring myth; or K. Jenkins, *Re-Thinking History*, 32, for the idea that truth dignifies personal judgments. Among Jesus scholars, Schüssler Fiorenza is the most emphatic about the critique of objectivism. She sees objectivity as the consequence of privileging male voices in the research and reads the drive for objectivity as ideological. While her study shows remarkable insight into the ideological use of method and into the actual hermeneutical process of studying Jesus, unfortunately, she still tries to make the case that her feminist reading of the Jesus tradition shows the patriarchal one to be wrong and that her reading is the best possible reading of what is there in the saga. In my reading of Schüssler Fiorenza, her hermeneutic is far ahead of her actual historical portrait of Jesus. Her efforts would be stronger if she limited her claims to the ideal that she was bringing a new and insightful conversation to the interpretation of the saga. Undoubtedly, she is mostly right about her judgment on the patriarchal research, but she has not quite separated herself from the old-fashioned objectivism she criticizes. See *Jesus and the Politics*, 51–55.

12. And, as we argue, *the thoroughgoing critique of questing founded on the retrojection theory actually is an early example of a post-modern criticism, since it interprets, without remainder, items in a historical Jesus as expressions of value.*

13. For instance, that the post-modern position has over-concluded the turn to the subjective or perspectival in the effort to criticize positivist historiography; that the post-modern position is ideologically closed to knowledge of difference, even as it claims to have moral interest in otherness; that it reduces all knowing to power relations, etc. See Windschuttle, *The Killing of History*, Appleby et al., *Telling the Truth*, or McCullagh, *Truth of History*, 14, 24.

ground between the objectivism of the positivist era and the Nietzschean constructivism of extreme post-modernism.[14] The difficulty, of course, will be to define that middle among options on a spectrum, but the search for a middle suits Jesus research particularly well.[15] We know the middle in Jesus research honors evidence (genuine memories in the Jesus saga) while admitting to the way that perspective and value give birth to evidence. We can call the position a critical or *constructive realism*, to note its nod to both objective and subjective elements in history writing. Popular imagination, whether secular or pious, works with a garden-variety realism that assumes the evidence for the figure of Jesus is *there*.[16] Such a view is naïve, of course. Against this view a middle position will insist that *historians and others invent Jesus in their imaging him*. But against extreme post-modern voices,[17] the middle position notes that the historian imagines Jesus in dialogue with the evidence.[18] Of course, the evidence in question can be "polyvalent," that is, having meaning under multiple possible engagements in different

14. See the moderate position between the objective and subjective elements in history writing in: Appleby et al., *Telling the Truth*, 271. One option we are rejecting is a turn to a Hans Frei-styled narrative or story-centered identity for Jesus, an identity that downplays the referential aspect of historical language about Jesus (as in Frei, *Eclipse of Biblical*, 311-18). See the critique in Marcus Bockmuehl, "God's Life as a Jew," in Arnal and Desjardins, eds., *Whose Historical*, 67. It is interesting to me that some philosophers and many theologians have taken a constructivist turn more than among typical, practicing historians. Indeed, many historians seem indifferent to or uninterested in the epistemological and hermeneutical difficulties of a historical realism, even a moderate one. But it is just as possible that the post-modernists have overstated the needed skepticism and are driven by ideological concerns of their own. Many historians seem to realize that the post-modern position finally puts them out of business . . . If we follow Paul Ricoeur's lead, where text mediates between writer and reader, we have an orientation that directs interpretation toward the middle ground: *Essays on Biblical*, 20. Such a middle proceeds without a self-evident Cartesian self on the one side that comes to know simply by receiving stuff from an independent world. The position we will advocate tries not to commit finally either to a correspondence model of truth or to a manifestation model but could be adaptable to a hermeneutically sophisticated realism or to a manifestation model with a sensitivity to historical "reference."

15. We will cobble together a middle inductively from inside Jesus research without making sweeping historiographical claims about all history writing.

16. The naïve realism is supported by a gospel-realism about the texts and a correspondence theory of language and truth.

17. A coherence theory of truth frequently lies behind the position. Even if coherence could be defended epistemologically on a meta level, it does not match the daily work of the historian who always tries to make sense of evidence.

18. Robert Stewart calls the engagement "interactivism": *The Quest of the Hermeneutical*, 126. See Willi Braun's description of the new past where interests of the historian give birth to the past: Braun, "Socio-Rhetorical Interests," in Arnal and Desjardins, eds., *Whose Historical*, 92.

historical imaginations.[19] Evidence is not monovalent in its reactivity, not denotatively prescriptive on the historical imagination: Jesus is not simply an item of furniture in the neatly organized room of our minds, not simply a blank page for unchecked retrojection of our whims or our will to power.[20] Rather the subjective elements of the historian give birth to the objective elements of the saga. Of course, there will be real bias and selection and the associated dangers, but the counter-direction is also possible in the middle position, namely, that historian's subjectivity liberates features in the saga.[21]

Nonetheless, elements of the post-modern orientation need to be preserved as critical checks within a theory concerning what happens when a historian constructs a Jesus. It is evident now that: 1. every Jesus-historian's construction comes from a perspective. Of course, perspective is not by itself the bias of positivist objectivism. Perspective is the where-are-you-coming-from moment and it must always be recognized and explicitated in good, contemporary history writing. Bias may be dimly recognized but it is not made explicit and it aims to bend the mind and will. It may be blind, but not necessarily so. Perspective may have a moral side, for good or bad. Consequently, *theologians must give perspectives an ideological critique*, and when they are found to be morally dangerous, they must be exposed as manipulative.[22] Good historians today are self-conscious about their interests

---

19. See Brundage, *Going to the Sources*, 3, for the notion of several and *new* pasts. Crossan uses the polyvalent term in his "critical realism" for the dialectic between evidence and value: *The Birth of Christianity*, 44. Polyvalence does open the door to multiple appropriate engagements with the elements of the Jesus saga, but the moderate position firmly rejects the notion that anything goes in the study of Jesus.

20. A post-modern option for history writing rests behind the position. The view, influenced by Nietzsche in philosophy and Saussure in linguistics, by Kuhn in the history of science, and by a range of historicists and cultural relativists within the social sciences, and given shape by the likes of Derrida, Foucault, and Lyotard, presents the position that identities are formed by the discourses generated in a society. Typically these discourses are shaped by the powerful. Post-modern sentiments show up in history writing in views that suggest that historical texts and history writers function ideologically to disguise power. Consequently, a history cannot claim to have objectivity. To speak of the truth of a historical narrative is to attempt to dignify what is, in fact, personal value or taste. Critics of these views suspect that the extreme post-modern position on the objectivity of history overstates the subjectivity of historical construction and its relativity as it is done in actual historical practice; they think that the no-truth position is logically incoherent and self-defeating; and they suspect that finally a seamless post-modern position epistemologically and morally closes out the very sensitivity to the other it claims to champion. Thus, it is at cross purposes with itself and does not mean what it appears to offer. What does it mean? A sensitivity to the value-encrusted and subjective elements of all our knowing and, with it, a sensitivity to forgotten voices.

21. Westerholm, "The Christ of Faith," 238.

22. See Schüssler Fiorenza's criticism of the epistemology of the quest as hegemonic knowing, that is, driven by a pursuit of objectivity which closes out dissenting voices

and set out their perspectives and methods, even as they work not to bend evidence at will. In this view we join a whole batch of newer Jesus historians who recognize perspective as inevitable (at least on the macro level of history writing) and who therefore recognize how hermeneutically murky is the line between fact and value in history writing.[23]

2. A perspective can have ideological bent and can be an expression of power relations, though we reject the reading that reduces all historical reality to ideology and power. 3. Historical research encounters evidence that has a *thereness* to it, neither reducible to, nor separated from the historian's perspective. It works with some real evidence from the past relatively indifferent to the handling by the historian's subjectivity. Of course, the discovery that evidence is resistant to historical handling emerges through the subjectivity of historians and others. Even the discovery that evidence offers resistance to our shaping comes through our shaping. Herein lies one of the great ironies of history writing: even the so-called objective elements of the historical record come through the so-called subjective features. 4. The perspectival and fragmentary aspect of Jesus research means that historians never finish the task of imaging Jesus. As Crossan says, "It is not that we find once and for all who the historical Jesus was way back then. It is that each generation and century must redo that historical work and establish its best reconstruction, a reconstruction that will be and must be in some creative interaction with its own particular needs, visions, and programs."[24]

A.1. The Issue of Framing

We need to identify the interaction between subjective and objective in Jesus research, if not in all historical work. Here we propose a view that is a middle ground between older positivism and the newer post-modern constructivism, one that honors both the objectivity of evidence and the perspectival shaping of the constructivist position.[25] We have to note, first of all, the scanty, erratic, and problematic character of so much of the Jesus

---

and supports patriarchy: *Jesus and the Politics*, 42. Such is an example of a moral consequence of perspective. The scholar of German literature, G. A. Wells, writes book after book demonstrating that Jesus never lived and that we can have no knowledge of him. Here is centrally an epistemological criticism, and one that is uninformed, unself-critical, and down-right ideological. See Wells, *The Jesus Myth* or *The Historical Evidence*.

23. See Carlston's observations on the blurring of the *office* of the historian because of the meta-decisions a historian makes in relation to past events, in: "Prologue," in Chilton and Evans, eds., *Studying the Historical*, 2.

24. Crossan, "Some Theological Conclusions," 19.

25. In our *constructive realism*.

evidence in the saga material. In the words of Patterson, the evidence for constructing a picture of Jesus is "like a jigsaw puzzle with most of the pieces missing."[26] Getting a bead on Jesus is more difficult than figuring most historical characters because the evidence is scant, slanted, and episodic. And, of course, the stakes are high, both for the liberally educated in our culture and for the faithful. Historians have to put together that jigsaw puzzle[27]—is it a five-hundred piece puzzle?—when we have only seventy-five pieces in the box, and no picture on the box cover! More troublesome yet, the pieces we try to assemble are somewhat of our own choosing,[28] and we are not certain they are from the same puzzle. Consequently, as John Meier puts it, there can be "no Switzerland of the mind in Jesus research."[29]

The Jesus puzzle befuddles the historian. No wonder some give up on questing. No wonder that some see any Jesus the historian finds to be his/her invention. Possibly, all history writing of the ancient world puts together puzzles; but the case of Jesus is particularly difficult.[30] Consequently, we must remember that the evidence is so fragmentary that every Jesus comes with a permanent uncertainty about it.[31] More so, the pieces are somewhat method-driven, that is, many of them *appear* according to the methodological choices made by the historian. The much debated issue whether to go with the canonical sources only or with extra-canonical ones presents a classic case in which *the choice of method shapes the evidence in question*. Despite the fragmentary character of the evidence, historians and others want to give a dense account of the pieces. It seems they cannot resist beginning to fit them together and fill out a picture. We might ask why we want a whole picture. Perhaps the reason is that the fragments themselves are so intriguing; maybe it is that the face in the pieces is a beckoning classic in our culture. In any case, we cannot resist the *drive to the whole*, and people with hostility toward Christian religion, and those indifferent, or from other traditions are just as apt to frame up a whole Jesus.

The pieces of the puzzle, then, do not mean anything (or mean much) without the shaping of the historian.[32] Even if scholars could agree on the

---

26. Patterson, *The God of Jesus*, 41.

27. Ibid., 41; Wright, *Jesus and the Victory*, 5. Cf. White, *Foundations*, 269.

28. As Patterson sees, *The God of Jesus*, 42. The pieces of the puzzle are, to some extent, actuated by the methodological choices the historian makes.

29. Meier, *A Marginal Jew*, I, 5.

30. Despite the reasonable claim of some, rejecting the maximal skepticism of an earlier era, we know more of Jesus of Nazareth than of any ancient figure.

31. See Allison, *The Historical Christ*, 36.

32. As Dale Allison puts it, the facts do not dictate their interpretation: ibid., 32. See a nice description of Jesus facts that do not tell us much of anything: Herzog, *Prophet*

pieces, they would be essentially unintelligible without the framing the historian gives. While it may be that we cannot think of the Jesus evidence as "literary ink blots,"[33] nonetheless, it is helpful to think of the Jesus evidence like the "duck-rabbit" of the psychologists.[34] Not nothing there, but shape nonetheless; yet the identifying of the shape eludes intelligibility until we apply a *"visual gestalt"*[35] in our construing the figure. Such a gestalt frames what would be random and disconnected fragments and details without it. The frame-supplying involves a constitutive construal of evidence in a particular way, rather in the way that Kuhn notes how paradigms work in the history of science.[36] And framing evidence in a particular way means that other ways of construal are precluded: the duck/rabbit cannot be both duck and rabbit without a shift in gestalt. We frame it in duckness.[37] In Jesus research, if not in all historical work, Thomas Kuhn's insight about scientific paradigms rules.[38] Historians do not assemble a Jesus inductively.[39] They lead with a frame.[40] Of course, the frame can be tentatively placed in the vicinity of Galilee; it can be revised; and it is always mediated through the pieces of the puzzle and through the history of Jesuses.

Importantly, the supplying of a frame or paradigm does not well up in self-evidence from the evidence. The frame does not emerge inductively.[41]

---

and *Teacher*, 3–4. See ibid., 5, for a list of the ways that Jesus historians lead with their frames.

33. As Witherington says against those of a more post-modernist bent who work with a non-referential model of language: Witherington, *Jesus the Sage*, 150.

34. I was happy to see the analogy occurred to Dale Allison too: *The Historical Christ*, 37.

35. Ibid.

36. Recognizing the importance of the paradigm is not to be confused with a return to sweeping and currently unfashionable, meta-historical gestures in history writing.

37. Arnal notes that the allegedly most certain fact about Jesus' life, the event in the Temple, is the perfect example of the duck/rabbit. Scholars do not know how to name, much less understand its meaning, without the frame: Arnal and Desjardins, eds., *Whose Historical Jesus?*, 311.'

38. Kuhn, *The Structure of Scientific Revolutions*.

39. Even as many historians give the impression that the evidence speaks and that they gradually let the evidence itself work up a fulsome picture of Jesus. Cf. Allison, *The Historical Christ*, 36.

40. Wright's main point against the atomistic Jesus researchers: the whole precedes the individual atoms: Wright, *Jesus and the Victory*, 10, 131. See Dunn, *Jesus Remembered*, 46–47, and Ben Meyer, *The Aims of Jesus*, 14, for a comprehensive identification of the many ways that subjective presuppositions shape history writing.

41. Allison, *The Historical Christ*, 36. Here I need to note the framing of even the low-flying *plenary* function of history writing. *The plenary function is the assembling of*

The difference between those historians who are optimistic about knowledge of Jesus or confident about his self-consciousness[42] and those who are pessimistic does not emerge from the evidence. The difference, however, is not a pattern in events to be discerned by the historian. It originates from the historian and in some sense it is within the choice of the historian. *Everything interesting is in the construal.* Historians really do invent Jesus.[43] Of course, self-critical Jesus historians make a case for their choices of framing and today serious work in the quest has to articulate *standards for better frames.* Actually, today many historians and philosophers believe that we can make critical judgments among frames: we are not simply victimized by the skin we inhabit.[44] Surprisingly, even when historians choose a biblical frame for identifying Jesus, they cannot escape the issue of criteria and warrants for a strong frame;[45] nor, ironically, would an appeal to a supposed self-designation of Jesus solve the issue of a strong frame, since biblical witnesses are plural, uneven, and mediated through a myriad of voices.[46] The appeal to biblical warrants, of the so-called canonical approach, solves little in this conversation, since it hides the questions of choice of frame in one of the biblical choices and asserts its appropriateness by the forceful fiat of faith.[47]

A frame is stronger when historians can make explicit the standards under which it is chosen. The standards are those of a good paradigm,[48]

---

the pieces, the holistic moment, where historians show the color of their paradigm, their theories of change, how they sort through causal explanations, and the like. Value rears its head, as does the set of questions from the research and from life that interest a historian. Admittedly, the plenary moment in shaping a Jesus is more fulsome than in many historical projects, where the plenary moment in the production of a Jesus reveals the values of the historian. Even a historian allergic to theology cannot escape this plenary function, as Ivan Strenski calls it in: "Mircea Eliade, Some Theoretical Problems," in Cunningham, ed., *The Theory of Myth,* 44. Cf. the post-Kantian effort to "understand" what has been explained: Ricoeur, *Interpretation Theory,* 70–72.

42. I.e., C. Stephen Evans, "Jesus Sources," in Moser, ed., *Jesus and Philosophy,* 39.

43. Even the fairly conservative scholar, N. T. Wright, calls Jesus history an "imaginative reconstruction"; *Jesus and the Victory,* 8.

44. See the relative standards for a stronger choice for a Jesus paradigm in Allison, *The Historical Christ,* 38: simplicity, scope, explanatory power, and parallels from the history of religions.

45. Without retreating into a pre-critical, harmonizing approach to differing gospel accounts.

46. Another way to express the failure of the Kählerian appeal to the givenness of the New Testament pictures.

47. See the position advocated by the group assembled at Princeton: Gaventa and Hays, eds., *Seeking the Identity,* 19.

48. With a nod to Kuhn, *The Structure of Scientific Revolutions.*

with a few criteria tied specifically to Jesus research. Not surprisingly, *a good frame is simple, incorporates comfortably as much of the pertinent evidence as possible (two criteria: scope and inclusion of evidence), and explains the evidence in a coherent and comprehensive way.* In the new history writing explaining is not the *give-me-the-facts* of older positivist historiography; rather it includes judgment and interpretations, contexts, worldviews, and perspectives on the part of the people of history as among the historians.

A frame leads the evidence.[49] Surprisingly, there are few facts about Jesus,[50] and the so-called *facts* about Jesus say almost nothing: not nothing, but *almost* nothing, until the historian supplies the connections, draws the dots into a line, into a coherent narrative flow,[51] that is, until the historian imagines them in a frame. Ben Meyer argues that the key moment in connecting the discreet items is *supplying a purpose* to the sayings and actions in the saga, since the saga does not bring to the table a purpose.[52] For instance, E. P. Sanders thinks the single, most secure fact about Jesus of all is the tantrum he throws in the temple. But what is it that happened in this fact? How do we say it? What word? Was it really a tantrum? A fit? A spell? Maybe Jesus was clumsy? Was he angry? Why? *A historian cannot name the intelligibility, much less the meaning, of the raw fact without the frame.* One of the gains of recent history writing and certainly of recent Jesus research is the **(Meta-Historical) Rule 12**, *that the whole must be in place before the part*. Specifically, historians are rejecting the inductive atomism of the past for a holism that begins with a large picture. They take the large picture in a heuristic fashion and see how, dialectically, it explains the evidence.[53] Reversing the induction of a skeptical past,[54] many historians now seek *to rule out what does not fit*. When they face a resistant body of evidence, they may have to revise their starting frames.[55] In the case of a Jesus frame, the

---

49. Dale Allison reminds us that facts do not dictate their interpretation and that texts never determine their interpretation: *The Historical Christ*, 32, 39.

50. Cf. Patterson's reminder, *The God of Jesus*, 258.

51. White, *Foundations*, 223, 225.

52. Ben Meyer, *The Aims of Jesus*, 14.

53. N. T. Wright has been particularly effective in this holistic approach: *Jesus and the Victory*, 125-44.

54. It is important to note that the era in which the priority of framing has been accented is also the era in which scholars of Jesus turn away from the atomism of the past and seek to find larger grids for meaning: Meier, *A Marginal Jew*, II, 317.

55. I think it is evident that the most (apparently) inductive of the Jesus researchers, the original Jesus Seminar group, actually worked with a holism that *began* with a vision of Jesus which informed their methods and decisions on details of evidence. For the most part, that vision was of a sage who was very different from the apocalyptic prophet with which they were raised academically.

choice of frame may actually create evidence, so to speak. That is, a frame may bring with it methodological implications and may launch evidentiary choices.

In Jesus research, frame choice requires some special qualifications. Biblical categories, for instance, have a place of privilege,[56] and, all things equal, historians do well when they fit Jesus into the biblical stream from which he seems to come. In contemporary Jesus research, historians must pass possible frames for Jesus through the critical fire of the history of the quest for the historical Jesus. Scholars have learned much, both positively and negatively, on the backs of earlier historians, and while in some circles it is fashionable to think of the quests for Jesus as cycles of repeating mistakes, nonetheless, there has been genuine progress in the last two-hundred-and-fifty years. The history of mistakes, and failures, and blind alleys alone makes for a critical check on selecting a frame. Today, **(Meta-Historical) Rule 13:** *Each Jesus that a historian crafts must be mediated through the history of Jesuses*. Further, in contemporary Jesus research more and more scholars turn to history of religions and social-scientific research for insight into possible frames. And today many Jesus researchers explicitly or implicitly filter their choice of a Jesus frame through a reading of the culture.[57]

Framing a Jesus is an imaginative act done by a historian. Historians do not discover or uncover a Jesus; they construct one. We may say they invent a Jesus, if we qualify the point with care. The activity of comprehending a Jesus, of putting the figure into coherence happens in the imagination, in an intentional, imaginative, holistic leap.[58] *It is imaginative but not fantastic*, since the framing happens in conversation with evidence. Framing a Jesus is done with interest, some interests of some kind, but interest is perspective and value, and not necessarily bias.

The conclusion to our reflections on framing forewarns us that an invented Jesus will incorporate many so-called subjective elements into

---

56. But only so far as they can also muster critical standards.

57. See the next section.

58. As Ben Meyer notes in "The Primacy of the Intended," in McEvenue and Meyer, eds., *Lonergan's Hermeneutics*, 85.

history writing.[59] Do not be surprised by the discovery of retrojected value,[60] by meditations on the nature of evidence, by judgments of usefulness of historical evidence, by interest in intentions, by decisions how knowledge works, by warrants for historical judgments, by hints of pre-understandings and existential questions,[61] by religious/moral interests,[62] by the interpretive hand in paradigm choice, in choices of methods and sources, in perspective, and in synthetic moments.[63] With luck and self-consciousness we will distinguish interest from bias, contemporaneity[64] from anachronism, reasonable value conversation both from the value-free claim and from manipulative value.[65]

---

59. We credit subjectivity in memory and mediated patterned memory (Becker, "What Are Historical Facts?," in Marsak, ed., *The Nature of Historical*, 37), in senses of significance of facts (Carr, "What Is History?," in Marsak, ed., *The Nature of Historical*, 110), in interests in problems and events of the past, in historians' perspectives and points of view, in beliefs (then and now), in selection of sources, and methods, in interpretive judgments, in the recognition of motives and intentions, in the recognition of patterns and causal connections in the evidence, and the choice of a paradigm, even in the purpose of history (Becker, "What Are Historical Facts?," in Marsak, ed., *The Nature of Historical*, 41). See Barnett, *Jesus and the Rise*, 5-6, for a convenient summary of subjective features involved in all history writing.

60. The real strength of the *Geisteswissenschaft* tradition of historiography is its primal recognition that the basic artifacts for study in history are expressions of human subjectivity, saved by subjects, of interest to human subjects. See Collingwood, *The Idea of History*.

61. Cf. the moderate position between the objective and subjective elements in history writing in: Appleby et al., *Telling the Truth*, 271.

62. The conservative philosopher Stephen Evans insists that "There is no story of the historical Jesus that can be isolated from faith" (p. 3). In his own way Evans relativizes the difference between fact and value and between history and faith in a way that complements the argument of this book. He is confident that the one essentially right historical Jesus is already a faith statement. I am not, however, convinced by his sense that there is an essential unity, a "basic narrative," under the differences in sources which can ground faith as reasonable: *The Historical Christ*, vi, 5.

63. See Henri Pirenne, "What Are Historians Trying to Do?" in Marsak, ed., *The Nature of Historical*, 32. See Dunn's list informed by Lonergan: Dunn, *The Evidence for Jesus*, 14.

64. We need to recall here Augustine's wise point about the structure of our relationship to the past: it is always the present of the past which is our primary datum. Cf. Marsak, ed., *The Nature of Historical*, 5. Consequently it is not possible to make an absolute separation of the past from the present.

65. See White, *Foundations*, 10; Schüssler Fiorenza, *Jesus and the Politics*, 5, 47; Allison, *The Historical Christ*, 19, 36. See also the quote from Benedetto Croce: "[O]nly an interest in the life of the present can move one to investigate past fact," in Marsak, ed., *The Nature of Historical*, 11.

A.2. A Construction, not a Portrait

Our comments about framing in historical research press us to reconfigure what a historian's picture of Jesus is really like. In the past, and at times in the very recent past, historians and others have assumed the job of the historian was to draw a portrait of Jesus, rather a literary version of what an artist does. In this *portraiture model* the historian realizes Jesus so far as possible by careful reconstruction of factual evidence. Here the historian must produce a Jesus by carefully assembling available factual evidence.[66] The historian tries: 1. to be accurate to Jesus on Jesus' turf; and 2. to be as close to accurate as possible. Good pictures are fair to what is out there in the evidence and assemble the fragments into a coherent whole: a picture of Jesus. Better pictures can be judged entirely by their adequacy to the evidence. *Jesus equals what historians assemble. In this view, the Historical Jesus is whatever historians put together, from the evidence, suitably selected and interpreted under critical methods.*[67] If the historian uses defective or problematic methods and frames in the historical work (i.e., heavy use of the dissimilarity criterion), the Jesus constructed will be defective or unsuccessful.

The portrait-building model seems intuitively common-sensical and has ruled most of the history of the quest.[68] It has won the quest because

66. Albeit dependent on historians' decisions on sources and methods for assembly.

67. See the critique of the seeing-picturing approach in Childs, *The Myth of the Historical Jesus*, 227. While Childs is right about the role of framing, that the apriori frame, held in faith, gives rise to fact, he overdoes the conclusion on this operation by concluding that all history is mythic.

68. Interestingly, both classic questing and the anti-questing positions share the same model of historical representation. Questers, more or less, believe that their historically reconstructed picture of Jesus reproduces the Jesus who lived, as far as the evidence allows. And anti-questers, more or less, deny that modern history writing can produce the real Jesus. In both is a classic mimetic expectation, as Schweiker calls it: Schweiker, *Mimetic Reflections*. The model seeks a picture which is real or unreal, depending on how it is judged according to the evidence, under a correspondence theory of truth and a referential understanding of language. As we know, the typical debates about the quest turn on questions of sources and methods and less on prejudgments, pre-understandings, and entry points into the hermeneutical circle. *The question is whether historians have represented adequately what is there to picture.* Questers say their pictures represent as best they can the real Jesus, while the anti-questers say no to the application to Jesus but see those pictures as sheer self-portraits of the values of the historian. In either case, there is no slippage or surplus of meaning, between the picturing of Jesus and its real meaning. Such is the traditional mimetic representation in most of the history of the quest, with *questers and anti-questers sharing the same logic of representation, almost a one-to-one correspondence that understands interpretation as an allegorical act of decoding the rationally encoded system of signs.* The reality of Jesus is locked into a past *there* event, which, when it fails, is little more than a narcissistic activity.

of the power of past historiographical and epistemological supports and despite growing suspicions of its adequacies. Indeed, even within a hermeneutically sophisticated historical environment, there remains a lot of truth to the portraiture method, particularly in the way that it attends to the evidence. It maintains that a Jesus can be recovered historically and judgments about better and worse assemblies can be made. Moreover, the project to *sketch a picture of Jesus has been, for the most part, the classic approach of questing for the historical Jesus.* The whole project of Jesus portraiture typically proceeds with the intention not to let history be cluttered by beliefs or heavily laden with value.

In the Third Quest, where method rules, the portraiture model survives, not by a simple appeal to the evidence, but by meta-decisions of method that actuate the pertinent evidence to sketch Jesus. Perhaps the most inventive contemporary Jesus in the portraiture mode is that of Crossan.[69] Crossan sets out his exacting decisions on methods and on dates of sources in a chronology and *Jesus* is the assemblage that obtains upon critical sorting of the themes on the earliest stratum.[70] What, however, would Jesus look like, if the methods were changed?

The failure of the portrait model, finally, is that it does not recognize its own value stake or it hides value in a questionable pursuit of objectivity.[71] Is it possible, maybe necessary, to think differently about the historian's task of writing about Jesus, that is, to move away from the portraiture approach, and to respond more fully to the newer developments in historiography? Recall the analogy of the famous duck-rabbit of psychology and philosophical conversations: the data in the Jesus saga are irretrievably ambiguous: They cannot be entertained, much less understood without constructing them as duck *or* rabbit (or a dozen other creatures), as it were. *To correct a historical portrait of Jesus actually means forming it within an entirely new construction.* This *"constructive"* approach, different from the portraiture model, presupposes a hermeneutical turn in Jesus research: **(Meta-Historical) Rule 14:** *it tends to emphasize that a Jesus is realized, invented even,*

---

69. Despite Crossan's hermeneutical nuance in his announced general statements.

70. On other points, Crossan suggests he wants to move toward a more hermeneutical approach. See *The Historical Jesus,* xxvi–xxxiv, for Crossan's articulation of his famous and controversial decisions of method and strata. To his credit, once Crossan sets in place his methodological decisions, his picture of Jesus follows in a one-to-one fashion.

71. Perhaps the historian most determined not to find Jesus relevant to us, E. P. Sanders, finds him relevant in a negative way, by ruling out wrong-headed and Christianizing views of Jesus for an emphatically judaized Jesus: a fully future restoration of Israel, a Kingdom, without any presence to it, that demands no participation on our part, etc.: *The Historical Figure,* 170–86.

within a circled conversation of resisting evidence and the values, perspectives, and concerns of the researcher. The intelligibility of a historian's Jesus depends on how well it picks up the duck-rabbit fragments and performs a coherentizing of the saga. The theologian adds a second step to this (**Theological**) **Rule 15:** *Theology requires that a (partially) realized historical Jesus must be completely realized in the resonances of the culture in question and the experiences of the faith community.* Thus, a fully realized historical Jesus is understood as constructed, as value-laden, and, additionally, as ripe for christological recommendation.[72] Correcting a Jesus portrait actually means forming it within a new construction.[73]

What about those historians who do not wish to let Jesus fly to christic heights? What about a Vermes, who is a Jewish Jesus historian, or a Sanders who claims no interest in a Christian deployment of the Jesus he crafts? Of course, what they intend to do does not solve the interpretive issues, unless one fixes all meaning on intention.[74] An invented Jesus has a sense not locked up by the inventor's design. Yet there must be a relative difference between the synthetic meaning work of historian qua historian and the actuating of that meaning in a worked-up, quested christology. When a Vermes or a Sanders constructs a Jesus, he puts in place—negatively, positively, or both—a Jesus who holds the shape of certain christological recommendations. A christic hand has been dealt in the construction of a Jesus, at least partially, even if historians have no interest in playing it. Some are historically coy—as under the ideal of neutrality. Some only play out christology negatively, as when Vermes concludes the Christian christologies are mistaken about Jesus.[75] Other historians offer only a blind hand for someone else to play. And a whole lot of contemporary historians offer their historical conclusions as direct theological applications.

In any case, *any invented Jesus brings a tag-along Christ*. Every attempt to make sense of Jesus constructs a coherent Jesus out of available materials; it is not exactly a drafting of the *real* Jesus. In the constructive model, if we abandon the unsuccessful copying notion embedded in the portraiture model, we must think differently about the realization of a Jesus and

---

72. Should a historian or someone else wish to pick up on the historically suggestive for christological purposes.

73. Or at least in re-figuring significant features of a Jesus.

74. Since the historians' Jesuses and, indeed, the classics of the quest have a sense independent of the consciousness of those who invent Jesuses, as Ricoeur insists: *Interpretation Theory*, 71.

75. See Vermes, *The Religion of Jesus*, 214; Wright correctly notices that Vermes enters the world of Christian christological claims in the very shape of his historical conclusions about Jesus: *Jesus and the Victory*, 118.

redescribe what really happens in the production of every Jesus. In conversation with pieces from the saga about Jesus, historians always imagine a Jesus in an intelligible form, saturated by value at every step of the construction. While the portraiture mindset dominated the first three epochs of the quest (the original quest, the no-quest, and the second or *new quest* periods of research), today the research appears divided between efforts that continue the portraiture approach and newer, more constructive approaches. More and more Jesus scholars have taken an explicit hermeneutical turn in their history writing, and more and more, they understand their Jesuses as constructions within a hermeneutical circle. To be sure, as historians, they often argue for their Jesuses on the basis of an objectivist appeal to the evidence,[76] but more and more they recognize their own hands in the invention of a Jesus. More and more, they recognize that each circle issues in a somewhat different Jesus, and properly so. In any case, *a historian's Jesus is the middle moment between the inchoate Jesus saga and explicit christological recommendations*. Not every historian, not then and not now, may wish to pick up on christological opportunities in a historian's Jesus, of course. And, we must remember, *historians as historians* do not frame opportunities as christological recommendations to a theology.

At this point we have to notice three fascinating features of christological endeavor related to historical Jesuses. The first is a truism that must be emphasized. The Jesus a historian constructs shapes the christology a theologian could develop in a christology informed by historical research, since, **(Theological) Rule 16:** *a christological opportunity must be there in the evidence for it to be received as a recommendation to theology.* A christology, of course, can go a number of ways independent of a historical Jesus, but so far as it seeks to be a quested christology, it must respond to evidentiary opportunities. Second, christological opportunities commonly appear at predictable methodological nodal points, and less in items of resisting evidence, in historical Jesuses, since, impossible as it seems, historians are more likely to agree concerning discrete items of evidence, than on plenary judgments of the whole ministry of Jesus. In the plenary judgments historians tend to wear their value conversation with the Jesus saga evidently on their sleeves. Third, Theologians have an easier job in understanding historical work that spells out the dimensions of the hermeneutical circle within which a Jesus is conceived. Simultaneously, **(Theological) Rule 17:** *Theologians have to conduct a genealogy of value on all historical Jesuses, whether in old portraits*

---

76. If this appeal implies that the evidence is self-evidently persuasive, then the appeal is a throwback to an earlier day of history writing.

of Jesus that hide value under objectivist presuppositions or in sophisticated, hermeneutical constructions.

It should be evident by now that, despite its common-sensible character and its longevity in the quest, *we are rejecting the portraiture approach*. It fails and fails repeatedly in the history of the quest, since every time critics discover retrojected value in a Jesus, they have to conclude that we have a failure to draw well a Jesus, according to its own epistemic commitments. It is quite easy to discover retrojected value, and consequently we must abandon such an approach, since its method does not take seriously the issue of framing a Jesus. *The mistake rests in the intuitive assumption that the historical Jesus = what is in the evidence.* The assumption first presupposes the evidence is ample, clear, and unambiguous and that historians hold in common the methods, epistemic conditions, and sources for the assembling of the evidence. Then, the assumption presupposes that the hand of the historian should be and can be light in the production of a Jesus. Even if these conditions could be met in history writing about an ancient figure, arguably an impossible ideal, the portraiture approach still puts the evidence exclusively on the objective side of the materials, while reserving the so-called subjective hand for the historian in his/her assembling of the materials. *Jesus* is there in the materials, and the historian puts him together without too heavy a hand. The *reality* of Jesus stands out there in objectivity, if the interpreter who expresses it does not overload it with his/her own value agenda. Behind the portraiture approach, even when it is done most sensitively, is the old fact/value split and the notion that history writing aims to be value free. Behind the criticism of portraits of Jesus, then, is a generalized and recast version of Schweitzer's retrojection critique.

Surprisingly, the portrait approach has been a great friend to people of faith who want to bail on a historical Jesus. In my view, *it is the failure of portrait-making that inspires or authorizes a fideistic escape into the given portraits of Jesus in the scriptural and ecclesiastical traditions.*[77] Consequently, skepticism about the historical Jesus and the fideistic response are cut of the same cloth.[78] Here we are rejecting of both options. The skeptical position

---

77. The surprising irony of the insulated position is that its defenders (rightly so) flee the portraituring of Jesus at the hands of modern historians into the hands of the earlier portraits of Jesus done in the oral Jesus saga and by the writers of gospels and the theologians. The former portraits are the problem, while the turn to the latter sacred portraits is the solution. Our position here is that *questing needs to free itself from the portraiture model*.

78. Centrist and right-wing Jesus scholars commonly recognize the skepticism of so much historical work on Jesus and seek to overcome it methodologically by inverting the logic of what is historical according to *the criterion of historical presumption*. For most of the quest, the picture of Jesus is that figure left when dissimilarly and related

we judge to be an overreaction to the collapse of historical positivism; the fideistic turn picks up the problematic historical skepticism but brings with it serious theological problems. *Both the turn to skepticism and the turn to a fideistic resolution to the failure of historical portraits presuppose the portraiture model.* An alternate approach is possible, however: a moderate constructivism[79] about historical work on Jesus.

A.3. Not Simply a Construction

At this point we need to flip over and consider the full-force constructivism which we will also reject. In the spirit of some post-modern voices, here *Jesus* becomes our working out of our selves and our cultural values and interests when we read the Jesus saga.[80] Jesus is the archetype onto which the historian retrojects his/her ego."[81] In this view, our role in the construction of Jesus is maximized, and so-called evidence is evidentiary only so far as we notice it, value it, use it, and put it to work in our expression. The evidence has little shaping power and the resulting Jesus is an indirect, externalized, self-or-cultural expression. In other words, in this model, the historical Jesus is the purely retrojected self-expressions of the historians who invent him. At this point, we realize that *post-modernism in Jesus research is really an extreme Schweitzerian critique of questing: the critique based on retrojection, thus, can be a post-modern reduction of writing a history of Jesus.*[82]

---

criteria have finished securing the real Jesus. The outcome is almost inevitably a reductive picture. Critics of the approach to picturing Jesus turn the approach around. The real Jesus is the one in the received narrative tradition, the saga, unless scholars can find reason to rule out some feature of the picture. See Meier, *A Marginal Jew*, I, 183, Luke Johnson, *The Real Jesus*, 124, and Wright, *Jesus and the Victory*, 60–63.

79. We could call the position a *critical realism* or an *interactivism* (Stewart's term, *The Quest of the Hermeneutical*, 126).

80. Usually associated with post-modern deconstructivism such as that inspired by Derrida, *Of Grammatology*, who denies that texts refer to realities beyond themselves, and Michel Foucault who rejects that there is objectivity to history: Foucault, *Language, Counter-Memory, and Practice*.

81. In my view, Hal Childs' inventive contribution to Jesus research, an attempt to read Crossan through Jungian archetypes, is flawed in its presupposition of the very fact/value split of positivism he seeks to deny and by the way he finds Cartesian dualism and "tacit positivism" in hermeneutically nuanced studies: Childs, *The Myth of the Historical Jesus*, 10. In Childs' reading, the quest turns into the expression of subjectivity, but I argue that he misses the power of resisting evidence because he finds an unvarnished Enlightenment project behind every quest.

82. And here, as in every area of contemporary letters, the line between modernism and post-modernism is blurred and overlapping. In some respects we can locate the retrojection thesis between modernism and post-modernism, and Schweitzer, its

Specifically, it claims that all evidence bends by will and that the Jesus we construct is our pure self-expression.[83] As many critics have noted, a full-force constructivist position is a hermetically sealed reduction of history writing. It is otherless. It lets in no fresh air. The values of the self and of the culture are perpetually recycled. In other words, a full-force constructivism is solipsistic. Even Schweitzer, who discerned the retrojection of value in every Jesus, seems to recognize the air-tight reduction of the retrojection thesis when he scrambles to secure the *real* Jesus behind our manipulations.

We are, thus, proposing a *moderate constructivist approach* which pulls back from the solipsism of the full-force constructivism, and places the constructive or inventive cast of Jesus-making in a dialogue with evidence in the Jesus saga itself. The approach is founded on two firm recognitions: first, the data in the Jesus saga are irretrievably ambiguous; they cannot be entertained, much less, understood without constructing them individually in a frame. No item is self-evident. In that sense, no item has old-fashioned objectivity. And second, there are data in historical records and in the Jesus saga: genuine objectivities. To be sure, the objective moment is not there in the positivist sense, but is an *objectivity-given-birth-by-subjectivity. The objectivity is conversational, and has its thereness in dialogue with the working of the historian.* Admittedly, as the historian works over the materials, their ambiguity begins to gel into clarity: that is the coherentizing we have spoken of. This *moderate constructive model* presupposes a hermeneutical turn in Jesus research, for it tends to emphasize that a Jesus is produced, invented even, within a circled conversation with the values and concerns of the researcher and the researcher's culture. The intelligibility of a Jesus depends on how well it picks up and performs a coherentizing of the saga elements. The truth conditions indeed appeal to *coherence*, but there is more. The undeniable persistence of evidence in the saga means there is a complex appeal to the *adequacy* of a Jesus construction. In Cadbury's words, "[E]very imaginative portrait of Jesus must somehow square itself with these persistent standards."[84]

The *moderate constructivism* we advocate names developments that are fuzzy but real among the historians. Today nearly everyone in the Jesus guild eschews historical positivism, of course, and the turn away from positivist history writing has been a set-back for the portrait model. Scholars on

---

inventor, is at once one of the last moderns and one of the first post-moderns.

83. Again, Schweitzer himself held to a notion that there was a real Jesus behind the self-expressive constructions.

84. Cadbury, *The Peril of Modernizing*, 45.

the left wing of contemporary Jesus research[85] tend to articulate a hermeneutical awareness, and thus give voice to positions closer to the moderate constructivist model. Scholars on the center and right tend to be closer to the portrait model,[86] while more and more they recognize their own perspectives in the invention of a Jesus. Historians with explicit theological interests tend to spell out the conversation they wish to conduct with the Jesus saga. Nonetheless, contemporary Jesus researchers are typically better about stating their methods and the epistemological consequences of them in their introductions and conclusions than they are in the details of the constructions. When they express their widest intentions, contemporary Jesus historians tend to identify their social, ideational and spiritual locations. They point to the historian's hand in the shaping of every Jesus. On the level of their intentions, then, they have made some kind of a constructivist turn. But in the midst of their technical judgments on sources and methods, they tend to lose sight of this turn. They press for a Jesus exclusively on *the evidence* and they debate with other historians on the basis of the evidence and who can read it most cleanly.[87] They charge other historians with bias and perspective and they discern retrojected value in other Jesuses. Thus, in the daily work of the Jesus historians *history is still written mostly within an objectivist mode.* There is, then, frequently a slippage between the wide intentional statements of Jesus historians and the conduct of their construction of a Jesus.[88]

The suspicion here is that the portraiture approach is epistemologically and hermeneutically problematic for history writing. Whether it is bad news for christology is a different matter. In the past of the quest, having historians assemble a Jesus out of the evidence, so to speak, usually presented theology with trouble, since the historians worked with the notion that the *real* Jesus was the guy pasted together from just those items of evidence within the saga that could be sustained by the application of criteria. Usually, such a real Jesus looked shockingly different from the received and perceived Jesuses of the ecclesial tradition. The portraiture approach, then, tended to create the crises of the quest in which a new, real Jesus confronted

---

85. The right-center-left designations here identify a spectrum of relationships of history to faith, each type differing according to the historian's interest in supporting (or not) traditional Christian beliefs and doctrines.

86. The classic example is the Jesus of E. P. Sanders, one of the most promising contemporary Jesuses.

87. The perfect example is the quest for the historical Galilee. Galilee offers resistance; the only question is who reads it best.

88. One senses that Jesus historians, maybe for good reason, have not figured out how to write history in any other mode but an objectivist one.

an old, allegedly unreal, ecclesial Jesus. Of course, revisionist theologians, often agreeing with criticisms of the received tradition, scrambled might and main to adapt the christological traditions to the new Jesuses, while various traditionalists erected sturdy walls against the newcomers claiming to be the real deal. Today that pattern of *crisis and reaction* continues, but in an abated form. A member of the Jesus Seminar can still rattle christological cages by posing the real reality of Jesus against the ecclesial or popular reality of Jesus, and at times, against the Jesuses of the academy.

So the portraiture approach often can be a challenge for christology. If a portrait of Jesus often makes christology more difficult, *the constructivist understanding can make it too easy*. Of course, a full-force constructivism allows an unimpeded christological conversation with Jesus, should anyone desire it. And surprisingly, an extreme constructivist approach can leap over the crisis-and-reaction pattern of past christological confrontations between Jesus research and theology. Indeed, that approach can easily make room even for very orthodox conversations with the historical Jesus.[89] A moderate constructivist approach must be more constrained, but, because it owns up to the value elements operative in framing a Jesus, historians and others can be tempted to dive directly into a christological application of historical insight. *The results of historical inquiry are value-laden, as we know, but they are also value-friendly.* A historian with theological views may discover in Jesus an inclusive ministry or a pattern of table fellowship and immediately apply that pattern to the Christian life. While the motive may be admirable, the method easily slides into the *historian's fundamentalism* we have criticized. Since under the constructivist approach a Jesus can wear values on his sleeve, *theologians have to be doubly alert to too easy christological applications*. Frankly, many historians cannot resist making christological recommendations, and their relative freedom from old-fashioned, just-the-facts historiography seems to encourage them. **(Theological) Rule 18:** *Theologians need to keep historians from acting as christologists even as they recognize that value-rich history writing is value-rich.* It is in the interest of good theology (much less good history writing) not to let historians slide into theological claims.

Not every historian wishes to begin a christological conversation with the Jesus he/she produces. But note a feature of the progress of our discussion: *the sort of Jesus a historian produces foreshadows the kind of christological conversation theology can have* (at least in part). Admittedly, theology enters a bit of circularity here, particularly when interests and values of the historian are placed on the theological table, and especially when certain

---

89. As Witherington's work and even aspects of John Meier's work shows.

historians are eager to play christological cards in some feature from their Jesuses. But despite the inevitable value character of history writing, history brings a framed Jesus to the table, and the manner of the framing sets the materials with which theology can deal in its quested christological moment. **(Theological) Rule 19:** *Theology need not get all its christology out of Jesus, but the quested moment must be in dialogue with actual features from the Jesuses of the historians.* Features of the Jesuses do not establish elements in a christology so much as they may line up as opportunities for christological formulation. But even though features of a Jesus foreshadow christological opportunities, these are not direct christological points.

A.4. The Issue of Resistance

Once we have emphasized the necessary framing of a Jesus, we need to resecure the notion that there is something *there* to frame. Imaginative construction, yes; *invention, yes, but not the work of fantasy*.[90] Here we stand against a pervasive constructivism.[91] *Not any old thing is a Jesus.* There are real. drawn lines to our duck-rabbit, after all.[92] To be sure, one can construe the duck as a rabbit, but only by a skip of the mind. One cannot make the duck-rabbit into a turnip or an elephant. The Jesus saga offers *points of resistance*: these are *constraints* in the evidence which limit what we can say,[93] and these points of resistance have a certain weightiness that historians must respect.[94] Importantly, they provide a relative defense against manipulative retrojection of value.[95] They push back against our interests and cannot be

---

90. We honor the objective pole here. See the point in Patterson, *The God of Jesus*, 260. His judgment on points of resistance: "We may not twist them into something we wish they were" (ibid., 258). Wright insists that our point of view cannot be forced onto unwilling material, not easily, not for long: *Jesus and the Victory*, 117.

91. Cf. Hal Childs (*The Myth of the Historical Jesus*), who rejects objectivity entirely in a collapse of the historian into history, via a Jungian depth-psychological recasting of the historical project.

92. Cf. Witherington's observation that, for all the shaping historians do in construal of the evidence, finally texts are not "literary ink-blots": *Jesus the Sage*, 150.

93. Cf. McCullagh, 4, 21. Patterson speaks of these points in the Jesus saga as providing "resistance to falsification" (Patterson, *The God of Jesus*, 252). I would emphasize the *relative* resistance, since Jesus historians are capable of bending most so-called facts. See Ricoeur, "The text presents a limited field of possible constructions" (*Interpretation Theory*, 79).

94. The famous quote from Philip R. Dick: "Reality is that which, when you stop believing in it, doesn't go away." *How to Build a Universe That Doesn't Fall Apart Two Days Later*, http://deoxy.org/pkd_how2build.htm.

95. Patterson, *The God of Jesus*: "We may not twist them into something we wish

reduced to our interests.⁹⁶ Consequently, we have two insights concerning the issue of resistance: first, resisting evidence alerts us to value in history writing, but, surprisingly, not in the way expected by the anti-quest position. Anti-questers (and others) assume that the discovery of value in the production of a Jesus authorizes for them their reductive reading of the Jesus into the values of the historian: the discovery of value launches reduction and thereby removes the item from the historical, according to the exact standards of positivist historiography. But if we move beyond such airtight reduction, resisting evidence in the Jesus saga can alert us to what we might call perennial *value locales* that every historian must face.⁹⁷ Not only does the historian have to react to the thereness of a persistence but, because there are only a limited number of points of hearty resistance, the historian immediately faces the question of how other interpreters have treated the same item.⁹⁸ Second, the first insight brings historians and theologians to value at the precise point of finding resistance to our value. Once we see that *we face value in facing fact*, so to speak, we realize that the question of what kind of value follows. We are in a position for a *"meta" conversation about what is appropriate and what is manipulative in value*, especially in the context of classic treatments from the history of the quest and from current discussions within the guild of historians.

Resistance presses undeniable points for explanation and interpretation. It is unreasonable to deny that Jesus lived, for instance. It is unreasonable to deny the event at the temple at the end of his life. But the minute we name the temple event, the minute we say something intelligible about it, we face both the thereness of the fact and the requirement to understand what resists via a framing of it. Even more intriguing is the fact that some of the facts of the Jesus saga are the expressions of a subjectivity: Jesus actually said certain things, like the infamous hating-our-mothers logion.⁹⁹ So, the "lines" of the duck-rabbit really resist, constraint, limit what we can say in

---

they were": 258.

96. Ibid.

97. Theissen notes a fact of the quest which secures resistance: every historian has to work over the same narrative events, the same sayings, the same issues of sources and method. On the one hand, we have here the power of the evidence to press for something like objectivity in questing (Theissen's emphasis in Theissen and Merz, *The Historical Jesus*, 12); yet on the other, that historians have to return to the same points over and over reveals value difference. Consequently, the *aid for objectivity simultaneously reveals a subjective voice*.

98. Here we appeal to judgments being informed by the history of the quest.

99. It is an insightful point from Patterson that there is resistance in the tradition wherever subjects are allowed to speak for themselves. A historian must work to let those voices be heard: *The God of Jesus*, 259–60.

THE TERMS OF THE CONVERSATION 61

our construal of them, so far as we are sensitive and self-critical historians. "We may not twist them [points of resistance] into something we wish they were."[100] They resist twisting at some point; likely they push back against our interest; they may stand voicelessly refusing our frames, demanding a reframing; possibly they can pose a falsification of a frame;[101] they linger, not well framed, as "retrodictive clues" that we are suffocating the voice of the past by our values.[102]

A.5. Support for Resistance

Method supports resistance, relatively. Doing history writing with explicitly set out criteria supports resistance, relatively.[103] The turn to method in Jesus research, while irritating to many, actually supports objectivity in history writing against those who would reduce history to the subjectivity of the historian. Keck thinks that careful and methodic study of history is "a major bulwark against ideology."[104] So far as we conduct our conversation with the past in an orderly, self-critical, explicit mode, we preserve and build on resisting evidence. With method we can check against our interests; we can support points of resistance against a collapse into our interests. Of course, methodic approaches to history writing can get stale and impose blinders; the methodic can ossify conclusions and build orthodoxies. But *only method can fix problems in the use of methods*: being increasingly self-reflexive and self-critical about the use of method provides the only known antidote to blinding methods, and only a paradigm revolution can explode the ossified. As is evident by now, contemporary Jesus research has taken a major turn to method, in part to counter the Schweitzerian charge of retrojected value. The turn to method, of course, does not immunize a historian from retrojected value (as some seem to think), since it sets the value question a generation back, behind conclusions about evidence to the choices of methods to determine what counts as evidence. But *the turn to method does make*

---

100. Ibid., 258.

101. Ibid., 252, though I am less optimistic than Patterson about this point.

102. See Mary Ann Tolbert's phrase: "Social, Sociological, and Anthropological Methods," in Schüssler Fiorenza, ed., *Searching the Scriptures*, 267; see also Schüssler Fiorenza, *Jesus and the Politics*, 104.

103. See Theissen and Merz, *The Historical Jesus*, 13, where Theissen sets out *criteria for better historiography*, such as: transparency of presuppositions, being free of arbitrary judgments, being able to be corrected by other scholars and by the sources, being sensitive to anachronism, working with a sense for the relativity of all sources, methods, and historical analogical imagination, and so on.

104. Keck, *Who Is Jesus?*, 38.

explicit a value locale to which every historian and theologian must react. It is unclear now whether contemporary Jesus research is on the cusp of a paradigm shift or not; nonetheless, having the guild of historians divided between the apocalyptic paradigm and the sapiential one has made all Jesus researchers more conscious of the issue of value and the need to articulate a defense of each reading at every value locale.

With the turn to method comes a simultaneous new attention to the history of the research, which also provides some support for resistance. Today historians cannot simply write history, since they must look over their shoulders at previous historical presentations. History today includes the history of histories and history writing is a continual revisionism. *The progress and the set backs of the past research act as a midwife to give birth to points of resistance.* Again, historians must use this critical check critically. But with proper use, the weight of the history of the research can press onto historians' criteria tried-and-true standards for explanation and interpretation, and the need to articulate judgments in public, that is, before an expert public.[105] The history of the research reminds historians of important questions, forgotten questions, and the consequences of particular choices of sources and methods. To work in a genuine community of scholars forces a historian to be public about warrants and judgments and to subject them to the fire of the guild's critique.[106] The fact that historians can and do change their views, the inevitable revisionism of history writing, confirms that resisting evidence can correct the conversation, even as it points to another fact about the research: *the role of values in every historical construction.*[107] At any point *consensus or relative consensus actually protects the objective*, even as we know well it can be a tyranny and a choking group-think. Short of a consensus on a point, having a spectrum of tested views gives the guild of historians relative confidence of their constructions.[108]

Both the turn to method and the turn to the history of the quest support resisting evidence and they direct researchers' value issues in the choices they make. Responsible Jesus researchers face choices from among various options and in light of the work of past scholars, particularly on hot-to-handle value locales. They must sift through options and articulate warrants for choices. Consequently, they open their decisions to the light of day and to the inspection of the guild of trained historians. For the sake of

---

105. See the point in McCullagh, *The Truth of History*, 4.
106. Patterson, *The God of Jesus*, 260–61.
107. Theissen and Merz, *The Historical Jesus*, 13.
108. Again, we need to have in place a critical check against the herd thinking of the guilds of research, what Luke Johnson calls the "creeping certainty" of a mode of framing: *The Real Jesus*, 131.

efficiency, we summarize a range of supports for points of resistance in a set of (Historical and Theological) Rules[109] *for historians and their theological admirers:*

1. **Historical and Theological Rule 20:** *Historians must be self-critical and public about their values and perspectives;*[110] *theologians must honor and encourage their efforts;*

2. **Historical and Theological Rule 21:** *Historians must be aware of the questions and interests they bring to historical work;*[111] *theologians must help them bring to light these interests and make critical judgments about them;*

3. **Historical and Theological Rule 22:** *Historians must be willing to change their positions and revise their minds in the dialogue with resisting evidence;*[112] *theologians need to check against historical orthodoxies;*

4. **Historical and Theological Rule 23:** *Historians must honor beliefs, worldviews, and values both within casual explanations and among the potential points of resistance;*[113] *theologians must guard that a Geisteswissenschaft not degenerate into the story of "fleas and ticks";*[114]

5. **Historical and Theological Rule 24:** *Historians must explicitly set out their criteria and make public methods for selection and valuing sources; theologians must evaluate those choices from a meta point of view and compare what is at issue in other choices;*

6. **Historical and Theological Rule 25:** *Historians must proceed according to public standards for better paradigm choice and better synthetic judgments, and to respect limits to reasonable synthesis;*[115] *theologians must*

---

109. See McCullagh, *The Truth of History*, 4.

110. In my judgment, even the most self-critical, contemporary Jesus historians are insufficiently aware about values and choices of methods. Cf. the same in Schüssler Fiorenza, *Jesus and the Politics*, 6, and Luke Johnson, *The Real Jesus*, 85.

111. Patterson, *The God of Jesus*, 261-62.

112. Wright, *Jesus and the Victory*, 117.

113. Ibid.

114. As Feuerbach puts it.

115. Good synthesis is not arbitrary but responds to general truth conditions and routine limits on interpretation which historians air publicly among the guild of scholars: McCullagh, *The Truth of History*, 6, 23, 27, 151. For a summary of these standards in biblical interpretation see Tolbert's "Criteria for Adjudicating Interpretations," *Sowing the Gospel*, 10-13. See Wright's rules for a good hypothesis: it must include as much data as possible, leaving few loose ends, without needless inventiveness, be simple, honor historical continuities, set events into the context, weave a coherent whole, and, if possible, shed new light: *Jesus and the Victory*, 367.

judge what is at stake in comprehensive historical judgments and in rival paradigms;

7. **Historical and Theological Rule 26:** *Historians must hone those judgments in the fray of public and open scholarly debate;*[116] *theologians must press historians to make all arguments in the light of day and with public rationales;*

8. **Historical and Theological Rule 27:** *Historians must strain judgments through the history of the research; theologians must guard the history of the quest and nag historians concerning the lessons and mistakes of the past;*

9. **Historical and Theological Rule 28:** *Historians must learn to trust relatively consensus among informed researchers;*[117] *theologians must meet every historical revision with immediate skepticism and press the new for defensible rationales.*

10. **Historical and Theological Rule 29:** *Historians must learn to be enriched by many different interpretations of the same thing:*[118] *theologians must offer historians their typical tolerance of ambiguity and plurality.*

B. The Role of a Theology of Culture

As Schweitzer discovered, quested Jesuses live as rich dialogues with cultural values. They are not simply evidentiary, nor are they simply about the past. Rather they are in the "perfect" tense, as Keck notes:[119] contemporary conversations of meaning with fragments from the past. Every quested Jesus, then, emerges amid the concerns and questions of a particular culture. Each Jesus, it turns out, is already a conversation with the values and concerns of a historian and his/her culture, even where the conversation is not on the table of method or in a historian's consciousness. Questing, thus, is

---

116. Patterson, *The God of Jesus*, 254, 260–61; Wright, *Jesus and the Victory*, 117.

117. McCullagh, *The Truth of History*, 23.

118. Given the varied points of view among historians, no single interpretation may command the stage and certainly no single interpretation will last. Therefore, it is useful to rely on several and to devote historical energy on better interpretations: see White, *Foundations*, 208, 252, 260, 270. The virtue of the plurality of interpretations is that they give us access to a genealogy of values in historical constructions—where do they come from and how do the build up a portrait of a figure or event?—including totalizing constructions that refuse alternate views (as Schüssler Fiorenza sees, *Jesus and the Politics*, 2, 69).

119. Keck's *Who Is Jesus?* has the subtitle: "History in Perfect Tense."

an act of correlation,[120] a dialogue between evidentiary moments of the past and contemporary concerns, though some historians may be minimalist or even dismissive of the way that the historian's stance and perspective shape the Jesus figured.[121]

(Theological) Rule 30: *When theologians elect to draw questing into a christological project, they necessarily enhance and make explicit the correlative activity already operative in the historian's questing.* They cannot assume at first that the historian's value conversation is itself theologically of value or of interest for theology; such an application, whether negative or positive, would be a historical-fundamentalistic category error. Rather, theologians begin the conversation with the historian's conversation with critique, central to a deliberate exercise of theology of culture. (Theological) Rule 31: *The critique aims to make judgments on the value conversation embedded in the historians' Jesuses.* Following Nietzsche's category, we speak of this step as *a "genealogy" of value*, for it seeks to isolate, name and judge the value of the values in the historical conversation. It asks the first question, with what values and perspectives the historian realizes Jesus as an intelligible, meaningful figure, before it can proceed to the subsequent question: whether a Jesus can be christic.

Then, on the basis of an independent social and intellectual portrait of the world of the contemporary Jesus research, (Theological) Rule 32: *Theology judges the descriptive-analytical adequacy of the cultural portrait implied in Jesuses.* How well do the values operative in a Jesus illumine the questions and values operative in an age? In other words, the theologian of culture treats historical Jesuses as cultural artifacts in the history of such artifacts and explains their meaning as expressions of the fundamental values of the culture. Often, the theological critics of questing offer alert insights into the value production of the historian's work, and, while the anti-quest party would reduce the Jesuses in question to the values of the culture, period, *revisionist theologians see in them signposts to the inevitable conversation that is every historical Jesus.* The theological question to the historical Jesuses is whether the historians have incorporated well values and perspectives as they mull the evidence and make the critical choices on method. Such criticism directs the judgment away from the one anti-quest folks want to make, namely an implicitly positivist one that insists the discovery of

---

120. Anticipating already the kinds of things about the conversation of theology with the culture, we know from Tillich especially that there is a conversation embedded in the historical enterprise itself that is not yet a theological correlation.

121. As Hal Childs rightly notes, positivist expectations hang around in quest circles long after historiographical positivism has been undermined philosophically: *The Myth of the Historical Jesus*, 226, for instance.

any retrojected value means anachronism and manipulation in historical research. The charge, claimed to be inspired by Schweitzer, typically insists that any time historians put themselves into the figure of the Jesus they invent, they lose Jesus. The alternate position here suggests that, in principle, it is *possible to discern the fine line between appropriate and inevitable value-rich conversations with the evidence and the manipulative ones.*

A quested christology adds a second step of culture studies: redescribing carefully the context of a contemporary theology. In this *meta* study we will identify this important step but bypass a comprehensive study of the culture of contemporary Jesuses. But we have to note two features: first, *revisionist theologians insist that a turn to context is central in every theological construction, but in the case of a quested moment of a christology, the attention to the culture is double, since theology seeks to learn from the historians' already inculturated Jesus figures.* Because the cultural aspect of questing itself anticipates the work of the theologian, theology can be richly contextual and speak out of and to a specific cultural setting. We have learned from Tillich and Tracy especially that the *aim of the cultural studies exercise is to discover the culture-as-problematic,* and that the formulation of what is questionable is interwoven with a sense for the solution. The theology of culture exercise, therefore, does not proceed under some supposed neutrality, but already the reading of the situation has been shaped by a possibility that transcends the present situation. Of course, to discover something christic (something that bears the "New Being," in Tillich's language) in a particular cultural setting is to discover something that functions as a or the solution for that which is taken as problematic about life in the world. Consequently, the analysis of the situation is circular: people do not take something as christic unless they have a sense for something that needs remediation. And people do not know what it is that is problematic unless they stand in relation to the remedy. The risk, however, is that in the double-level cultural analysis of a quested theology, it will be difficult to check against manipulative retrojection: that a double value dose will blind theologies: **(Theological) Rule 33:** *Revisionist theologies need carefully crafted critical checks for theology to find the balance between being culturally sensitive and boarding a cultural bandwagon.*

Second, even an abstracted meta study of the methods of deployment of historical Jesuses, such as this one, cannot avoid the values of the culture. A theology that attends to the quest is already embedded in modernity and into the waves and phases of the quest; even a formal study of method in use of a Jesus for christological purposes cannot escape the material location: where we are in the quest and what winds of the spirit circle in our culture. It is a product of the end of the so-called Third Quest, intensely, if not exclusively, often shaped by developments, for instance, in American culture and the American academy. To have concluded, as we have, that theology needs a more disciplined reaction to the quest locates us at a particular maturing episode in questing, at a time when the reigning paradigm for Jesus seems to be shaky, at best. Arguably, that questing has entered a methodological stage represents a time/space in the academy, in theology, in faith communities, and in the culture generally.

If we do not permit the reduction of each historical Jesus simply to the values of the culture or the historian, and yet recognize the way that value is embedded in historical results, we face the circularity here of the hermeneutical circle, with the swirl of cultural values, historical opportunities, and christological recommendations. Of course, it is somewhat arbitrary how we make sense of the mix, since, in principle, we may break into the circle at any point. Presumably, we might begin with the analysis of the context and eventually end with insights into how a Jesus picture might be christic. Or we might tease out the cultural values already operative in a representation of a Jesus. The best a theologian can do is simply begin, begin the analysis and see where it leads. Undoubtedly, beginning to analyze the Jesus research for a clue to the culture will be easier, since the research, however exhaustive, is nonetheless finite and may already hint at the value questions at hand in a culture.

The theological study of the culture of Jesus researchers alerts theology to significant cultural change, and with that, new spiritual and value questions emerging in the culture. The theological question is the one that Hegel put: how is Spirit instantiated in culture? Any effort to identify the significant spiritual currents[122] must ask the for-whom question. Whose currents

---

122. I would be quite happy to purge the English language of the term *spirituality*. I find it flabby and am usually repelled by those who claim it. But it is a term that is in the streets and usually represents the good stuff for which *organized religion* is the bad: spirituality vs. religion. We know, of course, what people hate about religion and we can honor their discontent with its formalities. But we also know that a spirituality grows into something very *religious* the minute the dust settles on some charismatic experience. In a short while, spiritual forms emerge as myth and ritual, and in a flash we have the dreaded *organized religion*. The consequence of these deliberations is this: we cannot accept the opposition between religion and spirituality. When people set the two in opposition, what they mean to express is that an *organized religion* is for them a dying or dead spirituality. A fresh spiritual explosion grows into a religion and a religion preserves a spirituality in narrative and in representative gesture. Consequently, spirituality usually fits within religion, although it may be independent: "In general, what is spiritual in religions has to do with articulating and relating to fundamental issues of the human condition and place in the cosmos. It has to do also with ultimate sources and characters of obligation; with emotive and self-definitional issues occasioned by glimpses of the limits of one's cultural world as manifested in contrasts between the sacred and the profane; with addressing the fundamental tasks, problems, or flaw in

are we identifying? A comprehensive cultural analysis would take theology into judgments about what and whose artifacts to notice and value,[123] and the assumption is that the cultures change in new configurations of the spirit. A revisionist theology does not preach the eternal selfsame message (whatever that might mean) but is ever adapting to new configurations of value. One way to interpret the burst of recent Jesus research, known as the Third Quest, is to explain it as a response to and symptom of major cultural changes in first-world cultures.[124]

C. The Notion of Retrojection[125]

The project here seeks to define theological conversations with historical work on Jesus of Nazareth. In the contemporary era of Jesus research, scholars of all stripes are extremely sensitive to the dangers of too easy conversations, where theology sneaks into historical research in incognito ways.[126]

---

human life; and with calling upon non-ordinary resources to address all these issues so as to approach perfection or fulfillment": Robert C. Neville, "The Emergence of Historical Consciousness," in Van Ness, *Spirituality and the Secular*, 137.

123. My own analysis identifies the following currents: the apathy, boredom, and empty diversions in our first world culture; our stress level and frenetically busy lives; the growing apocalyptic consciousness tied to environmental concerns and sociopolitical unrest; our culture wars tied to conflicts over modernity; our sense of cosmic battle of good vs. evil; the issue of terrorism and violence at home; our plugged-in techno-lives of virtual reality; the extent we live within sports and entertainment cultures; the necrophia of our culture and the taste for both tightly ordered experience and for extreme, decontrolling activities; the cultivation of ecstatic experience; our much-vaunted individualism and our simultaneous yearning for community and the whole; our quest for the pure, the natural, and the whole in many areas of our lives; our anti-organized religion theme, the privatizing of religion and the "sheilaism" (Bellah's term) of the spiritualism of the day; the new consciousness of diversity, the gospel of multiculturalism, and counter-reactions; our hostility to institutions; the deepening of our informality, the collapse of high culture, and the crisis over manners; the extent to which we live for celebrity and within a culture of recognition; the therapeutic and self-help theme balanced with the 12-Step mindset for addiction; a demonic experience of evil; our pastlessness, our relics, our icons, and the nostalgic yearning of our culture; the developing iconographic orientation of our minds; the love of nature, our pantheism, and the escape to nature and to exotic places; the simultaneous left- and right-wing activism; our complex reaction to changes in gender issues; the return of the supernatural and the revival of traditional religions; the uneasy life of secularist currents and indifference to religion amid the mainstreaming and suburbanizing of evangelicalism; the emergence of a culture of shame and the receding of a guilt culture; and the like.

124. See the section on American values in chapter 5.

125. Here we introduce the category that will receive a full treatment in chapter 4.

126. Typical of this era is the notion that retrojected value is ubiquitous in all aspects of Jesus research. See, for instance, Gowler, *What Are They Saying*," vii.

Today, in the post-Schweitzerian era of self-critical Jesus research, christological work informed by historical Jesus research has to be keenly aware of what belongs to the historical and what is a theological claim. Indeed, one of the most characteristic features of the conduct of contemporary Jesus research is that scholars have internalized Schweitzer's cautions against self-reflection through the figure of Jesus. Third Questers, for instance, hold every and no theological opinion, but as historians they are unified in their intention to distinguish historical work from theological treatments of Jesus. We have learned from Schweitzer that historical pictures of Jesus too often are little more than the retrojection of the values of the historian and his/her culture. Typically, then, they agree that their *historical studies are not and cannot be direct, constructive christological exercises*. Even the occasional christological recommendations that emerge from certain historians come with circumspection and caution. Therefore, our theological charting of how historical results can be deployed in a christology must be doubly careful, so as not to confuse what comes from history and what comes from faith.

In the famous words of Crossan, "It is impossible to avoid the suspicion that historical Jesus research is a very safe place to do theology and call it history, to do autobiography and call it biography."[127] Historians of Jesus today understand the critique of questing and are well-coached by Schweitzer's critical insight. They know how to sleuth out retrojection in Jesus researchers' works.[128] In fact, they are quite deft in zapping each other laterally with overlapping charges of value retrojected onto the figure of Jesus.[129] In effect, they pick up the charge of Schweitzer against the nineteenth-century Jesuses, and assume that the charge applies well in different contexts of questing, as if the critique of retrojection were a permanent hermeneutic of suspicion for any questing. *Retrojection is not simply a Germanic thing of the nineteenth century, not simply a modern risk of historical criticism, not simply a danger of theological liberalism; it is endemic to the entire project of historical and other forms of imaging Jesus (and presumably, other past figures and movements)*. Indeed, in this project we continue to abstract the critique of Jesus research and apply it to artistic, philosophical, theological, literary,

---

127. Crossan, *The Historical Jesus*, xxviii.

128. We do not need to repeat the many examples of charges of retrojection in the critical literature. Take as an illustration E. P. Sanders' aforementioned comment about Crossan's reading of Galilee, or Gowler's assessment that James M. Robinson could see the ideology and cultural values in other scholars' Jesuses but never in his own: *What Are They Saying*," 23–24.

129. Halvor Moxnes' fine phrase is "roll-your-own Jesus": Moxnes, "The Theological Importance," in Arnal, *Jesus and the Village*, 96.

and other cultural enactments of the image of Jesus. It may seem an easy and right extension when critics see Schweitzerian retrojection in, say, the Crossan Jesus at the end of the twentieth century.[130] It may seem obvious to those of us raised on Schweitzer to see that Michelangelo does *the same thing* when he packs a sculpture of Jesus with Renaissance value (i.e., the *weight room Jesus*). But we have to note here that we are generalizing the critique and extending it analogically into unfamiliar territory. And if we allow the extension into other picturings of Jesus, we have to live with a startling consequence: the consequence of the consequence is that *the teeth have been taken out of the criticism of the critics of the quest. No longer is retrojection the failure of the methods and orientations and epistemologies and faith of questers, but it comes with the territory of any image work with the figure of Jesus.*

While it may be evident to current questers and their critics alike that the critique of retrojection must be applied to the contemporary quest, both groups commonly do not take the *second analogical step to all imaginative work on Jesus.* Anti-questers, as we have seen, move quickly to the conclusion that historical critical research on Jesus is fundamentally wrongheaded, a mistake of history writing and of faith; but they have no interest in the notion that all treatments of Jesus are value constructions, since that view would undermine the Kählerian appeal to authority. Historians admit to the inevitability of retrojected value in history writing but typically read it as an indication of inadequate historical research. When historians let contemporary value creep into their Jesuses, other historians rush to correct the methodological failures of the historians, but usually they do not move to the conclusion of Schweitzer:[131] namely, that the discovery of retrojected value is sufficient reason to end questing itself. Rather, they read retrospection as an indication of failed or not-careful history writing and find the solution for retrojection of value to be improvement in historical method and technique.

Typically, historians get busy being better historians, not better hermeneuts, when they smell retrojected value. For them retrojection means failure in history writing which is, in principle, fixable. While non-historians often meet egregious retrojection of value in a Jesus with a retreat into the no-quest option, historians cannot resist the notion that better history writing can fix retrospection. Heavy with hermeneutical responsibility (under

---

130. Of course, Schweitzer himself hinted at the extension of his critique in the famous final comments on the search for Jesus: Schweitzer, *The Quest of the Historical Jesus*, 2001 edition, 478.

131. The recent work of Dale Allison is the exception: "The Embodiment of God's Will," in Gaventa and Hayes, eds., *Seeking the Identity*, 79–95.

[Theological] Rule 34): *Theology, however, must resist the notion that retrojection of value is simply a fixable, historical mistake.* Granted, there are instances where retrojection is indeed an opportunity for historical revision: the historians' intuition is right. These instances should continue to alert us to retrojected value and the need for continuing historical work. They should launch efforts to revise the reading of the evidence, to try out new methods. Granted, too, there are times when retrojected value is indeed manipulative and needs to be abandoned. But at some point *theologians have a hermeneutical interest to oppose the typical historians' reaction.* Too much of this reaction has been shaped by lingering positivist understandings of historiography; too much of the guild continues to find its warrants in a dated objectivism. (**Theological) Rule 35:** *At some point theologians have an interest in insisting that retrojected value can actually be a legitimate conversation with historical evidence.* It is value that emerges from us and is in dialogue with materials from the first century. That said, we next need to distinguish between *good* and *bad* retrojection, as it were.

The effort to distinguish between good and bad value conversations with historical evidence begins with the insights of self-critical historians of Jesus. Upon recognizing Schweitzer's insight and discovering retrojected values in other historians' constructions, many Jesus historians offer helpful criteria for history writing that would avoid retrojection of value. While theology must be suspicious of any motive to make history free of value, their criteria are useful starting points for the theological use of retrojection. (**Quest) Rule 36:** *A proper Jesus must be mediated today through the study of the historians who study Jesus.*

C.1. Self-Reflexiveness

The discovery of the retrojection thesis has stimulated hermeneutical sophistication among questers. After Schweitzer Jesus historians have had to become methodologically self-conscious.[132] Neither a historical picture of Jesus nor the rejection of questing can be done naively anymore. For instance, after Schweitzer no one can proceed immediately to the quest without worrying about potential narcissism in a historical Jesus. Routinely, every new Jesus book begins with an apology against the agnostic position; and every new book sets out critical checks against retrojection.[133]

---

132. Again, I would argue that contemporary Jesus historians tend to give voice to more hermeneutical self-reflection than the conduct of their actual historical judgments reveals.

133. I.e., Meier, *A Marginal Jew*, I.

Moreover, many critics, skeptical about historical reconstructions of Jesus, recognize they presuppose historical knowledge of Jesus with which they judge the historians' reconstructions to fail. Even the critics of questing, it is evident, must be explicit about the bases of their historical judgments of the historians' work. In other words, *today the question of the quest for the historical Jesus proceeds within maximal historical self-consciousness.*

For some this hermeneutical turn kills Jesus with method and layers of introspection. There is some truth in the point, since Jesus research has lost much of its immediacy and innocence. But the fact of the research today is that *historians cannot produce a Jesus directly in conversation with the evidence, but only through an intense methodological foray.* They must deploy an apology for every choice of method and a critique of each rejected position, since they know that the Jesus produced depends on the methods chosen. Moreover, today, the study of Jesus winds its way through the study of the Jesuses of the history of the quest. Indeed, increasingly today historians seem to realize this hermeneutical development.[134] We see increased self-reflection in their attention to method, to social and ideational location, and in their sense that they must locate themselves within the history of the quest. When theologians look in on this hermeneutically rich discussion, they do so in an activity of theology of culture.[135] For good or bad, we have **(Historical) Rule 37**: *Questing requires a hermeneutical turn today,* as a consequence of the methodological, cultural, and epistemological situation of the Jesus historians. Indeed, as the historicity of the Jesus researcher himself/herself and of the quest itself become part of the historical Jesus, Jesus research has matured into one of the most introspective of human endeavors. Again, some bemoan this development; we propose to make a virtue of the introspective turn.[136]

No doubt, a sensitivity to retrojection generates introspection among historians. Theologians see in the inward and self-conscious turn, not simply more nuanced and sound historical work, but the building stages of the realizing of a Jesus. In self-critical historical work on Jesus, *a Jesus has been actuated, at least partially, as a launched, meaning trajectory through the mediation of a historian-in-culture.* A Jesus no longer stands over there, in the past, all assembled in the only way the interlocking pieces can make a pretty picture. And the theologians no longer can assume they pick up a finished thing to apply to faith and to christology. Rather, historians draw the

---

134. Below, we add a further hermeneutical turn: the study of Jesus must be mediated through the history of the quest.

135. See below.

136. This book represents a meta-meta effort to chart the conduct of theology when it looks upon the already hermeneutically complex historical work being done on Jesus.

Jesus-aporia into a coherence as they ruminate over elements in the saga. The formulation of a Jesus is a hands-on creative act, as we have seen. It can be that the historian walks away from his/her artistry at this point, before it is fully realized. But in any case *the theologian picks up the artifact as a cultural critic and begins to study the Jesus launched by the historian.*

In **(Theological) Rule 38:** *Theological study aims to identify the way of being in the world posed by the produced Jesus, even if that way is only implicit in the historical figuration or inchoate in the mind of the historian.* Theologians take apart the Jesus analytically, in the genealogical step, to discern the values the figure intends. At this point, the theologian effects a value conversion and turns to consider the values, midwife to the historical production of a Jesus, as candidates, putative proposals that aim to launch a way of viewing the world and living in it. There is nothing mysterious about the *value conversion*, since in principle any human life can represent a way of being and any past figure worth historical research certainly poses to interpreters a way of seeing and a way of acting in the world. At this point, the theologian can determine whether and how elements of a Jesus can be used christologically. Of particular interest to the theologian are three points of judgment: first, how has a historian (in the specificity of the cultural and personal time/place) realized (or partially realized) the past figure?; here the concern is to identify how the historian actuates dead fragments as living history; second, what identifiable values mediate that actuation and how are they deployed?; and third, are there any historical moments that come to theology pre-packaged, as it were, as christological opportunities?

C.2. The Turn to Method

The notion of retrojection has captured judgments on questing. For many decades historians have sought ways to guard against retrojection. In worlds shaped by positivistic senses for history, any and all traces of retrojected value are judged as bias and as failed history writing. In other visions for history, the issue at hand in retrojection is manipulation of the past. Suspicion of retrojection naturally generates a turn inward in Jesus research; consequently, the inward turn seems to generate a natural interest in method. Scholars need to articulate just what they think they are doing, and particularly to demonstrate that their history writing avoids the charge of manipulation of the past for the sake of the present. Historians typically advocate a turn to method as a necessary evil in Jesus research in order to avoid the charge of retrojection. Method, they think, secures the objective moment against self-portraiture under the name of Jesus.[137] Method mediates and, historians seem to think, softens the hand of the scholar in the production of a Jesus. After all, when a historian makes explicit his/her methodological decisions, historical decisions proceed in the clear light of day and according to an ordered path. Method allows objectification of steps in history writing and works as an agent against capricious intrusion of value.

Contemporary Jesus historians typically value the turn to method highly, even as they sometimes ridicule it. By way of methodological choice, historians discover what is at stake in historical judgments; they explicitly face rationales and warrants for particular claims; they have a basis to argue with other historians and advance the progress of historical revision. There is no doubt that method explicitates certain value decisions and an ordered use of method gives the critic and the theologian a clarity and order for the evaluation of a Jesus.[138] But does the turn to method protect against the charge of retrojection? Does it anchor objectivity in historical results, as historians hope? Certainly it is true that the use of a publicly articulated method minimizes the power of hidden value in a Jesus construction. But it seems more of a stretch that the turn to method defends against retrojected value for the simple reason that history writing and certainly Jesus history are so saturated with value, that the battle over retrojected value sucks in the choice of method, even before the method can be applied to any saga materials. No wonder that different methodological assumptions yield incommensurable Jesuses and historians are unable to talk to each other.[139]

The position here argues that the turn to method does indeed smoothe out value capriciousness in the production of a Jesus but it also tosses the deep value issue back a generation onto the factors that shape the choice of method. Why are these methods chosen (i.e., using the main, certain actions of Jesus to build a frame, as Sanders does)? Why is this criterion privileged (i.e., the criterion of dissimilarity)? What goes into the choice of sources (i.e., the judgment that Thomas contains early and useful materials to make sense of Jesus)? In hermeneutically sophisticated Jesus research today the battlefield over value rests more in the choice of methods, than in the results of historical research. **(Theological) Rule 39:** *Theologians should welcome the*

---

137. Ben Meyer launched the contemporary era in Jesus research by arguing that improvement in methods and techniques of history writing will not resolve the fundamental dilemma of Jesus research (that the results of research will be in conflict with traditional Christian belief): Meyer, *The Aims of Jesus*, 14. That is, only a self-conscious change in the presupposed hermeneutic can resolve the dilemma.

138. Note Dunn's sense that different methods yield different Jesuses: Dunn, *Jesus Remembered*, vol. 1, 7.

139. Ibid., 11.

turn to method in Jesus research but not celebrate it as a resolution of the issue of retrojection. Likely the turn to method is no more than a relatively successful objectification within Jesus research and no obvious antidote to manipulative retrojection. Methodologically sophisticated Jesus research usually attempts to hold retrojected value in check. Critics and theologians must correct that ambition and aim it at the real problem: *manipulative retrojection.* In addition, they need to be cautiously suspicious that the historical use of method can be a false objectification, that is, an effort to hide the subjective hand in a scientized historical format. **(Theological) Rule 40:** *Theologians need to keep a critical eye on method in historical research and guard against the ideological use of method;* they must keep their focus on discerning when retrojected value manipulates the past.

C.3. The Sociological Turn

In reading Third Quest Jesus studies, one notices how commonly historians employ sociological insights, social histories, and comparative anthropological results in their historical reconstruction.[140] We associate the names of Theissen, Horsley, Freyne, Crossan, and others with the emphasis on social-world reconstruction as an aid to understand Jesus. This turn represents a perceived movement away from the individualism and existentialist orientations of Jesus research though the end of the New Quest under the impulse of studies of the social construction of knowledge.[141] Scholars of Jesus started to get interested in groups and movements, communities, class, gender, honor-shame, patronage systems, and effects of colonialism on people. Often they added comparative studies in cultural anthropology and synchronic cross-cultural methods in relative independence from historical paradigms.[142]

Arguably, Crossan's magisterial study of Jesus has been the most successful in integrating social-historical and comparative anthropological insight into a textual study, such that it seems impossible to return to an exclusively text-oriented study.[143] **(Theological) Rule 41:** *The sociological turn*

---

140. See: Stegemann and Stegemann, *The Jesus Movement* for a comprehensive, social-historical treatment of the Jesus Movement; and Malina, *The Social Gospel of Jesus.*

141. One thinks of the influence of Berger and Luckmann, *The Social Construction of Reality.*

142. Note that in the new era of Jesus research it is just as likely that apocalyptic will be read through sociological/anthropological methods and studies than through the tradition of religious ideas of the prophetic tradition of Israel: see Crossan, *The Historical Jesus,* 103.

143. See an outline of his use of such methods in *ibid.,* 4–13.

should be welcomed by theology. As we can imagine, sociological insights can offer to theology some of the largest frames for christological recommendations. Consider the way that the notion that Jesus was influenced by cynic philosophers revolutionizes the entire way scholars think about Jesus.[144] Who could unfold Jesus' mission today without positing a particular view on the social world of Galilee? Sociological insight can prompt the kind of revisions of conception revisionist theologians endorse. In addition to this positive (cataphatic) function of sociological insight, there is an interesting negative (apophatic) function afoot in Third Quest Jesus research, namely, that it can function as a critique of popular images of Jesus. This use gains traction among some Jesus scholars, academics who are skeptical or disdainful of popular piety. *The sociological Jesus seems to compete with the therapeutic, subjectivized, and psychologized Jesuses of popular piety.*[145] We will not dwell on this use. Suffice it to say that a newly minted Jesus may function in a theological and critical way to undermine the reigning images of Jesus in the culture.

One debate among scholars themselves centers in the precise social world that pertains to the life of Jesus, whether one should be looking at the wider Mediterranean world in the Levant or whether one should fix on the Jewish villages of lower Galilee. To a lesser extent the debate turns on how sociological results can be paired, if at all, with ideas and textual evidence. While few scholars frame the issue as an either/or, the differences among scholars rest on the relative weight they put on historical and comparative sociology or on traditional text-oriented results. Typically, scholars who emphasize sociological results produce a cosmopolitan, Hellenistic, and distinctly new looking Jesus, while scholars who work more with textual evidence usually offer more predictable Jewish Jesuses.

The choice of evidence seems to turn on the prevenient frame imagined for Jesus' hometown region. Here we have an enjoyable opportunity for retrojection, since *the search for the historical Galilee* is as elusive as the search for the historical Jesus. While the evidence itself may settle how Hellenized was Galilee, we have as yet no successful means to connect Jesus to the cosmopolitan wider world. Perhaps we can determine from resisting evidence how oppressive were the Romans, how much in economic crises was Galilee, how dispossessed and in class war were its peasants, how violent or revolutionary was the area, but we still do not know how to connect any of these themes to Jesus. It all turns on the frame one brings to the study

---

144. One of the liveliest discussions of the Third Quest is the proposal that the best analogy for the sage is with the cynic philosopher. See chapter 5 for the invention of Jesus-Sage.

145. See, for instance, the position of Borg, *Jesus: A New Vision*, 79.

of Jesus: just how conflictive and hellenistically complex does one imagine Galilee? Consequently, many scholars embrace the turn to sociology and social history and produce some startlingly cosmopolitan Jesuses, while others inspect the sociological work and turn back to textual evidence and construct a very Jewish Jesus. The former group tends to offer non-apocalyptic Jesuses, while the latter is friendlier to some kind of apocalyptic Jesus.

Theologians do not have a dog in this historians' fight. Nonetheless, **(Theological) Rule 42:** *they must remain critical of any effort to import sociological results whole-hog into christology, as if these results were faith's insights.* For instance, it is quite common for sociologically inclined historians to conclude firmly that the "love your enemies" logion is a political saying. While that may be true, we cannot assume the claim is simply a historical one at this point. If nothing else, the claims of sociologically inclined historians sound startlingly familiar in a generation of theology raised on liberation theology. While we cannot establish a causal link between liberationist themes and the kinds of things the historians are finding in Galilee, many historians' criticism of the apolitical Jesuses of the past and their construction of a politicized Jesus show that the liberationist hermeneutic floats in the air of Jesus research. Both the defenders and the critics of the sociological turn today must comment on the politics of Jesus, even if to deny he was political, in a way that would have been unthinkable years ago. It is no secret in Jesus research that a politicized Jesus does not look very *religious*, as we call it. Even if we note that modern notions of religion, as a private and subjective thing, have been retrojected onto Jesus, we still hear some stinging criticism of a political Jesus from middle and right-wing Jesus scholars. Similarly, the political Jesus is usually not really apocalyptic, in ways that we can easily understand. An apocalyptic Jesus wants to leave the world, after all, as Schweitzer knows.[146] Consequently, there are good reasons for theology to be suspicious, not least of all that certain historians may be selling theology wholesale as history.

Part of the suspicion about the sociological turn comes from the fact that social historians tend to overplay the results of their studies of life in Galilee. They overplay in two ways, the one mentioned above, namely, framing a Jesus with retrojected philosophical/theological themes, the other, an all-for-one mistake. That is, they tend to construct a Jesus or a fragment of Jesus too much isolated from the ideas and texts dominating the past Jesuses. **(Theological) Rule 43:** *Theologians need to be suspicious of the subtle hostility to ideas and textual evidence in certain of the sociological turns.* While the turn to sociology can concretize ideas, it does not replace them.

---

146. Unless a scholar attenuates the notion of apocalyptic.

As with all historical facts, sociological evidence speaks with a very small voice by itself.

There is a subtler aspect to the social-historical turn. It represents a pervasive paradigm change in history writing, away from the fascination with psychology and the great-man orientation of history. The focus is less on the genius of the heroic figure who bends history.[147] History is not the story of the hero's biography but of the way that individuals sit communally within a social and cultural network. When we translate this new orientation to Jesus research, we realize that much of the quest so far has been done in a great-man frame. His greatness becomes the foundation for the theological enthusiasm for him. But social history brings more attention to the way that Jesus was emplotted in a community, and if there is shouting about him, a good bit of that enthusiasm rests with those who received him. Feminist interpreters especially emphasize the notion that the christic is not an intrinsic quality in Jesus, his genius, but a relational happening in the interaction between Jesus and the community. Schaberg speaks of this happening as the "relational Jesus" and Brock speaks of it as a relational "erotic love." In both these instances Jesus research has been somewhat or completely de-centered from the person of Jesus.[148]

One can see that the sociological turn brings up the decision whether to portray Jesus with a politics or not: an explosive theme. Typically, the Third Quest Jesuses are more political than those in the past. Jesus either has a kind of religious politics or he opens the door to political critique and change. As we have seen, he is less likely to be an isolated, mystic, religious individual who is otherworldly and more likely very engaged in his social world. Today, even conservative scholars' turn to praxis in the world, and their critics commonly see the hand of a generation of scholars raised on liberation theology. Among scholars on the left, the themes of empowerment, of colonial oppression, of marginalization, of patriarchy, of domination paradigms, of class struggle, and economic dispossession fill the pages of the new Jesuses. It is common for contemporary Jesus researchers to think of Jesus as subversive, as an iconoclast who deconstructs something in his world.[149] Individual historians may see different targets of his critique and

---

147. Even a moderate Jesus scholar like Leander E. Keck is critical of heroic historiography; he sees it as is a liberal theological tendency: Keck, "The Second Coming," 784.

148. See Brock, *Journeys by Heart*, and Schaberg, *The Illegitimacy of Jesus*. We have endorsed the de-centering of christology by insisting on a dialectic between subject and object. Jesus is not the Christ as Jesus, so to speak, but as received as Jesus as the Christ.

149. Mack, *The Lost Gospel*, 119–20. Mack wants a subversive, countercultural Jesus who yet does not launch a social or political or reforming-religion campaign.

his aphoristic quips. Still, very few see Jesus as an active politician, despite the fact of his countercultural orientation.[150] Therefore, scholars disagree about the extent to which Jesus carries through on changes in the social order, with scholars on the left more likely to see in Jesus' actions political dimensions and scholars on the right and center more interest in the religiously reforming character of his ministry.

C.4. The Use of the Alien Criterion: Antidote to Retrojection?

Jesus historians find a further defense against retrojection when they locate in the Jesus saga materials that defy retrojection. They turn to an imaginative tool, a criterion, to secure the integrity of their historical research. They decide to seek in the saga the irreducibly different about Jesus: different from us, from our values, from our historical expectations, and certainly different from the doctrinal Christs. Schweitzer inspired the move, as we know, when at the end of his great study of the lives of Jesus books, he confidently identified the real Jesus to be the strange apocalyptic figure.[151] Charlesworth expresses the criterion best: "I am persuaded that I have not created a Jesus who serves my faith but have been confronted by a historical figure when Jesus appears offensive and strange."[152] How did Schweitzer know that the alien one was the real Jesus? How did he know that the liberal Jesuses were unreal, retrojected modern value constructions while the glimpse he had of the real Jesus escaped retrojection? How indeed? By appealing to the untamably different character of the real Jesus. The real Jesus is the alien one, *the one unknown*, who is beyond analogy, beyond our retrojective powers of domestication.[153]

Here we are not focused on the apocalyptic prophet and whether Schweitzer's choice can be sustained. Rather, what is of interest is the formal methodological move he makes and gives to the rest of the quest. We speak of this as the *alien criterion*, for it seeks in the Jesus saga the different that resists domestication.[154] The criterion is a hermeneutical relative of the much

---

150. This point is fodder for the critics of questing.

151. Perhaps the definitive articulation of the alien criterion can be found in: Schweitzer, *The Quest of the Historical Jesus*, 2001 edition, 478.

152. Charlesworth and Weaver, eds., *Images of Jesus Today*, 21.

153. Cf. Jeremias' confidence that the eschatology of Jesus would be a bulwark against modernizing: *The Problem of the Historical*, 19.

154. Schweitzer first sets out the notion that the alien Jesus can defend against domestication on *The Quest of the Historical Jesus*, 2001 edition, 478. See also Gowler, *What Are They Saying*, viii, 14.

debated, New Testament criteria of dissimilarity and of embarrassment[155] but generalized away from judgments about particular items in the Jesus saga. The criterion of dissimilarity, for example, looks at individual sayings in the saga and asks whether they are likely genuinely from Jesus. If an item from the saga does not match the views of Second Temple Judaism or of the earliest church, likely it goes back to Jesus. The generalized version of the alien criterion follows Schweitzer's lead and focuses on the wide-frame issues for construing the figure of Jesus: great themes even on up to paradigm choice. A historian can be confident of the objectivity of his/her historical construction so far as the Jesus produced shocks with difference.

Naturally, the alien criterion appeals to historians.[156] As a meta-methodological choice and value, it directs research toward the starkly different in an attempt to protect historical work against retrojection and to deliver a real Jesus whose reality is confirmed by his historical difference. Like the turn to method, the search for the confirming difference objectifies the capricious way that value can intrude on historical Jesus research. In fact, *the alien criterion bolsters the turn to method, by bringing to the selection of method a trump that defends against retrojected value.* As we have seen, the turn to method objectifies Jesus research somewhat but, apparently, it itself cannot escape the arms of retrojection unless it simultaneously seeks the alien. The truly alien is so unfamiliar or distasteful that a historian could not have invented it, nor could deep values of the historian slide into the Jesus construction. So one day historians achieve Jesus as a de-Christianized Jew, and on the next, he is a traditional Mediterranean peasant, or really an ancient person whose strange world is peopled with demons, and so on. The real Jesus differs from us sharply; he may offend our sensibilities, and he certainly is a critique of our modern fictions, as Schweitzer knows. When Jesus is shown to be so unlike us, historians are cheered. They are confident they have not succumbed to the dangers Schweitzer warned against. Of course, not every historical Jesus (nor element of a Jesus) appears as shockingly alien as Schweitzer's own Jesus. Nonetheless, it is important that historians show they have been *surprised* by the Jesus they produce: *surprise proves they are not mirroring themselves in the name of Jesus.* To be *embarrassed* is even better. Often it is a mark of historian's pride that Jesus shows up in church unrecognized . . . or that he is countercultural.

---

155. Embarrassment is an extreme form of the dissimilarity criterion: see Meier, *A Marginal Jew*, I, 171ff.

156. As Meier says: in guarding against domestication, "The quest for the historical Jesus, almost from its inception, has tended to emphasize the embarrassing, nonconformist aspects of Jesus": ibid., 199.

Historians and analysts of the quest have not yet noticed the extent to which the quest has been driven by a search for the alien. Undoubtedly historians and others will discuss it eventually, given the vigor of the discussion over the use of the criterion of dissimilarity in gospel research.[157] Undoubtedly, the research will begin to recognize its strengths and limits, ones analogous to the virtues and risks of the use of dissimilarity. Just as dissimilarity builds objective confidence by accenting the detailed sayings of Jesus that are *unlike*, so searching for an alien Jesus can reassure. Of course, the criterion tends to recognize the reality of Jesus in his radical difference from us in the contemporary world but is less reliable in discerning commonality or continuity both with his world and with us. And sooner or later the research on Jesus has to notice that we become accustomed to radical difference and the alien begins to lose its edge and thereby its power to assure the research. Recall that not so long after Schweitzer discovered the alien apocalyptic prophet, historians and theologians settled into inventive ways to become comfortable with an apocalyptic Jesus. Here we face the backside of the drive for the alien: *the power of the imagination to domesticate the alien.*[158]

Theologians must keep an eye on historians' use of the alien criterion. Jesus historians favor the alien criterion to demonstrate that they have avoided distorting bias and perspective. For historians the alien criterion is an anti-retrojection device. However, **(Theological) Rule 44:** *Theologians must guard the use of the alien criterion and check that the criterion does not blind historical research to the same, the similar, and the continuous.* The criterion can be charmed by exotica and miss the value in the ordinary. While Schweitzer himself stumbled onto the criterion, its disciplined use today may exaggerate discontinuity in its search for difference, since it happens onto a position that implies that *everything same is subject to retrojection.* Schweitzer, for instance, got so convinced that he had cleared a space against the retrojection of value that he could not appreciate the world affirming elements in the Jesus saga (much less of apocalyptic). And while theologians want to affirm the historian's work effort not to manipulate evidence, they will want to see that historians do not lose sight of Jesus' similarity to his age or even to us. Further, they may have to correct one feature of the use of the criterion. As it was conceived, the criterion meant to protect history from the retrojection of value, and perhaps today still may seduce historians

---

157. Few topics in the quest have received as much discussion as the debate over the criterion of dissimilarity. Every historian begins every Jesus book by commenting on the debate and the critics of the quest attack its use.

158. Cf. Moxnes' argument for the domesticating character of historical research: Moxnes, "Theological Importance," 97.

into imagining they are free of the value question in their history writing. If the criterion gives historians a false sense that they have dispensed with value, so far as they have found the categorically different, theologians must call history writing back to a more sophisticated value conversation with ancient materials. **(Theological) Rule 45:** *Theologians must check that the historians' use of the alien criterion not create a faulty assumption that a Jesus is free of value.*

The theologian, therefore, has to be a critic of the conduct of the historians without claiming any special insight into the what-happened question. The use of the alien criterion alerts theologians to areas of inquiry where they have special expertise: in meta areas beyond the daily conduct of history writing, in historiographical and hermeneutical business, and in the philosophical underpinnings of the writing of history. After all, what is truly alien is a historical show-stopper: beyond analogy and where language fails. But the theologian is more accustomed to traffic in otherness. Take, for instance, the issue of the healings in the Jesus saga. During the first epochs of the quest, historians, under Enlightenment epistemologies, dismissed the healing stories as typical folk-tale heroics. More recently, under changes in the epistemological and historiographical climate, Jesus historians have noted more and more that the healing stories show resistance in the saga. They persist against our values, particularly against the concerns of the modern academy. Yet, no Jesus historian has a sophisticated, non-reductive category or conceptuality to capture the resistance of the healing story. So, historians report voiceless thereness in Jesus as healer without knowing what to do with the report.

It becomes a central theological task to do something further with the alien. Theologians, of course, have to *admire the historical construction of the alien.* Despite the theological critique of hanging the historical hat on the alien, *the theologian notes that in the radically disanalogical and discontinuous historians confront an aporia, the absolutely other.* They enter a liminal situation that appears similar to a primal religious experience. They are speechless, rather in the way that Schweitzer has to shift gears into poetic meta-historical language at the end of his study.[159] First of all, **(Theological) Rule 46:** *Theologians must discover the values operative in what surprises the historians.* Then, again, they must *pursue a genealogical step*: why do these items in the Jesus construction shock or at least unnerve us? Next,

---

159. Dunn offers a brilliant insight into how the alien criterion has functioned: in an effort to purge Jesus of Christianisms and to judaize Jesus, historians have turned to the alien Jesus to preserve a surplus of meaning useful for Christian theological purposes: Dunn, "Can the Third Quest," in Chilton and Evans, eds., *Authenticating the Activities,* 36–37.

(Theological) Rule 47: *the theologian must interpret the balancing of the shock of the new/alien with the domesticating power of a familiarizing imagination.* There is no question that historians often get excited when they encounter the alien, and if they can say anything at all about it, they tend to drop into meta-historical or mythic language.[160] Schweitzer, for instance, was so awed by the freakish Jesus that he felt he had had a glimpse of something absolute. He speaks of confronting the realized Jesus as "a mighty spiritual force," as a fact that "can neither be shaken nor confirmed by any historical discovery," and "independent of any historical knowledge or justification."[161] More recently, C. Stephen Evans thinks he has a christological cipher to God when he retrieves the supernatural as historical from the Jesus saga. It is easy to be moved by "a mighty spiritual force" that "streams forth from him and flows through our time also."[162] But theologians have gotten burned by enthusiasm before and know that they must test the spirits. It is too easy for the interested to inflate what is other into the Other, or to say it christologically, it is too easy for historians and others to mistake something of interest

---

160. We intend to notice *myth* here and not be critical of it except where historians recognize that role of myth in history writing. *Myth enters history where historians situate the plenary work of history writing into a larger world.* Most Jesus researchers, zoom higher, when they package a Jesus. Often there are clues of deep value, final value, suggestions of modeling and imitation, recommendations that Jesus' way could fix something, a reclaiming of ideals and suggestions that Jesus may have really gotten the world right. These values (and their negative forms) go beyond the plenary function of history writing. The only category I know which captures these meta meta-historical clues and expressions is myth. In a general way I am allying with the Eliadean tradition of myth as cosmicizing, but without the intense focus on cosmogonic myth among archaic people and without Eliade's suspicion of history: Eliade, *Cosmos and History*. See Claude Levi-Strauss, "The Structural Study of Myth," in Sebeok, *Myth*, 87. To capture the myth-making in Jesus research I am dependent upon Paul Ricoeur's project to recover the larger world of symbolic language and to recover a revised Kantian sense for the productive imagination. Here I appropriate his sense for the possibility-discerning aspect of metaphor for the large foundation narrative that is myth. *Myth projects a world; a historical myth projects by "retrojection,"* if I can return to that category, that is, *by imaginatively producing a myth related to the past which is a project for the will: Essays on Biblical*, 30, 36, 102. Such a project enlarges our world: "the outline of a new way of being in the world," as Ricoeur says about Heidegger: *Interpretation Theory*, 37. The creative aspect of myth rests on the "semantic innovation" of metaphor, according to Ricoeur: ibid., 63. David Price writes of *the future of the past*: "The key to the imagination is figuration; every act we commit is a projection of a figured future. A recreation of the past, therefore, would be the projection of the future in the past. In other words, to comprehend fully the reality of the past, we must participate in the processes whereby individuals, peoples, and entire cultures, and societies *figured* through imaginative projections of their wills": Price, *History Made*, 3.

161. Schweitzer, *The Quest of the Historical Jesus*, 2001 edition, 489.

162. Ibid., 479.

in the historical record as itself christic. **(Theological) Rule 48:** *Theologians therefore need to be alert to the points where the use of the alien criterion presses an interest to sacrilize a point of otherness.* Even a miraculous Jesus is not the Christ, as the gospel narratives knew. So, theologians need to be suspicious and, surprisingly, must take Schweitzer's suspicion a step beyond his application. Even the discovery of the categorically different from us, from our values, functions within our value constructions. We set what is alien, even if only by way of an indirect, negative value, and thus, our discernment of what is other is subject to retrojection.

Retrojected value is ubiquitous. Even the techniques to avoid retrojected value are subject to retrojected value. The turn to method can be value-laden. The use of the alien criterion too does not escape value. Therefore, **(Theological) Rule 49:** *Theologians must be suspicious of the use of the alien criterion.* The criterion does offer relative help in managing manipulative retrojection of value, but not an airtight escape from value. But because of its relative help, theologians need to hold suspicion critically and lobby for balanced historical judgment.[163] Once we have noted our balancing of suspicions, we are able to indicate *that the historical identification of otherness can be an opportunity for theology.* After all, theologians and people of faith have more conceptual tools in the box than simply the historian's analogy. One thinks of the role of narrative and myth, of the investment in symbolic or figurative discourse, and of the long-standing attention to apophatic approaches to the Other. What is *the historian's aporia can be a launching place for theological reflection.*

C.5. The Difference Criterion: The Softer Alien

Possibly, the search for the alien is too extreme for history writing. It is an experience of otherness, where historians, like Schweitzer at the end of *The Quest*, face a limit, locate the *aporia* at the end of historical research, and then close down explanation in a flurry of figurative or mythic words.[164] Historians have found their liminal experience and they do not know what to say about what is beyond analogy. The apocalyptic is one such aporia; Jesus as a healer is another. More often historians today turn away from the alien to a softer imaginative relative, a *difference criterion*, which also

---

163. Powell, *Jesus as a Figure*, 18.

164. Despite the negative sounding judgment here, myth has virtue precisely as that which takes over when historical explanation comes up to its limit. The real danger of mythic language happens when people take the mythic as if it were historical. In the fullest sense, *the past is saved and kept alive by mythicizing the historical.*

promises to protect Jesus against themselves and their values, and to secure the integrity of their historical research. The criterion works like the alien criterion but it gives historians and theologians more to work with. It seeks the novel or the unlike, not the categorically different and operates on a double level: what, if anything, is new in Jesus in relation to elements in his world; and what is new in our picturing of his life and ministry.[165] What motivates the turn from the alien to the different in the research? We would be guessing motives in a complex matter, but we do know that historians have difficulty knowing what to say about what is beyond analogy since the pursuit of the novel operates in tension with the natural analogical strengths of historians. They are not required to enter the world of poets or theologians. We do know that Jesus research has been haunted by the crazed apocalyptic prophet of Schweitzer; and a discerning eye to the history of the research will notice that historians and theologians found the apocalyptic paradigm useful only so far as they could boil off the apocalyptic frenzy. The suspicion is that *the difference criterion is a tamer, domesticated alien criterion*, one more apt for historical inquiry, on the one hand, and yet able to deliver some of the rewards of the alien, on the other hand.

The criterion helps us to locate the emergence of *new* Jesus meaning on the horizon: new to Jesus, as it were, and new to us. We have to name both moments of newness, even if there is an overlap between the two.[166] For instance, Weiss' departure from the liberal Jesuses depends on his reading of evidence in the saga through different eyes, within a different frame, that of a genuine apocalypticist. The new Jesus threatened reigning theologies and cultural values, as we have seen. More recently, many Third Quest historians, often rejecting that consensus Weiss launched for the twentieth century, appeal to a sapiential Jesus as a break with the apocalyptic. Here, Jesus is doubly different, separated both from reigning Jewish and early Christian apocalyptic forms and from the reigning views of Jesus research. We quickly recognize that in the history of Jesus research difference is diverse and quite multi-layered; at least it includes: 1. the difference a Jesus represents over against ecclesiastical Christs (and to a lesser degree, cultural

---

165. Schüssler Fiorenza sets out an intriguing feminist version of the difference theme: the fact that women are different from the male figure of Jesus may mean that feminist wrestlings with the historical Jesus are freer of bias: being a feminist can be a critical check against too easy retrojection of unthinking patriarchal, etc. assumptions: *Jesus and the Politics*, 12. Schüssler Fiorenza, moreover, argues that a rich socio-political reconstruction of the world of Jesus protects against retrojection of value, too, since a social portrait can check against the malish attempt to picture Jesus as the charismatic, great-man individualist: ibid., 23.

166. Since it is central to the understanding of history here that history writing is a dialectical engagement with evidence.

values); 2. Jesus' historical difference from the worldviews around him; 3. Jesus' difference from modern values; and 4. Jesus' difference from reigning scholarly reconstructions of him.

The first difference names a classic Enlightenment ambition of historical research on the gospels: to clean the dogmatic tradition of unreasonable christological claims.[167] While this motive typifies the early quests, it continues powerfully today in the work of some Jesus researchers.[168] In the first kind of difference, the different in a Jesus represents a value taken against a dogmatic formulation. The value operates negatively and becomes the basis of a critique of theological or pious christologies. Of course, if a value from a Jesus can negate a christological position or formulation, then it no longer operates on the historical level of generality on which it was conceived: not as reasonably composed claim about Jesus, but as a christological marker. That is, someone, perhaps the historian or a theologian, has actuated a framed and intelligible element of a Jesus within the world of faith (in a positive or negative application).

Suppose, for instance, that a historian determines that it is incredible that Jesus is a healer. If a person takes that fact to undermine a christological position, then that person has actuated a possibility in a Jesus. What is *a possible opportunity in the imaging of Jesus* has been snatched up as a *christological recommendation*. Someone has judged that healing in Jesus is a christic issue and the loss of healing damages a christological claim.[169] While such a judgment may seem natural to modern Christians,[170] it is neither obvious, nor necessary for, say, Muslims, who have no trouble holding to the miraculous in Jesus but do not read it as christic. In another example, historians may hold that Jesus' status as a peasant is important to make him intelligible, but in the eyes of one theologian, his peasantness seems to be incidental and of no use for a christology. In that case, a fact provides opportunity but neither a critic nor a christologist uses it in christological production. But another thinker (i.e., Crossan) sees the peasant character of Jesus to be central to what makes him interesting to the faith; indeed, we find all sorts of hints of a liberation theology slightly under the surface of the "Mediterranean Jewish Peasant."

The second form of difference suggests that Jesus actually departs from historical options available to his culture and is (relatively) unique.

---

167. We consider this function fully in chapter 4.

168. I.e., see the sophomoric enthusiasm of Funk's *Honest to Jesus*.

169. More recently some Jesus historians have reversed the direction of the same logic: determining that Jesus was a healer allows them to make christological claims for him.

170. Here modern Christians usually ignore the biblical critique of miracle.

Difference here often identifies positive value in Jesus. The value might be as simple as a revisionist historical reconstruction of an ancient figure, but it also might be the basis of a value application for contemporary culture and church. Take, for instance, one major issue of every Jesus: is there anything suggestive about Jesus' difference from John the Baptist? If a scholar is interested in christological opportunities, conceivably, Jesus' difference from his mentor might support a non-apocalyptic christology or soft-apocalyptic christology. How a Jesus sets up Jesus' difference from his world becomes a magnet for value, since we see difference according to our values, since we may over-value the difference we notice in Jesus, and since we are apt to totalize from the difference we notice to establish a comprehensive christology on the basis of noticed difference. Of course, the minute we qualify the status of difference, we have to remind ourselves that difference is interesting and might be true.

When we determine difference, are we somehow retrojecting value onto Jesus? More difficult to judge will be whether in our enthusiasm we have over-valued difference. Does an item we find suggestive in a Jesus have central value, marginal value, or simply prove to be incidental? Are we over-reading it because it speaks to us? Are we over-emphasizing its value among other values? Consider whether Jesus is a typical, first-century Jewish male in his relationships to women and to outcasts. Does he depart significantly from the pattern of males in his culture? Is his departure from the typical itself compelling, or possibly, simply incidental, or actually a side consequence of some other value in Jesus? As we have learned in the last years, people simply do not thematize Jesus' relationships with women until they have developed a gender-sensitive hermeneutic and have started to notice a difference. And today, virtually every Jesus on the market makes a big deal about Jesus' free-wheeling, non-patriarchal behavior. Some see in it a christologically suggestive value and even build an entire christology of liberative practice on the basis of this difference.[171] Some are so impressed with his liberative practice that they judge the practice itself to be christic, independent of Jesus.[172] Such a christological application may have risks: how do we know that the difference we notice says anything significant about Jesus (instead of us)? This question returns us to the problem of retrojection, but now with some novel topspin. We can imagine that we retroject onto Jesus when we find in him familiar and cherished values. Here retrojection operates within sameness. But a more complex form of retrojection may happen when we place on Jesus cherished differences from us, those values

---

171. Schüssler Fiorenza, *Jesus and the Politics*.
172. I.e., Brock, *Journeys by Heart*.

we do not represent but would *like* to represent. Here Jesus is different from us, but different from us in the way we want ourselves to be different, thus according to prized values we do not instantiate. So, in a gender sensitive climate interested in the critique of patriarchy Jesus appears as egalitarian[173] and inclusive, but not, say, as ascetic. We can see that the difference-we-like found in Jesus can become the basis of a prophetic christology.

At this point we will have to refine our up-coming analysis of the retrojection thesis to accommodate the rhythm of same and difference. We can easily see the most evident form of mirroring that goes into a Jesus.[174] The values we like we find instantiated in Jesus; he likely is a larger version of these values and can stand to inspire us. Here retrojection lives within a saming self-reflection: Jesus is like us, and different ages see different things in him and may pick up on these differences differently. Different eras may seek more sameness in a Jesus, according to perceived spiritual needs: a friendly Jesus and an emaciated Jesus can both be christic, but with a different grade how like us he is to be. Indeed, a Jesus who manifests intensely the same quality we value in ourselves enters into a difference from us, a difference that can become an ideal.

We will want to keep track of a further and subtler form of retrojection, one that operates where we locate substantial difference from us, a difference we value. Here the retrojection involves, not valorizing our favorite themes, but the launching of values against which we wish to be judged, or against which we understand we must be judged. These values are lacking in us but they are the ones by which we wish to be stretched, judged, criticized; conceivably, the faithful and theologians may have confronted these values in resisting evidence from the Jesus saga itself.[175] Thus, we may participate in a patriarchal culture and, out of a growing gender sensitivity, decide it is the gender inclusiveness in Jesus by which we wish to be criticized. At the same time, we may not notice the asceticism of Jesus because we do not value the ascetic and do not want to be judged by ascetic standards. The subtler form of retrojection, consequently, appears wherever we select the ideals against which we will be judged by a Jesus.

Evidently, a Jesus who differs from his contemporaries or from the Christs of the Church cannot escape the retrojection critique, since in a large degree scholars shape the different. A third kind of difference aims

---

173. See Crossan's "open commensality": *The Historical Jesus*, 341.

174. Allison, for instance, notes how like is drawn to like, when theologians are attracted to particular Jesuses or familiar elements of a Jesus: Allison, *The Historical Christ*, 29.

175. Here we have a fairly strong argument against the complete reduction of questing into the values of the historian, as is typical among the anti-quest voices.

to protect historical research better against retrojected value and functions apologetically against critiques founded on the retrojection thesis; it is a defensive strategy meant to counter criticism. Here a historian points to *themes in a Jesus which defy being reduced into modern values and ideals.* The different in Jesus proves we are listening to genuine historical evidence and not simply looking at ourselves in a mirror. In the most low-flying application, this defense against retrojection functions as a check against historical bias: thus, the search for the different may be nothing more than an epistemological-methodological orientation in quality historical research. But at times, under more strenuous effort, *a defense against retrojection turns to difference to prove that scholars and others have not manipulated the figure of Jesus in picturing him.* Here we have a *moral check* designed to free Jesus from contemporary values, to demonstrate that Jesus can have his own voice different from ours. Why would historians make such a point? Presumably, because they take an interest in unvarnished difference: they want a Jesus who represents value that does not reduce to self-reflection. *Difference means that they have succeeded in their historical work, yes, but difference also means that they have uncovered something valuable that resists reduction to self-reflection.* Here we find a value that can inform us (i.e., scholars, society, church) normatively: as Jose Miranda says, "The Christ that cannot be co-opted by the comfortable is the historical Jesus."[176] In the broadest sense, then, *the moral application of the retrojection thesis opens the door to a christological interest.*

To the original three differences, we add a fourth that functions within the waves of scholarly research in which one generation works through problems of the generations and concludes there is need to overturn the work of a previous generation. This difference, too, is logically independent of the retrojection issue, but has been historically connected to it in the history of Jesus research. In my view, it is perfectly reasonable to hear the Oedipal plot acted out as one generation rejects the work of the previous one.[177] But the useful feature of the appeal to this difference is that it may signal to all when a new Jesus is emerging in the history of the research. Difference can be a sign of a paradigm shift in Jesus research, since the shift often appears as the discovery of a hitherto-unrecognized difference in Jesus' relationship to his world (difference 2) or in an unrecognized value retrojection in the last generation's Jesus studies (the issue of difference 3). *Difference produces difference*: a categorically different Jesus emerges when

---

176. Miranda, *Being and the Messiah*, 9.

177. I read the allergic rejection of the apocalyptic paradigm by some of the sapiential types as just such an Oedipal move.

difference has been isolated and then certain scholars are in a position to raise again the consequence of this difference for a dogmatic Christ (difference 1), or to notice that difference has been flattened in a fashionable theological use: the domestication theme again. We see, then, that the four senses of difference frequently are interrelated.

When the research on Jesus focuses so on the importance of difference, it brings with it certain risks, softer versions of the ones that circle about the alien criterion. The immense conversation about the famous criterion of dissimilarity (for determining genuine Jesus sayings) has uncovered many of these difficulties. For instance, heightened attention to unique sayings in the Jesus saga may disguise familiar, common things Jesus may have said, by noticing only the elements in Jesus that depart from Second Temple Jewish themes or that of the early Christians. So, too, the application of the difference criterion, in any of its forms, may divert attention from Jesus' sameness. Jesus' status as a Jew among Jews can be at issue, for instance. Oddly, then, there must be a *critical check on the application of the difference criterion*, itself designed as a critical check, since the criterion may be overdone and make scholars blind to elements that Jesus shares with his world. It may overdo his difference and consequently be *too hopeful for value opportunity found within his alleged difference*. Perhaps little is at stake whether Jesus said this or that saying; but much could be at stake in assessing the larger issue of his whole mission/task/orientation. If a construal of his entire life work were dependent on his difference from his contemporaries (i.e., was Jesus an apocalypticist?), it would stand to win or lose on major value opportunities.

Further, we have to notice that attention to difference may mask, not simply commonalities, but coincidences, accidental overlaps and historical continuities. A focus on Jesus' difference from, say, other Jews of his world can miss points where he incidentally or casually presupposes themes of his world or of Second Temple Judaism. Attention to Jesus' difference from our worldviews and values may make us blind to the themes where he chances to hold similar views or where our views have been influenced by the history of the effects of Jesus. We may be blind to accidental values, to uncaused coincidences or consonances of value, or to historically derived continuities of value. For instance, in the era of the Third Quest, it has been fashionable to see in Jesus someone who prefigures our sensitivity to gender issues. Can we contemporary people claim a genuine similarity between Jesus and us? Or is Jesus' attention to gender issues no more than a homology to our interest in gender, such that there is no genuine value contact between Jesus and us? The retrojection theorist immediately smells an effort to make Jesus a contemporary feminist and to reduce the picture of Jesus to a modern self-portraiture. While there may be (much) truth to this critique, it cannot see fully the possibility that Jesus may represent values consonant with us despite our wishful retrojections. We want a Jesus who feeds our gender transformations and, despite our wishes, not because of them, Jesus does indeed represent a gender transformation in the Mediterranean world.

Here in this blocked or partially blocked vision we have identified a serious limitation to the application of retrojection theories. Such theories cannot see some or certain elements in a Jesus. At times they are blind to resisting evidence. And to be able to see what they cannot see would undermine the adequacy of the reductive approach of the theory. Indeed, there would be a surplus of meaning: further, retrojection theories require a meta-theoretical position to found their critique. They insist that they can spot the errors of value retrojected onto Jesus, yet they imply that their spotting equipment is historically accurate and free of retrojected value. In other words, critique itself brings value and a theory of critique brings heavy value. For instance, as we have noted already, critique values difference and is suspicious of sameness. Sameness, it turns out, is as complicated as difference: it flattens value and unique value in Jesus; it also signals that we are being self-reflexive; it means we scholars have nothing new to say about Jesus; and so on.

One of the remarkable features of the new Jesus research of the last thirty years has been the coincidence of the four forms of difference in the work of many Jesus scholars. Currently, many researchers are dissociating Jesus from Second Temple Judaism at the same time they are abandoning last generation's consensus picture of Jesus, even as they smart under new applications of the retrojectionist critique. And some take the new Jesuses to be cause for critique of churchly and popular Christs. Forms of difference support each other and the discovery of difference in one area frequently triggers difference in another. Thus, when earlier scholars get Jesus' relationship to his world and to Jewish themes wrong, suddenly we have a new generation of Jesus researchers with a life's task to revise the paradigm or to create a new one. Jesus appears newly and noticeably different from the reigning ways of his world and suddenly historians must think differently about him. And just as soon as the new Jesuses emerge, other scholars attack their questing as little more than renewed efforts to modernize Jesus. In response, these scholars have defended themselves with a complex new appeal to difference which resists retrojection.

C.6. Lessons from the Quest

Part of the self-conscious, methodic attention to retrojection and the attention to the alien and the different is the disciplined study of the history of the historical study of Jesus. The history of the quest brings lessons and is therefore comprised of a certain spiraling progress. Despite what the anti-quest crowd thinks, the quest is not one damn thing after another. More or less scholars are learning from the past of their craft, from things questers do right and from their mistakes. More importantly, perhaps, they learn the *questing* version of a hermeneutic of suspicion. Through Schweitzer, scholars, including quest-oriented historians, have learned how to recognize retrojected value and how to apply the critique of retrojection. After Schweitzer every Jesus historian worries about anachronistic treatments of Jesus; every Jesus historian can spot them in other researchers' works; every historian makes efforts to avoid retrojection:

C.6.a. (**Theological**) **Rule 50:** *The most useful, quested Jesuses for christological employment are ones that are crafted within a heightened sense for the history of questing.* Since Jesus research can be subject to the retrojection Schweitzer identified, it is relatively protected from its own tendency where it is done with meticulous, methodologically reflexive, self-consciousness in the full light of the structure of retrojection and of the history of successful and failed quests. Scholars pose the best Jesuses for christology amid methodological alarms. A Jesus who stands among all the quested Jesuses is most likely to make the contributions to christology outlined above. That Jesus will internalize the self-reflexive lessons of past quests.

C.6.b. (**Quest**) **Rule 51:** *Historians and theologians should not be trapped by the periodizing of the history of the quest or by individual divisions and labels of methods/styles/goals/eras.* The more one knows about the history of the quest and the quests, the more one sees significant lines of continuity among all the epochs and overlaps of orientation. Indeed, scholars tend to periodize the quest and label movements and style for meta-historical reasons. Typically, the drive to periodize and label the history of questing serves ideological purposes, to distinguish, to separate, and to criticize others.[178]

---

178. See the self-serving way Robert Funk divides contemporary Jesus researchers between the "pretend questers," all the conservatives and moderates who are doing nothing but protecting ecclesial orthodoxy from the collapse of neo-orthodoxy, and the good guys, the "renewed questers," who agree with Funk on method, sources, and aims for the quest: Funk, *Honest to Jesus,* 64. In Funk's reconstruction, all the conservative and moderate questers have not entered the new "paradigm" for the research that began about 1975 but are engaged in rear-guard defenses of orthodoxy.

C.6.c. (**Quest**) **Rule 52:** *The most useful, quested Jesuses for christological purposes will have internalized changing senses of the historical.* Not all history is the same. The minute questing can be freed from positivistic models of historiography, it is open to drawing in the deepest lessons of a historical consciousness: that the historical is crafted in and amid interests and intentions of meaning, that the ahistorical and mythic have a history, that history itself has a history.[179]

C.6.d. (**Theological**) **Rule 53:** *The best Jesuses for christological purposes have been honed by the public, academic discussion of the historians and theologians.* Christology does well when it relies on quested Jesuses that stand the scrutiny of public debate. The position here argues that the sturdiest pictures, the ones closest to the center, the ones tied mostly strongly with consensus, are to be viewed typically as most reliable for theological work. The theologian should look first to the consensus and to the reigning paradigm for his/her Jesus.

Of course, this rule has risks. First, by favoring consensus Jesuses christology is adrift in times of paradigm shift. It was perfectly reasonable that certain theologies once worked with the liberal Jesus of the nineteenth century or the apocalyptic Jesus of the twentieth century, but today we may be between paradigms. We are seeing little consensus and little of an agreed-upon paradigm emerging. The transition in Jesus research feels theologically like that happening in the 1900 to 1920 era when Wrede, Weiss, and Schweitzer stirred things up for liberal christologies. Then, a second risk is that favoring the consensus may squelch badly needed odd, extreme or marginalized pictures of Jesus. We need the Schweitzers and the Macks of Jesus research, ones who go against the stream. We need their capacity to force clarity, to challenge the consensus and to bring out suppressed tones. In addition, the odd Jesuses may well be the leading edge of the new paradigm, as Schweitzer's was.

C.6.e. (**Theological**) **Rule 54:** *Questing for a Jesus cannot simply be left to the historians.* The rule here argues that one cannot trust historians to be historians. Or said with more nuance, one needs outsider checks to keep historians on track. Of course, we do not debate that New Testament scholars and historians of Judaism and Christian origins need to do virtually all the spadework on constructing a Jesus. But the history of the quest has been a discouraging story of self-forgetfulness: historian after historian, fully aware of the dangers of retrojected value, fully critical of other scholars'

---

179. See Patterson, *The God of Jesus*, vi.

modernizing of Jesus, go on to construct Jesuses that seem like mirror images of themselves. The irony is powerful. Only the scholars who are trained historians can do the spadework on Jesus and the only guard there is against retrojection is heightened consciousness of retrojection; we have a guild that professes to have learned the lessons of Schweitzer, and each historian is keen to see retrojection in everyone else's Jesus, but relatively blind to his/her own. No wonder that many would abandon questing.

Methodological self-consciousness and public academic debate among historians can help relatively to counter retrojection of values onto Jesus; but a further check can be put in place by drawing in philosophers and theologians. Not only do they bring outside eyes, but eyes particularly attuned to the study and history of values. It is no secret that the best critiques of retrojection, then and now, have emerged from outside the guild of historians.

C.6.f. **(Quest) Rule 55:** *An application of the alien criterion: Be suspicious if one's invented Jesus matches closely the needs of the day.* Here we have a rule that extends Schweitzer's insight about the structure of retrojection. We have to be historically suspicious when we find in Jesus exactly what we look for or think we need in a Christ. Any intimate coordination of the sought and the found should sound alarms, and while it is perfectly possible that the historically found could be what we want, the larger record of the quests has been a persistent pattern of questers getting from history what they want, what they think we need.

The lesson from Schweitzer is to begin with suspicion. *Too cozy a seek/find correlation is bad news.*[180] If a scholar thinks the creedal Christ of ecclesiastical tradition must be destroyed, be very suspicious when the same historian finds Jesus to be an iconoclast.[181] A different Jesus—the alien one—more reliably breaks out of the seek/find expectation. As we have seen, surprise is good, and surprise over the difference historians find in Jesus is very good.

C.6.g. **(Quest) Rule 56:** *Be suspicious of any certain claims for the real Jesus.* Despite all the warnings historians and theologians continue to make irrationally confident claims for the *real* Jesus. They are certain of their single Jesus and they sneer at other Jesuses. Such certainty surely is blindness and works to undermine the willingness of scholars and church people to be

---

180. The post-liberal critique of the Tillichian method of correlation comes to mind.

181. Cf. for instance, the disturbing lack of self-reflexivity about a reflexive issue in Funk, *Honest to Jesus*, 31.

serious about questing. Bravado about one's construction of Jesus may arise out of scholarly stag behavior and have only a rhetorical basis; more troublesome, it may express a hidden historical positivism—we have finally gotten to the unvarnished facts about Jesus! Worse yet, it may be an ideological expression that implies some judgment about the *meaning* of Jesus hidden in a construction of his history. The first is without basis unless the second or third factors lie behind it. The second is epistemologically and historiographically naïve, while the third is little more than a christology or antichristology playing in the field of history.

C.6.h. **(Quest) Rule 57:** *Be suspicious of the suspicion of questing.* Christological employment of Jesus research must begin in suspicion of the methods and moves of the historians. It seeks to identify the values operative in Jesus research and takes the lead in constructing a genealogy of those values, even when historians eschew the task or seem only partially aware of the issue. Theologians must be sleuths of anachronistic retrojection onto the figure of Jesus. Of telling importance are the points where Jesus researchers exhibit suspicion of something in the Jesus saga; the inverse, also revelatory, points to too-friendly or too-easy historical appropriation of something from the Jesus saga. Points of suspicion and suspicion of suspicion are alarms that cause the theologian to redouble the concern not to be manipulating the figure of Jesus; but they do not necessarily signal historical mistakes. Suspicion can overlap with historical accuracy; and an easy element to grasp in the Jesus saga could just as well be true as an alien one. We put up close scrutiny under the mode of suspicion; but we do not necessarily dispose of the suspected.

C.6.i. **(Quest) Rule 58:** *Avoid an artificial separation of historical and theological themes on the turf of Jesus studies.* Of course, a historian can eschew theological questions and even questions of value and relevance in Jesus research; we have to honor those intentionalities.[182] We have to honor also the ideal of neutrality in historical research as a noble asymptotic value: it aims to keep bias under control. And of course, modern questing stands opposed to ahistorical christologies which, naively or self-consciously, posit the historicity of the Jesus saga under the theological pressures of the dogmatic tradition. But once we oppose blunt positions and extreme expectations, we find ourselves in a gray middle where the difference between history and

---

182. John Meier, for instance, continues to insist that a "purely empirical, historical quest" can and should "prescind from" or "bracket" what is known by faith: Meier, "The Present State," 464.

theology becomes murky.[183] Scholars seeking to avoid bias cannot; scholars who claim to be strict historians wander into christological territories; values intrude on all the constructions; and the difference between historians who embrace christological possibilities and those who reject them or are indifferent to them is miniscule. Therefore, no longer is it reasonable to separate (so-called) strictly historical study and theologically intended history writing on the figure of Jesus. We save time and effort when we recognize that no one can treat the figure of Jesus without a thickness of value. As Boring puts it, even if we can distinguish the strictly historical from the value-laden and theological in theory, we cannot do so in practice.[184] Value, ideology, theology, anti-theology all saturate every step of the construction of a historical Jesus and inform every step of the method.

Crossan once set out a critical judgment on questing, that historical Jesus research too often has been a safe place to do theology and call it history.[185] Following insight in the spirit of Schweitzer, his point regrets that so many Jesus scholars, wittingly or not, sneak theological views into their historical reconstructions. And we can easily sympathize with Crossan's regret when we think of *extreme* positions. But today few historians advocate a historical objectivism, on the one hand; more historians are apt to hold to an ideal of unbiased history writing. And critical scholars no longer think that historical research can smooth all the wrinkles of the New Testament images and produce a Chalcedonian Christ, on the other. In the gray middle the values, ideologies, and theologies of the historians shape the construal of the figure of Jesus. Why? Because the shape of the Jesus depends in large part on the meta-decisions concerning the sources and methods, and a historian's disposition to these decisions arises out of themes that are not strictly historical. Whether meta-decisions make history in all cases of historiography is beyond the turf of this book, but it appears definitely to be the case with the history of Jesus. For all the reasons we know already, the construction of a Jesus is maximally a dot-to-dot creation of an image, dependent on holistic judgments prior to working inductively with any of the

183. The claim pertains here only to the particular case of Jesus research and may not apply more generally.

184. Boring, "The 'Third Quest,'" 347.

185. Crossan, *The Historical Jesus*, xxviii. There is reason to believe not only that Crossan himself has done what he complains about (doing theology in historical research) but that he recognizes that the line between theology (or value reflections) and history is much more permeable. Jesus researchers are particularly good at noticing the theology and values operative in other Jesuses. Cf. John P. Meier, "All too often the first and second quests were theological projects masquerading as historical projects": "The Present State," 464.

dots on the page. And the Jesus constructed tags along reliably according to the meta-judgments made.

All the major either/or points of the contemporary discussion require the historian to roost on a plank which is not strictly drawn out of the evidence. Good scholars disagree on whether to see much use in the gospel of Thomas; they differ on whether to go with a minimalist foundation (for a sharp image) or a maximal scanning of all the evidence (for an eclectic image);[186] they divide over the use of Q and whether there are levels of Q-ness, whether Kingdom language carries any sort of an apocalyptic smell to it or not; should we focus only on the canonical gospels, should we privilege the actions of Jesus—the list is endless. And no interpreter of the quested Jesuses can any longer assume the historians are simply arguing over methods and sources and judgments about individual items in the saga. The fight is over values in the broadest sense and thus is theological or pre-theological in character. Of course, we could take this observation and side with the anti-quester crowd; but we are no longer able to go along with Crossan's regret, certain that the other historians are theologians while better history will give us the pure history (on which theology can be founded).[187]

Once we have made the point about the value-laden character of Jesus research, we need to make a Kantian move. On one hand, the evidence in the Jesus saga is strictly atomistic: dots without connections, so to speak. The connections do not *come from* the evidence but, in good historiography on Jesus, they are never independent from the evidence. The connections which begin to make an intelligible portrait of Jesus *come with* the evidence, *as if they are synthetic apriori conditions of the evidentiary process.* An appeal to the evidence cannot by itself be the basis of an adjudication of the quality of any type of construction or comparison among constructions. *The evidence itself does not judge which transcendental conditions are to be preferred.* But conditions that provoke coherent, intelligible, plausible use of the evidence are more viable.

Of course, we do not have a court that can absolutely cancel some dot-to-dot pictures. Yet we have an intuitive reaction against anything-goes interpretations of the past. Not everything goes when it comes to the past. The past is not simply an ideologically informed invention of our power

---

186. Powell, *Jesus as a Figure*, 169.

187. Cf. Boring's nice but different reconstruction of the valuing in each historical step: Boring, "The 'Third Quest,'" 350. In my judgment Boring is on track in his recognition of the value saturation in producing a Jesus picture, but underestimates the values operative in the lowest level of isolating the data and separates theological value from other cultural and methodological values too much.

interests.[188] Surely, we can be skeptical of *unfinished* portraits, pictures that leave much unaccounted for (adequacy-to-available-evidence criterion). We can imagine, in addition, certain relative standards for better picturing (i.e., consensus among informed scholarly community,[189] enduringness, simplicity of explanation, holism, aesthetic appeals, etc.).

The discovery that certain values and conditions put together a Jesus does not by itself falsify the picture. The discovery that contemporary concerns have been retrojected onto Jesus does not by itself undermine the Jesus produced under those concerns. No Jesus emerges without those applied connections that give birth to the evidence. The *conditions therefore operate the evidence but do not simply determine the evidence*, in the helpful distinction of Eugene Boring.[190] Discovering the triggering mechanism that makes sense of the data ought not to launch us into a reductive reading, as if the only value rests in the triggering mechanism and none in the evidence. This reading of constructing Jesuses does indeed soften the difference between the historian's Jesuses and the Christs of faith, between the historians' work that seeks to be objective and those that integrate faith's insights into the quest, between those who seek to check their values at the door of the quest and those who embrace them. Softening the lines comes with the territory, when one admits to the holistic or synthetic activity of historical imagination required in Jesus research: "[T]he dots do not connect themselves."[191]

C.7. The Genealogy of Values

Behind the above criteria is something like a "genealogy of values," a modification of the Nietzschean project. Theological interpreters first must discern the values encased in a historical Jesus. Then they must bracket them in suspicion that holds in check the immediate notion that these values refer to first-century Mediterranean life. Then theologians must take the values to the culture of the historians and, with study, figure out whether that culture generates the values or interest in the values. The discovery that Jesus values have their origin in our contemporary culture provides the critic with

---

188. I will not repeat the critique of extreme post-modern positions (chapter 2).

189. Boring, "The 'Third Quest,'" 350–51.

190. Ibid., 347. I am taking the categories in a way that departs somewhat from Boring. Cf. his view: "[T]he penultimate constructive phase that assembles a historical portrait on the basis of data that survive the criteria of authenticity as well as the 'data base' from which all else proceeds are already conditioned (not to say determined) by theological perspectives."

191. Boring, 349. In our reading here faith values are among the many values operative in construing a Jesus.

a gleeful critical rush, of course. It is the perpetual excitement of criticism and, in our case, the reductive basis of the anti-Quest position. But this discovery is only mid-way through the interpretive process.

Were theological interpreters to end with the reduction of a historical Jesus to the values of the historians' cultures, they would slide into one of three positions: 1. the fully insulated position, in which historical work on Jesus has nothing to do with the Christ of faith; 2. the modified historical position, identified with the position of Martin Kähler, in which the necessary historical moment of Christian faith and confession is defined away from so-called secular history writing to the historic picturing of Jesus as the Christ in the gospels and in the earliest church;[192] or 3. the skeptical position, in which the apparent evaporation of a link between the values of the historical Jesus and the first-century Christians means a post-theological or post-Christian conclusion.

A fuller interpretation begins with a critique of the reductive reading. Namely, the sheer discovery of the coincidence of value in a historical Jesus and same value in the historians' cultures does not end the issue with the value. The position here is that theology cannot let the critique of retrojection have the last word. **(Theological) Rule 59:** *Theologians need to learn from that critique but must criticize it, too.*[193] To dispense with historical study of Jesus altogether because of the coincidence is to over-react, over-conclude. First of all, values in a historical Jesus participate in an on-going cultural sweep from the earliest biblical days down to the present. Significant values precede Jesus. Second, the cultures which have constructed the historical Jesuses have been informed by his and by biblical values. Third, it is logically possible and historically probable that our value interest is also Jesus.' Fourth, even where our values differ from his, we can bring perspectives informed by our values into conversations with his values, conversations rich with our perspectives and concerns.

Just as problematic as the reductive approach is the ready application of values of a historical Jesus to contemporary life. *The reductive approach over-concludes while the ready application of a Jesus to our scene over-applies. Theologians need to learn from that critique but also must criticize it too for direct christological application of Jesus' values to us.* The former approach finds cultural familiarity in the values of a Jesus and flees too quickly, while

---

192. It is a point of debate whether the second formal position is logically different from the first, insulated position.

193. The theological position insists that there are hermeneutical and historiographical issues at stake in rejecting the reductive reading. The positive side of the reductive position insists that good history writing ought to be free of value and perspective: a position on historical method that theology rejects on epistemological grounds.

the latter too eagerly takes as theologically normative the ready values a historian finds in Jesus. We all remember the early days of gender-sensitive interpretation of biblical materials: the easy dismissal of biblical sources for their patriarchal values and the easy application of the notion that *Jesus was a feminist*. At this point in the research both approaches seem wooden and fundamentalistic. One makes this judgment even as one holds to the possibility that there may be values in Jesus that need to be repudiated, just as there may be some that can be indirectly applied to contemporary christological purposes.

It remains to be seen whether there are indirect christological opportunities in the historical work of Jesus research. Some researchers, then and now, seem to suggest that their work is theologically rich, even as others take no interest in such theological activity or, alternatively, they work with theological positions immune to or indifferent to historical work on the figure of Jesus. The ones that hint at possible christological entailments of historical research on Jesus obviously present the most to work with; yet the ones that somehow separate Jesus research from christology provide a more interesting challenge for contemporary christology. Beyond these indirect hints is the possibility of an explicit christological application of elements of a historical Jesus in ways that stretch beyond the work of historians themselves.

3

Warrants: Why Should Theology Care about Historical Jesuses?

Anyone who reads the history of historical research on the figure of Jesus is apt to be overwhelmed. The claims for such research are so incommensurable, the results so divergent that a theologian may abandon help from history for the work of christology. The era of the Third Quest alone has seen the construction of radically different Jesuses by scholars who cannot agree on suitable sources, methods, or even on the value of historical research on Jesus. No wonder that some theologians are tempted to insulate christology from historical research, more out of despair over the welter of conflicting opinions than of the quality of the historical reconstructions. The larger project of this book, rejecting the way of insulation, attempts to map how theologians can move through the thicket of Jesus research. In this chapter we address the specific question of why: why should theologians bother plowing through the mass of Jesus books? What christological good could come from it, especially in light of the considerable limitations of questing?

C. Stephen Evans suggests that there have been four types of response to questing: *defense, rejection, revision, and separation.*[1] Indeed, he reads questing as an activity of modernity and the four as the types of response to the terms of (historical) inquiry launched in the Enlightenment. While there is virtue in his typology, the project we are embarking on embraces elements of all four types that Evans distinguishes. As such, it does not fit a type exactly, except that it allies itself with those who are willing to take a look at the effects Jesus research might have on the practice of christology. These effects might be to defend, to reject, or to revise the inherited

---

1. C. Stephen Evans, *The Historical Christ*, 27–46. Eventually we will be arguing that a revisionist theology must embrace all four of his types, whereas Evans responds with an inverted defense mostly by changing how history writing works.

christological traditions. One can imagine, moreover, elements of each of the four that a christology may have to reject: i.e., blind defense against all evidence, biased hostility to Christian claims, and a willingness to sell the christological farm on the modernist market, to name the most obvious criticisms of the three. Since this project would inspect the prospects for a christology in light of Jesus research, it stands against the position of the separationists. But even here, I will argue, a quest-informed christology must learn from this type. Consequently, as the argument unfolds, we will reject the slotting of the discussion into Evans' four types even as we will attempt to preserve the best of the insights of his typology. As such, the project presents itself as a *revisionist* work because it continues the work of modernity on christological inquiry, in the tradition of modern theologies.[2] As we will see, the modernist cast of the project is hardly purebred, in that it has incorporated a fulsome sense of the failure and limits of revisioning, including an honoring of the separationist point, even as it claims continuity with pre-modern interest in the figure of Jesus.[3]

A. Factual Warrants

Our question, why should theology care about historical Jesuses, has a familiar ring to it. It is, of course, a modern way to ask the famous question of Tertullian, "What has Athens to do with Jerusalem?"[4] By now, readers will recognize that we are answering with: *a great deal*. In this section on warrants we begin with *a few factual states-of-affairs that encourage theology to concern itself with historical research on the figure of Jesus*. Behind each of these is a dilemma for theologians, particularly for those interested in or haunted by Jesus research. *It is the puzzlement that begins with the question of whether to take theologically seriously quested results and ends with the uncertainty of how to deploy knowledge about Jesus in theology. How does the non-expert judge among the many portraits of Jesus?* The fact is that theologians are adrift; they suspect that their likes and dislikes are random or trendy or shaped by already-held values. How does theology move beyond a capricious, pick-and-choose relationship to historical knowledge of

---

2. As opposed to C. Stephen Evans where we find an arcane reconstruction of the business of historical knowledge (informed by the so-called Reformed, spiritualist epistemologies) that re-secures virtually everything in classical christology as plausible, warranted, and knowable.

3. In other words, questing with its flawed retrojection is not simply an activity of a dated and flawed Enlightenment project, which can be dismissed by post-modernists or by people who are theologically frightened of modern critique and enlightenment.

4. As Allison reminds us: *The Historical Christ*, 8.

Jesus? Many theologians feel a great need for a map through the research and through the methodological issues for theology.[5]

A.1. The Meta-Warrant: A Negative, Factual Warrant

At the end of the Third Quest Jesus research remains a bewildering array of options for understanding Jesus. However we identify the cause of the array at the end of the dominance of the apocalyptic paradigm, contemporary Jesus research presents an overwhelming *plurality of options for Jesus*. Historians, critics, and now theologians face too many different, even incommensurable Jesuses: too many, too different, too rapidly passing in fashion.[6] The sheer plurality of Jesuses is a problem that daunts even informed historical judgments. Neither lay nor theological readers know what to make of the many Jesuses. Theologians especially are haunted by Allison's question, *"Which Jesus should baptize our theology?"*[7] The options are so many and the choice among them dependent upon so much technical knowledge, the theologian is adrift. Whose expertise should theology trust among the many?

Theologians are apt to favor voices among historians who offer Jesuses framed with values theologically pleasing, according to the favored cast of a theology. Predictably, people with liberal Christian views gravitate to a Marcus Borg, while conservative Christians get excited about Wright or Witherington. But such a favoring approach is capricious and tends to create *a false friendship between christology and the results of historical research on Jesus*. Sometimes the friendship is the strange familiarity among enemies. Values that a theologian or an anti-theologian brings to a historical Jesus get theologians to resonate with particular Jesuses or elements of a Jesus on the assumption that Jesus represents, endorses, or grounds said values. The pacifist Christian likes to hear of a Jesus who demands turning the other cheek; the warrior Christian wants a Jesus who brings a sword to the earth; the advocate of family values is pleased with a Jesus who is anti-divorce, and so it goes. And while all theologians and people of faith gravitate to favorite elements in the studies of Jesus, such favoring is little more than

---

5. See the similar diagnosis in Hellwig, "Historical Jesus Research," 90.
6. Cf. Allison, *The Historical Christ*, 10–11.
7. Ibid., 9. The actual formulation of the question makes the rhetorical point about the plurality of Jesuses but the argument of this book rejects the substance implied in Allison's question. So far as his question represents a serious approach to theological options in light of historical work on Jesus, it expresses a version of what we are calling a historian's fundamentalism.

prooftexting from the *scripture* of a historical Jesus, with no more sophistication than we find in popular Christian use of the Bible. We agree with what we agree, even in the negative voice.

We need rules and warrants to take the use of historical Jesus materials to a sophisticated level. Theologians and people of faith are out of their element when they have to make sense of the many, sometimes incompatible Jesuses: that there is no consensus (and never has been) about even minimal points of history, that the options for Jesus are more diverse than ever, that the paradigm does not hold, that the fashion in Jesuses keeps changing—all are distressing features for theology's reaction to the quest. What historian does the theologian trust? And why? How does the theologian keep up with changing Jesuses without latching onto outdated historical orthodoxies or running after the latest fashion? Favoring what we like risks that theologians will assume that something in the historians' results is directly christic. Oddly, *this enthusiasm for finding a quick Christ in a Jesus is actually an instance of manipulating the resisting evidence.* (**Factual**) **Warrant 1:** *Our first warrant, then, is a meta-warrant, the need for warrants.*

A.2. Situating Theology's Interest in Historical Research on Jesus

It is a fact that historical research on Jesus continues, now into the third century of the quest, and, while there is nothing normative about the fact that historians keep writing about Jesus, there is a (**Factual**) **Warrant 2:** *The persistent impulse from the fact of continued questing by historians.* Particularly powerful is the nudging from historical revision. Historians do with Jesus what historians always do: they churn up old constructions and offer revised pictures of the past.[8] Old Jesuses get revised, especially under the press of new sources, new approaches, new methods. In other words, Jesus historians are professional, revisionist historians. A new generation of historians brings new values and sensitivities to the materials; they ask new questions.[9] Indeed, they want to have a new conversation with the Jesus saga. New peoples want to have a crack at inventing a Jesus. Some of these new Jesuses just well up in the values a historian brings to the quest. Other times a new Jesus is an in-your-face critique of an old Jesus and the culture that extrudes it. In this writing, we will not bemoan the constant revision of the figure of Jesus, but embrace it.

---

8. Chilton notes that people are already making historical judgments about Jesus and the only question is whether they make good ones: Chilton, *Studying the Historical Jesus*, 5.

9. Brundage, *Going to the Sources*, 3.

Indeed, we can imagine a day when one Jesus may be in conflict with another Jesus; perhaps there will be a plurality of Jesuses, even a plurality of truthful Jesuses, since historians invent under different locales and conditions.[10] We can imagine new Jesuses, such as those of the Third Quest, posing a major revision within the guild of historians, perhaps an overturning of the century-long apocalyptic paradigm.[11] Or possibly an apocalyptic Jesus will be refurbished to live with or along-side the sapiential Jesus. In any case, we embrace the remarkable vitality of the imaging of Jesus, not simply because historical work is important per se, but because there is important value business being conducted in the imaging of Jesus. The direction of our argument here is to claim that *inventing a Jesus is one way of discovering/ inventing an identity of a self or of a people, through the self-reflexive objectification that happens in an imaging of Jesus.*

New historical Jesuses represent new dialogues with the evidence of the Jesus saga and new opportunities for value conversations with church and culture mediated through the Jesuses. Of course, the sheer facticity of continuing historical research propels further research, and, inevitably, historical revisions. Part of the revision should be explicit conversation about the interface of value and evidence, with special attention to whether a historian's position is warranted. But many impediments stand in the way of the value conversation. Revisionist historians should have a shrewd eye for a value discussion, but they commonly resist the temptation to debate positions on value and instead, usually offer revisions by exclusive appeal to so-called objectivist issues of evidence and method. After Schweitzer and in contemporary Jesus research, the value conversation comes easier than in the past.

Revising historical Jesuses indeed opens the door to value conversations on the part of history writing. But the fact that historians continually revise their estimations of Jesus does not itself warrant theological involvement in the quest. Rather, theology has to trip its own switch in order to pick up the work of the historians. Nonetheless, the sheer fact that historians produce an image of the religious founder and, more so, that they continue to revise that image puts into the lap of theology an undeniable colossus to which it must react. When theology perks up and recognizes in Jesus research something at stake for christology, then it redoubles the genealogical task the good historian has begun.

---

10. See ibid., 3, for notion of several and "new" pasts.
11. Cf. ibid., 4.

A.3. The Historical Impulse: Faith Seeking Understanding

The Enlightenment and the rise of a historical consciousness pressed onto critics and faithful alike the recognition that the gospels were not *historical* as the term was beginning to mean. Now, we can debate whether traditional Christians understood the gospels as historical, whether they intended to tell a historical story, or whether they held to a *pre-critical realism* (Frei's term). Whatever the term and orientation, we can be pretty confident that traditional Christians assumed and believed that the events told in the gospels happened. But we know various forces of modernity undermined the realism of the Jesus story with a different understanding of how knowing and historical knowing work. In this shift a fissure opened between the narrative and the events to which it points, between the older model of knowing (supported by classic epistemologies of the West) and the new models of knowing, heavily influenced by the rise of science.

Living with or overcoming the fissure has occupied the best minds of the modern world and it has issued in *models of denying, rejecting, co-opting, defending, relativizing, criticizing, and accommodating the Athens pole on the part of the people of Jerusalem*. In this study we do not have to tag along with any one of these approaches, since the thrust of our argument holds for any reaction to the fissure. If we adopt a traditional model of knowing, the fissure is, perhaps, smaller, but we still cannot avoid Tertullian's question. If we board the Enlightenment bandwagon, the fissure is so starkly before us that the only coherent options are for pyrrhonist skepticism or fideism. And if we work out a mediating position, a revisionism founded in criticism of either the traditional model or the modern one, we still must sort out the historical from the mythopoeic. We do not escape the problem of history, nor do we escape thinking about the way people imagine Jesus: when they think historically about Jesus, do they put themselves into the picture?

Of course, we can avoid or deny the *questing version of Lessing's ditch*.[12] But for those who are convinced that we must walk with historical research, there is no turning back. The fact is that we can and do think historically,[13] and the faithful and theologians naturally want *to employ continued research in history to help them understand their beliefs:* **(Theological) Warrant 3**. For

---

12. In Lessing's famous words, "If no historical truth can be demonstrated, then nothing can be demonstrated by means of historical truths . . . Accidental truths of history can never become the proof of necessary truths of reason": Lessing, *Lessing's Theological*, 53.

13. Without entering the question here whether all historical thinking is the same, whether some peoples do not think historically, and whether the orientation of the rise of historical consciousness may be waning.

moderns the Anselmic quest to understand requires that the faithful dive into the ditch, so to speak. They cannot avoid it. They cannot pretend it does not exist. Here *we argue that the only way to manage the crisis-producing ditch of historical consciousness is by historizing every feature of the fissure*: the traditional faith elements, the models of knowing and reason, even the faith-reason conversation itself. In other words, the most satisfactory approach to the challenges of history is through the history of history and of historical research, thus, through more historical research in the clear light of day.[14] Such is a methodological commitment. But the fact is that this continuing research is already being done. Only good historical research can figure out the provenance of things in the saga, the questions of both the pious and the skeptical in a historically possible era, and even of the history of history and of historiography. The research is going on and the questions are being asked.

Theology picks up the historical questions and re-asks them in light of the questions of understanding a faithful person might formulate. Here we will categorize these questions by type of expectation the faithful might have:

A.3.a. *Corroboration*: Can history illumine the meaning of Christian claims about the Christ?

A.3.b. *Defining the Parameters of Faith/Reason:* Can historical research help mark the extent of reason and what belongs to faith?

A.3.c. *Continuity:* What things do the historians say that help us understand why the Christians declared Jesus the Christ?

A.3.d. *Defense:* Can historical research help Christians defend their belief against criticism or attack?

A.3.e. *Making an Apology:* Can Christian claims be reasonable?

A.3.f. *Criticism:* Can historical research clarify issues related to troubling doctrine and events tied to Jesus?

A.3.f. *Sharpening or Selecting:* Can historical research help us understand the images of Jesus in Bible and tradition? Can it help us sort through all the different images and names for Jesus? Conceivably, more sophisticated and theologized faithful may ask for nuanced questions of historical research on Jesus:

A.3.g. To *buttress* certain preconditions for christological claims, or

A.3.h. To develop possible *entailments* of christological claims, and finally

---

14. See Patterson, *The God of Jesus*, 5.

A.3.i. To set out the *conditions of the possibility* for the reception of christological claims.

So far as people ask these questions, they are asking historical questions about Jesus; indeed, as the last thirty years show, there is a real hunger for interesting things to say about Jesus. Historical research can, in principle, address this need. In other words, that the faithful often ask serious theological questions of engagement with history suggests that the quest can become a *microcosm and laboratory for faith's modern wrestling with historicity*.[15]

A.4. The Pure Desire to Know

The simplest rationale for questing is that it is possible. *Historical research on Jesus is a possible human activity of inquiry. The warrant is a simple appeal to curiosity and honesty:* **(Factual) Warrant 4**. Historians participate in the most fundamental liberal arts curiosity to figure things out. Theologians and some of the faithful share this desire to know, and add another motive, that faith must understand itself.[16] When historians claim they know something, theologians and others want to react, they want to know what the historians know and how. Knowledge brings intention which places a moral demand on Christians. Enough said. There is a distinctly religious version of this warrant, namely, the *faith seeking understanding* model: (Theological) Warrant 3 above. A quested Jesus can contribute to the historic task of theology, to bring the faith into understanding.[17] In particular, it can inform curiosities and assuage doubts about Christian origins. Even the most devout wonder what has generated Christian claims.[18] And some in the fold are positively puzzled about aspects of the Jesus saga. All it takes is an attentive reading of the gospels and one may wonder why Jesus is not interested in his family, why his hometown rejects him, why his disciples fight with those of John the Baptist. How can we preach on Mother's Day when Jesus says to hate one's mother and father? . . .

Part of theology's embrace of the sheer good of knowing is its openness to historical research and to the methods of history writing. Formally, this openness requires theology to honor whatever makes for good historical research. Of course, when theology embraces historical methods, it does

---

15. And with modernity itself.
16. Gaiser, *The Quest for Jesus* 6; Meier, *A Marginal Jew*, I, 198.
17. Patterson, *The God of Jesus*, 9.
18. Ibid., 1.

so critically, at once encouraging historians to do their best work on Jesus but daring to make critical judgments about the conduct of history writing. They bring perspectives to bear on the research from outside the guild of historians and a special eye how values shape ideas. Commonly they are trained in suspicion and are practiced in ideological critique. If the Jesus historians rely heavily on the criterion of dissimilarity to discern the earliest Jesus from the other Jesuses, then the theologian starts with appreciation. As the historians pile up the critical evaluations of the use of that criterion, theologians shift gears and make independent judgments on the judgments of the historians.[19] While theologians must trust what the guild of historians is doing, they can join the forces of criticism that press for changes in the conduct of research on Jesus. Such is what they have done with the movement away from the positivist paradigm in history writing. **(Theological) Rule 60:** *Theology's affirmation of historical research, then, includes honoring the self-correcting stance of history writing.*

More narrowly, *theology endorses a history-of-the-research criterion central to revisionist history writing*: **(Theological) Corollary 60a.** In Jesus research, the history of questing is a story of some advances and a catalogue of errors to be avoided. Reading a Jesus through the centuries of questing for the historical Jesus provides a framework for developing the research.[20] *The worst posture for theology is the sweeping claim that there is nothing new in Jesus research, that it is, in fact, a narrative of ever-repeating errors:* **(Theological) Corollary 60b.** Moreover, *theology endorses the hermeneutically self-consciousness criterion of recent historical work:* **(Theological) Corollary 60c.** In Jesus research, spelling out one's stance, one's pre-understandings, and one's social and intellectual location as a historian is a good, as is identifying one's entrance into the hermeneutical circle. It is truth-telling, to be sure, but it also provides the surest defense against manipulative modernizing.[21] Explicit self-reflection allows the members of the guild to debate directly on the issue at hand and enables a transparency to the historical work. Theologians endorse these values as the best way to avoid the too easy dismissing of Jesus research on the part of some.

To the curiosity warrant and that of valuing of history writing, Meier adds *a third criterion*: that the first two must be combined.[22] **(Historical)**

---

19. See, for instance, the summary of the discussion in Meier, *A Marginal Jew*, I, 167–95.

20. Ibid., 4–5.

21. Meier writes, "In a sense, though, the most important hedge against rampant subjectivism is an honest admission of one's own personal stance, one's point of view and background": ibid., I, 5.

22. An idea of John P. Meier, ibid.

Rule 61: *A good Jesus researcher must know how to avoid the pitfalls of the history of the quest, and must, upon hermeneutical self-reflection, turn possible lessons onto his/her own portrait of Jesus.*²³ Simply to find anachronism in other scholars' Jesuses is insufficient until the suspicious eye turns back onto its own Jesus. We see a corollary of the above points, namely, that **(Historical) Corollary 61a:** *we are no longer to expect a neutral portrait of Jesus*, one that is immaculately conceived, free of stance, and perspective. In the past some theological voices have cheered the move from positivist history writing to the recognition of the so-called subjective features of all history writing. But theologians should not celebrate prematurely this turn, as it can disguise a false friend of theology. True, theology welcomes history writing freed from objectivist notions, but a hermeneutically explicit history writing brings its own risks, namely, the sticky issue of control of interpretation and authority.

Historians commonly insist that better methods make for better history writing. There may be some truth in this view, but it is inadequate and pre-hermeneutical by itself, as Ben Meyer argued in 1979.²⁴ The great divide among contemporary Jesus researchers is whether or not they "try to exclude [the interpreter's] influence in making scholarly judgment . . ."²⁵ Some, like John Meier, take as an ideal the notion of minimal interpretation for historical research on Jesus, while others regard the ideal as distracting, impossible, and adopt instead a more conversational approach to writing a history of Jesus. In the battle whether historians should exclude their stances as much as possible, *we opt for the view that excluding one's stance is neither possible nor desirable* [**(Theological) Rule 62**] and go with Ben Meyer's choice, that more progress will be made where historians spell out and argue for issues of stance, perspective, choice of method, and the like.²⁶ *Theologians, too, must trust the scholarly consensus within the historical guild,* **(Theological) Rule 63**, and must criticize only when the underlying values have gone unexamined. Short of a consensus, theologians honor a spectrum of views from the guild, **(Theological) Corollary 63a**, with an eye to the likelihood that *they may have to honor a plurality of historically responsible constructions of Jesus at a given time:* **(Theological) Corollary 63b**, the plurality rule. Trusting and honoring include pressing historians to be explicit about values operative in their constructions; *theologians support especially the genealogical effort to uncover those values:* **(Theological)**

---

23. Meier, *A Marginal Jew*, I, 5.
24. Ibid., 13.
25. Ibid., 6.
26. Ibid., 13–14.

Corollary 63c. *Theologians also honor consensus methodological choices from the guild, but support the criticism of method from within the guild:* **(Theological) Corollary 63d.** Fortunately, theologians rarely have to make original criticisms of historical work, as the guild is endlessly busy now in reflexive criticism of every step of questing. Therefore, *theology must support internal historians' critique of the conduct of questing every bit as much as trusting the scholarly consensus:* **(Theological) Corollary 63e.** Finally, *theology must remain open to paradigm change:* **(Theological) Corollary 63f.**

Concerning specific methods and source decisions within the guild of questers, theologians best remain above the historical debates. *The major source decision of the day is whether to stick to canonical sources for Jesus or to add an exploration of non-canonical ones.* A version of this either/or is the decision whether to rely heavily on scholarly reconstructed sources (i.e., Q) or stick more with the narrative-driven Marcan or synoptic accounts. This question of sources leans into the issue behind the issues of method: namely, whether the historian proceeds to construct a Jesus with a more atomistic approach or through a more holistic-narrative approach. If historians opt for non-canonical sources or privilege scholarly reconstructed sources, they are apt to undertake an assembling job when they construct a Jesus: framing from the atoms on their plates, usually the ones judged to be most authentic or earliest. The most obvious person who follows this approach is Crossan: *Jesus looks like the assembled fragments of the earliest sources.* In an earlier era Jesus looks exactly like an assemblage of what passes the criterion of dissimilarity. Today quite a few researchers have departed from the atomism of much of the quest and turned to a narrative-dependent approach with a new tool, *the historical presumption criterion.* Here, a Jesus emerges, not from what the historian assembles from the fragments, but from a holistic judgment informed by the mainlines of the gospel narrative (usually from Mark). The judgment comes from a wide sifting and sorting of signals in the saga, to be sure, but it is supported by the uses of the historical presumption criterion: namely, that historians need to make a convincing case to rule out an item from the record.[27]

Theologians have no dog in these historians' fights. They wait and see. They support and they search for values alive in every choice. At times they criticize when they see unexamined values or manipulative ones. But they do not prefer one historical result over another, even when on the surface a decision makes things difficult for theology. Of course, when historians choose to go with canonical sources and with a holistic assessment tied to the gospel frame, theologians often are cheered. But the enthusiasm is

---

27. Ibid., 183.

premature and misguided, since it collapses the proper christological work of theology into the results of historical research. Theologians reject this direct application of history to christology, even as they are suspicious that the *turn to historical presumption can be an evangelical manipulation to confirm the gospel storyline as given or to secure traditional Christian doctrine.*

B. Theological Warrants for Theology's Interest

We begin our series of overlapping theological warrants with a meta-warrant, which we term simply:

B.1. The Fundamental (Theological) Warrant

At some point Christians become curious and *theologians feel pressed to determine whether the Christ of faith somehow matches what Jesus of Nazareth was about historically:* (**Theological**) **Warrant 5**. We can call the curiosity a concern for confirmation from history but the concern can be put in any number of ways with more nuanced categories. For instance, the warrant may emerge from apologetic needs, whether to calm troubled insiders or persuade unconvinced outsiders. Or it may come from the sheer academic interest in the intelligibility, meaning and truth of Christian claims. It may come from a theological vocation drawn to conversations with history, philosophy, and culture studies. In fact, any of the above uses (chapter 2) can be followed back to the fundamental warrant.

The issue at hand in this motive is whether there is some *connectedness* between the figure of Jesus and the kinds of things Christians have said about the Christ.[28] In Wright's phrase, is there a reality "behind the icon" of Christian faith?[29] Quest-interested christologies proceed on the assumption that "faith in Jesus Christ is intimately connected with the factual events of his life."[30] They are christologies that risk historical investigations into foundational-appearing events. The philosopher C. Stephen Evans, hardly a fan of the typical quest for Jesus,[31] nonetheless has articulated the fundamental warrant well: 1. *Christians need to know why knowledge of the gospel story is important for faith and theology,* and 2. *whether Christians "who claim*

---

28. Patterson, *The God of Jesus*, 1: the aim of historical studies on Jesus is to determine "what it was about Jesus that moved them so deeply that they could only name it as 'God with us.'"
29. Wright, *Jesus and the Victory*, 16.
30. Galvin, "'I Believe,'" 374.
31. As it is done among Jesus historians.

to have knowledge of the truth of the story of Jesus of Nazareth may be quite reasonable in making such a claim."³²

Of course, the language of confirmation sounds foundational, particularly in an era in which certain pieties, theologies, and philosophies are allergic to foundationalism.³³ Thus, to certain religious people on the fideistic end of the spectrum, talk of confirmation appears to undermine the leapy character of faith. To theologians of a hyper-Protestant bent, the drive flies in the face of a reigning religious epistemology: Melanchthon's view that knowledge of the Christ should be defined by the benefits of the Christ.³⁴ To many philosophers confirmation language appears interested in a religious Cartesian deduction from indubitable foundations. Against these views, *a theology open to questing poses an orientation toward knowing for Christian faith that rejects self-warranted faith of any kind, that rejects collapsing christology into soteriology, and that is willing to swim against elements in philosophical anti-foundationalism*, because of the virtues identified in the warrants listed below. For now we point out that the language of confirmation need not mean the Cartesian drive for certain knowledge, for the self-evident pillars from which all certainties can be drawn, now so fashionably criticized by post-modern intellectuals. Rather, *confirmation* can be a catch-all word for the range of uses for quested knowledge, identified in the list in chapter 2 (p. [X-REF]). In each of the following theological warrants, we restate the fundamental point in a series of overlapping sub-warrants which unpack the point.

B.2. The Kergymatic Warrant

Here we begin with a quick and obvious claim that founds theology's interest in the quest: *the early Christian kerygma makes historical claims for Jesus*: **(Theological) Warrant 6**.³⁵ That the kerygma makes historical claims implies it is not entirely in the language of the meaning of the Christ, not entirely of the language of faith. Indeed *the kerygma does not ground the kerygma*, so we are forced by the logic of Christian salvation to consider the grounding this human life and ministry, since the kerygma points to a historical foun-

---

32. C. Stephen Evans, *The Historical Christ*, vii.

33. John Galvin puts the foundational point concisely: "[T]hat some empirical information about [Jesus] is, in one way or another, of foundational religious and theological significance." Galvin, "'I Believe," 374.

34. Melanchthon, *The Loci Communes*, 68.

35. As Fuchs noted in his first famous position against the Bultmannian no-quest doctrine: Fuchs, *Studies*, 25.

dation.³⁶ *Questing can be a way to rename and secure the historical claims of the kerygma.* Indeed, the kerygma's confessional language usually takes the form of (apparent) historical claims. In the famous position of Günther Bornkamm, faith does not begin with itself.³⁷

B.3. The Soteriological Warrant

Revisionist theologians turn the Melanchthon dictum around and insist that, in the order of being, if not of knowing, christology proceeds *before* soteriology, since something launched the saving benefits.³⁸ In the order of being, as it were, founding events of the Christ are logically prior to soteriology, while in contrast, in the order of knowing, the recognition and transformation of the soteriological moment is indeed prior. *Christians claim that salvation is possible because of events that happen in the history of Jesus of Nazareth:* **(Theological) Warrant 7**.³⁹ They make this claim from the theological and confessional traditions that insist not all things christological are rooted in the resurrection. While the resurrection of Jesus may trigger christological clarity, quested christologies insist that *not all christic value comes from Easter*. Even in a theology dominated by resurrection-faith, the horizon of Easter stretches back to the story of Israel and its prophetic-apocalyptic hope and forward to the fulfillment of the Kingdom.⁴⁰ Considerable value rests in the larger story of Israel, and, quested christologies argue, in Jesus' ministry within that story.

Therefore, *questing can be a reminder that biblical notions of salvation are never strictly trans-historical*. We may disagree whether biblical salvation finally ends in a transcendental understanding of salvation; but there is little doubt that biblical salvation is tied directly to what becomes of this world. Questing can remind theology of the dangers of otherworldly notions of human arrival, particularly at a time when things are going so badly for us in this world.

---

36. Jeremias, *The Problem of the Historical*, 12.
37. Bornkamm, *Jesus of Nazareth*, 21–23.
38. Melanchthon, *The Loci Communes*, 68.
39. C. Stephen Evans, *The Historical Christ*, 69.

40. See Richard Hays' critique of Luke Johnson's over-reliance on the experience of the Risen Lord as a sufficient basis for faith: "Faith and History," in Gaventa and Hays, eds., *Seeking the Identity*, 46.

B.4. The Anti-Docetic Theme

The second, main warrant for *questing is that it can be a powerful, modern means to guard against the heresy of docetism:* **(Theological) Warrant 8.**[41] Indeed, at the hands of some Jesus researchers, a robust historical Jesus can correct the lazy docetism of popular piety[42] and of reified ecclesiastical pronouncements.[43] There is little doubt that most piety has viewed Jesus as a walking/talking god, a representation of the most "omni" divinity of classic theism. This Jesus can do and can know without limits. He is "a God." Against this view good historical research on Jesus humanizes him, and, despite the doctrinal repudiation of docetism, after Easter Christians have had particular difficulty noticing and crediting the humanity of the Savior. *In a quested christology the theologian inquires whether historians can determine evidence that makes certain Christian claims plausible or reasonable. This determination is a theological task, not a historical one.* For instance, against docetic tendencies, what evidence of a robust humanity can the theologian discover in the historian's Jesus? Actually, docetism is so pervasive and so unrecognized in our culture and theologies that, when a historian reveals a human feature of Jesus' life, the pious scream of heresy and do not recognize the irony. In this case, historical Jesus research can bring faith and theology back to old-fashioned doctrine. It can remind the faithful of elements of the biblical record. Even non-theological or anti-theological historical work on Jesus can contribute to good theology, particularly to the enduring anti-docetic project of Christian religion.[44]

We know, of course, that the church rejected docetism in its battle against gnosticism and gnostized Christian faith. Its rejection was re-secured in the "fully human" doctrinal language of Chalcedon.[45] Crossan reminds us that Catholic faith rejected gnostic style and the notion of the savior as an apparent human who reveals the route of escape from this world. Historical

---

41. The classic articulation of the docetism argument comes from the one who led the return to questing by the students of Bultmann: see Käsemann, "The Problem of the Historical Jesus," 46. See also Meier, A *Marginal Jew*, I, 199.

42. One can argue that popular docetic Christian religion opens the door to very blatant and manipulative retrojection.

43. Cf. Keck, *Who Is Jesus?*, 127; Patterson, *The God of Jesus*, 5; Powell, *Jesus as a Figure*, 74; Borg, *Jesus in Contemporary*, 172.

44. The anti-docetism point receives support from all quarters: cf. a conservative like Watson, "Veritas Christi," in Gaventa and Hayes, eds., *Seeking the Identity*, 113, a once-quester who has abandoned the quest, Allison, *The Historical Christ*, 85, and a revisionist Catholic, Elizabeth Johnson, "The Word Was Flesh," in Donnelly, ed., *Jesus*, 151.

45. See below.

study of Jesus, in principle, can recall the church's commitment from its earliest battle.[46]

B.5. The Incarnational Warrant

Related to the anti-docetic point above is an argument based on the Christian doctrine of incarnation: *the logic of incarnation involves theology in historical claims:* **(Theological) Warrant 9**.[47] With Paula Fredriksen, we can say Christian claims require historical study.[48] An incarnational theology begins with a God who is invested in human life.[49] The Christian God is human and lives in real history from day one of the life of the world and of the life of Israel.[50] Real human life is social and enmeshed in historical reality. Behind the christic claims of the church must stand a real human life in real history, and, it follows that that life, so far as sources allow, must be open to historical inquiry. *The doctrine of the incarnation locates the religious significance of the Christ precisely in the historicity of Jesus.*[51] Admittedly, there are escapes from the logic here: into cynicism, into skepticism, or into some kind of fideism. But if we reject these views as non-starters, then theology has to turn to historical research. Indeed, the argument goes, in a historically conscious era, *it is no longer sufficient for theology to make vague assertions about the historicity of Jesus of Nazareth.* If the God in question is somehow human in a historical life, and if we have research tools to illumine his historicity, we have a responsibility to do so. It is not simply that historians can do questing; theology demands that work, honors it, and runs with the risks of historical research.[52] The warrant, then, is an extension and application of a doctrinal commitment of the Christians. In a historically possibly world, not to quest implicitly turns christology into the ahistorically mythic.[53]

---

46. Crossan, "Some Theological Conclusions," 18.

47. The early and principal incarnational argument of Ernst Käsemann aims at the docetic and mythical orientation of most of historic christology: Käsemann, "The Problem of the Historical Jesus," 15–47. This argument was a staple of the New Quest scholars' rejection of the no-quest position of their teacher Rudolf Bultmann.

48. Fredriksen, *From Jesus to Christ*, 214–15.

49. Patterson, *The God of Jesus*, 5; Hays, "Faith and History," in Gaventa and Hays, eds., 46.

50. See Gaiser, *The Quest for Jesus*, 7.

51. Jeremias was one of the first to underline the point in the era of no-quest: Jeremias, *The Problem of the Historical*, 15. Cf. C. Stephen Evans, *The Historical Christ*, vi.

52. Gaiser, *The Quest for Jesus*, 7.

53. Caird, *Jesus and the Jewish Nation*, 3; Wright, *Jesus and the Victory*, 11.

Seen from this viewpoint, the tradition that follows Kähler proves to be inadequate: an insulating position, motivated by noble concerns, to be sure, but inadequate chiefly on the basis of the very warrants that commend the quest.[54] The entire incarnational commitment of Christian faith begs historical questioning, as Fredriksen puts it.[55] And specific Christian articles of belief require "historical correlation" in Dale Allison's way of putting it.[56] In time, we will ask the next question, "How much history does theology require?,"[57] and we will refine the language of correlation.[58]

B.6. The Chalcedonian Warrant

Based on the *church's Chalcedonian decision, the argument begins in the doctrinal insistence that it is unacceptable to short-change the human nature of the Christ* and in a critique of much of history's theology as "crypto-monophysitism," in John Meier's term.[59] Of course, the doctrinal point can be made in the anti-docetic language of the second century (B.4. above) but here we extend the issue into the christological debates of the fifth century: a full human nature must be actual in a history, and the divine nature must not smother it, or we have the monophysite heresy.[60] It is insufficient to assert the humanity of the Christ; it may also be insufficient to claim the humanity of the Christ in an essentialized form, that is, in an im-personal or non-personal way, as critics of Chalcedon put it. *A full human nature must be actual in a history, and must be found, located, identified, emphasized, so far as possible:* **(Philosophical and Theological) Warrants 10 and 10a**. In a his-

54. Patterson, *The God of Jesus*, 37.
55. Fredriksen, "From Jesus to Christ," 214-15.
56. Allison, *The Historical Christ*, 32.
57. In the apt words of Allison, ibid.
58. The language of correlation, while connecting this project to Paul Tillich's theology, needs refinement, to avoid the notion that historians find items in a one-to-one correspondence with items in faith's doctrinal tradition. Only rarely would there be a one-to-one connection between the evidence of the historian and the claims of faith and theology. Instead, we are more likely to find opportunities which can be taken as recommendations in the historical work and received in theology as continuous, launching points that are finished within a christology, such that we have some *overlap between the prologue of the historians and the completion of the theologian.*
59. Meier, "The Present State," 487.
60. Cf. Elizabeth Johnson, "The Word Was Flesh," in Donnelly, ed., *Jesus*, 151. Johnson makes the intriguing point that a monophysite mindset is essentially more hierarchical than Chalcedon and classical theology already is. The image of the divine nature dominating and minimizing the human is an elitist christological parable of the God/world relationship and the very opposite of the kenotic image of the incarnation.

torically conscious and capable world, doing historical research on the figure of Jesus can be a powerful means to accent the historical value implied in Chalcedon's concern for the full humanity of the Christ. As many critics argue, finding a means to assert the human person of the Christ may be in the spirit of the intention, if not the accomplishment, of Chalcedon.[61] Historical Jesus research can discover, not only a human named Jesus, but a person for the Christ.[62] A hearty historian's Jesus can protect against the intense monophysitism of popular piety. We see clearly the monophysite tendency when we notice the dual reactions to contemporary Jesus research, namely, a combination of outrage that Jesus has been desacrilized at the hands of his historians and of genuine excitement to learn of a flesh-and-blood figure with whom people can relate.

The case here claims that historical research on Jesus can be a mode *to secure the humanness of the human nature* of the Christ. At this point it matters not whether Chalcedonian formulations themselves short-change the human side,[63] since we are pretty clear about the intentions of the Fathers. This sub-warrant flies particularly well in a historically capable and enabled modern culture.

B.7. The Christological Warrant

Many theologians continue to be convinced that it is necessary for modern theology to conduct christology *from below* or that a christology must include a from-below component. Here we will not enter the extensive discussion of the virtues and limits of a from-below approach to christology.[64] What we can be clear about is that *historical Jesus study is one of the best ways to proceed with a from-below approach because of the concrete and complex way it can picture human life:* **(Theological) Warrant 11**.[65] More generally, questing well, strong in endeavor but modest in claim, can inspire theology to conceive of a revisionist christology.

Consequently, self-critical study of the historical Jesus ought to teach us how beginning steps in a christology should proceed: by *analogical*

---

61. See Hellwig, "Historical Jesus Research," 90. Hellwig writes: "To be truly human is not to be in some sense essentially human, but to be existentially, specifically, and concretely human." Admittedly, the intention of Chalcedon may be more to embrace than the means by which the fathers established the full humanity of the Christ, since, as we know, they held to an anhypostatic human nature.

62. And not a Person in the classical christological sense.

63. Since the human nature was enhypostatic in the Divine Logos.

64. See Pannenberg, for instance: *Jesus-God and Man*.

65. Cf. Elizabeth Johnson, "The Word Was Flesh," in Donnelly, ed,, *Jesus*, 152.

likening. It can alert us to wherein we are finding *difference and sameness* in the Jesus figure. Given the likening character of all analogical thinking, difference from us intrigues the theologian. In time, we will have to analyze the pattern of same and difference, but for now, we anticipate our argument that difference is always a difference in relationship to some same and, when historians discover a difference in relation to a same, theologians may have in front of them the leading edge of the christic for our day.

Of course, not all theologians will want to probe the findings of the historian's analogy for christological insight. Many will retreat to the pictures of the canonical transition. However, revisionists believe that there is danger in insulating our Christs from Jesus research. Now, we can identify the particular danger of historical-Jesus-less christologies, namely, *the possibility that we will freeze the Christ in someone else's, dated Jesus form*. Revisionists sense that the spirit of the Christ requires us to find a shape for Jesus to address contemporary faith and experience. Schweitzer's apocalyptic Jesus may have been just the ticket for criticizing a too comfortable, nineteenth-century, European Christianity. But today, as liberals and conservatives both live in dread about the future of our societies and our world, perhaps the world-denying difference discovered in Schweitzer's Jesus may no longer minister to the apocalyptic numbing and paralysis most of us feel. Possibly, historians and others are just now inventing a new historical Jesus who can speak to us today.

B.8. The Theological Warrant

Various modern theologies, at least since Hegel, have felt the need either to criticize classical theism's understanding of God or at least to press theism to think about the idea of God in a distinctly Christian way. Part of this revision drives away from the language and thought patterns of classical theism. Is it possible to think of God in more biblical thought forms, ones that include the life of Jesus? Even more daring are efforts to historize Trinitarian thinking. As *Christians must construct the doctrine of God, there must be room for the history of Jesus within the life of God, or we are dealing with what is not appropriate for a Christian doctrine of God:* **(Theological) Warrant 12**.[66] One way to honor the theological warrant is to effect the historical demand through Jesus research.

A subset of this theological warrant is a critical version: a Jesus who acts against God. This view first appears in Baron d'Holbach in the midst

---

66. Possibly, a new criterion for what is *theo-propos* for the Christian understanding of God.

of the French Enlightenment. Usually a most hostile critic of Christianity, d'Holbach nonetheless on occasion warms up to the figure of Jesus. He finds values in the historical Jesus he uses against Christian religion, of course: nothing new here. But the new happens when d'Holbach aims a Jesus against the God of the classical theism. He finds Jesus, more often, reasonable and moral, and one who can mediate a new view of God through an application of a theo-propos[67] *criterion, the* **(Theological) Corollary Warrant 12a:** *The real Jesus can teach what is appropriate in a God and can press for a purging of incredible and reprehensible elements in the doctrine of God.* To be sure, d'Holbach does not want to believe in God, but he is certain the God he rejects is really a better God than the one of classical theism. Theologians need not follow d'Holbach's bizarre direction but on good doctrinal basis they can still appreciate that *a Jesus can transform God*, as it were. The transformation need not be an ontological transformation, if conservative views would be offended by such, but it could be at least an epistemological breakthrough mediated through the Christ.

B.9. The Anti-Marcion Warrant. See the gnostic point below.

C. Meta-Theological Warrants

C.1. Christian Humility

Schweitzer recognized that the study of the historical Jesus often ends in Wredean skepticism: the historical Jesus eludes historians and, if they boldly draft one, they fall into the trap of self-portraiture under the retrojected figure of Jesus. Of course, we remember that Schweitzer turns to the categorically odd apocalyptic figure of Jesus as the protection against modernizing Jesus. Today, the Wredean skeptic can no longer view the apocalyptic Jesus as a magic potion against retrojection, as it was for Schweitzer. Rather, we argue, all historical Jesuses modernize Jesus. And when we extend Schweitzer's insight to include even the apocalyptic Jesus, then we have plenty of skepticism without an object. At this point, the theologian, short of abandoning the quest for the insulated, turns the skepticism into a lesson of self-critical modesty: *the study of the study of Jesus reconfigures the skepticism about modernizing into a self-critical modesty about any picturing of Jesus:* **(Meta-Theological) Warrant 13.** Questing for the historical Jesus ought

---

67. D'Holbach, *Ecce Homo!*

to relativize our picturing of Jesus. As we stare into the gallery of all the Jesuses which bear family relations to their inventors, we quickly learn that christological certainties come and go, and that *we better not absolutize the Jesus we work with*. Strikingly, the virtue of historical modesty coincides with a theological modesty.

C.2. The Plurality Warrant

Increasingly, scholars have become aware of the many christic images of Jesus within the New Testament and within the doctrinal and theological traditions. Increasingly, scholars have also recognized the tensions among the images of the Christ in the creeds, and councils, and the early theologians, on the one hand, and those of the New Testament, on the other. More and more people are aware that cultures and sources and historians are not on the same questing page in imagining Jesus. The issue for theology *is how to sort through and evaluate the plurality of Christs* in questions such as these: what shall it make of the sheer plurality? Is it theologically unnerving to have many Christs, as it were? Are there some better, even more Christian, ones among the many? What are we to make of the differences among classic or recurring Christ images and at what point do differences become theologically problematic? Are some differences more theologically sensitive and at what point do differences make a difference?[68]

Crossan speaks of the quest as a "scholarly bad joke,"[69] and he makes this comment in a voice of regret. That is, he is disturbed by the capricious and plural, even incommensurable findings of the quest. He regrets the lack of consensus and the rapid overturning of paradigm and assured results. Descriptively, Crossan is right. But he thinks getting methodic about history writing may contribute to fixing the wild plurality of Jesuses. But we have suggested that Crossan's solution to the welter of Jesuses is problematic, since we have seen that a *strict adherence to method can be as pluralizing as it is unifying. Method will not eliminate the plurality of different Jesuses. But it will make explicit what is at stake in every Jesus historian's offer and will be an aid in a genealogy of values.* Differences in method yield different Jesuses. Therefore we have to admit to this recognition of the inevitable plurality of Jesuses in the research and the only resolution is to make a virtue of the

---

68. C. Stephen Evans, *Historical Christ*, 4, puts the historical Jesuses next to the church's Christ in the "marketplace of ideas" in which we can begin to judge the truth of the Christian story; oddly, he assumes that there is *the* church's reading of Jesus as the Christ.

69. Crossan, *The Historical Jesus*, xxvi.

plurality. It is true that we find ourselves in an era when the plurality of Christs is especially evident. We are more aware of the plurality than in the past and, arguably, there are fewer restraints on the production of new Jesuses. And the vast and cumulative historical research on Jesus reveals the variety of pictures and, even more unnervingly, the elements in their genesis.

While the anti-questing position commonly pounces on the welter of historical Jesuses as evidence of the futility of questing, its reaction proves to be no help, inadequate precisely because the New Testament pictures of the biblical Christ themselves are plural in value and in provenance.[70] The pictures implied in the doctrinal traditions are plural. To freeze arbitrarily the frame of christology on one set of pictures is to hide from history. Today literate people are conscious of the many, and the older strategy to deal with the plurality of Christs—*harmonizing*—no longer satisfies a historically conscious time. Of course, in some sense, the church has been conscious of the many Christs from the start: Tatian, after all, constructed his *Diatessaron* in the first half of the second century. And more or less, a harmonizing approach has dominated centuries of interpretation of the life of Jesus, one which presupposed that differences among the synoptic gospels and that of John could be ironed well enough to give the impression of the story of a single human life. To this day, harmonizing is the pervasive pastoral defense in most sermons and confirmation classes. While few could cement the fragments of the gospels into a seamless single story today, nonetheless, to this day, the conservative approach typically assembles "a basically coherent narrative."[71] Here, the harmonizing of Tatian has given way to an essentializing approach, in which the basic facts about Jesus are culled and ordered from the several gospels following a Marcan plotline. Those who dip under the plurality of christic Jesuses do so only by *asserting* an essentialized unity underneath the plurality. Whether the unity convinces or seems like a bland or authoritative imposition of unity onto difference remains to be seen.

A theology interested in modern Jesus research tackles the problem of the plurality of christic Jesuses with a strategy different from the old harmonizing one or the modern essentializing ways. Again, the problem here is a perennial one for any christology but that modern Jesus research offers a new opportunity to deal with it. But the quest rejects the harmonizing solution to the gospel plurality with insight from form and redaction criticism: sorted into different taxa. And the quest sketches a historically reconstructed, not an ideational, unity amid the trajectories of difference. By theological

---

70. So also Luke Johnson's position.
71. C. Stephen Evans, *The Historical Christ*, 5; cf. Powell, *Jesus as a Figure*, 12.

extension, it can also pose a strategy to sort through the plurality of ecclesiastical Christs by measuring these Christs against the reconstructed unity that is a historical Jesus. The former task is rich in value, as we know, but in its purity it is never more than pre-theological, while the latter task is decidedly theological, if often anti-theological. As history moves beyond the descriptive/analytical and savors the bigger issues about the Jesuses in the New Testament collection, we move into a new function, no longer strictly historical. Today, after all the critiques of questing, Jesus historians may at times recognize when their work slides into the theological room; some embrace the extension. But too often we still find a remarkable lack of self-consciousness among historians (i.e., scholars who recognize theology hidden only in others'—not their own—historical claims) and a loss of self-criticism in the heat of detailed historical reconstruction. Since these historians found judgments on certain Christs of the ecclesial tradition, they are operating in the theological arena.

From day one modern historical critics were impressed that the differences among the gospels could not be synthesized in any easy manner. They refused to soft-pedal differences and to read them as epiphenomenal. They were certain that a harmonizing approach would not work, as differences among Jesuses were taxonomically irreconcilable. Indeed, subsequent study of the gospels deepened the sense for the layers of the gospel tradition and of the redaction of earlier materials. Viewed from the vantage of this heightened sense for difference, the harmonizing approach appears to be simply unsophisticated and ahistorical. *Questing can be an alternative strategy to confront the plurality of the Christs (in scripture and theology). It honors, not minimizes, difference, and reads it thickly as a cipher to layers of differing historical deployments.* Instead of a flat, minimizing reading of gospel narratives, intent upon finding "common ground,"[72] *careful questing can deliver potential historical configurations that anticipate judgments among the many Christs:* **(Meta-Theological) Warrant 14**. Some configurations are earlier, to be sure, and, while we do not need to enshrine the earliest as the best necessarily, the early can be purgative. Other configurations show how a Jesus functions christicly in a particular context and can be foundational for particular constructive christologies.

In any case, *the quest can help sort among the Christs of faith and theology*. First, Jesus research honors the plurality of christic Jesuses in scripture and tradition without rushing beyond them in a harmonizing move or under them as if difference were epiphenomenal. Jesus research judges each image of Jesus and each element of a Jesus picture according to the cultural

---

72. C. Stephen Evans, *The Historical Christ*, 5.

and value configurations which support them, and does so in order to press to a unity founded in the *plural historicality of christic Jesuses*, namely, historians' best shots at what happened at this time/place. The unity is founded in the enjoyment of the plurality not in the denial of it. The advantage of the questing route to unity lies in its use of a genealogy of value to determine what is at stake in each christic Jesus. In other words, *Jesus research employs a retrojective critique on every image of Jesus to discern its genesis, its value content, and the world it intends. When it opens up how each Jesus functions in its concrete setting, it arms theology with the configurations it needs to make informed normative judgments among Jesus pictures.* However, historizing the picturing of Jesus does not produce direct theological judgments, or we would be returning to the historian's fundamentalism. Rather, *it informs theology of the value and provenance of each Jesus.* On the way to a historian's Jesus, we learn how a Matthean Jesus represents a gospel relatively distinct from that of Paul. And once we get to a historian's Jesus we have a perspective to illumine what is at stake in the contrast between Matthew's view of Torah and Paul's in light of contemporary theology's effort to reclaim the Jew in Christian understandings of salvation. In other words, once theologians understand the genesis and plurality of the Jesuses, they are better equipped to face the problem of plurality in a theological way.[73]

C.3. Questing and Interreligious Dialogue

A special subset of the apologetic use is the possibility that *historical work on the figure of Jesus may be a useful mediator in interreligious dialogue*: **(Meta-Theological) Warrant 15**.[74] The fact that historians frequently use comparative or neutral categories in their explanatory mode puts quested christologies in a favorable place for conversation among the religions. What is typical of *religious founder figures*? How does charisma found a sect? Under what conditions does the supernatural emerge typically, and so on? The fact that historians now speak of Jesus' life in relative independence from Christian categories may act as an aid in dialogue among the faiths. That historians drop into neutral or comparative categories when they identify Jesus, far from a loss for Christian faith, actually helps explain him to outsiders and to people of different faiths. *A historical Jesus, then, can mediate the theological conversation with others.*[75]

---

73. As they are well on the way to discovering what are opportunities in the Jesus saga to be taken as christological recommendations.

74. As suggested but not developed by Meier, *The Marginal Jew*, I, 5.

75. Admittedly, the anti-quest crowd will scream that the use of neutral or

C.4. The Complexity of Truth

(Meta-Theological) Warrant 16: *Questing for Jesus can clarify what is at stake in each way within a typology of ways of being Christian, each anchored in a rather different picturing of Jesus.* It does so by offering a historical developmental of each picture, and by showing how each picture lives within a particular cultural world. As we have seen, Jesus research solves the problem of the plurality of images of Jesus in a layered approach which, so far as possible, traces trajectories of meaning backward to the earliest recoverable level. The many-ness exhibited in the Jesus saga cannot be harmonized and should not be essentialized, but can be arranged in layers of development from the earliest to the most recent. The unity of the many is that of the source and in relation to the many trajectories of presentation, some of which are heterodox by later standards. The consequence of any layering, as we know, is frequently that favorite items of the Jesus saga get *docked*: that is, they get placed far from the historical Jesus. Indeed, the history of the quest has been the story, however uneven, of the demotion of favorites from the earliest list. The most famous example, of course, is the gospel of John, but recent examples are legion: the loss of Matthew's and Luke's distinctive materials, the loss of the narrative story line of Mark, the loss of certain parables and, in some views, of the passion story, etc. Whatever the current state of loss in the research and independent of efforts to salvage this or that item, scholars place some items far from the historical Jesus and well into the life of the church.

Fortunately, the loss looks different to scholars who do not work with the old fact/value split. Those with a different hermeneutic, one sensitive to the values of any picturing of Jesus, no longer can see the earliest as factual in the old sense and the developed is simply the expression of later value. Indeed, the loss looks different if researchers free themselves of the notion, often tied to a positivist or a romantic search for the pure origins,[76] that the earliest is retrojection-free, and thus value-free. Historians must free themselves of another notion, the protestant idea that development is loss of purity. Instead, *the discovery of layers of traditioning, of various gradations of probability poses the question of truth to those who attend to the results of the quest, and it does so in a useful way.* In a world of simple-minded, and at times, primitive notions of what is true, believers and others need to face the idea that some truths are not factually true. Yet there may be truth in

---

comparative categories and insights distorts the sui generis reality of the figure of Jesus. Theology would have to address the problem of the typicalizing of comparative methods just as it does concerning historical research.

76. A version of what Wilken calls *The Myth of Christian Beginnings*.

the *black* and not simply in the *red* Jesus.⁷⁷ Some truth may be of a different order. Historical studies contribute much when they pose the notion that, if we dig like archaeologists, we may discover items in the saga that are *closer* to Jesus. But we may also find things in the saga that ring true but are far from Jesus. In any case, we cannot return to the saga with a flat notion of truth.

C.5. Jesus against the Jesuses: the Cleaning Warrant

Because of the nature of the sources, the historical situation of the earliest followers of Jesus, and the high stakes of the game, the figure of Jesus eludes crisp historical portraiture as much as it provokes the imagination. As we have seen, the discovery that historians retroject their values onto the figure of Jesus has been bad news for questing: in positions that are immunized against historical research. There is another reaction, however, the one endorsed by quested christologies. Here Schweitzer's discovery of retrojection is not taken as the death-knell of questing for christology but as *the inspiration to do questing better by remodeling what happens in retrojection*.

That position argues that Schweitzer uncovers a historical, not a theological, mistake in questing. *Here we read Schweitzer's discovery of retrojection not as theology playing at history, but as failed historiography*. Thus Schweitzer was wrong in his famous claim that questing is the *"school of honesty"* for theology.⁷⁸ Questing does indeed bring honesty, not for theology directly, but for history writing.⁷⁹ Here we argue that historians and theologians need to turn the sleuthing for retrojected value into historical reconstruction (instead of worrying upfront about the theological consequences) and indeed, to *re-aim Schweitzer's insight into an internalized critique among the historians*. To be sure, critics and theologians can note mistakes in history writing and can heighten consciousness about the way that values shape the construction of a Jesus. But the correction and the construction of a better Jesus can be done only by historians. And, here is the important point: *theology protects the historians' efforts continually to improve historical research on Jesus*. Why? *To prevent people from reading*

---

77. To play on the famous procedure of the Jesus Seminar.

78. Actually Schweitzer's critical position bespeaks the very category error, confusing history with theology, against which he complained.

79. And for theology that has lost its bearing by grabbing the results of historical research, as if they were directly christological. In this sense Schweitzer was as confused about proper boundaries between history and faith/theology as the liberals he criticized.

retrojection of value as a theological mistake. Let history be history; encourage historians to do their task better. Revisionist theology has an investment in the notion that history and theology are different enterprises and that one ought not to confuse the two. If theology lets people apply value failures of historians to faith and theology, the difference between writing history and doing theology has collapsed. Surprisingly, then, even though we know that historical research engages in retrojective framing of the figure of Jesus, only better historical research can guard against manipulation of the past.

Consequently, *theology has much at stake in letting history be history. Only historical research can correct mistakes in historical research.* In a historically conscious and able era only further historical research can establish new insight into the figure of Jesus, on the one hand, and can correct extreme, unsustainable, and manipulated Jesuses, on the other. Again, theologians have no dog in the fight among historians. The continued working of the community of historians, however flawed, is the only mechanism which allows Jesus to break out from historical orthodoxies and which calls back failed constructions. We know historians are capable of mistakes, especially about Jesus. Yet a self-reflective quest, fully done within the light of the history of questing, is the only defense against historical mistakes: that is, only more and better and more self-reflexive historical research can correct historical mistakes. Questing amid the vicissitudes of the history of questing sharpens the quest; questing with a well-crafted retrojection-hermeneutic of suspicion sharpens questing further. Questing with a developed sense for the pervasiveness of value sharpens the quest.

The aim of better questing is to narrow and sharpen the Jesuses into a spectrum of sustainable conversations with the evidence, particularly in an era when no consensus is forthcoming. Roughly speaking, the sustainable ones pick up on resisting evidence even as they balance evidence with interests that are on the table. The working over of the available Jesuses continues the historical work on a meta-level, where historians can test each other's work for presuppositions and possible retrojections of value in particular Jesuses. As we can imagine, the standards for *sustainable conversations* are complex, not simple. Sustainability in historical presentation no longer is an appeal to the single criterion, whether the historian has gotten the facts right. Responding to the resisting evidence is one standard, and responding to all the resisting evidence adds another. The need to frame the evidence is important, but a sustainable conversation leaves room for difference of frames and methods and for the confession that we do not know some things. Being sustainable means being explicit about starting points and methodological choices, and testing them against the guild of historians and the history of the quest. It means being explicit about perspectives and how one finds a frame or a paradigm. Sometimes the sustainable simply has to trust the consensus of canonical judgments and informed views, even as it looks to avoid doctrinaire formulations. It focuses especially on the traditional *value locales* within the Jesus saga: i.e., how shall historians approach the miracle traditions?, how do they frame Jesus' *second-mile ethic*?, what is the meaning of the temple disruption? and so on. Finally, sustainability requires an analysis of the community of faith at the present time and a thorough sense for the dominant values of an era and a culture.

The task, to procure sustainable options, is a historical good in itself, but it also serves faith and theology. *Continued historical research sharpens the attention of christology by focusing it on those Jesuses that are more probable dialogue partners for its christic project. And, at the same time, a new Jesus can work as an iconoclastic force to break apart religious and theological orthodoxies:* **(Meta-Theological) Warrant 17**.[80] In our current debates, for instance, theology might need to work both with an expansive sage Jesus and a moderate apocalyptic Jesus: options that seem to wear well today. Of course, some will complain that the procedure here gives historians the trump card and makes christology *wait* for the guild of historians to sift through their reconstructions for sturdy ones. Indeed, Eugene Boring speaks of this historical sifting as a virtual "apostolic" role for historians and he is not happy to enshrine the guild with this authority over faith and theology.[81] But in fact, in a historized era, theologians and others are in no position to make subtle historical judgments and cannot solve the historical issues by asserting ecclesiastical claims by fiat.

C.5.a. Honoring Good History

Good theology embraces warrants and criteria of good history writing on Jesus. Revisionist theology cannot be hostile to quality historical research of any kind, but instead, out of its fundamental affirmation of the desire to know, it encourages good history writing. It turns over history to historians even as it presses historians to do their task well (i.e., especially to avoid dressing theological judgments as history).

---

80. Meier writes, "Indeed the usefulness of the historical Jesus to theology is that he ultimately eludes all our neat theological programs; he brings all of them into question by refusing to fit into the boxes we create for him" (*A Marginal Jew*, I, 199). Again, "[H]is importance lies precisely in his strange, off putting, embarrassing contours, equally offensive to right and left wings" (ibid., 200).

81. Boring's thesis in: "The 'Third Quest,'" 341–54.

C.6. Breaking Christological Symbols: Christian Iconoclasm

The Jesus saga has just enough evidence in it to keep questers busy and not enough evidence for sharp and unanimous constructions. The figure of Jesus remains elusive, no matter how many times we circle the block. Soon it occurs to questers and very soon to students of the quest that efforts to reduce the enigma by *the application of a single categorical system fail.* What evidence there is and what is required to assemble it defy every attempt to name or identify the person in a single stroke. Jesus is not quite a cult leader; he is not quite a prophet; not quite a sage, etc. And when scholars choose one category, its failure is clear to the rest of the questing community: they have done a classic part-for-whole mistake. Some scholars have even reacted to the failure of a category to capture the figure of Jesus by assembling an eclectic package of multiple categories.[82] In any case, the ever-elusive figure of Jesus ought to keep theologians humble, just as continued questing reminds historians of the failures of the quest.[83]

When we step back from the historical debates (i.e., whether Jesus is a charismatic holy man, a prophet, or a sage), we become aware of a larger lesson for faith and theology, here on the turf of christology: the brokenness of finite language to capture the hero of faith. *Jesus research makes christology face the limits of language,* not only because of the spotty sources of knowledge but because of *the inadequacies of any category to capture the elusive figure:* **(Meta-Theological) Corollary Warrant 17a**. And while we may be accused of making a virtue of necessity, nonetheless theology and faith need some humility. The many images of Jesus in the sources and the formulations of the creedal and doctrinal traditions all are broken symbols that more or less approximate what the faithful try to say in every generation. Jesus research reminds us that Jesus fits no known category[84] and that we better not freeze him into the form of any categorical Christ. Indeed, some interpreters find something christic in the (apparent) fact that Jesus explodes all Christs.[85]

---

82. Borg's four stroke approach is the most well-known here: *Jesus: A New Vision*, 15.

83. Nick Overduin, "Review of *The Jesus Quest*," 201. Note here the overlap among apophatic uses of Jesus research.

84. Cf. Wright, *Jesus and the Victory*, 144; Meier, *A Marginal Jew*, I, 200.

85. Ibid., 200.

C.6.a. The Mistaken Christ

Questing for the historical Jesus can pose to christology the notion that Jesus was mistaken about something in his world. Schweitzer presses the point in a sharp way, of course, when he offered the crazed apocalyptic prophet as the real Jesus. That one was painfully and nobly mistaken about the end of history. And to this day those who continue within the apocalyptic paradigm more or less work around the elephant in the room: the world did not end and Jesus was wrong. Of course, we can join one of the many twentieth-century models that put spin on this alleged fact; and possibly a non-apocalyptic reading of Jesus may survive subsequent research. Whether or not that mistake holds up, we still may have to face the notion that Jesus was mistaken about something. That historical research on Jesus poses this issue allows theology to confront some of the fundamentalisms of the day.

Today, even the most generous and kindly questing for Jesus has the power to challenge the fundamentalisms locked into secular and pious notions of religion. Once we move beyond the broad hermeneutical issue, we have to face narrower decisions on the overlaps between historical inquiry and theological construction: what mistakes?, why is Jesus mistaken?, are some mistakes relatively insignificant while others judged to be weighty?, what interpretive moves does a historian use to judge certain mistakes as not significant?, what are the favorite acceptable mistakes of an epoch? What values informed these questions and where do they come from? Most interpreters today do not wince if Jesus does not have modern, physical knowledge of our world. But should he be faulted if he works with pre-modern notions of health or of how economies or colonial empires function? Do we let him off if he labors under an antique worldview full of demons and prodigies, but expect him to be dead-on in his moral vision or in his insight into the human heart? And more generally, *can theology's Christ live with a mistaken Jesus?* Can it claim any of its traditional categories (i.e., divine nature talk) and, by way of its anti-docetic theme, still assert certain to-err-is-human mistakes?

C.6.b. Protection against Manipulative Retrojection

Questing for the historical Jesus can remind both historians and the faithful about the dangers of uncritical modernizing of Jesus: (**Theological**) **Corollary Warrant 17b**. We have already established that it is impossible to imagine historical work on Jesus without values. So the warrant here cannot teach us to expect no retrojection of value. Nonetheless, questing can put before our attention different Jesuses from the ones we know. New Jesuses shock us in such a way that we are forced to relativize our picturing of Jesus. Self-critical questing, sensitive to how we invent a Jesus, may be a critical check for us to discover what values support the Jesus we know of. How have we mirrored ourselves in our Jesus? Potential difference from our mirrored image may prompt a revisioning of our image. Certainly it makes us aware of the issue of retrojection, so that we have a permanent critique of naive, unself-reflexive imaging of Jesus. Whether we can expect questing to generate the notion of the inevitability of retrojection remains to be seen. More self-consciousness about questing should make us leery of retrojection, enough so that we face our inaugural either/or: *retire from questing into a historical-Jesus-free zone or embrace the project of retrojected Jesuses.* The latter turns on converting the recognition of retrojection into consciousness of and resistance against manipulating Jesus.

C.6.c. Honors List: Christological Halos

Related to the destruction of the icons is the manner in which *historical study of Jesus can force theology to sharpen the focus of christology onto essential christic matters:* **(Theological) Corollary Warrant 17c.** When historians do their analogical work, when they frequently smash some (christological) icons, theologians and the faithful typically have to face what aspects about the Jesus event Christians judge to be foundational of the christic. Specifically, are there things in the pre-Easter Jesus which are christic? If so, what things?, how many, as it were?, how necessary for christology?, are they constitutive of christological claims? Then, to what extend do items in the historical record become luminescent only after Easter? Boring reminds us of the ancient artistic tradition of painting the Christ and the saints with halos to signal the luminescent. Of course, historical research has trouble painting halos on historical figures, and often strips them off in the writing of history. But theology has to decide whether it requires haloes in the historical record about Jesus—keep searching!—or whether it can live with pictures of Jesus that reveal places where haloes could be painted in, as it were, by intelligent appropriation of historical results by post-Easter eyes of faith. *How transparent to God does the life of Jesus have to be?*

C.7. Christian Renewal

Ironically, *historical study of Jesus, the very thing that can be so destructive, can also be a means for Christian renewal:* **(Meta-Theological) Warrant 18**. While one should not overdo this hope, nonetheless it is conceivable that a newly refigured Jesus can inspire moribund pieties or reach out to the culturally alienated or indifferent. This use is particularly favored by questers on the left wing. If scholars right of center tend to employ Jesus research to shore up various religious and academic orthodoxies, those on the left often see a vast need to change Christianity: to modernize it in the mode of liberal theology; to restore it by leaping over unfortunate doctrinal reifications in the mode of a protestant reformer; to correct tendencies in theology and piety in the mode of a doctrinal guard; or simply to energize the faithful and bring theological renewal.[86] Effective historical research can be a fruit-basket-upset for Christians: clearly the intention of some members of the Jesus Seminar and implied in some of their publicity stunts to bring Jesus research out of the academic closet. Out of the turmoil can appear renewal.

Clearly, a new Jesus can stimulate theology to keep up with the times. In the past, theology has had only a few postures when it has faced genuine historical change. Mostly it denies change, either in the culture or in the scripture. Or it reads changing reality as epiphenomenal in an essentializing view of human nature and a harmonizing unification of the biblical message. When Protestants smell change, they usually flip open the Bible and read selectively in a proof texting manner. Catholics, of course, have a most successful tradition for handling change through the teaching magisterium of the Church, unless the magisterium becomes ossified. But in the modern era, historical critical research on the Bible has generated a new model of response on the part of the faithful: *they can respond to changes in their world as they respond to changes in historical knowledge.* No doubt, *the historical study of Jesus can press the church to react to a changing world.* Indeed, the recognition of development and plurality of voices in the biblical tradition goes hand in hand with the faithful's attempt to embrace a changing world. In other words, a good historical Jesus can prompt theology to react in a revisionist way; it can be preliminary to realizing a Jesus in a time of new experiences and new world constructions.

---

86. Meier, *A Marginal Jew*, I, 200.

D. Philosophical Corroborations

Many of the theological points above can be restated in philosophical language, since a philosophy of religion or a philosophy of theology too would be interested in sharp category distinctions and in the good sense of keeping the historian from sliding into philosophical claims of a metaphysical or epistemological sort. Philosophers interested in religion have interest in critique and the proper limits of reason. Here we have a **(Philosophical) Corroborative Warrant 19:** *That philosophical reflection can support theology in clarifying key categories entailed in the theological use of the quest in order to avoid category errors.* Indeed, the critique of religion, of the biblical narrative, and of the Jesus saga has been enacted most commonly in the modern world by philosophical reason peering into the world of religion. With philosophical insight philosophers like Kant, Hume, and their followers cut away troublesome features of the doctrines of faith and the images of Jesus. One need only think of the way that scientific standards of knowing and Enlightenment notions of reason supported the critical moment in the quest, whether we turn to the critique of miracle in Hume, the mythological interpretation of Strauss, or the anti-quest position of Bultmann. In these and other cases we see that critique lives both in and out of faith.

Many philosophically inclined will want philosophy's help in *defining belief properly.* This second contribution, a philosophical task beyond clarification, arises in the process of Jesus research, since the faith/history relationship emerges naturally there. One thinks of Hume's doctrine of belief as knowing on a scale of probability. As we know from Hume's "On Miracles," it is unreasonable to believe beyond the evidence. In the twentieth century, Van Harvey's *The Historian and The Believer* sets out a fundamental rule for history writing as it bears on belief: it is immoral to believe something for which there are no warrants.[87] That claim is a philosophical way to restate this entire chapter on warrants.

D.1. The Anti-Idealist Warrant

Christian faith and theology are invested in realities that purport to be instantiated in the world. *Biblical religion is worldly and the metaphysical bias of Christian religion points away from an abstract idealism,*[88] if by idealism

---

87. The basic claim of Van Harvey's, *The Historian and The Believer.*

88. Wright rightly notices an "anti-historical idealism" in both the group who wishes for only the pretty Christian icon and in those whose only goal is to reduce the Christian Christ into a flat "silhouette": Wright, *Jesus and the Victory,* 133.

we mean an otherworldly or essentialist devaluing of history and material life: **(Philosophical) Corroborative Warrant 20.** If anything, the Christian logic sponsors a critique of idealism (in the popular sense): on its good days, Christian faith is skeptical of mere ideas, however noble, until they have been concretized.[89] Finally, faith does not point to good ideas, not to a pleasing picture, not a good story, not a good ethic, not a warm spirituality, not a repeated creed, or the decisions of a boss. Of course, Christian religion may be all of those things and has been all of them at times. But its center, its inner logic, is that something happened in and around this Jesus figure. *Happened* takes us to history, real history.[90] What happened in and around this guy that got the earliest followers so excited?

It is easy to see how theology can find allies, not only in good history writing, of course, but more so, among philosophers, especially those critical of classic Western notions of reason. When Lessing imagined an ugly ditch between the contingent truths of history and the eternal truths of reason, he insisted that we could not bridge from history to reason. A consequence of this view of reason appears to be that philosophy can do nothing about and nothing with Christian claims for history, except to translate particular factual items into necessary general truths. The possible and contingent character of history does not measure up in such a vision of reason. In Lessing and in the classical tradition of philosophy, the flow of reason is away from particularities. But the logic of Christian faith proposes that the flow of reason, as it were, has been reversed (that the Logos as become finite and human) and if it were up to the incarnational logic of Christian gospel, reason should not be thought of as a drive to abstract from particularity to the necessary and universal, as it was for the classical tradition. Of course, theology does not have epistemological views of its own and would not tell philosophy what it should do, but nonetheless, its natural allies are with those critical of the classical flow of reason. Among some of these views reason drives at concretion and becomes instantiated in the particular. In this surprising reversal, *historical study serves the search for truth by a focus on the concrete and criticizes the way of abstraction.*

Philosophers, of course, will debate the virtues of idealisms. Theologians, regardless, worry about the risks of an idealistic reading of Jesus as the Christ. Their concern is for the way that it essentializes away from the particular: does this orientation not undermine the incarnation? Cadbury

---

89. That truth is concrete is fundamental to Hegel's critique of abstract idealism, inspired by Christian religion.

90. C. Stephen Evans makes the point in this way: the meaning of the gospel narrative cannot be separated from its historicity; thus an idealism fails for Christian revelation: *The Historical Christ*, 47.

rightly recognizes that an idealistic reading of Jesus as the Christ masks a modernizing Jesus that pulls him out of the particular world and universalizes his action, his words, his meaning. But the universal is allegedly timeless and provides no resistance against retrojected value. In other words, it is subtly manipulative. In Cadbury's insightful words, Jesus' "permanent timelessness is merely a euphemism for *our* perpetual anachronism."[91] Arguably, the classic quest has been biased against setting Jesus in his social world, in favor of abstractions, ideals, and heroes[92] and must be corrected both by friends and critics of the quest.

D.2. The Anti-Myth Corollary

This corollary warrant repeats the idealist point by rejecting that Christian faith is centrally invested in archaic events in Urzeit, and is not preserved primarily in the illo tempore language of myth.[93] *Whatever is true about the Christian thing, its logic, takes us to real time and real history* and, as Christians define it, "faith includes a relationship to empirical reality":[94] **(Philosophical) Corollary Warrant 21**. As we know, the *it* is not about eternal truths, despite the temptation of theologians in certain eras to hide in idealist or mythic versions of the gospel.[95] The gospels themselves are not in a mythic form but some kind of historical genre.[96] Of course, the Easter experience, whatever we say about it, has the power to mythicize the Christ; but *a robust historical Jesus can bring the Christ back to earth*. Theologically, it presses two crucial points onto theology and faith: 1. a negative one: whether Christians can discover a non-mythologized meaning for Easter; and 2. a positive consideration, whether and in what way the pre-Easter Jesus is in some sense continuous with the resurrected Christ. The former

91. Cadbury, *The Peril of Modernizing*, 34.

92. See Schüssler Fiorenza's argument in *Jesus and the Politics*, 32–33.

93. Rejected is the notion that Christian religion has deep investment in cosmogonic etc. reality and the language of archaic people, so famously charted by Eliade, *The Sacred and the Profane*.

94. Galvin, "'I Believe,'" 376, Keck, "The Second Coming," 784, and Meier, *The Marginal Jew*, I, 199.

95. C. Stephen Evans, *The Historical Christ*, 71–72.

96. Hays, "Faith and History," in Gaventa and Hays, 46. Interestingly, Mack and Crossan take the anti-myth character of questing to go beyond the usual judgment on the gospels as some kind of historical genre: Crossan deconstructs the passion as historical (*Who Killed Jesus?*, 6–13) and Mack takes the Wredean tradition to its extreme and insists that the whole narrative cast of Mark is early Christian myth-making. Instead, he poses a cleaner, leaner picture of an itinerant cynic philosopher from the aphoristic sayings: *The Lost Gospel*, 10.

is an apophatic exercise that explores the boundaries of reason. Actually Easter is the most conspicuous issue of so-called supernatural phenomena which beg for explanation.

Historical research can define what can be given explanation and what is beyond the limits of reason. Some time ago, historians, for instance, found a way to explain the exorcisms, typically by re-encasing them in a modern psychology.[97] Today they want to explain the healings, if not the nature wonders, and they routinely claim that Jesus' reputation as a healer is historical. The miracle accounts and reputation are factual. With the help of the philosopher the historian charts what can be explained and what cannot. And that the historian puts that distinction into the lap of theology and the faithful serves the faithful in a surprisingly helpful way, even when the distinction comes at faith in an apparently harsh way.

We have noted that historians frequently enter the territory of the meta-historical when they want to say much about Jesus. Their framing of a Jesus may involve the *language of myth*. That is, the manner of their framing a Jesus presupposes a sense of what it is to be at-home in the universe with a picture-policy for navigating in the world, and it does not matter whether historians are explicit about this meta moment or they embrace it. Sometimes historians operate in the mythic simply by rejecting the mythicizing of Jesus done by others. *We accept this use of myth as evoking a foundational story for our traffic in life in the world.* But the anti-myth corollary above aims at a slightly different point: it is not a critique of the mythic as such, but *a critique of groundless, eternalizing myth, in which there is no origination, no connectedness to history.* Consequently, the anti-myth warrant takes a shot against archaic efforts to make the life of Jesus an ahistorical myth of eternal return and against post-modern indifference to the grounding of the figure of Christian faith. In other worlds, theology has an abiding interest in what we call *historical myth*.

The consequence of the anti-myth warrant takes us back to the debate between the questers and the anti-questers. With new insight we now read *the Kählerian position of insulation as an unbeknownst retreat into the mythic*. That is, by insisting on an absolute discontinuity between the historian's Jesus and the Christ of faith, the anti-questers mythicize faith by founding faith in faith's own expression, the picturing of Jesus in the gospels.[98] In other words, the christic Jesus founds the Christ.

---

97. Through a psychological paradigm.

98. See Leander Keck, "[I]f there were only discontinuity between Jesus himself and the proclaimed Jesus Christ, the gospel would be a myth imposed on history, and Jesus would not be the church's sovereign but its hapless victim." Keck, "The Second Coming," 784.

D.3. The Criticism of Religion

Questing can contribute a healthy lesson in the critique of religion: **(Philosophical) Corroborative Warrant 22**. Most theologies of the past have not been very good at remembering the biblical criticism of religion. And churched Jesuses especially tend to flatten the critique of religion arguably discoverable in the figure of Jesus.[99] Questing for the historical Jesus can be a useful hazing for theology according to its founding intentions: discovering a Jesus who can clean house on bad christologies. The emphasis in this warrant is to clean religion. While some (i.e., Reimarus or d'Holbach) use a historical Jesus to dispose of religion or Christian religion, more see in Jesus the possibility to reform religion along the lines of biblical critique. Usually the reformation is of a moral sort, but as likely it is the use of a Jesus to uncover the ideological character of religion or of some religion. The former looks like a prophetic critique of religion, while the latter centers in an ideological critique. Here we have a fascinating positive use of retrojection. When scholars and others discern the structure of retrojection in constructing a Jesus, they become values sleuths armed with a genealogical suspicion of value. They can take their discerning new insight, externalized in a Jesus, and swing back to criticize the religion and the culture which is mirrored in the figure of Jesus.

Thus, *ideological critique can proceed through the objectifications of Jesus against Jesus,* in which one value exposes another unconscious one. To be sure, such a mediated ideology critique can end with a repudiation of religion, but it is just as likely to be an agent of the *reformation of religion.* In any case historical work on Jesus can help us see how our self-projects cloud, if not undermine, religion. Insight into the mechanism of retrojection, therefore, can give us the opportunity to distinguish good and bad retrojection, since we can see the values in our self-project. Are they manipulative and lead to ideological use of religion or are they benign? While insight into modernizing Jesus is not foolproof against manipulative religion, it does place before us what is at stake in domesticating Jesus religiously. One way we can actually see ideology in religion, and an effective way at that, is to continue to do historical work on Jesus, and the way that the figure of Jesus plays in power and value. Read theologically, this insight can be an old fashioned *critique of idolatry.*

---

99. Here we do not need to settle the questions whether Jesus fights some with "scribes and Pharisees" and, if so, over what issues, whether Jesus affirms Sabbath law and kosher, purity, ritual, Temple, etc., whether he essentializes or spiritualizes Torah, whether he offends Mediterranean mores, or whether he somehow simply transcends Torah.

D.4. Defense against Critique

Religion and especially Christian religion frequently come under philosophical criticism. Sometimes the criticism comes in the form of a skepticism of some sort, founded in certain claims about how we know. Sometimes critics go after religion for its incoherence or for moral failures. In the nineteenth century critics discerned various kinds of false consciousness or ideology operative in religion. These criticisms are familiar. *When religious people attempt to defend themselves against criticism from the outside, they employ a range of philosophical, historical and linguistic arguments. Perhaps, the most powerful criticism is the charge that religion is some kind of illusion. One such defense can be Jesus studies:* **(Philosophical) Corroborative Warrant 23**. Some Jesus historians and their theological allies seem to think that historical Jesus research can prove, or at least, confirm the truth of Christian religion. While we have rejected such a view as the wrong kind of expectation for continuity between Jesus and the Christ, and suggest the view represents a historian's fundamentalism, nonetheless, Jesus research can dispel misunderstandings of Christian origins and ideological bias against Christian religion. It is capable, then, of relativizing certain attacks and opposing positions.

Instead of a direct approach, we argue that it is possible for certain claims of Christian religion to be plausible or grounded. Minimally, we can determine whether certain Christian claims can be correlated with other truths. No doubt, Christian faith was triggered by the Easter experience, whatever we take that to mean. But was the response *appropriate*? How do we know the whole business is not illusory, especially since its trigger is so difficult to make sense of and is not *historical* in any common sense? A decent historical Jesus can take us a long way toward establishing the reality and truth of Christian claims. It can establish the sheer existence of Jesus of Nazareth, in a time when there are still some absurd deniers out there. In principle, it can discover whether Jesus' ethic has some reason to it. More importantly, it can discover the deeds and words that generated the enthusiasm for Jesus, independent of the resurrection, which independence helps Christian theology defend against the charge of illusion.

D.5. Apologetic Othering

Here we identify a need which uses historical and philosophical work, but which functions as a theological warrant in the tradition of Justin Martyr. Questing can be a component of theology under its apologetic mode: **(Philosophical) Corroborative Warrant 24**. There are times when theology may embark on an apologetic task. A fairly standard set of circumstances generates this mode: the need to persuade outsiders; the need to mollify doubt; the need to minimize the impact of critique; the need to bring to clarity points of confusion or tension within the tradition, and the like. When theology shifts into its apologetic mode, it may turn to quested Jesuses for help. It is the turn to the methodic, explanatory work of history writing that promises to shed light on Christian christologies. To bring to understanding, in all the ways that modern historical research can do, and to explain under a public commitment to honor the voice of evidence of the past, can illumine the terms under which christological claims have been launched. That illumination can be the stuff of an apology.

In the apologetic mode theologians take a dialectical step away from christology itself, from its claims and categories, and play away from home in the modes of the historian. The road game may be motivated by any or all of the standard apologetic concerns: an effort to see better, to explain to the faithful, to relativize critiques, to defend against attacks, or to persuade an outsider. In principle, all of these concerns can be enriched with a voyage into the kind of explanatory historical work typical of questing. Theology sponsors the voyage, learns from it, and draws the results of the othering into itself.

E. Historical Arguments

E.1. The Anti-Gnostic Warrant

The Anti-Gnostic Warrant restates the theological warrants and the anti-myth point: **(Historical) Warrant 25**. Christian religion is not primarily an escape from the world despite the fact that piety sometimes seems to think so. Faith in Christ is not "a contentless cipher, a mythic symbol, or a timeless archetype."[100] But historical study of biblical religion, especially of Jesus, can reinstate the worldly appreciation of creation and bring the faithful back to this world.[101] It may be that Christians have enjoyed cosmic battles and mythicized atonement theories, but sooner or later they need to be brought back to some ordinary conflicts in Galilee and to some very evil Roman colonialists. Jesus, not even in some of his apocalyptic forms, is no escape

---

100. In John Meier's words, *A Marginal Jew*, I, 198.

101. It is interesting to note that the Jesus scholars whose Jesus is the most abstracted from historical plot and narrative are the ones who favor the priority of Q and Thomas, the two most *gnostized* sources; see Meier, "The result is a dehistoricized, timeless message of self-salvation through self-knowledge and ascetic detachment from this material world": *A Marginal Jew*, I, 134. See also Henaut,

from caring for the world. The church said no to gnosticism, even as on good days it had to be vigilant to protect that decision. One suspects that the contemporary obsession with spirituality, both in the faith community and out, presents a new gnostic challenge for Christianity. In any case, good historical research on Bible narratives and on the saga about Jesus can bring the faith back to this earth. So many of the above, overlapping points affirm the need for securing the historical for Christian faith, against the spiritualists of the post-modern era.[102]

E.2. Concretion

The above warrants press faith back to the world. Here we restate these warrants in different language. *Historical research on Jesus can return the experience of faith to the world:* **(Historical) Warrant 26**. We see in the historians' Jesuses a figure who has real encounters with town and family. Jesus acts in the world with both compassion and anger; his actions are concrete, not mythic, not idealized, not abstracted from social life. When historians draw a Jesus, they picture him in a causal world where his speaking and his acts live concretely in people's lives. He does not *save* them from the world, but turns them back to the world. Historical research on Jesus can concretize Jesus' ministry and the ethical project associated with him for the simple reason that historians trade in the concrete language of causal, worldly connections. Modern historians rarely operate with mythic language and often are not comfortable with any meta-historical spin to their causal explanations. Indeed, their habit of looking for facts in the ordinary sense becomes a great ally for theology, since it matches the anti-mythic, anti-otherworldly, incarnational theology of Christians.[103]

To speak of concretion is to speak the language of philosophy and with an ideal of modern social history (see below). But the point has value for theology.[104] The danger in retrojection, according to Cadbury, lies in the tendency to pull Jesus out of the specific terms of his life and culture in its drive to modernize him. Such a tendency, Cadbury argues, is that we are abstracting Jesus into what we take, usually unawares, as a universal humanity with which we can identify. Hellwig notes, "To be truly human is not

---

102. "'Historical Jesus,'" in Arnal and Desjardins, eds., *Whose Historical*, 267.

103. Meier, *A Marginal Jew*, I, 199.

104. Recall the argument of George Lindbeck in *The Nature of Doctrine* that the particular (say, the redemption in Jesus Christ) must be constitutive of the universal claim, and not vice versa. Lindbeck's position supports the case for the centrality of concretion, even if he would reject the revisionist cast of this entire project.

to be in some sense essentially human, but to be existentially, specifically, and concretely human.[105] We do identify with Jesus but at some cost to his particularity. When we pull Jesus out of his particular world and essentialize him in his universality, we do so against the grain of biblical religion and especially the doctrine of incarnation. Obviously, we are restating the critique of idealism, of mythic sensibilities, and so on. As we have seen, Cadbury regrets any and all retrojection and wants to eliminate it by turning to historical work that attends better to the social world of Jesus and to the gospel texts themselves—what he calls the "standing enemy" of modernization.[106] While we can understand the social turn and the turn to resisting evidence, we have to note another lesson of hundred years of the quest: namely, that even the power of specific facts cannot resist retrojection.

The turn to the particular and the concrete, a virtue in itself, bears some complexity for theology, when, for instance, it faces feminist criticism of christology. So far as the sensible drive for concretion in historical research yields a single male figure, feminist theology poses a concern about the incarnation. How is it possible that one honors the specific humanity of the Savior without being androcentric? The sought-after particular comes as a particular male, not a female. What of female others? Feminist research criticizes the androcentrism of traditional christology, as we expect, but also the implicit heroic model of the individual Savior. By now there are a range of responses to these criticisms: the ideological critique of the patriarchal Christ symbol, the turn to androgyny and women's imaging of the Christ, the abstracting from Jesus' male particularity and treating it as incidental to the christic, usually in a prophetic style of christology, the decentering of the incarnation from a once-and-for-all individual happening to the continual reception of a community, and the like.

A theology interested in the historical Jesus should check itself against making Jesus the heroic individual: **(Theological) Corollary Rule 26a**. While at some point Jesus *is* heroic for Christian faith, theology today has to move beyond the notion that the faithful are simply passive receivers of the goods that flow from the hero. Relational and functional soteriological moments are easy components of a revisionist christology, even one that flies to ontological heights. Historical Jesus research can concretize christology.

---

105. Hellwig, "Historical Jesus Research," 90.
106. Cadbury, *The Peril of Modernizing*, 44.

E.3. The Social-Historical Argument

We have seen that the traditions of faith that emerge out of the Bible envision worldly and historical notions of salvation; they turn to historical experience, and not centrally to mythic experience. These motifs consort with the social-historical turn in history writing of recent decades. On biblical grounds the turn argues that biblical notions of salvation are at least in part worldly and invested in the social order. As we know, biblical religion pictures a God who is deeply invested in the history of a people. The problematic for humans is historical and the resolution happens in history, even if it somehow transcends history. Jewish thought has as much invested in historical research as does Christian theology. Where there is historical faith, there must be historical study.[107] To make the biblical historical point concrete, historians of Christian origins today participate in the social-historical turn in historiography, not, one hopes, at the expense of intellectual and literary history. *Jesus research can participate in the effort to enrich and concretize the notion of salvation:* **(Historical and Theological) Warrant 27**. The sense of history writing today is that we have not explained a thing and hence, do not know it, until it can be explained in its particularity. We need to understand, for instance, that Jesus dies in a real execution, with real causes amid conflicts and violence among powerful people. To explain entirely by mythic or cosmic transactions is not to explain the death at all, and as many people have noted, abstraction can be a moral, not only a cognitive, failure.[108] Historical research then can be a corrective to the mythic and meta-level of much of the doctrinal tradition.

There is little doubt that the social-historical turn has created history writing interested in ordinary people, and away from the historical genius or hero. Such a turn implies a criticism of older models of historiography. Contemporary Jesus research fits nicely into that correction. We have noted that the social historical era brings with it more attention to values, and more attention to the reception of historical events. The followers of Jesus make him the Christ, just as the faithful receivers of the de facto Christ in each historical Jesus actuate it in an explicit christology. Interestingly, earlier eras of the quest were desperate to secure how Jesus would be unique; they were wedded to the dissimilarity criterion. Today the buzz word is *egalitarianism* to identify the pervasive critique of elitist values in Jesus research of

---

107. Boring, "The 'Third Quest,'" 352.

108. The atonement explanations can have a sadistic ring to them and they can valorize suffering. See Elizabeth Johnson, "The Word Was Flesh," in Donnelly, ed., *Jesus*, 158–59.

the past.¹⁰⁹ Part of the new egalitarianism is that Jesus historians are likely to want to make their Jesuses available to the public. The public is not only the church public but a more general public, and some historians seem to have an almost missionary zeal to bring a robust, surprising Jesus to the masses.

E.4. The Ideological Critique of Culture

When we understand how retrojection works, we quickly recognize that launching a historical Jesus can be a ready, if indirect, critique of pervasive values in the culture. Good historical research continues to stand against manipulative values with new insights. Of course, it recognizes in resisting evidence the shape of values it honors in shadowy form, but *by way of the objectification of a Jesus figure, interested parties can bring the shadowy values of a culture to light and expose dominant values of the culture as ideological.*¹¹⁰ *A historical Jesus can be an obscure means by which the culture criticizes itself.* The culture critique is particularly powerful when the critical value can appeal to the archaic as legitimacy. Indeed, the historical Jesus can be a means to criticize the reigning Jesus research of an age.¹¹¹ *Jesus research, then, can contribute to the critique of culture:* **(Cultural Historical) Warrant 28.**

E.5. The Jewish Jesus Warrant

The quest has intrinsic value for the study of the first century of the common era in the Mediterranean world. It also can have high value for theology as a means to establish the study of available Jewish life in the Second Temple era. As we know, there are few Jewish sources from this century, from before the Jewish War. Jesus and his movement are important for Jewish history. But more to our point here, the quest helps us with a deep and enduring requirement of theology: *to establish Jesus as a Jew and reestablish him in his Jewishness:* **(Historical and Theological) Warrant 29**. Reclaiming Jesus as a Jew not only is a literary and historical challenge, since the materials about him are saved seemingly exclusively by Christians, but it looms as a major doctrinal and ethical challenge: not only to rebuild Christian relations to

---

109. Cf. Henaut, "'Historical Jesus,'" in Arnal and Desjardins, eds., *Whose Historical,* 267.

110. Meier thinks a good historical Jesus subverts all ideologies, even fashionable ones like liberation theology: *A Marginal Jew*, I, 199.

111. Meier makes the nice point that historical Jesus research can call the research and christology back from the extreme views that crop up around the figure of Jesus: *A Marginal Jew*, I, 199.

Jews but to counter the Marcionism of Christian piety and theologies. The Jewish Jesus Warrant becomes *an Anti-Marcion* **(Theological) Corollary Warrant 29a,** *in the belief that historical research on Jesus is an efficient and reliable means of reclaiming Hebrew Scripture and Israelite religion for Christian theology.*

We say *establish and re-establish* to name the struggle to secure a fully Jewish Jesus for the church's Christ during most of the twentieth century. Each phase of the quest has begun in a heightened urgency to set Jesus fully within Palestinian Judaism and with a critique of the failures of the last phase. Meanwhile, scholarly knowledge of the Jewish world has been an immense growth industry for Jesus research, and while we can know much more about Palestinian Judaism than in the past, the task of locating Jesus within it is scarcely easier. There are as many proposals for putting together a picture of Palestinian Judaism as there are of the historical Jesus; the quest for the historical Galilee is as complex and elusive as the quest for a historical Jesus. To be sure, a historian must construct Judaism and Galilee as he/she is constructing a Jesus.

One mantra from the quest repeats: *My Jesus is more Jewish than yours.*[112] And while recent phases of the quest have sought to judaize Jesus, the progress has hardly been steady. More recently, voices from the left have denied that Jesus should be situated with Palestinian Judaism (Mack), or have insisted that his Jewish world is richly Hellenized and cosmopolitan (i.e., Crossan).[113] Scholars from the middle and the right of the spectrum perceive these efforts to be a dangerous de-judaizing of Jesus.[114] It is beyond our work here to contribute to these on-going debates, of course. But we can note what is at stake theologically. A richly Jewish Jesus is one fully immersed in a social world, however hotly debated its contours, and who fits within the biblical experience of Israel.

A Jewish Jesus is concrete, and the drive to make Jesus Jewish fulfills both the historical impulse to set him in a social world and the incarnational impulse of theology. "No true Jewishness, no true humanity."[115] Of course, historians could select some other specific social world for Jesus (i.e., that

---

112. For instance, Marcus Borg suggests that even the hyper-Jewish Jesus of E. P. Sanders is not Jewish enough, because Sanders sees Jesus entirely in terms of Jewish *ideas,* and thus in abstractions from the social world: Borg, "Portraits of Jesus," 5.

113. Raising the complex question of how Hellenized was the Judaism of Jesus' time, and the issue of the Hellenization of the lower Galilean region.

114. Meier, "The Present State," 485. Meier insists that the question of continuity and discontinuity is so complex today that we cannot work with an apriori theory of Jesus' relationship to Judaism: A *Marginal Jew,* I, 173.

115. Meier, "The Present State," 487.

of the cool Hellenized cynic-sage) but even that world would have to be constructed as concretely as possible, to match the Christian theological demand for a worldly saving economy.[116] Theologians cannot solve how to reconstruct the social world of Jesus. But they do have a stake in concretion, as far as the evidence permits. If the evidence suggests that Jesus is not a Jew or not much of a Jew, we have a theological crisis about the inner logic of christological claims. If Mack's position were to be sustained historically, for instance, the christological jig is up for the Christians (as Mack knows). Mack's position, however, has not been sustained and seems unlikely to receive support. The more likely theological concern comes from critics who see in the cynic Jesus of the left wing almost an academic abstraction from any social world at all, not to mention the haunting possibility of an anti-judaic bias in some of the new research.[117] An abstract Jesus, known mostly from a handful of random, knifing aphorisms, floats in atmospheric irrelevance, the argument goes.

The drive to construct a Jewish Jesus certainly can bring concretion to the figure of Jesus. But we need to add three qualifications. First, in principle, setting Jesus into a clear Jewish world is not the only way he could be concretized historically. A non-Jewish social world, however, would make things very difficult for christology, as we have seen. Second, we have to recall Hellwig's observation, that making Jesus Jewish can be a subtle ideology, in which anti-Christian or anti-dogmatic orientations can play a Jesus-against-the-Christ critique.[118] And, third, we have to remember that the Judaism to which historians turn in constructing Jesus is a plural thing. Perhaps, it is too far to say we have Judaisms, in the plural, in the first century, but at least we have major internal differences among Jews of that era. There were few normative features about Jewish life and practice, unless we state them in such a high level of generality that we say little. So we have Holmen's question, *into which Judaism do we place Jesus?*[119] The qualification of the plurality of Jewish ways brings a limit and an opportunity to our reflections: Jesus could be fully Jewish and still depart from other Jewish people or ways. This fact means we have to be careful in the application of the difference criterion. *Not all opposition and difference between Jesus and other Jews need be proto-Christian nor does it mean that Jesus is departing from Jewish ways.*

---

116. If we set aside what damage to Christian claims a Jesus not set in Israel would do.

117. Meier, "The Present State," 485.

118. Hellwig, "Historical Jesus Research," 91.

119. Holmen, "A Theologically Disinterested," 180–81.

The drive to judaize, noble in itself, is fraught with difficulty. It can be a subtle anti-Christian or anti-dogmatic move to value the apophatic negative of Jesus-against-the Christ. And if we avoid that danger, we risk getting little out of the difference criterion. If Jesus is a Jew among Jewish options, we have little to explain why Jews opposed him (if they did), why we have an opposition tradition, and why is he executed (the *execution criterion*).[120] If any of the above possible results hold up in the research, Christians need to look elsewhere for christological promise.

E.6. The Jewish Warrant

As we know, contemporary Jesus researchers have produced a Jewish Jesus in what must be the third wave of re-Judaizing New Testament studies. What the researchers think is new in their approach is that they reject looking back from the early church to its foundation. *Jesus does not fit within the story of the church*. Rather he fits within options of Second Temple Judaism: that is his world, his social world, his political frame, the location of his eschatology, if he has one. Today we know so much more about this Judaism, about the plurality of options within the turf, and scholars generally have begun to work with a generous sense that Judaism is a living, grace-filled religion.

But treating Jesus within Judaism is tricky. The new canon of scholarship insists that Jesus must fit comfortably within the Judaism of his day. Notice that from the start contemporary Jesus researchers *bracket any special insight into Jesus bred in the church*.[121] Jesus must be a typical Jew, even if he can put his own topspin on being Jewish. The difficulty for the researchers will be to handle well three different criteria: first, the *execution criterion*, namely, why did this good Jew, fully within the options of Judaism, get into trouble, raise the ire of some and get himself executed as a criminal? Second, the *opposition criterion*, which seeks to explain whether Jews (some or all) came into conflict with Jesus and, if so, over what issue. And third, what I call the *Christian origins criterion*, namely that an adequate Jesus portrait must account for the possibility of the emergence of Christian groups. Concerning the opposition and execution: if scholars make Jesus a

---

120. Johnson notes that the work of history writing inevitably typifies Jesus and makes him so bland that he surprises no one, offends none. So far as the Jesus historians proceed analogically, they strip away the possibility of explaining why Jesus was executed: Luke Johnson, *The Real Jesus*, 49.

121. Wright notices the tendency to camouflage Jesus into invisibility: Wright, *Jesus and the Victory*, 91.

good, observant Jew, they have difficulty accounting for Jewish opposition to him and for Jewish complicity in his death. Then, if Jesus is such a good Jew, short of a miracle, why did the Christian movement get off the ground?

We notice how difficult are the issues. If scholars offer a sensitive and generous picture of Judaism, do they not minimize the problems a reformer-prophet might want to fix? If scholars accent the problems within Judaism, do they not feed centuries of Christian hostility to Judaism? If Judaism is a living, gracious religion and Jesus a loyal son of Abraham, how do we account for the emergence of a step-child religion out of it? And if Jesus is a good Jew among good Jews doing good Jewish things, what justification is there for Christians to read him christicly?[122] Apparently, the more winsome is one's reading of Judaism, the fewer are the christological opportunities. Can Jesus really have debated with the Pharisees over their wooden and legalistic interpretation of Torah?[123] Can scholars really blame Jews for Jesus' death, after the Holocaust? A very delicate matter.[124] Contemporary Jesus research has tiptoed around this question in such a fashion that we have to see there is a *moral criterion* at work in history writing: an *anti-Semitic criterion*. No Jesus researcher is willing to say anything about opposition to Jesus or about his death that will fuel crazed hatred of Jews. The cognitive version is an *anti-Judaic criterion*, which insists that no Jesus researcher can say anything which suggests that Second Temple Judaism is a dead or wooden religion.

It is no easy matter to account for opposition to Jesus and for his death without falling into the buzz saw of these criteria. The effect of the criteria is to press Christians and others to be extremely careful how they treat the Judaism of the Jesus saga and how they receive the work of Jesus historians. They must treat Judaism gently and accurately yet without falsifying the history of the effects of Jesus. The criteria, crafted in good historical

---

122. Meier, *A Marginal Jew*, I, 172. Meier notes the irony of a research project committed to locating Jesus within Judaism which depends heavily on the criterion of dissimilarity. Meier also thinks that the Jesus Seminar types wandered away from this primal intention of the Third Quest (*A Marginal Jew*, III, 3); it is difficult not to agree with this judgment. Cf. the judgment of Wright that the entire Wredean heritage of questing, all the way through the left wing of contemporary research, has lost the impulse behind the Schweitzer heritage: to place Jesus squarely within Judaism: *Jesus and the Victory*, 29, 79, 89.

123. Thus the effort by some to see the controversies with scribes and Pharisees to be late first-century retrojections onto Jesus and to identify the deep issue, if there is any, in the disputes with the Pharisees to be independent from respect for and obedience to the Torah and, instead, a dispute over the status of added, oral law which the Pharisees favored and Jesus rejected.

124. Thus, the drive to blame the Romans with little or no Jewish help.

research and in the history of Jewish-Christian relations, set a minefield before theology. It is inconceivable today that the faithful and theologians could walk through it safely without the aid of historical research on Jesus and on Second Temple Judaism.

4

Retrojection

We have already introduced the notion of retrojection in chapter 2, where we hinted that retrojection is more complicated than it first seems. Now we need to examine the complexity of the notion and head toward a reconsideration of the meaning of the critique founded on the retrojection thesis. Particularly, we will be critical of the common assessment of retrojection in the production of a Jesus and will be reconstructing the value of retrojection.

A. The Structure of Retrojection

Schweitzer taught suspicion to the quest. In 1905, in his famous study of the early lives of Jesus, Schweitzer started to notice that Jesus historians, as they busily reconstructed the Jesus of history, ended up concocting a Jesus who more or less mirrored their views: something of a cultural self-portrait under the name of Jesus.[1] What Schweitzer noted about the nineteenth-century lives of Jesus critics continue to see in the Jesuses of contemporary Jesus research: those Jesuses look surprisingly like their historians. Schweitzer's alert eye recognized the liberal theological and cultural values in the nineteenth-century Jesuses, while our alert eye can discover the feminist-liberationist-inclusive-pacifist-ecological, etc. values of the Third Quest.[2] The suspicious eye applies a theory that looks for the truth, not in what it sees, not in what appears, but in what is below the surface. The truth of such Jesuses is the value put on him, not what he is and means in himself.

---

1. John Meier writes, "[T]he historical Jesus readily becomes the clear crystal pool into which scholars gaze to see themselves": Meyer, "Reflections on Jesus," in Charlesworth, ed., *Jesus' Jewishness*, 86.

2. What Paul Barnett notes as "an astonishing expression of subjectivity by agenda-driven scholars": "Finding the Historical Jesus," 6.

Real value is expressed through an indirect means, the Jesus figure; or, to turn it around, *the Jesus figure is an externalization of cultural and personal values of the historian.* These values are the truth of these Jesuses and they explain their shapes.

Because the hermeneutic looks similar to Enlightenment patterns of criticizing religion, scholars commonly speak of this theory of explanation as a *projection theory*.[3] The category, however, is problematic even if we intuit what is meant by the term, since there is nothing immediately pro- or forward-looking about the mental act in question. A better term would be *retrojection*.[4] Historians appear to be throwing contemporary concerns backward onto a figure separated by time and space, doing what Krister Stendahl used to call "playing Galilee." A pressing concern, a value for our world, the historian discovers already foreshadowed in Jesus. According to the retrojection theory, we can explain this discovery, not as a true discovery of something new out there, but as a launching backward onto Jesus of very close-to-hand values. Admittedly the launch may occur within the shadows of the mind.

As the theory goes, the historian and others[5] fill up the empty Jesus form with their values. Of course, it is not just any values we place on Jesus. We select the most cherished ones, dear to an individual or an age. One day Jesus is a warrior; the next he is a friendly pacifist. One day he is a mother-hating celibate; the next he is into family values. Look at the history of the artistic representation of Jesus and note that one day he is a Roman lad (i.e., the fresco, "The Good Shepherd of the San Callisto" from the catacombs), the next a Byzantine emperor as the Pantocrator (i.e., the Daphni mosaic in Greece from c. 1080 CE). One day he is the emaciated, rotting monk on the cross (i.e., Grünewald's) and the next he is Michelangelo's muscular Jesus-jock who dwarfs his cross. At each step of the way, historians make connec-

---

3. I doubt that projection theories of religion are very useful to explain questing, though there is a family similarity between projection theories and the retrojection theory I am outlining here.

4. As a retired Feuerbach scholar, I am suspicious of any use of the common language of projection for critiques based on a theory of intellectual objectification. My suspicion starts with the clue that Feuerbach does not use "Projektion" but a range of other terms, both informal and technical, for the externalization that happens in religion; then the suspicion notes that there is great variety among objectifications and among theories of objectification. The Freudian one, arguably the one which captures educated opinion, is very different from the Feuerbachian one and gets tied into a notion of illusion. It is the *heart of my argument that the retrojective encounter with Jesus typical of Jesus research is anything but a projection or illusion. Rather, it is an imaginative act of objectification by which we converse with a past figure and thereby realize him.*

5. I.e., artists and theologians.

tions between a saying or an event to an intention, connections which are not *there* but are brought apriori by the historian.[6] Not only are the values put on Jesus the values we care about, but they tend to be ones that ideate human aspiration, ones tied to senses of what it is to be human. These values close to us are put at a distance, thrown back onto a foreign place, *Galilee*, a place just as empty as the form of Jesus.

We have to guess why people retroject value onto Jesus. Cadbury suggests that the root cause of the modernization of Jesus is ignorance.[7] He may be right in part, but he misses the mark for the research of the last century where scholars have been intensely self-consciousness about the issue of retrojection. Historians are hardly ignorant and yet they modernize Jesus—and do so even as they caution against retrojection and as they discover retrojection in other scholars' works. Commonly, historians defend themselves against the critique of retrojection by using Cadbury's escape. He claims that quality historical work is the best antidote to modernizing Jesus. In contemporary research their second line of defense appeals to the hermeneutical circle: bias and perspectives are inevitable, come with the territory of writing history on ancient figures, and the best historians can do is to be explicit about value. These two defenses provide relative help in the problem of retrojection. But we will have to go further for a fuller explanation of the ubiquity of retrojection.

When we happen on to the uncanny coincidence between our cherished values and those of Jesus, advocates of the retrojection theory read this happenstance as no coincidence but as *an obscure mental act of objectification: historians and others have placed these values onto Jesus in Galilee. Important for the theory is the notion that the act of externalization happens unknowingly or mostly unknowingly.* Those who find in Jesus familiar, comforting values do not know or know fully that they put those values on him. In part the lack of consciousness may be a function of the sheer objectification, of putting at a distance what is close at hand; but it also may arise from the exotic location for the objectification. Presumably, first-century Palestine is so alien a location that it masks *the actual exoticizing of values*. That is, *Galilee* is a sufficiently strange and unknown locale that the likening that happens there, in imagining the figure of Jesus, goes largely unnoticed. But there may also be human values operative in our unknowing objectification; it could be that what happens in producing a Jesus is of such high-stakes earnestness for many that *a kind of self-forgetfulness* descends

---

6. Sanders criticizes typical apriorist history writing and counters it by historical rigor and the right approach built out of the core, undeniable facts about Jesus: *The Historical Figure*, 9.

7. Cadbury, *The Peril of Modernizing*, 28.

over the business of making sense of Jesus. In any case, over and over both uninformed lay people and expert historians find a Jesus who is friendly to their dearest concerns. The surprising thing is that the Schweitzerian warning too often does not remind people of the dangers of retrojection, and too often among informed historians it becomes converted into "a relentless use of methodological skepticism."[8] Indeed, being self-conscious about the danger of retrojection seems too often to drive the professionals into a hyper-objectivist concern for method and certain results. In other words, *the turn to method is an internalizing of Schweitzer's critique of questing.*

Playing Galilee does seem to disguise the exoticizing of our values.[9] Certainly it lends authority to our values when we discover that our favored ones turn out to be rooted in an almost mythic Urgrund.[10] The first payoff of the procedure gives the historians and others a sense of familiarity with the Jesus figure. He is like us in a world like ours. We can easily claim him as one of us, who, like us, has trouble with his family and his hometown, and so on. The *likening of Jesus associates him with our life projects.* A second payoff happens in the midst of the likening: we find our main concerns *valorized*, since they are rooted in a foundational locale and anchored in the primal structure of reality. In some sense, our values are validated. We learn from Jesus that we are right. The associative move reminds us that our concerns for life are well aimed, in fact, that they rest in absolutes, especially since Jesus participates in those values. Externalizing the values onto Jesus is a mental act of abstraction. The values are isolated, universalized, and raised to their maximum when we bestow them on Jesus. Larger than life, he embodies the maximum, the highest instance of the value.

Likely, *Jesus is a hero of our own making and our own liking.* He leads us in our projects and fixes our problems. When Cadbury and Schweitzer discover our self-mirroring, they react in regret and seek to protect real values in Jesus, different from the ones we find in the Galilee play. *They note that the real Jesus plays in a moral theater quite different from the script we have given to him.*[11] The enemy of the real Jesus is the way we force upon him a

8. In Keck's fine phrase: "The Second Coming," 786.

9. The point here is dependent on an insight of Schüssler Fiorenza, who depends on Edward Said's insights about the way the oriental works for the European, *Jesus and the Politics*, 13. Schüssler Fiorenza recognizes the romantic hermeneutic that is much impressed with the charismatic great man, ibid., 7. When one hears Crossan and others of the social-scientific turn in Jesus research wax eloquent about Jesus as a Mediterranean peasant, it is no stretch to see how Jesus is being orientalized as the "noble savage" who brings critical leverage against mainline Euro-American culture: so Kwok Pui-Lan, "Jesus the Native," in Segovia and Tolbert, eds., *Teaching the Bible*, 83.

10. Ibid., 83.

11. See Cadbury's powerful list of all the good ideas and modern values we cannot

universalizing abstraction so that we can be valorized. When we attend to difference, the difference of another distant era, with an eye to value difference, we protect the real Jesus.[12]

Here *the associative likening flips over and, by virtue of an intensification of value, Jesus becomes different from us.* The dissociation of Jesus from us at this point fosters the third payoff: namely, Jesus becomes the ideal of the value, one who can inspire us as our archetype, edify us as our model, and judge us as our ideal. And while "retrojection" is to be preferred over projection language, the dissociative step turns us to the forward-moving meaning of projection. The ideal lurches forward as our inspiration-model-archetype to stretch us to new recognitions and especially to new moral heights. *The dissociated difference measures the exact amount of recognition we need and moral growth to which we can aspire.* Typically, then, the play at Galilee ends with a lionizing of the Jesus figure. In Charlesworth's words, "Jesus had been created in the likeness of an admired sophisticated contemporary man."[13] *Since he is endowed with the maximum of the values we have placed on him, he becomes the hero of the life project we set for ourselves.* He is unlike us, in that he has intensely or maximally what we can muster only at a reduced rate. And his unlikeness can lead us to heights of faith and practice.

So, humans do indeed "roll their own Jesuses."[14] Retrojecting value onto Jesus is ubiquitous. Historians do it, even ones who are conscious of Schweitzer's lesson. Informed theological judgment falls into retrojection of value nearly as easily as does popular piety. Artists retroject value in such an obvious way that the retrojection hypothesis is virtually undeniable.[15] Even historians who eschew theological consideration of Jesus fall into value commentary and rhetoric, as we have seen.[16]

---

really find in Jesus: *The Peril of Modernizing*, 90–111.

12. At this point we see the inadequacies of Schweitzer's and Cadbury's efforts to resolve the issue of retrojection. *They have to presuppose that their resolution and all the means they use to get it are free of retrojected value.* But this view we have judged to be unacceptable for contemporary Jesus research, since the sheer decisions what to use to find the real Jesus underneath the modernizing are fraught with value.

13. Charlesworth, "From Barren Mazes," 222.

14. In the fine phrase of Moxnes, "The Theological Importance," 96.

15. Interestingly, Cadbury noticed that the "modernization" of Jesus began at Easter: *The Peril of Modernizing*, 17.

16. Moxnes quite rightly notes a point we have been arguing: that it is impossible to separate historically driven Jesus researches from theologically driven ones, and that there is *an implicit theological commentary in every Jesus*. Moxnes notes that the language of questing inevitably and eventually enters a "cosmotropic or soteric" sphere: "The Theological Importance," 97. Notice that *theological* here can mean *antitheological*, too.

Three generations of scholars learned the retrojection critique from Schweitzer. They got scared of what Henry Joel Cadbury called in 1937 "the peril of modernizing Jesus." Cadbury saw in the quest of the historical Jesus an unrelieved opportunity for historical anachronism, a temptation to make Jesus like us modern humans.[17] Many gave up the quest altogether; many others joined those in becoming retrojection-inspired critics of questing. And every time scholars renewed the quest, the Schweitzerian sleuths exposed the anachronisms with the retrojection theory in hand.[18] Concerning recent Jesus research the sleuths have discovered a ton of American values,[19] patriarchal values,[20] bourgeois values, European-colonialist values,

---

17. Cadbury, *The Peril of Modernizing*. Cadbury's insight was anticipated by Tyrrell, *Christianity at the Crossroads*. Significant for the argument of this book is the fact that Cadbury, like Schweitzer, did not turn the retrojection critique onto his own picture of Jesus, who *really* was an apocalyptic, Jewish social ethicist. We are unable to imagine how Cadbury's theory can escape the retrospective trouble he finds in all picturing of Jesus. His insistence that historians should stick to the text alone as the basis of historical reconstruction now seems naïve and unsophisticated, unable to stand Cadbury's own criticism of modernizing. Cf. Charlesworth's deconstruction of Borg's modern Jesus, "Jesus Research Expands," in Charlesworth and Weaver, eds., *Images of Jesus*, 21. *The ubiquity of retrojection is a major thesis of this book*; where scholars confidently find retrojection in others' work but not their own, we find support for our argument. Both Cadbury and Schweitzer have to distinguish the retrojected, modernizing value from the real historical in what is a classic divide between fact and value. Indeed one can argue that the entire historical Jesus discussion since the New Quest has been shaped by a similar fact/value division. Consider the separation of the kerygmatic and the authentic in the tradition of the studies that follow from Käsemann, and the recent use of the dissimilarity criterion which divides the historical bedrock from the later expressions put onto Jesus. Francis Watson calls the separation a kind of "de facto atheism," since it views the interpreted as fantasy: "Veritas Christi," in Gaventa and Hayes, *Seeking the Identity*, 114. Watson's insight is apt but its critical edge misses that advocates of questing and the anti-quest position commonly share an understanding of the relationship of faith and history, if on opposite sides of the same coin.

18. Many a scholar has made a career sleuthing out the contemporary values packed into the new Jesuses. Surely we should apply the retrojection critique to their criticism too.

19. See Luke Johnson's list of American and American academic values: *The Real Jesus*, 43. See Mack's concern to use historical Jesus research to break the hold of the "Christian Myth" on American culture: *The Lost Gospel*, 254, or Borg, *Jesus: A New Vision*, 200, where Borg's concern is to criticize the popular American image of Jesus: 2. See Henaut's claim that Mack's Jesus exactly fits the America of the 1960s and on, where countercultural values were all the fashion and grim judgment (as in apocalyptic) clearly went out of fashion: "'Historical Jesus,'" in Arnal and Desjardins, eds., *Whose Historical*, 263.

20. Schüssler Fiorenza, *Jesus and the Politics* is the most obvious source here.

liberal values,[21] academic values,[22] baby-boomer values,[23] secular values,[24] liberation-revolutionary themes,[25] pacifist themes,[26] you name it.[27] And after three generations of judaizing Jesus, scholars are still finding Christian

21. Cf. Catherine Keller's critique of the "heroic individualism" in Crossan's Jesus: Keller, "The Jesus of History and the Feminism of Theology," 75; Schüssler Fiorenza thinks the great-man tradition in Jesus research is anti-Jewish, anti-women, and loses the egalitarian thrust of the Jesus movement: *Jesus and the Politics*, 65. See also Arnal and Desjardins, eds., *Whose Historical*, 314, for the academics who hate apocalyptic and "turn Jesus into a slightly disgruntled, liberal, university professor." See the following American values in the left-wing Jesus: the church/state separation, the classless society of individual opportunity, and a modern Western unwillingness to interpret the Bible: Horsley, "Jesus and the Politics," in Charlesworth and Weaver, eds., *Images of Jesus*, 79.

22. Luke Johnson, *The Real Jesus*, 43. Arnal thinks Jesus as sage appeals to academics who hate the apocalyptic prophet because of its association with right-wing views: Arnal and Desjardins, eds. *Whose Historical*, 313.

23. Allison notes that the left wing of Jesus research is dominated by boomers who have a visceral dislike of conservative American religion and that value prompts scholars to ignore eschatology, christology and soteriology: *The Historical Christ*, 65. Again, the point is that many new Jesuses are not too "religious."

24. It is typical of right-wing Jesus scholars to criticize left-wing Jesuses as "secular" efforts to appeal to liberal and academic culture: see, for instance, Wright's critique of Sanders: *Historical Figure*, 118. See Arnal and Desjardins, eds., *Whose Historical*, 309–10, for a discussion of how religious is the Third Quest Jesus and how Jewishly religious is he. The drive to judaize Jesus runs into a criticism from the left that a "religious" Jesus is an anachronism. We see the issue as rival retrojections onto Jesus.

25. Luke Johnson, *The Real Jesus*, 65. See Horsley's contribution especially: Horsley, *Spiral of Violence*.

26. Cf. Wright, *Jesus and the Victory*, among mainline Jesus researchers, 446.

27. See, for instance, Schüssler Fiorenza, *Jesus and the Politics*, 6, 12, 59–60, for a concern that Jesus research must become self-conscious of how it perpetuates marginalization of women and others globally; see Kwok Pui-Lan, "Jesus the Native," in Segovia and Tolbert, eds., *Teaching the Bible*, 76.

themes in the quested Jesuses of contemporary historians.[28] Thus, Dale Allison says, "[Y]ou can do anything with Jesus..."[29]

Schweitzer posted for Jesus research its permanent challenge: *how can a historian break free from the self-mirroring we call the historical Jesus?* What can historians and others do, if at all, to break free from the pervasive value imposition on Jesus? After all, if there is no escape from retrojection, then is *the historical Jesus* any more than *a hermetically sealed value externalization of a historian's world construction*? Suspicion wins by reducing a Jesus without *surplus of meaning* to the values of the historian and his/her culture.[30] In this light *Schweitzer becomes a pioneer of what we are calling post-modernism or deconstruction in history writing these days.*[31] Oddly, suspicion generates suspicion. When the critic reduces each Jesus in an air-tight way to the cultural/personal values of the historian, such suspi-

---

28. Historians have been in the midst of a three-generation arms race to create the most Jewish Jesus and to uncover the hidden Christian bias against things Jewish in quested Jesuses. An insightful critique comes from Dieter Georgi who sees anti-Judaism hidden in the historians' commitment to great-man traditions of historiography, on the one hand, and to a radicalized theory of Jesus' ethic, on the other: Georgi, "The Interest in Life," 51–83. The attempt to judaize Jesus has been so pronounced in post-holocaust research that we are seeing the first signs of a counter-movement. See Wright's critique of "philo-semitism" in Jesus research, where he identifies points and people who sell the Christian farm, who reduce history writing about Jesus into Christian contrition and absolving Jews for the crucifixion, or who talk things Jewish but subtly construct a Jesus unrelated to distinctive Jewish themes: 119. Another conservative Jesus scholar, Dunn, agrees: *"Can the Third Quest,"* in Chilton and Evans, eds., *Authenticating the Activities*, 36–37. Note the significant overlap between scholars emphasizing the Jewish Jesus and scholars who frame Jesus in terms of the apocalyptic paradigm: Arnal and Desjardins, eds., *Whose Historical*, 313.

29. Allison, *The Historical Christ*, 16. We have every reason to believe that American culture wars influence the decision to frame Jesus as apocalyptic prophet or as sage. The right-wing advocates the apocalyptic frame while the sage frame appeals to the left. The former, tied to the most traditional historiography, is often more Jewish and religious and otherworldly, while the latter, with more post-modern style, is more liberal, worldly/cosmopolitan, and more socially engaged: see Arnal and Desjardins, eds., *Whose Historical*, 314–17.

30. Critics conclude there is no surplus of meaning in a quested Jesus beyond the values of the historians and that the revealing of those values requires that we dispose of such a Jesus. Neither conclusion is necessary and both live within a closed, historicistic presupposition about history writing: the former presupposition seems to deny anything new in history is possible, since there is no slippage between what is produced by the historian and the reality of his/her cultural values. The historian can discover nothing new about Jesus, since to discover new amounts to a claim to have succeeded in placing oneself outside of the picturing. The latter, finding no use for a historical Jesus, disposes of it.

31. An incomplete reading, I would argue, since it ignores Schweitzer's effort to say something real via the "alien criterion."

cion opens the door to further suspicion: namely, it is easy to assume that, without a non-reductive suppositum, the Galilee play is no more than an ideology. It is indirect, needlessly complex, obfuscating. *What starts as a critique of a suffocating game of self-reference turns into a moral critique of an ideological use of Jesus for power or profit.*

At the end of his famous study of the lives of Jesus, Schweitzer allied himself with the "thoroughgoing eschatology" of Johannes Weiss' portrait of Jesus. That is, against what he called the "thoroughgoing skepticism" of Wilhelm Wrede,[32] he agreed with Weiss that we should be thinking of the real Jesus as an apocalyptic prophet.[33] How did he know? In turning to the apocalyptic prophet, Schweitzer simultaneously articulated the *first defense against the retrojection thesis he had invented*. He might have ended his study of the studies of Jesus with his revelation of the historians' self-mirroring though Jesus. But Schweitzer himself had to struggle to define the line between retrojected value and historical facts that do not smell of the historian. Schweitzer was certain there was a real Jesus behind the self-reflection. He could not sit in silence about Jesus. Indeed, he had to define the line, since neither silence about Jesus nor accepting the church's pictures of Jesus would satisfy him. Why? Because he was certain both the church's pictures and the scholarly treatments were wrong, inaccurate, and thus did not represent the real Jesus. The church got him wrong; and certainly the nineteenth-century historians missed him completely.

Despite the fact that Schweitzer authors the retrojection approach to the quest, he will not let himself be backed into an agnostic room (associated for him with Wilhelm Wrede's skepticism about the gospel storyline).[34] Though his criticisms are stinging and though his reputation to a large degree rests upon his uncovering the interpretive problem in all questing, Schweitzer seems to recognize that he must defend himself against Schweitzer. The Schweitzer who reduces the quested Jesuses to retrojections is able to recognize a retrojection and can distinguish it from the real thing. Consequently, he ends his book with a haunting picture of a real Jesus who resists retrojection.[35] This Jesus is the apocalyptic wild man, so distasteful and strange that he fits into no one's ideational hopes. In Schweitzer's retrieval, the real Jesus is so different from and so discontinuous with our values and self-understandings that he can be no pious or cultural self-reflection. In

32. Wrede's discovery that a theological motive shaped the best source for the study of Jesus—the gospel of Mark—was a shaking blow to gospel-realism.

33. In those days Schweitzer used "eschatological" for what we typically term "apocalyptic" today.

34. And certainly not the insulated room.

35. Schweitzer, *The Quest of the Historical Jesus*.

his difference from us and from our world-constructions Jesus is immune to our manipulation. Here *difference secures historical accuracy and it does so against self-reflection*. If it did not, Schweitzer would never be able to distinguish his and Weiss' picture of Jesus from all the unacceptable, quested Jesuses.

Of course, one cannot be so certain of these mistakes about the reality of Jesus without presupposing a correcting measure. How could Schweitzer claim to know what the real Jesus was like? Similarly, how could Cadbury know his sketch of Jesus was not one more instance of modernization?[36] More precisely, how could he or anyone know these views about the real Jesus were more than or different from the typical retrojected treatment of Jesus? Schweitzer has to escape his own discovery of retrojection. Obviously, the critic in Schweitzer propels him negatively to claim to know more about the historical Jesus than some want from the author of the retrojection theory. Certain anti-questers in the Kählerian camp like to imagine that Schweitzer's discovery of retrojection ends questing for all time. But not Schweitzer. Some seem to think that the so-called *no-quest* period follows necessarily and permanently from Schweitzer, but this view adds value far beyond what Schweitzer envisioned.[37] Schweitzer is unwilling to be Wredean in his skepticism. Therefore, he must discover a basis for his critical judgments about other pictures of Jesus. To be truthful about it, *the retrojection thesis requires a non-reductive surplus of meaning*[38] *on the basis of which it can launch its critical endeavor*. So Schweitzer, the one who invents the retrojection theory in Jesus research, must protect himself and it from the reductive power of his own critical insight into the workings of Jesus research. And without a pedal point that grounds the retrojective critique, Schweitzer cannot say anything about the real Jesus. What we have termed the *alien and difference criteria* (identified in chapter 2) founds Schweitzer's *post-critical retrieval of what he has deconstructed*.

We can judge with confidence that Schweitzer and Cadbury were right about retrojection: they were right to deconstruct the historical Jesuses with the retrojective critique. Schweitzer was also right to come up with this alien criterion and to use it to unearth the real Jesus, so different from the one squeezed through modernizing value tendencies. We understand what they were escaping, the power of the domesticating imagination. But we also

---

36. Cadbury weakly hopes that good, methodic historical investigation "should be a kind of corrective" to the anachronism of Jesus research: *The Peril of Modernizing*, 15, 25.

37. As Bultmann brings Kant, Luther, Kierkegaard, existentialist currents, etc. to the no-quest table.

38. Ricoeur's famous phrase.

wonder whether there was a positive support for Schweitzer's confidence that he was dealing with the real Jesus. We know that both Schweitzer and Cadbury are caught by the limits of their hermeneutic. Both participate in the romantic hermeneutical tradition (back to Schleiermacher and others) with its concern for intentionality and religious experience. This interpretive approach directed attention to Jesus' self-consciousness and his developing messianic consciousness. And, while Schweitzer fills Jesus' messianic consciousness with content at odds with both the ecclesial traditions and nineteenth-century liberalism, he is no less fixed on what Jesus thought he was doing, as he threw himself on the "wheel of history." Both he and Cadbury understood that there was something historically *there* to the Jesus saga despite the anachronism of the moderns. When, according to Schweitzer, Jesus calls God's hand at the end of his life, he does so with a sense for the actual mission of the man whom he names, "the one unknown."[39] When Cadbury speaks of the counter danger, the danger of over-archaizing Jesus, he names the positive support for the search for a real Jesus. Historians do not and cannot leave Jesus as the alien unknown. While Cadbury and Schweitzer wrongly assume that the real Jesus is the one left over when good historical work trims away the modernizing, they are right to insist that we cannot understand the unknown one.[40]

Schweitzer does little with the tiny, positive revelation he finds. It hardly launches him to a post-critical christology. Perhaps, he finds so little to grab ahold of in Jesus' confident swagger that he could not imagine a constructive christology. We do know the positive support for a real Jesus is important, since Schweitzer spends most of the end of his book refuting Wrede's skepticism. Indeed, the additions to the second edition (1912) focus entirely on his critique of Wredean skepticism, particularly on the issue of whether we have historical knowledge that Jesus knew what he was about. So Schweitzer has much at stake in the positive plank of his vision of the real Jesus. But, instead of taking what he thinks he knows about the real Jesus (say, a messianic consciousness) into christological waters, Schweitzer takes the real Jesus as a cipher to secure his famous moral-mystical piety.

Most questers and anti-questers today agree with Schweitzer's insight concerning retrojection. Questers routinely employ the difference and the alien criteria, even if anti-questers are not as impressed with their benefits. The impasse between Schweitzer's approach and that of Wrede continues to bedevil the quest: Wright even turns the choice into a permanent either/or

---

39. Schweitzer, *The Quest of the Historical Jesus*, 2001 ed., 487.

40. As they understand understanding, namely what delivers an unvarnished Jesus.

for all of Jesus research.⁴¹ That is, either skepticism about serious knowledge of Jesus or a Jesus saturated with retrojected value. Explicitly or implicitly affirming the way of Wrede, the anti-quest crowd ducks out of questing. In the judgment of the conservative wing of the Jesus researchers, left-wingers are on the path toward Wrede's skepticism.⁴² Usually, conservatives more or less walk with Schweitzer but feel they can, on the one hand, enrich the positive content in the historical record, and thus, on the other hand, avoid the sting of the retrojection charge (by careful method).

Theologians need to be skeptical of both left-wing and right-wing optimism about the theological use of the Jesuses: **(Theological) Rule 63**. Particularly they must be on guard against history parading as if it were theology. In other words, they must guard against historian's fundamentalism, wherever they find it. During most of the quest the results of Jesus research have worked to reduce what theology can say christologically. Most of the historian's fundamentalism appears, then, on the liberal side of the ledger, and it continues even up to the contemporary Jesus Seminar types. Robert Funk's pronouncements, for instance, represent the left-wing temptation to fundamentalism; the irony here is that Funk has turned to one form of fundamentalism to attack another form. But today there are as many Jesus researchers of a theologically conservative stripe who are just as tempted to be fundamentalistic about the results of historical research. The theologies within the Jesus researches of Craig Evans or Ben Witherington represent this second type. As usual, revisionist theologians find themselves embracing a hybrid that mixes the concerns of all the camps. *Against the anti-quest position, revisionist theologies are not persuaded by undue historical skepticism (vs. the Wredean impulse), and are mindful of retrojected value coloring Jesus histories (with Schweitzer); here we have* **(Theological) Rule 64**. *Moreover, against most questers, revisionists are not convinced that better method fixes retrojection and delivers a Jesus of direct (positive or negative) christological significance* [**(Theological) Rule 65**]; *but with most questers they favor continuing to refine method and to make explicit the values and orientations of historical researchers. Almost alone, revisionists reject the fundamentalistic application of historical results while still holding to their interest in discovering whether historical results can support christological possibility:* **(Theological) Rule 66**.

41. Wright, *Jesus and the Victory*, 20.

42. Today, the Schweitzer-Wrede battle plays out in the battle between the left-wing Jesus researchers who favor the atomism of the Wrede heritage (i.e., most of the Jesus Seminar) and the holism of the Schweitzerian tradition of conservative scholars, like Wright, C. Stephen Evans, and even a centrist like Sanders. More interesting is that each choice inspires a retrojection critique.

Historians with theological interests and theologians differ where they see retrojected value and what to do next, after they uncover values in historical treatments of Jesus. A theology that looks in on this historical discussion faces a *first either/or: to quest or not.* The one choice, that of the anti-quest position, thinks, in effect, that the discovery of retrojected value in the historians' Jesuses kills the wisdom of questing for good. When scholars notice that Jesus has been modernized, the critique ends the issue of modern historical research on Jesus. The retrojective eye sees all and the critique reduces the historical Jesus without remainder. The fiction of the *historical Jesus* is an ever-receding horizon. Or maybe it is a black hole, filled only with the imaginations of those who are foolish enough to say something about him. Those taken by historical skepticism either offer a bare Jesus or retire from questing.[43] Those who wish to continue theological conversations in light of the rocky (reduced and retrojected) findings of the quest face a *second either/or: either they turn full of hope to more careful historiography with better methods and more self-conscious approaches to deliver a more secure Jesus for christological purposes, or they elect to rethink what happens in retrojection:* **(Theological) Rule 67**.

The revisionist option, chosen here, applauds the former efforts to be better historians but suspects that value is ubiquitous, on the one hand, and remains critical of the assumption that better method will cure retrojection, on the other. Indeed, as we must note, both the search for an *objective* story of Jesus and the concern for the modernizing of Jesus are values of modernity. As we have argued, method is not the answer to value, as the turn to method simply puts the value question back a generation onto the values operative in the choice of method. In due time we will continue to recast retrojection in a revisionist way, without the positivist hangover locked into historical discussions about Jesus.[44] More importantly, revisionists will want to deploy insights from historical research on Jesus but to do so without the fundamentalistic application of historical results directly to christology. Here they part company both with many enemies and friends of Christian faith and theology.

---

43. Like Dale Allison, apparently.

44. Consider the long-standing, New Quest-influenced methodological orientation to the sayings of Jesus. Possibly, the turn to the sayings reflects Enlightenment troubles with the supernatural. Possibly, the confidence in the sayings tradition is a remnant of a Romantic hermeneutic. In any case, scholars routinely turned to the sayings with an assumption that they could read back from the parables and the aphorisms to the intentions and aims grounding the ministry of Jesus.

B. Analysis of the Retrojection Theory

The retrojection theory is a critical theory, applied to history writing.[45] As such, it attempts to explain, not history, but history writing as an aid to understand the placing of contemporary values in the historical presentation of Jesus of Nazareth. The theory is a critique, a hermeneutic of suspicion, in Paul Ricoeur's phrase. It places the work of historians under a hermeneutic of suspicion and seeks to explain features and tendencies of the Jesus saga, composed by historians, as expressions of the values of the historians. The theory decodes historians' Jesuses into the values of historians and their cultures with an aim to explain why a Jesus takes on a particular cast (among all the possible casts). If a critic were to claim that the Jesus in question could be reduced without remainder to the values of the historian, the critique would be complete. But such a fulsome claim entails the position that elements of the Jesus saga provide no important resistance to the shaping values of the historians. Perhaps, we should not say *no* resistance, since the important concern is whether evidence of high significance has resisting value. In the reductive application of the retrojection thesis, critics of questing conclude that historians' values define the figure of Jesus at all the crucial points of meaning. A completely reductive reading, therefore, collapses the historical Jesus into the values of the historians and the influences of their era. In other words, in what is a clean and airtight reduction, the historians' Jesus really is completely modern.

If a critic, whether historical or theological, were to suggest that the real Jesus were quite different from the historian's modernized Jesus, he/she would cross a threshold, beyond the purely reductive, into positive historical claims. At first, the step seems insignificant, but it brings us into a new room, one that requires a new logic, a retrieval *beyond suspicion,* which instructs a historian how to honor certain evidence in a certain way. *We see already that the retrojection theory is not what it appears to be, not a complete reduction of a Jesus to the values of the historian.* Consequently, the theory has to be broader than its advocates sometimes say. It must include *a critique of itself that recognizes its own limitations. First, how is it possible that, given the ubiquity of retrojection, historians can discern real light from the past:* **(Quest) Rule 68**?[46] Apparently, *the airtight reduction does*

---

45. And by extension, to literary, artistic, and faith expressions.

46. Within the basic theory of retrojection, critique requires a non-retrojective basis for the discovery of retrojective value. We note the significant fact that Schweitzer and Cadbury, the two inventors of the retrojection thesis, both go on to speak of *the real Jesus* while recognizing that their construction too might be a retrojection of modern value. Even the great critic of questing, Martin Kähler, turned to a claim that the real Jesus was "uninventable" (*unerfinnbar,* as Michael Labahn notes in: "Martin

not capture all that happens in the interpretation of the Jesus saga.[47] When a historian or theologian claims a Jesus does not match the real Jesus, he/she joins Schweitzer who, in claiming that the liberal Jesus is not the real Jesus, has some access to the real Jesus. It may be true that the progressive values of nineteenth-century Europe are foreign to the real Jesus, but how does Schweitzer (or anyone) know that? On what basis?

Once the new account identifies how non-retrojective light from the past is possible, it must turn to a second challenge: *why this light and not some other?* When Schweitzer turns to the alien Jesus as the real Jesus, he implicitly enshrines *radical cultural difference as a formal value and difference from modern bourgeois European values as a shadowy material value.* He might have grabbed onto other values (i.e., where Jesus is most like us, or where he reveals his Jewishness most clearly). Consequently, *we ask for warrants for the non-reductive choice of the real,* warrants that check against the arbitrary. Such a new account would have *to identify how we have access to real elements about Jesus* that are not smothered by retrojected value. Presumably, such an account would not want to abandon the insight into retrojected value or deny/ignore retrojection. And finally, if we are not already lost in the turns of consciousness here, the new account would *have to show how the turn to supposed real elements about Jesus (to avoid retrojected value) can itself escape retrojection.* When, for instance, Schweitzer sings his praise of the unknown one who dares to turn the wheel of history, is it not Schweitzer's faith and christology speaking, and not his historiography? Whatever it is that delivers a real Jesus (i.e., the alien criterion) is weighted with value, however real it may be.

Apparently, *anyone who claims to know the real Jesus must have some basis for that claim.* If we set aside the attenuated notions of knowing held by some of the insulated positions,[48] we face claims grounded in evidence

---

Kähler," Craig Evans, *Encyclopedia*, 351). The fact that these anti-quest figures shape a real Jesus without self-consciously owning up to the retrojection possible in their own constructions supports the thesis of this book. Modernization of Jesus, then, is a self-reflexive exercise. Cadbury insists that the task begins almost immediately with Jesus' followers and that it proceeds typically in an innocent and unconscious manner. Schweitzer names the motive for the anachronism, that the gospels do not tell us what we, or someone at least, want to know about Jesus, and that they are riddled with gaps in the storyline. Scholars may argue from silence or read between the lines. Most likely, people will simply fill in the gaps *with modern content* by inference and conjecture. In Cadbury's and Schweitzer's analyses of the modernizing of Jesus, it is primarily the *psychological conjecture* which fills the gaps.

47. Particularly when the light goes against the expectations and values of the researcher.

48. The basic position here argues that history should not be unrecognizable to historians.

presupposed in the critique of other views grounded in evidence. Both sets would be colored with values. But the important point is that we are unable to maintain that a historical judgment behind a real-Jesus judgment is free of retrojecton. Critical judgments applied to other scholars' value laden Jesuses are not neutral. For one thing, they do not escape retrojective value woven into the values they apply to the judgment that someone else's Jesus is *unreal*. A critic employs values in discerning issues to criticize and in applying methods. Moreover, the Jesuses implied or articulated to counter the ones discerned under critique carry value from the historian. And in an intriguing meta-turn, we must note that explanation under the mode of suspicion and critique itself carries values. *The application of the retrojection thesis does not escape value and, hence, is itself hardly immune to retrojection.*

For instance, since there is retrojection in any picturing of Jesus, how would one know this or that item belongs to the real Jesus (so far as the real is that which escapes retrojected value)? Indeed, how do we know that the real is what escapes retrojected value? Would such a theory account for the values in our culture Jesus may have influenced? How would we know whether Jesus too might endorse our retrojected values? Finally, how do we know whether the whole notion to recognize retrojections in historians' Jesuses may not be a typically modern retrojection? Evidently, the application of a retrojection theory onto a popular or a historian's Jesus cannot sustain the critical judgment it seeks to pose without retreating into one of two safe houses: either the immuned one associated with Kähler or the one claiming access to the historical knowledge supposedly secured against the retrojective critique. The former option becomes silent about the historical Jesus by turning to a *gnostic theory of history, open only to the faithful*, while the latter refuses to take the retrospective critique home. The one saves the day with a fideist reliance on the given pictures of the early faith community, while the other saves the day by fencing off certain historical judgments from critique.

At this point we see that the problems employing the insightful retrojection critique are serious enough to require that we rethink what happens in retrojection. That is, were the theory to adapt to the above critical points, it would no longer be the same critique. If we believe that the theory is inadequate and we are not persuaded by the above attempts to rescue it, we may turn to an *alternate reading, namely, by taking the retrojection theory to completion and by not protecting any feature of any historian's Jesus from the critique.* A complete application presses the critique onto the New Testament pictures, to those of the early doctrinal traditions, and to theological constructions; and it scrutinizes the retrojective theory itself. The critical eye for values in history writing will not stop at any historical safe house. It eyes the imaginative constructions of theology and artistry as well. Here we open the door to critique and let it claim the entire room; no Jesus hides in any closet. In a complete application there are no sacred cows on the basis of which other people's value retrojections can be exposed with Olympian vision. No, once we open the door to retrojection, critique sheds explanatory light on every space in the room. Unless we slam the door shut by force (as in the insulation position). For good and bad, the retrojection thesis takes all room and eventually relativizes every claim to see Jesus unvarnished by one's perspective and value.[49]

We can find some good news in the relativizing power of the retrojection thesis. It consumes everything, even itself, eventually. Without sacred spaces to appeal to, every aspect of everyone's Jesuses can be evaluated for the way that values operate in the construction of each aspect. No item is off limits, and thus we are freed of the arrogance-parading-as-piety-or-science that smugly finds retrojected value in other scholars' Jesuses without recognizing the same in one's own. As we have seen, even the capacity to recognize the log in the other guy's eye is a function of one's own blindness. At some point in this recognition we can move on and begin to make genuinely critical moves about the retrojective critiques we have before us. Luke Johnson thinks critique is over and done when he shows the American academic values operative in the Jesus Seminar-styled Jesuses. But he does not examine why he discerns and becomes uncomfortable with the Americanisms in those Jesuses, he does not examine whether there may be overlap between resisting evidence and American values, and he does not examine how his turn away from the historian's Jesus presupposes the historian's Jesus. Most importantly, he does not examine the modern Enlightenment hermeneutic presupposed in the very retrojection theory he uses negatively to escape into the sacred space of insulation.

A thorough use of the retrojective criticism turns on retrojection itself. Just as the critique will not allow any item to escape its view, so, too, eventually it turns on itself and begins to ask about the *values that inform the invention and deployment of the pattern of criticism*. We can locate the critique within a family of critiques emerging in the nineteenth century under the spirit of the Enlightenment. A thorough use of the critique criticizes the critique in much the same way that reason's critique of religion turned on itself eventually. At that point *the critique has been transformed, but not lost*. Its critical power can survive, reconfigured in a new room. Theologians,

---

49. Obviously, we can apply the notion of a complete retrojective reduction to any item of history and, indeed, the duck-rabbit nature of Jesus research makes for an exceedingly smooth application. Were we to leave a complete application of the retrojection critique without further comment or retrieval, we would have a pure, post-modern (i.e., Derrida-like) reduction of history writing.

if not historians, will begin to understand the main point: *avoiding retrojection entirely is not a realistic goal,* and not a treasured goal of Jesus research. Such a position arises from hermeneutical good sense and from the recognition of the engagement of the interpreter in the history presented. It is also prompted by the facts of the research on Jesus made especially evident in the study of the history of the quest.

Theologians will appreciate the importance of the alien and the different without being fooled that these criteria will deliver the value-free. Once they own up to the pervasiveness of value, they will see the *need for setting standards of good and bad Retrojection,* **(Quest) Rule 69**, especially if they are not persuaded by the anything-goes-as-Jesus position of some post-modern historiographers. The criteria we seek do not make for perspective- and value-free historical reconstructions, as some historians hope. Rather, they identify moments of better retrojection, as it were, explicit points of choice that promise appropriate, contemporary, historical conversations with the Jesus saga. And negatively, the criteria aim to identify the worse retrojection as manipulative, or what amounts to willful and organized manipulation, an ideological use of Jesus.[50]

> **69a.** *Now, we need standards for better retrojection: all things equal, better retrojection is the opposite of manipulative retrojection.*
>
> **69b.** *Better retrojection does not avoid what we call retrojection but is self-critical about the value issues in the production of any Jesus.*
>
> **69c.** *It makes explicit the choices of method and source and spells out the stance and aim of the production so that all can see and judge.*
>
> **69d.** *It respects the research of the guild and especially consensus views but not in a doctrinaire way.*
>
> **69e.** *Better retrojection locates a Jesus in relation to the spectrum of classic Jesuses and filters a Jesus through the history of Jesuses.*
>
> **69f.** *It identifies how a researcher enters the hermeneutical circle. Of particular importance, scholars must make explicit how they are reading contemporary culture and how that reading plays away in the streets of Galilee of the first century.*
>
> **69g.** *And at each step on the way better retrojections set out warrants and publicly argued criteria of adequacy for every decision. And better retrojection is especially careful to justify when a Jesus departs radically from the Jesuses:* **(Quest) Corollary Rule 70.**

---

50. See: Barnett, *Finding the Historical,* 6.

The trigger that opens these criteria clearly is historical self-consciousness. Undoubtedly, becoming self-conscious in history writing is a gradual process but a thorough sense for the history of the quest, among other studies, equips consciousness to be reflexive about the production of a Jesus. The historian must set out methodological choices, subtler perspectival and valuing decisions, and decisions about sources in as explicit fashion as possible. *Each choice must be taken back to its weight in value.* The theologian will help in this genetic task, as needed, and with the comparison of the weight of the chosen against that of the rejected.

C. Consideration of the Same

Next in the logic, we turn to *sameness*, to points of familiar continuity in the picturing of Jesus. It turns out that sameness is as complex and multilayered as is difference and includes at least how a Jesus is related to his culture(s) and how a Jesus is related to our knowledge. Here we focus on the latter with a criterion that value conversations with the Jesus saga show an imaging of Jesus thus: *by identifying the ways in which a Jesus continues known ways of imaging Jesus*: **(Theological) Rule 71**. Here we respond to the convincing critique of the criterion of dissimilarity in gospel research and seek a standard to accent in questing how a historian's Jesus (or a feature of a Jesus) sustains familiarity among the Jesuses. We look for continuities and similarities as ciphers to value.[51] Oddly we may have to work back from noticing difference before we can analyze the same. It is not easy to see the familiar without the jarring presence of difference, since the magic of the domesticating imagination lulls us into thinking the different is really same. But with difference we can return to the same, identify it first, and then begin to unpack its meaning.[52]

The meaning of uncovered sameness is substantial, to be sure, if the same has roots in the Jesus saga. But quickly it becomes formally tied to the historian's working of evidence. Questions such as these may elicit what we look for in our criterion:

---

51. Charlesworth, "Jesus Research Expands," 4. Charlesworth thinks the criterion of dissimilarity is falling out of fashion and emphasizes that it unfortunately exaggerates the difference between Jesus and Judaism, 1–41; see also Borg, "Jesus and Eschatology," in Charlesworth and Weaver, eds., *Images of Jesus*.

52. Note that the theologian faces much the same issue as the gospel researcher who knows that dissimilarity is an effective but sometimes blind criterion to apply to the sayings of Jesus.

1. In what sense is Jesus the same as something in the world around him, such as in the values and beliefs of his Jewish family and town in Galilee?
2. To what resisting evidence does the historian point to ground a Jesus in his world?
3. Are there new methods, new sources, new insights which show him sharing orientations of his culture and religious traditions?
4. Are the similarities presupposed, claimed or defended in a historian's picturing?
5. How has a certain continuity been treated in the history of the research?
6. Do we see signs that a historian allies his/her notion of what is the same with a tradition of thought or research style?
7. Is the resisting evidence in the saga so powerful that a position has a life of its own?
8. Is there a sturdy consensus on method or on source choice?
9. Has the position sustained critique?
10. Are we dealing with the dominance of a school or the influence of a major scholar?
11. Do we see some guild or herd mentality?
12. Is there a period of stasis in the quest that accounts for a persisting consensus on a point?
13. Has there been a change in the academic culture or in the culture generally to prompt a re-assertion of the same among certain historians?

These and a dozen more questions help us account for the *continuity of a historical position*. Why, for instance, did the *eschatological prophet* Jesus last for a hundred years, and why does it evoke passionate defenses under critique today among some? That a historian identifies Jesus as *prophet* responds to trajectories in the biblical and saga evidence. But that a historian elects the prophet category to capture Jesus cannot be confirmed simply by an appeal to the evidence, since there are so many other options. Instead, we need to probe the genesis of the values that sustain the use of the category, and since what sustains something is often not so noticeable as what changes things, *the theologian needs a schooled eye for indirect clues*: the recent shift to the *sage* category, for instance, is one such clue. We could unpack the prophetic category around each question and come up with a fairly good genealogy of the power, the viability and the survival of the apocalyptic paradigm.

D. Reconsideration of Difference

We are now prepared to return to the difference criterion and reformulate it for theological purposes. Of course, Schweitzer invented the criterion and gave it to New Testament scholars of the New Quest era; it dominated the Jesuses of the second half of the twentieth century by directing scholarly attention to points of discontinuity in the saga. In its bald form the criterion assumes that the categorically different in the saga from Jewish concerns or from early Christian concerns not only marks reliably the real Jesus but the most real. But, as we have seen, the criterion may cull out the different against the similar/same and may give a skewed image of Jesus, one that ignores ways in which Jesus shares values and themes with people of his era.

Nonetheless, the difference criterion may serve gospel research, if critically applied and balanced against the sameness criterion. It serves theology, however, in quite a different way. The new way begins when *theologians turn a critical eye on difference and thematize difference as an issue in the historical construction of a Jesus:* **(Theological) Rule 72**. Schweitzer, of course, taught historians and theologians about the search for difference, but today our theological expectations are more modest than in the past, and our eye will be aimed differently from Schweitzer's or from that of a gale of Jesus researchers who follow his search for the alien. *Here we focus our attention on difference as value locale of any framing for Jesus on the horizon.* We have seen how Weiss departed from the liberal Jesuses with a turn to the apocalyptic prophet, and more recently, how many Third Quest historians break with apocalyptic for a sapiential frame for Jesus. Each new Jesus is doubly different, separated both from reigning Christian forms and from the reigning academic views of Jesus research. Each represents a paradigm shift.

These dramatic changes alert us to the notion that in the history of Jesus research difference is not all the same, but is multi-layered and may include: 1. *the difference a Jesus represents over against ecclesiastical Christs (the difference-from-Christ type of difference);* 2. *Jesus' historical difference from the views and values around him (the difference-from-his-world type);* 3. *Jesus' difference from modern values and worldview (the difference-from-modernity type);* and 4. *Jesus' difference from reigning scholarly reconstructions of him (the difference-from-the-academy type).* In the following paragraphs we will examine each of these types; but here we notice that, when we begin to pull apart at least four types of difference, each functioning differently, we realize that the *difference criterion is no single critical tool* as it was for Schweitzer. Indeed, Schweitzer's primary concern was difference-from-modernity as a way to secure Jesus in his reality; when he had a sense for the alien figure, he would turn this difference against the churchly Christs (difference number one) and against the theological orthodoxies of liberal theology (difference number four). Schweitzer did not see rich value in difference number two, and differences one and four for him had no theological promise. Once Schweitzer had in hand the real Jesus, elements of differences one and four fall away as epiphenomenal mistakes.

Before we treat the four differences we have to add a qualification. In the era of the New Quest, scholars used the difference criterion to establish discontinuity. The different could signal the discontinuous between both the Jewish-Jesus and Christian religion. *The assumption here is that continuity between items in the Jesus saga and familiar themes within Judaism or in the early Church should be suspect.* Scholars then looked for what did not fit into the world around Jesus in the saga and declared them likely genuine.[53] They pointed to a lack of parallels to Jesus' message within Second Temple Judaism. They were high on the Abba experience,[54] on the table fellowship, on certain apparent violations of holiness codes, and especially on Jesus swaggering claim to authority. The assumption was that the unique or the different in Jesus would hold secure christological claims. What the church wanted to say about Jesus as the Christ could be secured by *Jesus' exceptionalism*.[55] Were he not exceptional, the church's claims would be without foundation.

It is just this position we are rejecting when we point to difference and to continuity. While we understand why scholars turned to difference, we note that the theory devalues Jesus' ties to Judaism, and indeed, the continuity of his ideas and effects on the earliest followers who become the church. So far as it contrasts Jesus with options within Second Temple Judaism, it is vulnerable to further research on the religion of Israel. In fact, the hoped-for moments of uniqueness and difference have not stood up well to the criticism of those who know Judaism best. So far as difference can be blind to what continuities may obtain between Jesus and the early followers, the criterion can be criticized just as fairly from the point of view of its vision of Judaism. Both difficulties of the difference criterion represent a blindness. We accept the main lines of these criticisms but make a more important theological point. Namely, *the trouble with the use of the criterion*

---

53. Despite the fact that historiography hates the unique: see Meier, *A Marginal Jew*, I, 174.

54. One of the last to fall, a Christian favorite, is the specialness of Jesus' so-called "Abba-experience," out of which a whole generation of Christian christologies has been founded: cf. Barr, "Abba Isn't 'Daddy,'" 18–47; Borg, *Jesus: A New Vision*, 45; Wright, *Jesus and the Victory*, 149. That is, every charismatic, Jewish holy man sensed an intimacy to the God of Abraham and viewed himself as Son of God.

55. Jeremias, *The Problem of the Historical*, 23.

of difference both in relation to Judaism and to the early church is that people typically over-read the criterion. It is a historian's criterion, after all, but too often the use of the criterion wanders where it does not belongs, namely, into theological territory; and people assume that they can and must apply the insights of historical inquiry directly to value/theological issues. Specifically, difference usually works apophatically to rule out things, namely continuities with Judaism and with the early church.

The theological point cautions that the use of difference, particularly in the search for the unique in Jesus, confuses the theological with the historical in the effort to launch what we call a direct application of christological promise. The failure of the search for continuity among the scholars of the New Quest was that they took what the historians said about Jesus and applied it to norm christology and the whole of theology;[56] that is, these questers applied historical insight directly to christology. We are not willing to apply any direct kind of continuity (or discontinuity) based on relative historical and contextual judgments, because of our concern not to confuse the historian's realm with that of theology and faith. *Remember difference, even the unique, at best may pose theological opportunity, but does not confirm the christic.* So as we listen to historians, we learn that it is unlikely, maybe by definition inconceivable, that the categorically unique will or can be found about Jesus, and we must realize that theology and faith may have to be content with something less: the *distinctive*. Therefore, theologians must also learn not to be unduly charmed by shiny revelations about the unique in Jesus, since these are the tempting stuff of a category error.

1. The difference-from-Christ types names a classic Enlightenment ambition of historical research on the gospels: to clean the dogmatic tradition of unreasonable christological claims. The quest for the historical Jesus fits within the larger biblical-critical project of modernity. From Reimarus on, the classic motive has been to cull out unacceptable elements of the christic Jesuses and present a truer, realer Jesus. This difference, for instance, lives powerfully in the work of some members of the Jesus Seminar.[57] In this kind of difference, *the different we see in a historical Jesus measures its value against a dogmatic formulation.* Difference here operates negatively, of course, and becomes the basis of a critique of theological or pious christologies. The critical function of difference seems very familiar to any student of the quest. But less clear is the way that difference operates within the retrojection critique itself. A Reimarus, a d'Holbach, a Strauss, or even a Robert

---

56. Ogden, *The Point of Christology*, 50. In so doing, arguably, they moved away from the important mediation of an analysis of the structure of existence carried forth in the message of Jesus.

57. See the sophomoric enthusiasm of Funk's *Honest to Jesus*.

Funk cannot simply announce that they do not like, say, the supernaturalism of the Jesus saga or the higher christologies of the gospels; they cannot simply reject the distasteful in the saga. Rather *they have to be convinced that the real Jesus too did not like the very features in question*. Hence, those who run with the first kind of difference need to play Galilee with their values. They objectify them and find them played out in the story of Jesus where they are only dimly recognized. The real Jesus eschews wonder-seekers and is shy of claim for himself.

Tellingly, many of the harshest critics of the christic Jesuses, like d'Holbach, reveal a surprising affection for the figure of Jesus. They may represent divided consciousnesses, at once impatient or angry with the pictures of Jesus they find or receive from scripture and culture, yet admiring of his countenance after they have uncovered the real Jesus. We see real affection mixed in their hate. D'Holbach is certain that the real Jesus embodies the true moral life. Funk is certain the real Jesus will lead to a rebirth of a misguided Christianity. *It is easy to be charmed by the affection for Jesus of the harsh critics*; possibly we should just enjoy their affection without raining on that parade. *But the theologian must press the retrojection critique full-hilt. We need to suspect this affection for the real Jesus as a retrojective move set in place by the use of the retrojection critique itself.* That the critic arms the retrojection theory with the concern for difference (as in difference one) means that he/she finds what is already loaded in the gun: namely, a Jesus-so-far-as-he-differs-from-the-ecclesial-Christs. Funk gets the Jesus he seeks. At this point we understand the affection for Jesus on the part of the harsh critics: *it is a gentle affection for themselves in externalized form.* The Jesus they find in their historical work mirrors themselves to themselves.[58]

In order successfully to objectify the dearest values, those driven to use the first difference to clean the Christian house often resort to a *theory of deception*. The early Christians somehow get it wrong about Jesus; the evidence shows him to be different. Of course, *part of the deception rests in being deceived about how playing Galilee actually works*. Sometimes the deception is imagined on a model of a cooked-up conspiracy (as in Reimarus); more nuanced and modern critics may substitute an appeal to a false consciousness theory for the deception: Jesus and his followers see and intend a world that is inverted, as Feuerbach and Marx discover. The difference between the two styles of deception theories, one tied to the Enlightenment and the other more typical of the nineteenth century, rests in how they account for the mistaken impressions of the early Christians. But both

---

58. We will develop this notion in the second volume of this work. Here we only need to note that a Jesus functions within *a self-picturing in the midst of a bifurcated consciousness*.

deceptions involve some kind of unknowing, conscious or semi-conscious, retrojected onto the Jesus saga, but ironically the application of the theory of deception typically goes unnoticed by the historian. What appears in Galilee under the mode of objectification always looks strange at first. In other words, historians typically do not see what really goes on in Galilee.

Once a deception theory helps historians isolate Jesus' difference, the criterion serves as a platform for applying the retrojection critique. The measure of difference becomes the extent to which there is a suppositum on which their criticism can do its business. It is an assumed reality retrojected onto the Jesus saga, as we see, but it is taken as real, as a genuine reality about the saga, revealed by the real Jesus. Part of the *double deception (unknowingly retrojecting value in the critique of retrojected value)* rests in the way that historians so often wander into theological territory when they are retrojective critics. We can see that the minute they apply their insight into the real Jesus to the ecclesial Christs, they no longer operate on the level of generality on which the critique was conceived: not on the historical level but on that of an implicit christology. Harsh critics so often move beyond historical judgments and attempt to discredit *unreal* christic Jesuses.

Suppose, for instance, that a historian decides that it is incredible that Jesus is a healer. If someone takes that *fact* to undermine a christological position, then that person has actuated a christological possibility in a Jesus: that person has judged that healing in Jesus is a christic issue and the loss of healing damages a christological claim. *The critique arms the historian with enough leverage to make a haphazard extension of the point into a theological position*. While such a judgment may seem obvious to historians and maybe to the faithful, it is neither obvious, nor necessary for, say, Muslims, who have no trouble holding to the miraculous in Jesus but do not read it as christic. Similarly, a historian may hold that Jesus' status as a peasant is important to make him intelligible, but his peasantness may be judged by some to be of no use for a christology. In that case, a fact provides no christological opportunity and neither a critic nor a christologist uses it in christological production.

The extension of a historical position into a direct christological application is an example of what we have been calling a category error: a confusion of what belongs to historical research and what belongs to the theological turf. Such an extension represents the classic impact of the quest on christology: *something known to historians cancels something in theology*. Here we have one of the cleanest characterizations of the historian's fundamentalism we are rejecting. Theologians do not start with applications of the known, anti-theologians do not work to reveal the unreality of the christic Jesuses, without a confused fundamentalism. *The theologically* interested begin with a wait-and-see attitude toward the historical elements of the Jesuses: listen to them, pick them up critically, conduct a genealogy of values on them in light of work on a theology of culture, and then begin to reconfigure viable conversations with the Jesus saga within a comprehensive theology.

At this point we notice that the difference-against-Christ type has been transformed. It no longer identifies an immaculately conceived Jesus untouched by retrojected value. It no longer triggers the brash criticism of ecclesial Christs. Rather, *difference of this kind alerts us to value locales which may have possibility for christology.* We say possibility, since we are rejecting the notion that elements of a Jesus can be directly applied to a christology. Nonetheless, if those elements can be sustained by the guild, they can become opportunities for christological reflection when they have been situated in a comprehensive christology. At this point, possible insight from the Jesus historians could revise ecclesial doctrine.

2. *The second difference, difference-against-the-world,* looks to determine whether Jesus actually departs from practices and values of his culture. In what sense is he different from, say, Galilean Jewish villagers or Mediterranean peasants? Does he stand out or go against the way of the world? Is he unique or, better, relatively unique? Theologians do not have to determine whether and how Jesus is different, of course, but they have to listen carefully how historians put the issue. *Theologians also need to sift critically the locales of difference pictured in historical Jesuses:* **(Theological) Rule 73**. When they look over historians' shoulders, they discover that most of the locales are quickly recognizable. They repeat over and over while surprises happen mostly in times of paradigm shift. To have Mack argue that the earliest Jesus community was *not* Jewish shocks the patterns of same and difference. Historians take notice and begin to debate the historical revision, and theologians notice that some historians really are saying new things. Why? What evidentiary and cultural elements prompt a new conversation with the Jesus saga? The guild of Jesus researchers will work through the theory and determined whether it can be sustained or sustained in some form, while theologians will be more interested in the factors that led to the new theory.

The construction of difference in a Jesus may signal opportunity for a theologian. In particular, difference may signal a new value-rich conversation with the Jesus saga. The historians, of course, will be debating sources and methods, as they do, to decide whether a revisionist historical reconstruction of the ancient figure is appropriate. But in and with the debates of the guild there will be the light of value that can launch possible meaning for contemporary culture and church. For instance, every Jesus historian has spun out Jesus' relationship to John the Baptist: the value locale is very predictable. Historians and interested theologians know to zero in on the Jesus/John relationship. As Jesus is constructed at the hands of a historian, is there anything suggestive about Jesus' relationship to John? The resisting evidence seems to suggest we have a telling value locale.[59] Evidently, the historians have to decide whether Jesus' *departure* from John is rich with meaning or mostly incidental. This difference has high value and theologians want to notice what values go into that choice. Issues of high-significance difference are doubly interesting to theologians, as is the hard-to-access saming value that lies under the choice of the different. Notice that a historian cannot say, cannot name the Jesus/John relationship without sliding into the language of value. Was his departure from the Baptist movement a *break*? Can we figure out why Jesus accepts baptism from John? Do we know why Jesus associates himself with the John movement? Was he a disciple of John? Why does Jesus not baptize? What happens to John's message of judgment? What do they break about, and so on?

A scholar with theological interests sees lots of christological promise in the Jesus/John theme. But how to take it? For many eras of Christian theology, Jesus' relationship to John was unthematized and without rich value for theology, since theology accepted the ecclesiastical spinning of the relationship, namely that Jesus identified with John's cause, that he was baptized in his identification, but that John came to defer to the one for whom the heavens opened up. Theologies affirmed the same for generations, until historians started to notice differently Jesus' difference from his mentor. *They see a difference because they are seeing differently.* At that point theologians get busy and start the value analysis: why now in contemporary Jesus research does this difference get noticed? How convincing is the resisting evidence? What is going on in the culture which allows different visions of the same texts? The questioning goes on.

Not surprisingly, many historians cannot resist being christologists at this point, and they play a card in a direct christological application: *this* fact of history means that *that* item of faith must be reconfigured. The historian discovers that the message of Jesus, say, rejects doom and gloom asceticism and thereby suggests that Christian faith set aside the message of judgment of John the Baptist.[60] Such a fundamentalistic use of historical results should make us wince, but read charitably, it provides us a clue wherein theology will have a great value struggle today. Who says (and why) that Christians

---

59. Two items seem to pass the embarrassment criterion: that Jesus accepts baptism from a senior figure and that, when Jesus departs from the Baptizer, his followers fight with John's.

60. Cf. Meier, *A Marginal Jew*, II, 400-401.

should be shy of judgment? Without solving the historical question of whether Jesus was an apocalypticist or not,[61] theologians know what is at stake in the supposed *paradigm shift from an apocalyptic Jesus to a sapiential Jesus: it is the issue of whether or not Christian religion is judgmental.*[62] Some historians want a Jesus who supports a non-apocalyptic christology or at least a soft-apocalyptic christology and think Jesus wants nothing to do with a religion of judgment.[63] Theologians might be interested in that theme, too, but not so immediately, not so directly. For starters, the move is to discern the way value collects at certain points. First, how persistent is the resisting evidence? *Persistent evidence of difference can be defined by being intense, clear, distinct, long-lasting in the guild, and widely honored by the historians. If all other factors are equal, more persistence in evidence gives us more reliable difference to work with for theological purposes. We need to notice that, in principle, difference-against-the-world difference probably does not disappear easily under the power of the domesticating imagination* (as in the first kind), since, if the guild continues to sustain an item of difference, it remains as a fixed feature of Jesus' relationship to his world: **(Theological) Rule 74**.

Once we see that historians can learn to see differently, we ask the next question of them: are they seeing difference according to their values? Yes, of course, we have to say yes. But we know *we cannot reduce resisting evidence simply to the valuable*. More interesting are the less obvious factors in the discernment of difference. For instance, is our interest in and our noticing of the different commensurate with the power of the resisting value? **(Historical and Theological) Rule 75:** *If there is an imbalance between interest in difference in a historical Jesus and the power of the resisting evidence, we know we are putting much value into the conversation with the item of difference.*[64] In the classic retrojection theory, *imbalance is proof that historians are anachronizing and that good history writing must attempt to purge the imbalance by eliminating retrojected value*. But in our revision of retrojection, we do not expect the elimination of value; more importantly, we would not prohibit an imbalanced conversation (high interest, but less powerful resistance) if it were done in the light of consciousness and conscience.[65]

61. And what the apocalyptic might mean for Jesus.

62. We could unpack the notion of judgment to connect with our politics, the reigning moralities, our newborn interest in spirituality, our capacity to love life in the world and the like.

63. On the assumption that Jesus moves away from the doom-and-gloom, desert theology of John's apocalyptic message to a warmer message for the villages.

64. Halvor Moxnes' intriguing analysis of gendered space in the Jesus saga is one such example of imbalance: *Putting Jesus*.

65. One thinks of the gender-sensitive conversation Schüssler Fiorenza conducts

Therefore, we ask a third question: if we over-value the difference historians notice in Jesus, have we paused to consider *the risks and the virtues of an imbalanced conversation?* What is at stake if in our enthusiasm we have mis-valued or over-valued difference? What if we over-read pacifism in Jesus? What about excitement for asceticism in Jesus? What if we see Jesus as a friend of nature? *The worst case in each of these is when we simply read into the Jesus saga what is not there. Difference would be illusory and hold the potential for manipulation without check.* While reading into the Jesus saga presents the harshest case, it is also the easiest to fix. A little historical knowledge can cure this worst case. More troublesome is when we meet elements in the Jesus saga that sound familiar to our causes. At that point the historian must put on a critical brake, to determine whether the similar turns out to be no more than a *homology*. Again, such judgments are the proper work of the historian. *And Jesus historians can protect theology and church by cutting away the false friends that show up in so many sermons and church forums.*[66] What about items that have clear resistance in the saga? I see "love your enemies" and I want Jesus to be a pacifist. Here we need the historians to help us determine whether we are really understanding the meaning of the logion, whether this provocative item has central value, marginal value, or simply proves to be incidental. Are we over-reading it because it speaks to us? Are we over-reacting to its value among other values? Have we pulled an item out of its wider context to make it valuable to us? In these and related questions, only the best, hardcore historical research will do. And if theologians think they know what "love your enemies" means without the help of historians, they are deluding themselves.

Consider whether Jesus is a typical, first-century Jew in his relationships to women and to outcasts. Admittedly, we have to have a lot of historical knowledge to ask this question, but eventually experts do ask the question. As we have learned in the last years, people simply do not thematize Jesus' relationships with women until they have developed a gender-sensitive hermeneutic and start to notice a difference. Jesus *seems* to be different about gender issues. How do we know we have latched onto a significant value and not simply retold our values to ourselves by way of Jesus or that we have found an incidental difference? Today, virtually every Jesus on the market makes a big deal about Jesus' free-wheeling, non-patriarchal behavior. Some

---

with the Jesus saga, a conversation marked by more interest than resistance, but one badly needed in our situation.

66. The danger of homologies, between an item in the Jesus saga and our cultural values, is the negative reason why quested materials cannot be imported directly in theology as christic. The positive reason, of course, is that even well-quested and promising items take their full meaning within a comprehensive christology.

see in it a christologically suggestive value and build an entire christology of liberative practice on the basis of this difference.[67] Some are so impressed with his liberative practice that they judge the practice itself to be christic independent of Jesus.[68] However, *theology needs to put the brakes on such direct christological application;* it is risky without some critical checks, even if we endorse the values in question. Does Jesus depart significantly from the pattern of males in his culture? Is his departure from the typical itself compelling, or possibly, simply incidental, or actually a side consequence of some other value in Jesus? How do we know that the difference we notice says anything significant about Jesus (instead of us)?

These questions return us to a revision of retrojection, with insight for a more nuanced notion. We know about our retrojecting onto Jesus when we find in him familiar and cherished values. *Retrojection begins within sameness, often with an unspoken assumption of sameness. But a more complex form of retrojection happens when we place on Jesus cherished differences from us, those values we do not represent but would like to represent.* Here Jesus is different from us, but different from us in the way we want him to be different, thus according to prized values we do not instantiate. *Yet what we do not exemplify in ourselves are our same values of difference, the same ones we value. We notice then the intimate and dependent relationship of same and difference in the imaging of a Jesus.* So in a gender-sensitive climate interested in the critique of patriarchy, Jesus appears as egalitarian[69] and inclusive, but not, say, as ascetic. Here we see how *playing Galilee with Jesus not simply confirms us in our values, but leads us.* Indeed, we are beginning to build a prophetic christology founded on the basis of the difference-we-claim as instantiated in Jesus. This christological frame, easily picked up by a comprehensive christology, can support two expressions: first, the obvious one, where Jesus leads as the prototype of the ideal we value but do not possess yet. Jesus becomes *the great Includer of the marginalized* and *the Author of the inclusive way.* And second, a subtler, more important christological function: in the Galilee play of difference and same, new Jesuses become the *Vanguard by way of which value extends beyond its first historical instance.* Surprisingly, the *imbalanced conversation* can offer a means of extension by way of an essentializing. So the real Jesus can be something of a feminist, even if he were not one! Such an extension extends the meaning of *realizing Jesus* by showing how a value can be extended in the spirit of Jesus.

---

67. Schüssler Fiorenza, *Jesus and the Politics.*

68. I.e., Brock, *Journeys,* where Brock expands erotic power from a personal quality to a quality of a network of people.

69. See Crossan's "open commensality": Crossan, *The Historical Jesus,* 341.

Imbalanced conversations with the gospel materials happen when our interests seem greater than what the Jesus saga offers in resisting evidence. Of course, older historiographies would rule out such conversations by insisting our reaction (say, probability of knowing, even valuing) must be commensurate with the secured evidence. The worst imbalance, of course, would be if we are deluded or if we manipulate by decisions on method and source and criteria to make the saga say what we want it to mean. Less problematic, but still serious, would be a part-for-whole mistake in which we find a modest amount of resisting evidence and totalize from the bit so as to support the conversation we want. Less serious still would be the random application of an item to our cause, an instance of the capriciousness of the historians' fundamentalism. With such a complete array of dangers, *theologians will need to be cautious about imbalanced conversations, but still not rule them out of court.*[70] Why? Because only by continuing to extend our conversations with the Jesus saga can faith and theology respond to the new. There is nothing wrong with imbalanced conversations if we do not oversell them. *An imbalanced conversation is certainly possible in theology if: if it were clearly marked as a conversation in light of the elements in the Jesus saga, if it avoids hidden, illusory, and manipulative smothering of the elements of the saga, and if the conversation receives a high warrant from our work on a theology of culture and contemporary experience of faith.* Continuing to find new conversations with the saga is the faith's way to grow into new forms. One can sing well of the work of the Spirit in the extension of the conversations[71] or more flatly of the embrace of historical revisionism by revisionist theology. In any case, the point is the same: *we have to reject the view that our interest must balance perfectly with the power of resistance, in order that we can avoid being trapped in a past, in an ever-repeating fundamentalism.*

New Jesuses offer an opportunity for faith and theology to break free from fundamentalisms of all kinds and adapt to new realities. Of course, theology does so carefully. Lest we hear that theology chases every burst of wind, it adapts to the new only under a high mandate from its critical cultural studies. Lest we hear the charge of sell out and accommodationism here, we need to remember that changes in our cultures can also generate

---

70. A comprehensive discussion of imbalanced conversations with the Jesus saga would take us to the wider discussion of method in a (quested) christology and would add a range of theological criteria well beyond the chief one we deal with in this work: intelligent, self-reflexive conversation with resisting evidence in the saga. Remember: if a historical Jesus cannot instantiate a cherished value well, theology may still conduct a christological conversation with the value through its non-quested moments, since, as we say, Christians are not required to get all their theology out of Jesus.

71. Such extensions can be read as the spiritual work of the resurrected one.

the possibility of our hearing resisting evidence differently or better.[72] *We are dealing with a real dialectic between evidence and value.*[73] And lest we assume that christology is continually dancing to each new historian's Jesus, be reminded that the quested moment in christology is never more than a component of a more comprehensive christology. Indeed, we need to be particularly alert to tempting new nuggets from Jesus research, since historians and theologians so easily totalize from the difference they notice to comprehensive christological claims on the basis of that difference. Such would overstretch the role of the quested elements of christology.

So christology interested in the quest walks a tightrope: cautious about change but willing to change, willing to risk new conversations with the saga without knowing exactly where they head. Should theology pay attention when the historians are comparing Jesus to a cynic philosopher? Should theologians get excited when historians introduce class hermeneutics or post-colonial insights to clarify the situation in Galilee when Jesus was born? Should they take seriously the scholarly reconstructions of levels of Q logia and tie them to developments in an actual Q community? These and a hundred other historical decisions might be fading fads in Jesus research; they could be stark and manipulative decisions of value put onto Jesus; or they might be much more. We know they represent for us at least typical *cultural questions of value being played on the away field* of issues of method and source.[74]

3. When scholars determine that Jesus is different from the Christs of the church or that he is different from his contemporaries, they do not have in place difference that is immunized against the retrojection thesis. A third kind of difference, the difference-from-modernity type, aims to protect historical research against retrojected value and functions apologetically against critiques founded on the retrojection thesis; it is a defensive strategy meant to counter criticism. Here a historian points to themes in a Jesus which defy being reduced to modern values and ideals. The different in Jesus proves we are listening to genuine historical evidence and not simply looking at ourselves in a mirror. In the most low-flying application, this defense against retrojection functions as a check against historical bias: thus, the search for the different may be nothing more than an epistemological-methodological

---

72. One thinks of the way that the gender revolution taught us to see what was *there*, but what Christians had missed in the history of interpretation.

73. This is the double dialectic again, since evidence comes valued even *before* it interacts with values in history and theology.

74. To decode what is at stake in the battle over Q: the issue is whether or not Jesus is an apocalypticist, since in the common reconstructions of the Q tradition, what is thought to be earliest some scholars claim is actually non-apocalyptic.

orientation of quality historical research. But at times, under more strenuous effort, *a defense against retrojection turns to difference to prove that scholars and others have not manipulated the figure of Jesus in picturing him.* Here we have a moral check designed to free Jesus from contemporary values, to demonstrate that Jesus can have his own voice different from ours. What would prompt historians to make such a point? Presumably, because they take an interest in unvarnished difference: they want a Jesus who represents value that does not reduce to self-reflection. Difference means that they have succeeded in their historical work, but difference also means that they have uncovered something valuable that resists reduction to self-reflection. Here we find a value which can inform us (i.e., someone, society, church) normatively. In the broadest sense, then, *the moral application of the retrojection thesis implies the possibility of a christological interest.*

4. A fourth kind of difference, the difference-from-the-academy, functions within the waves of scholarly research on the same topics in which one generation overturns the work of a previous generation. It too is logically independent of the retrojection issue, but has been connected to it in the history of Jesus research. One of the most useful features of *the appeal to difference is that it may signal to all when a new Jesus emerges in the history of the research. Difference can be a sign of a paradigm shift in Jesus research, since the shift often appears as the discovery of a hitherto-unrecognized difference in Jesus' relationship to his world (difference 2) or in an unrecognized value retrojection in last generation's Jesus studies (difference 3). Difference produces difference: a categorically different Jesus emerges when difference has been isolated and then certain scholars are in a position to raise again the consequence of this difference for a dogmatic Christ (difference 1).* We see, then, that the four types of difference frequently interact.

When the research on Jesus focuses so on the importance of difference, it brings with it certain biases. The immense conversation about the famous *criterion of dissimilarity* (for determining genuine Jesus sayings) has uncovered many of these biases. For instance, heightened attention to unique sayings in the Jesus saga may disguise familiar, common things Jesus may have said, by noticing only the elements in Jesus that depart from Second Temple Jewish themes or that of the early Christians. So, too, the application of the difference criterion, in any of its forms, may divert attention from Jesus' sameness. Oddly, then, there must be a critical check on the application of the difference criterion, itself designed as a critical check: it may be overdone and make scholars blind to values that Jesus shares with his world. It may overdo his difference and consequently be too hopeful for value opportunity found within his alleged difference. Perhaps little is at stake whether Jesus said this or that saying; but much could be at stake in assessing his whole mission/task/orientation. If a construal of his entire life work were dependent on his difference from his contemporaries (i.e., was Jesus an apocalypticist?), it would stand to win or lose on major value opportunities.

Further, we have to notice that *attention to difference may mask not simply commonalities, but coincidences, accidental overlaps, and historical continuities*. A focus on Jesus' difference from, say, other Jews of his world can miss points where he incidentally or casually presupposes themes of his world or of Second Temple Judaism. Attention to Jesus' difference from our worldviews and values may make us blind to the themes where he chances to hold similar views or where our views have been influenced by the history of the effects of Jesus. We may be blind to accidental values, to uncaused coincidences or consonances of value, or to historically derived continuities of value. For instance, in the era of the Third Quest, it has been fashionable to see in Jesus someone who prefigures our sensitivity to gender issues. The retrojection theorist immediately smells an effort to make Jesus a contemporary feminist and reduces the picture of Jesus to self-portraiture. While there may be (much) truth to this critique, it cannot see fully *the possibility that Jesus may represent values consonant with us despite our wishful retrojections*.

Here in this blocked or partially blocked vision we have identified a serious limitation to the application of retrojection theories. *Such theories cannot see some or certain values. And to be able to see what they cannot see would undermine the adequacy of the reductive approach of the theory.* Indeed, there would be a surplus of meaning: what is not reducible to retrojection could be historical and accurately so, and, in addition, could be a value opportunity. Further, *retrojection theorists require a meta-theoretical position to found their critique*. They insist that they can spot the errors of value retrojected onto Jesus, yet they imply that their spotting equipment is historically accurate and free of retrojected value. In other words, critique itself brings value and a theory of critique brings heavy value. For instance, as we have noted already, critique values difference and is suspicious of sameness. Sameness, it turns out, is as complicated as difference: it flattens value and unique value in Jesus; it signals that we are being self reflexive; it means we scholars have nothing new to say about Jesus; and so on.

We have seen both the interplay of same and different so far and the complex relationships among kinds of difference. The next observation notices that sameness takes its meaning in relationship to a certain difference. We have a type of sameness attached to each difference: namely, one type of sameness refers to the commonality between an aspect of a historical Jesus and a (traditional) christological claim. For instance, both historians and theologians say that Jesus died on a cross. A second sameness looks for commonality between some aspect in the evidence from the Jesus saga to that among Mediterranean and first-century Jews. A third sameness identifies the opposite of the Schweitzerian concern for domestication, some historically determined feature of a Jesus which, because it is so *like us*, enables us to associate with Jesus. For instance, Jesus is born to a real family, he finds a mentor, he goes on a vision quest as a young man and so on. Finally, the fourth names features of a historical Jesus that endure and reappear in successive waves of historical research and through paradigm changes. An example of this theme may be Jesus' attention to the marginalized.

So far we have figured out that there are many kinds of difference, each with its own sameness and that the kinds of difference overlap at times, all of which live within the turf of historical research on Jesus. We are ready now to move closer to the theological entailments of the web of difference and same in historical research.

E. Is It a Peril to Modernize Jesus?[75]

We return to the leading question posed by the retrojection: is it a peril to modernize Jesus? *Modernizing Jesus is a complex analogical activity*. Historians, and others of us less aware, treat the figure of Jesus analogically. That is, we discover likenesses to ourselves, to our values and aspirations, in the figure presented in the gospel narratives. Perhaps we are not discovering likenesses so much as imagining them as we go. Whether we are discovering likenesses or imagining them depends on whether we face resisting evidence in the Jesus saga. In any case, the discovery of likeness in Jesus brings with it the possibility of anachronism.[76] We take what we find as similar and throw it back onto Palestine in the first century in order to know. That which we retroject onto Jesus bounces back to us with normative power. When the mirrored image comes back to us, it does not come back with distortions: as, say, a poor reflection of ourselves. *Rather, it comes back abstracted, enhanced, improved, so that the mirrored-back Jesus is an idealized version of what we value.* When we retroject likeness onto Jesus, we also imply an unlikeness: Jesus is like me, but so much more than me. On the basis of the unlikeness, Jesus transcends us, can stretch us, lead us, even judge us. But notice that in modernizing Jesus, we set the standard, both of the likeness we find in Jesus and of the unlikeness.

75. Cadbury, *The Peril of Modernizing*.
76. Elsewhere we discuss whether the anachronism or modernizing is good or bad.

Evidently, in the business of playing Galilee, we have more than simple historical anachronism to interpret. *We have a strange and indirect form of human self-production via a detour through an objective image. Modernizing Jesus is not simply the historian's analogical tool in action, but also an anthropological puzzle by way of which selves and ultimately cultures produce themselves.* Were that not enough complexity, a little suspicion brings us further into the modernizing of Jesus, namely, to a christological plot hidden in the historical issue of anachronism. By now it is evident where we are headed in this analysis of modernizing Jesus. *That which we find in Jesus to be like us typically becomes the foundation for what the dogmatic tradition calls the human nature of the Christ. That in which we find Jesus to be different from us can become a candidate for the divine nature in him, in the language of Chalcedon.* Same and difference, then, unfold much more than they appear at first glance.

E.1. Association and Dissociation

Jesus like us; Jesus different from us. In association, we find the familiar in Jesus. In dissociation, we find something unlike us. The unlike factor immediately strikes us as theologically interesting, but on second thought, the like is of christological interest also. In historical studies the difference factor comes carefully calibrated by association, and the interconnected character of association and dissociation in the research actually aids theology, since christology has always wanted a Christ who participates in human life even as, in some sense, he transcends it. *The analogical work of the historian finds its accent in relation to the dis-analogical.* It likens, and likens to our knowledge and experience, but it does so against a backdrop of difference. Certainly the anachronism hawks who hunt for retrojected value in our historical and theological work have a case. They rightly note that when we liken the historical Jesus to us, we open the door to retrojection. But those in the analogical tradition press the point that analytical likening is the only way to know the unknown, and that the retrojective possibility is worth the risk. By likening we can extend our knowing, as we know, and the likening grabs at (apparent) similarities. Since we do not, perhaps cannot, encounter the absolutely different and would not know what to do with it, we have no choice but to advance our knowing with what we take to be likenesses.

If we know by likening generally and likening Jesus to us specifically, we open the door to retrojection, yes, but with a critical sense for the structure of retrojection, we can be at once emboldened to know and yet cautious about the possibility of misconstrued and manipulative knowing. As we proceed to reflect on our likening and knowing, we begin to watch the ways that *association and dissociation swirl in interdependence.* For instance, we are quick to enjoy Jesus' *suffering* the little children to come to him, but we must ask why we are so drawn. Is his the same love of children we claim? Or is there some other value operative? And while we think of children, how quickly we turn in pain to Jesus' rejection of his mother. Perhaps, with a psychological shift some of us can stomach an exorcism but most of us back away from zapping a fig tree for not having fruit in the wrong season. Possibly our dissociation from the fig tree incident tells us something we are unable to see yet close up; possibly it represents difference that is so extreme we cannot face it without softening it interpretively in our sermons. Our point is not whether or not historians can deal with nature miracles. Rather it is that in every point of association, wherein we sense that Jesus is like us, lurks a specter of some dissociation, of some difference. And in every point of dissociation, wherein Jesus is different, lives a frame of possible likening, however we stretch to explain it.

How complicated it is to find a good sermon on Jesus' words and deeds! Today the informed theologian and, hopefully, the preacher must listen in on the work of the historians and, at times, lead them in assessing the pattern of our association and dissociation as we read the gospel tradition. At each point in the saga, we ask why we respond to this sameness, why to that difference. For example, perhaps today we can deal with Jesus as an exorcist, but what about him as a healer? Today, we may be troubled by his recommendation to hate our mothers, while cursing fig trees seems simply fantastic to us. As we think about our associations and dissociations, we first have to ask self-critically why and how we affiliate with particular items in the Jesus saga. And then, it occurs to add a third angle to the back and forth of association and dissociation, namely, the expertise of professional historians. We need to know what a historian can tell us about the status of children in the Mediterranean world. We need to know about the patterns of family life in that world and what would disrupt them in order to make sense of the puzzling acts and sayings of Jesus. We need to know how the people of the bible put their reality together to order to know what to make of the wonders that seemed to burst forth around him. The historians can judge whether there is resisting evidence in the saga and how strongly it resists.

Once we realize we must listen to the historians, we face at least three factors in the dialogue of association and dissociation. *First, the historians' patterning of association and dissociation; second, their judgments on resisting evidence; and third, theologians' receptions of the historians' patterns.* Theologians make their own judgments on the associative work of historians, of course, and they may squabble among themselves over this or that item. Is there something christologically interesting about the fig tree incident, or the hate-your-mother logion, for that matter? In each theological reaction a christology waits to burst out in every picturing of likeness and unlikeness in Jesus. Older pieties know Jesus is christic because of the supernaturalist elements of the saga, while informed opinions have winced at that notion. Somewhere in the christological warring, Jesus historians, often unknowingly, are cooking up new christologies for the twenty-first century. The historical question is whether these are warranted by resisting evidence. The theological question is whether or not these christologies are good ones, and whether they are Christian christologies or not. The pastoral question is whether church and secular audiences will find the newer Jesuses palatable.

How is it possible that we can modernize Jesus? What are the conditions for the possibility of modernizing Jesus? Three conditions come to mind: first, the simplest one is ignorance. If people know nothing about the ancient Mediterranean world, nothing really of bible or theology, there is nothing to stop naive and/or dangerous modernizing of Jesus. Modernizing Jesus is easiest where people are not historically attuned, where people work with ahistorical and atemporal worldviews, and where they are not self-critical of bias and anachronism. The power of naive modernizing is typically unchecked. Of course, historians are learned about the bible and the ancient world; they have learned historical critical methods and, the recent ones are hermeneutically sensitive. The question is whether knowledge and all that methodological self-awareness can defend against harsh modernizing. Second, to modernize there must be interest in Jesus. For us to modernize Jesus, we must be sufficiently interested in him to bother to think about him. The opposite of interest is indifference, not hostility. The interest we need might be a historical one, generated by such a major player in history. Or it might be faith's genuine interest in Jesus. Third, among people of faith, it is apparently easier to modernize Jesus where people work with docetic christologies. If the faithful work with an abstract or idealized Christ, and not a sweaty human Jesus, they have few defenses against uncritical modernizing.

Then, we need to note several characteristics of the historical task of recovering the historical Jesus, characteristics which make modernizing possible:

1. As we know, the sources of knowledge of Jesus frequently do not show any interest in the questions that bother us, whoever we are. The sources have their own agendas.

2. Further the sources give plural and sometimes competing pictures of Jesus. Did Jesus forbid all divorce or not? When we fix on one Jesus, we are either selecting one among many or we are harmonizing several.
3. In fact, it is not entirely clear which are the most reliable sources for knowledge of Jesus.
4. And, of course, each source has its own bias; the historian must cut through bias with a critical reading to free each source for the task at hand. In its own way each source modernizes Jesus. Some do so with lavish, insider enthusiasm for Jesus, while others with indifference or bitter hostility to him.
5. The historian has to judge what method or methods to use to plumb the Jesus saga. The options are selections packed with value.
6. Finally, facts, especially historical facts, come prepackaged in interpretive networks. The facts simply never speak for themselves and never have.

These and other conditions mean there is plenty of room for the historian to do exactly what the naive believer does: shape a Jesus who is enough like us to lead us to do whatever we wish. Even critical historians may modernize Jesus as they decide upon the issues listed above. Consider the issue of choice of sources for our knowledge of Jesus. Naive modernizers simply plop open the book and put what they think Jesus is saying into whatever Galilee is playing that day. Historians, however, make critical judgments about sources according to criteria. Crossan's Jesus, for instance, comes out as he does in large part because Crossan thinks that the Gospel of Thomas and a hypothetically reconstructed early layer of the hypothetically reconstructed Q sources contains the best early sources for knowledge of Jesus. John Meier, another American Catholic, thinks only the canonical gospels are acceptable sources and that Thomas is derived from them much later. Both have good, critical reasons for their choices, but what disposes a historian to honor one set of reasons over another? Here is the crack through which a modernized Jesus enters critical historical work. Here dispositions, values, worldviews, even religious commitments creep into the picturing of Jesus. Consequently, historians of Jesus give us very different Jesuses, even as they struggle with the same issue of resisting evidence. Each picture has its own topspin.

So, now, is it a peril to modernize Jesus? Cadbury thinks it is, but he also sighs that the modernizing of Jesus is virtually inevitable. True, a historically sensitive researcher can resist the temptation to some extent, can avoid some anachronisms, and certainly can avoid manipulation of the past.

Cadbury feels such resistance is possible so far as we come to a self-critical relationship to our own prejudices and presuppositions, learn thoroughly the mentality of Jesus' era, and let the gospel records themselves act as our "standing enemy" of modernization. Obviously the first two standards help in a formal way. The third standard can be only relatively useful, since the very "thereness" of the saga in the gospels can contribute to modernizing as easily as to the resistance against modernizing. Thus, Cadbury's solution is of only modest help toward the very problem he has diagnosed so well. It helps, for instance, to detect the uncritical modernizing of uninformed opinion, but it would be virtually useless in judging modernizing done by historically informed researchers. Consequently, *Cadbury's guidelines function as a reminder that imaginative Jesus portraits should be historically informed but do not go very far in assessing the modernizing imagination among historically sensitive portraits.* Why? Because they beg the question why critically informed Jesuses come out so differently and they ignore that *the appeal to evidence in the saga is an appeal to the already modernized.* We would need further guidelines for us to meet the full hermeneutical stage of the discussion.

In the end Cadbury can go no further than a question-begging hope that historical research will help *fill the gaps* in our treatments of Jesus. Negatively, he is certain we cannot simply import our materials onto Jesus and we cannot simply *believe* our Christ onto Jesus. But positively, he has no more to offer: "The gap must either be left empty or be filled partially and tentatively by painstaking historical research and imagination."[77] We can leave Cadbury with a partial gain: his notion that good historical research functions as a limiter to modernizing helps us with the pre-hermeneutical phase of our issue but does not help us choose among historical pictures of Jesus, nor with the theological problem of determining when a christology is Christian. There is a historical optimism about Cadbury's work and era but the optimism is ironic: it anticipates the bittersweet insight that historical research must fix the very problem historical research uncovers.[78]

---

77. Cadbury, *The Peril of Modernizing*, 191.

78. We may wonder why the life of Jesus research did not anticipate the difficulty. Schweitzer, it seems, gives us the clue why the historical phase of the research proceeded with an unchecked optimism about historical work: namely, that this phase was vexed by the effect of historical work on dogmatic claims for the Christ. Historical work on the figure of Jesus was to be a *"school of honesty" for theology*: "It turned to the Jesus of history as an ally in the struggle against the tyranny of dogma." But Schweitzer does not share Cadbury's optimism about historical work. Despite his progressivist sense that the life of Jesus research is headed somewhere, *Schweitzer is not able to see a historical way out of history.* As is well known, he is so convinced of the power of the modernizing reflex and of the virtual impossibility of the historical task, due mostly to the character

Before Cadbury Schweitzer offers his Jesus as an exemption to his own discovery of the modernizing reflex: thus, he gives no indication that his portrait is just another objectification of Schweitzer's own values and world. On the contrary, his Jesus is the historical Jesus, the right one, as one can tell from the confidence with which he completes his book. And of course, he does not make explicit the basis for his confidence. We may suppose that his confidence is founded on two things: first, Schweitzer is certain he has gotten through the modernizing to the solid historical subbase, the incontrovertible factual evidence. Here he is confident of the work of the alien criterion. And second he seems confident that his sensitivity to the modernizing reflex makes him immune to the very pattern he complains about in, say, Reimarus or Renan. Once we notice that Schweitzer assumes his portrait is exempt from anachronism, we recognize, first, that he operates under the same optimism about historical work as a Cadbury. Then, we must recognize that Schweitzer's optimism about historical research includes a progressivism: he really believes that historical research on Jesus is progressing and is leaving behind its mistakes. Specifically, Schweitzer implies that the progress of the research moves away from blatant anachronism, and in fact, he is less worried about anachronism as he traces the story of Jesus research up to his own day. By the end of the nineteenth century, he tells us, we have left behind the "fictitious lives of Jesus," the "imaginative" lives which "play fast and loose with the history." Tellingly, his battle with Weiss is not played on the field of a historian's critique of the work of imagination, but of one historian disagreeing with another one's reconstruction of the evidence.[79]

---

of the sources, that he despairs of recovering a historically clean portrait of Jesus: in the words of his famous thoroughgoing skepticism, "This ticket office is now closed." Nonetheless, even Schweitzer settles on a historical portrait of Jesus—that of his famous, wheel-of-the-world passage. The entire passage is worthy of quoting once again:

> "There is silence all around. The Baptist appears, and cries: 'Repent, for the Kingdom of Heaven is at hand.' Soon after that comes Jesus, and in the knowledge that He is the coming Son of Man lays hold of the wheel of the world to set it moving on that last revolution which is to bring all ordinary history to a close. It refuses to turn, and He throws Himself upon it. Then it does turn; and crushes Him. Instead of bringing in the eschatological conditions, he has destroyed them. The wheel rolls onward, and the mangled body of the one immeasurably great Man, who was strong enough to think of Himself as the spiritual ruler of mankind and to bend history to His purpose, is hanging upon it still. That is His victory and His reign" (Schweitzer, *The Quest of the Historical Jesus*, 1968 ed., 370–71).

79. We must notice that there is a considerable tension between the anachronism argument in Schweitzer and that of the historical progressivism. The anachronism argument sounds Schweitzer's famous sensitivity to the negative character of Jesus

How does Schweitzer know that he can escape the perils of modernizing Jesus? How does he know that historical work finally can check the imaginative? Indeed, how does he know that Jesus research is making progress and not spinning another self-reflexive Jesus who is simply someone's or some age's alter ego? Again, Schweitzer gives no clues and thereby demonstrates that he himself has not taken the hermeneutical turn he recommends for the lives of Jesus he studies. We can only guess at the warrant that is supposed to buttress his closing arguments. After all, his is a historically self-conscious Jesus and one done on the basis of the misfired retrojections—but such factors are not the complete answer. The criterion for the genuine Jesus implied in Schweitzer's effort is the anachronism issue turned backward. Anachronism turns Jesus into the familiar; the real Jesus stands up where one finds an alien Jesus. Schweitzer reverses the reflex and secures the so-called real Jesus by making him the ever-alien. Anyone who knows the Schweitzer text marvels at the fascinating alien he simply calls "the Man": a terrible misfit, misunderstood and misunderstanding, ever receding from our grasp, a moving target, never to be domesticated. *That which refuses to be anachronized is taken as the real Jesus.* And finally, for Schweitzer, since eschatology and history are incompatible, the real Jesus is beyond analogy, beyond the historian's analogy. Consequently, we see that Schweitzer has taken something like the dissimilarity criterion of recent NT scholarship and driven it to an extreme. The only Jesus who escapes anachronism is the one who is so unappetizingly weird that no one would claim him. And Schweitzer's Jesus is horrific.

Peril or not? We have to answer with a yes and a no. We say yes, retrojection is indeed a danger, especially when it is naïve, blind, and manipulative.

---

research: consider, for instance, the theme that runs through his entire book: "There is nothing more negative than the result of the critical study of the Life of Jesus." Because of the peculiar character of the sources, the researcher is left with a messianic Jesus who is the imaginative invention of Mark principally, or with a purely eschatological, and hence anti-historical, Jesus who is the enemy of Christian religion. So far as Schweitzer seems to universalize the retrojection onto Jesus, it is difficult to imagine how one could make genuine progress toward discovering the *real* Jesus. So far as progress is possible in the research, there must be some defense against unchecked modernizing. How can Schweitzer assume his Jesus escapes what he finds in every other Jesus? Of course, his is a historically self-conscious Jesus and one done on the basis of the history of the misfired retrojections—but such factors are not the complete answer. *The criterion for the genuine Jesus implied in Schweitzer's effort is indeed anachronism turned backward. Anachronism turns Jesus into the familiar; the real Jesus stands up where one finds a strange Jesus.* Barton's title, *The Man Nobody Knows,* carries a wonderful irony in it, for Barton, thinking we all had missed the real Jesus, works to familiarize Jesus but actually turns him into us. Schweitzer, however, reverses the reflex and secures the so-called real Jesus by making him the ever-alien.

Its potential mistakes are of epistemological and moral sorts. That is to say, believers and insufficiently critical historians can stumble, first, into cognitive mistakes when they picture Jesus naively: sheer deception and various false consciousnesses, which are often innocent in their naiveté. For instance, their picturing of Jesus may involve them in reifying and legitimating certain values which show up as superstition or anti-intellectualism. Or second and more worrisome, naïve retrojection can draw people into moral dangers. They may think, for instance, that the picture of Jesus valorizes a certain vision of the bourgeois nuclear family.

Behind both the cognitive and moral mistakes lies an unaware manipulation of the figure of Jesus, the very manipulation that Cadbury warned of. In an imaginative grasp of the figure of Jesus people unknowingly familiarize Jesus, burn off his edgy difference, and condense his image into something of cozy relevance. This manipulation is indeed a danger but, arguably, less so than unreflective retrojection among those who should know better. When scholars, raised academically on the lessons of the quest for the historical Jesus, slip into naïve retrojection onto the figure of Jesus, we do not know if we should be irritated ("they should know better!") or intrigued that they are putting in place the staging for genuine christological conversations with the figure of Jesus, triangulated through their own values. When we find explicit and self-critical retrojective conversations with the Jesus saga, we know we have moved into new territory, a landscape of potentially *good* retrojection. Here we have historians and others who see clearly the value terrain in their conversations with Jesus; they are self-reflexive about the genesis of value and concerned that their dialogue with Jesus materials could become manipulative. They see the risks and are willing to proceed. A studied attention to historical difference and the employment of the alien criterion support their willingness.

We have moved far enough in the quest for the historical Jesus to say with some assurance that *there is a qualitative difference between naïve retrojection and informed retrojective conversations with the past*. When Bruce Barton makes Jesus a successful twentieth-century American businessman, we find naïve retrojection that must be dispensed with. But when a John Meier sweats through hundreds of pages of gender research in relation to the gospel pictures of Jesus, we find a serious modernizing conversation that can inform christological constructions. And, thus, we are in a position to say a qualified no, that it is not a peril to modernize Jesus. *Done well, modernizing conversations are the mode in which Jesus is realized in historical research and in faith and practice.* Therefore, we need to be critical of the critique of modernizing Jesus without denying that historical anachronism presents risks for the understanding, for the appreciation of difference, and for the moral life.[80]

F. The Need for Reconstructing Retrojection[81]

If we are now ready to revise modernizing Jesus, how does it proceed? 1. First, in the midst of the complexity of putting together a Jesus from the unfinishable Jesus jig-saw puzzle, historians and others supply an *intentional reading* of a word or a deed of Jesus (or all of them). The modernizer guesses at an intentionality that causally motivates some historically identifiable event. Jesus throws a temper tantrum in the temple on his first trip to Jerusalem, at the beginning of Passover. That seems to be a fact. But to call it a *temper-tantrum* is already to intentionalize the event. To read it as symbolic, or to read it as a critique of filthy lucre is to intentionalize it. Of course, we are guessing at something we do not have access to, since we do not know what is going on in Jesus' mind. 2. But supplying intentionality to events is part of a larger mechanism of modernizing. Historians and others tend to retroject onto Jesus psyches in a modern style: this is *a psychological conjecture*. Here we make an analogy between our psyches and those of the actors in the gospels, and assume that their minds work pretty much like ours. For instance, it is typical for Jesus researchers to take the discreet sayings of Jesus, deemed to be genuine, and discover a unity among them such that Jesus is commending what we call *a lifestyle*. Or scholars gather the sayings and connect them to discreet deeds of Jesus and, poof, we have *a mission* of Jesus, maybe even *an identity* and *a self-consciousness*, which we can know. Now Jesus might have had a lifestyle and a mission, but the construction of these always goes through layers of an interpreter's retrojected notion of

---

80. Cf. Gowler, for an argument that modernizing is inevitable and needful if it avoids domesticating Jesus and blatant anachronism: Gowler, *What Are They Saying*, 14.

81. Here I offer a critique and reconstruction of the critique called the retrojection theory. What should we call the hermeneutic of retrieval operative here (in Ricoeur's language)? Schüssler Fiorenza considers quite a range of terms for *revisioning* the movement in and around Jesus of Nazareth. After considering several options, including the radical post-modernist one of Derrida, *rewrite*, she settles for reconstruction: *Jesus and the Politics*, 59. I am happy with that term for the multiple and continual process of *inventing a Jesus*. It carries enough of the imaginative to identify the role of the historian's values in the object of historical inquiry and it avoids the post-modern extreme in which history writing is no more than fictive expressions of the will to power. The term *reconstruction*, moreover, emphasizes that inventing a Jesus rebuilds with materials already on the shop bench in an act that is imaginative but not sheer fantasy.

psychological coherence. The interpreter unifies the fragments of a story by means of the psychological conjecture.

3. The psychological conjecture is part of a larger historical technique: the *historian's analogy*. To determine the eventness of some event, historians tend to assume that the way things go for us in the events of the world is pretty much the way things went back in Jesus' time. The psychological conjecture is an analogical activity in which people, perhaps unconsciously, liken Jesus to the modern person. The modern psyche is taken as the standard for redescribing Jesus' person and ministry. It is a reflexive retrojection, which fills in with modern content at the point of assigning a motive, as we have seen. Motive-giving is a blank check for modernizing. Here we need only note that the analogy throws onto Jesus a psychic coherence that attempts to unify all the fragmentary and externalized features of the Jesus saga. Of course, it is no secret by now that the gospels show virtually no interest in the interiority of Jesus but tell of episodes in an externalized, action-oriented manner. They know nothing of the turn to the subject, of the invention of the individual, of depth psychology, of the discovery of the unconscious mind, of modern natural and psychic causality, and so on.

So when people discover in Jesus familiar elements of the modern psyche, they really operate with a three-step retrojection: first, they actually create a psyche, in the modern sense, which is not *there*; second, they unify episodic materials around a vision of personal identity which answers the questions moderns lust after, namely, concerning the purpose and aim of an individual's vocation; and third, they assume that such a unifying identity centered in a self-consciousness best captures the meaning of events. The perpetual theme for the moderns, of course, is to explain events by uncovering the intention that lies behind them in a self-consciousness: we expect that we will know what Jesus is about if we could know what he thinks he is doing. We would know what to make of Jesus if we know what Jesus makes of himself. We should not be surprised by the retrojection of the modern psyche, since modern scholars are inventing the *historical Jesus* at the same time as the modern individual human is emerging. *At this point in the activity of modernizing, modern preferences will occasion an associative retrojection onto Jesus, while modern aversions will evoke a dissociation.* Finally, we can expect that the pattern of association and dissociation will frame up dogmatic opportunities: a place holder for theology's divine and human natures of the Christ.

Therefore, 4. modernizers tend to *universalize human nature*. Not only do they assume the same sort of psyches, then and now, but they assume that human nature is pretty much the same, then and now. We have a continuity of the human essence, whereby humans are essentially the same, facing the same sort of issues and challenges. An uncritical modernizer universalizes unabashedly by unconsciously sifting out and accenting associative features in the Jesus saga; critical historians, however, try to be sensitive to historical context and guard against anachronism and to honor innovation and change, even at the expense of the use of the historian's analogy. 5. Obviously, modernizers *read between the lines*, as we say. More exactly, reading between the lines means that we provide the interpretive framework that coherentizes the discreet fragments in the Jesus saga, as we have seen. 6. Obviously, modernizers *argue from silence*. When people handle the Jesus story, they fill in the gaps. They fill in the gaps with applied intentions, with psychological retrojections, reconstructed contexts, with causal inferences. 7. Finally, in all of these moves modernizers determine *what is at issue* in the history of Jesus. They intentionalize, they psychologize, they provide the frame, they read between the lines, they argue from silence—all of these things they do but they do so to determine what is worthy of historical investigation to begin with, and what are the fundamental issues of value and meaning operative in the life.

Naturally, Jesus historians have been in a virtual arms race to show themselves free of the modernizing retrojections, the very retrojections they find so obvious in the other historians.[82] They have put up standards and tests to show that their Jesuses are free of retrojected value.[83] Consider Mei-

---

82. Crossan, for instance, speaks of the tendency of Jesus research to retroject values as "something of a bad joke." Questing for a historical Jesus allows historians to "do theology and call it history, to do autobiography and call it biography" in trenchant phrases that scholars quote over and over: *The Historical Jesus*, xxvii–xxviii. Ironically, many think Crossan's Jesus is one of the most artful expressions of the very retrojection he decries: Allison, *Jesus of Nazareth*, 10–33, 65, and, Allison, *The Historical Christ*, 19; Schüssler Fiorenza, *Jesus and the Politics*, 108. Consider the advice of Robert W. Funk: "Beware of finding a Jesus entirely congenial to you": *The Five Gospels*, 5. One should notice the irony that this caution is from the writer of the outrageously PC *Honest to Jesus*, one of the most blatantly retrojective documents of recent Jesus research.

83. The first and most famous was that of Schweitzer, the *alien criterion*, as we have seen. Some scholars express the *surprise criterion*: the fact that they were surprised by the Jesus they found in their researches proves that they did not invent him in their image. Still others offer a softer version, a *difference criterion*: that Jesus is so different from the historian is proof of freedom from retrojection. Schüssler Fiorenza sets out an intriguing feminist version of the difference theme: the fact that women are different from the male figure of Jesus may mean that feminist wrestlings with the historical Jesus are freer of bias: being a feminist can be a critical check against too easy retrojection of unthinking patriarchal, etc. assumptions: *Jesus and the Politics*, 12. Schüssler Fiorenza, moreover, argues that a rich socio-political reconstruction of the world of Jesus protects against retrojection of value, too, since a social portrait can check against the malish attempt to picture Jesus as the charismatic, great-man individualist: ibid., 23. James Dunn offers insight into how the alien criterion has functioned: in an effort to purge Jesus of Christianisms, in the drive to judaize Jesus, historians have turned to the alien

er's catalogue of standards that should help historians manage retrojection. Meier poses the following criteria: 1. *The history-of-the-research criterion.* The very history of Jesus research offers a catalogue of errors to be avoided. Critical rereading of *the quest for the historical Jesus* provides a framework for developing the research. 2. *The hermeneutical self-consciousness criterion.* A researcher who is capable of spelling out his/her social and intellectual location and entrance into the hermeneutical circle can do what is possible to avoid sheer and uncritical modernizing of Jesus. As Meier says, "In a sense, though, the most important hedge against rampant subjectivism is an honest admission of one's own personal stance, one's own point of view and background."[84] 3. Then, Meier thinks *criteria one and two must be combined*: good Jesus researchers must not only know the pitfalls of the history of the research but must, upon hermeneutical self-reflection, apply possible lessons to their own portrait of Jesus.[85] 4. Implied in the first three criteria is a point, a negative one that commonly shapes contemporary Jesus research: there can be *no neutral Jesus portrait*.[86] Objectivity in the old sense, in the sense of the detached, Enlightenment ideal of being free of bias, is simply not a possibility, since every objectivity represents some stance. The question becomes what to do with the discovery that there is no neutrality. The great divide among contemporary Jesus researchers concerns whether or not the scholar ought to "try to exclude [the interpreter's own standpoint] influence in making scholarly judgments . . ." Meier, for instance, insists that one must work to exclude one's stance, while others insist that such concern is neither possible nor desirable. The former option seems to fit within the expectations of classic, modern historiography, while the latter might be termed fully a hermeneutical, post-modern approach.

5. Then, Meier suggests that the chief means of excluding an interpreter's stance is the appeal to *commonly held criteria*. We shall name this criterion as *the scholarly consensus* one and note that it refers to the employment of fairly narrow criteria for authentic Jesus materials which have emerged in twentieth-century New Testament research. For now we hold in check whether the appeal to scholarly consensus can actually exclude certain interpreters' stances or whether it is simply a formal guideline standard for stronger-looking Jesus research. 6. *The plurality criterion.* So far as a Jesus portrait must be a hermeneutical one, that is, self-critically self-conscious,

---

Jesus to preserve a surplus of meaning useful for Christian theological purposes: Dunn, "Can the Third Quest," in Chilton and Evans, eds., *Authenticating the Activities*, 36–37.

84. Meier, *A Marginal Jew*, I, 5.
85. Ibid.
86. Ibid.

the researcher and his/her construction of the work are engaged in the portraying. But one engaged Jesus portrait may differ from another one. Consequently, we appear to be facing, for the first time, the notion that no single *historical Jesus* can or should carry the day: no one of the many can claim privilege (a factual claim) nor, perhaps, should it claim privilege (a normative judgment). "As in the 1st century, so today: no one's Jesus — no one Jesus — suits everyone."[87]

7. Finally we identify the *historical presumption criterion*. Nearly every Jesus researcher today speaks of a new spirit afoot in historiography. Not only are current methods of work less atomistic, but the mood of the research has, more or less, taken a *swing away from the skeptical presumption*. If earlier the burden of proof typically rested with the researcher who had to make a case to prove that an item ought to be included in a historical portrait of Jesus, today virtually all researchers work with a shifted burden of proof. To be sure, different scholars put the burden at different spots on the scale; but it is fair to say that more of them turn the issue on *justifiable arguments for excluding an item*.[88]

G. Reconstructing Retrojection

Where are we, now that we have seen the historians' efforts to secure a sure defense against retrojection? Despite the fact that the historians have armed the quest with layers of methodological sophistication and critical checks, we remain skeptical that they are securing objective historical results. Actually, today quite a few historians themselves are skeptical of the objectivity of historical work on Jesus, as we have seen. Nonetheless the fact is that they fight so on the basis of evidence, real historical results, that they charge each other with modernizing Jesus, that, as critics recognize, they so easily mirror their own cultural- and self-values in their Jesuses, that they even use retrojective values to root out other historians' retrojected values: all of these undergird our suspicion. We have even seen that the trusty alien criterion cannot resist retrojected difference. Possibly, historians can make retrojection-free research an asymptotic goal of historiography and they can learn to do better history writing with the above criteria, but in the last years I have become convinced that there is more happening in the retrojection

---

87. Meier, *A Marginal Jew*, I, 3.

88. The Jesus Seminar group typically rejects historical presumption, I should note. And, of course, it is possible to favor including traditional materials in a historical portrait (unless they fail for other reasons) without turning historical presumption into an evangelical warrant to confirm the gospel storyline as given.

of values onto Jesus than the sleuths admit to. We need suspicion, yes, but we also need to suspect suspicion. To leave the quest with simple suspicion of retrojection is a partial view, somewhat blind, and somewhat reductive.

We need a way to recover the good stuff happening in retrojection. Here we will rethink the retrojection theory as a step toward our guidelines for a quested christology. The business we have called *retrojection must be rehabilitated*. From the history writing side, the quest for the historical Jesus must do history writing better: more self-critical, hermeneutically sophisticated history writing, such as we have described above. Writing the history of Jesus can neither eschew value nor let value fly without a critical ground. The theological side troubles more, since the insulated position haunts the theological deployment of the quest and does so from a hermetically sealed room. No historical discovery, no historical results, indeed, no theological warrants for historical research can crack the way of insulation. Only a different notion of faith allows theology to open the door; but it dares not open that door without critical checks against foolish historical and theological claims. Fortunately, the anti-quest position can bring a kind of sobriety to the use of quested materials in a christology, even if it cannot be allowed to win the day. Naturally, the historical form of this sobriety is a rule for theology; **(Theological) Rule 76:** *Theology must sustain the suspicion of retrojection throughout the entire process by which it puts quested materials to use christologically.* Theology should not leave behind suspicion. Historical bias is still bias; anachronism is still problematic. When retrojection of value is bias or anachronism, it has to be called out, as revisionist historians and anti-quest theologians know. Theological bias, too, is bias. But exposing bias and anachronism cannot be tolerated in the name of perspective-free, value-free, objectivist standards of history writing. **(Theological) Rule 77:** *Therefore, theologians (and historians too) must rethink bias as perspective, to use an innocuous word for explicit, self-critical engagements with historical evidence.*

The above rule must be yoked with a reconstruction of the critical posture of alert scholars of all kinds: namely, **(Theological) Rule 78:** *Theologians (and historians too) must distinguish perspective from bias and anachronism which must now be identified as ignorant and manipulative retrojection of value.* In other words, while perspective is explicit, inevitable, even healthy, bias and manipulation are bad retrojection. Both are instances of groundless modernizing. Sometimes ignorant retrojection of value is charming and harmless, but because it has no defenses against dangers, it can be manipulated. Manipulation of any sort is morally problematic, of course, but manipulation of the past is an unvarnished and often unconscious power move. At this point we see the permanent use for a retrojection theory: namely, in

(Quest) Rule 79: *Properly reconstructed, the retrojection theory must be an enduring ideological critique within Jesus research.*[89] By recasting the retrojection theory we preserve the insight of the Kählerians: that manipulative retrojection is not good history writing, and that good theological suspicion supports good history writing.[90] But now we are prepared to reject the larger Kählerian judgment that retrojection is inherently the manipulation of the past for some present purpose.

If we return to what we have argued in chapter 2 about historical method, we now have to claim that *problematic retrojection has run with the subjective elements against objective elements.* There is, then, bad retrojection, where subjective elements smother the objective, and the Kählerians rightly reject it. But the criticism of retrojection cannot be founded on some vision of value free historical work.[91] The retrojection we must embrace, *the good retrojection, as it were, is really an explicit, self-conscious, public, value dialogue with historical evidence.*[92] The dialogue is, first of all, a first-order historian's conversation with the materials and methods of historical research as they bear on points of resistance in the evidence.[93] Wearing their interests and perspectives on their sleeves, historians seek out resisting evidence and listen to it; they allow points of resistance to speak; they do not wander too far from those points. Their first reaction should be to notice and to notice with suspicion, uneasy about asserting quick opinions about meaning. Historians next should turn to the views of the guild to see in the light of day what others are saying about the meaning of a particular point of resistance. Is there a consensus or almost consensus on the meaning of an

---

89. Where questing serves clear ideological purposes, scholars should intensify the suspicion. Of course, we may debate what will to power is active and who profits from an ideology, but the principle stands. See, for instance, Schüssler Fiorenza, *Jesus and the Politics*, 14, where Schüssler Fiorenza suspects that Jesus has become a commodity in a bourgeois and patriarchal academic business. Luke Johnson makes the same point in: *The Real Jesus*, 70.

90. In this case, theological suspicion encourages the self-consciousness.

91. Or faith hermetically sealed away from historical criticism. The question is whether we should maintain the retrojection word for the *good* kind of retrojection we are embracing. After all, the term arises out of a dated notion that good history writing should be value free. I judge it important to keep the term to accent the notion that there is no value free inquiry.

92. See Wright's sense that Jesus research proceeds as a dialogue between the informed, self-critical student and the sources: *Jesus and the Victory*, 117.

93. Historians and theologians have to judge when points of resistance promise potential retrieval and when they do not pertain to our situation. It might be a historical point, for instance, that Jesus thinks the world is flat but we have to acknowledge that there is not much meaning there.

item? The consulting continues: how have scholars over the history of the quest treated the item?

With a resisting item in mind, the historian and others can turn to the next question: how can we make sense of the item? Making sense of it means explaining it analytically (i.e., where does it come from, how does it emerge, how does it function?, etc.) for sure, but eventually it means second-order understanding of the item in a fuller sense (what is the meaning of the item, why does it take the shape it does, what values shape the item, etc.?). Now, in the case of evidence from the Jesus saga, if not all historical evidence, *all three steps (noticing, explaining, and understanding) are value-rich interpretive exercises on the part of the historian.* The writing of history is laden with value and value does not simply appear suddenly at the end of the process when someone asks about the significance of an item of fact. As we have seen, what is a fact to notice is already colored by value choices of the historians. So while resisting evidence has a thereness to it, it has only a faint voice there until it is noticed, explained and understood. Noticing, paying serious attention to evidence is a value exercise. Explaining items involves choices of method and sources, especially in the duck-rabbit terrain of Jesus research. Understanding a Jesus item involves issues of paradigm choice and wider complexities of interpreting religious founders and charisma.[94]

Every step, from noticing to understanding, is a value engagement with items in the Jesus saga. Meta-historical framing encases every historical construction, but historical work on charismatic founder figures is especially electric, since it commonly involves cryptic and scattered evidence as well as charged issues of worldview, belief in God, metaphysical judgments, moral recommendations, etc. Some historians get caught up in questing for Jesus and wear their christologies on their sleeves; they unpack waves of recommendations for church and culture as they spin out a Jesus. They are moved by him, sometimes in hostility, sometimes in inspiration.[95] Historians, especially those on the left or the right end of the historical/theological spectrum, slip into explicit theological and value recommendations, when they put a Jesus together out of the puzzle pieces. But even historians who claim no interest in the doctrines of the Christians, even those connected to other faith traditions seem to look expectantly at their invention: for relevance, critique, social commentary, moral recommendations, and so on. Virtually all historians claim relevance of their historical constructions, of course. But more so, virtually all historians see themselves cleaning or propping up some christological house: even the Jew Vermes has christo-

---

94. Not to mention epistemological and metaphysical issues.
95. Anti-theology is a theological position, of course.

logical opinions.⁹⁶ Consequently, we know that virtually all questers think historical knowledge (of Jesus) has significance, if not normativity, for faith.

*What is it that turns on the meta-historical switch in historians,*⁹⁷ especially when historians are questing for Jesus? Of course, the anti-questing critics see nothing but raw theology parading in the new historical Jesuses.⁹⁸ And some historians do claim to recognize bias and anachronizing in the work of the Jesus historians. Both of these judgments have some validity. But it is more likely we have in front of us a combination of other factors: that we have only, say, seventy-five pieces of the Jesus puzzle to work with, that the sources for study are not very amenable to historical research, that we have so much, even too much, cultural and religious expectation about the figure of Jesus and that charismatic religious founders elude easy analogical study and that they cannot be studied in any manner without the most profound confluence of value issues. The list of factors can go on. It is therefore tempting, even inevitable, that historians comment in some way about the Christs people find with a historical Jesus.

The Jesus historian today must know the evidence, of course, but must also know how value issues have informed the judgments of others in the guild and in the history of the quest. Again, studying Jesus today requires facility in interpreting the scholars who study Jesus, since a stronger Jesus comes through the history of New Testament research and of the quest. The historian aims his/her knowledge of this history of the research primarily toward identification of the ways in which values in the past have entered the conversation with items in the Jesus saga. Precedent helps relatively and provides a platform for the genealogical step: where have the values come from in the historical judgments?; how have they arisen?; what kind of a world do they intend? The genealogical step aims to ask whether the values have seen the light of day, whether they are warranted, and whether they can be reprised in a new Jesus.

We are now ready to summarize some standards for good retrojection and for good value conversations in the construction of a Jesus, those presupposed in a proper deployment of a Jesus in a christology:

1. We identify the first and most obvious standard: **(Quest) Rule 80**, *Better retrojection, as it were, happens when historians and others, schooled in the suspicion of retrojection, are self-conscious of the issue of value in the production of a Jesus, their own and others.'* Consciousness of the issue

---

96. Vermes, *The Religion of Jesus*, 208.

97. Patterson states simply that the *search for God* lies behind the modern historical quest for Jesus: *The God of Jesus*, 11, 56.

98. Schüssler Fiorenza, *Jesus and the Politics*, 69; Luke Johnson, *The Real Jesus*, 55.

does wonders, not to eliminate value (as some think), but to bring to light *value locales* in historical research: places in the construction of a Jesus where we may expect value issues to well up, places where differences among Jesuses reveal differences of value conversation. We make no progress in the business of retrojection if we cannot see it. Here we seek to move beyond naïve retrojection.

2. **(Theological and Quest) Rule 81:** *Careful and critical use of the history of the quest can be a guide by which we can anticipate value locales.* It is no secret of the quest that scholars have been able to see retrojected value in other scholars' works better than in their own. The history of the quest tutors us in value discernment, particularly when it is partnered with the work of the critics of questing. The critics have been very discerning of retrojected value. After centuries of questing, most of the value locales start repeating: historians and others in-the-know know they must face the same issues that other Jesus historians face. For instance, does Jesus think of himself as messianic?; or, who does he call into his inner circle and for what purpose? Once we apply insights of the history of the quest, we can do the genealogical step, to take values back to their cultural and personal roots, and to bring those values into comparison with other scholars' constructions.

3. The hunt for value goes better when historians and others are *armed with an actual theory of retrojection*, not simply with a suspicion. An organized theory heightens suspicion. It takes technique and practice to learn to decode well the sophisticated and esoteric Jesuses of informed historians. More importantly, it takes a critical, Enlightened mindset to want to explain the apparent by the appeal to the disguised value. We argue that suspicion is stronger and more truthful where it moves beyond the *gotcha* orientation that seeks only to expose and dispose of recognized value constructions. Instead, the theory of retrojection needs to be re-aimed as we have done above.

4. The suspicion should aim, first and foremost, *to cull out retrojected value that is manipulative.* **(Quest and Theological) Rule 82:** *Historians and theologians need to move beyond the issue of uncovering the modernizing of Jesus and begin to focus on manipulation of the past.* That is, the retrojection critique converts to an ideological critique sensitive to power relationships. What is manipulative should be exposed and flushed: in whose interest is the construction? How is it exposed? By a complex double dialectical test against, first, the power of the resistance of the evidence, and, second, by a frank conversation with elements of one's exercise in theology of culture. Of course, the latter

recommendation is open-ended and would have to be charted more carefully.[99]

5. Certain value locales, seemingly invited by the Jesus saga itself, are particularly revelatory of value. Over the years these locales are very predictable and heavily worn. To focus on how historians or others handle such locales provides immediate access to particular value, which is easily compared to the contributions of others in the guild of historians and from the past. Such comparison opens the door to analytical judgments concerning what is at stake in particular readings of an item in the Jesus saga.

6. The use of a *spectrum of views*: Relatively, a value conversation with the Jesus saga is more promising when it finds support within the spectrum of informed historical opinions.

7. The use of *consensus:* Theologians can relax a bit about dangerous value when they attach their christologies to things of consensus within the guild of historians. Nonetheless, they need to keep a critical eye on herd mentalities and dissenting opinions, particularly in times of cultural change.

8. *Reshaped expectations about retrojection:* Retrojection is better where it lives in explicit value conversations, as we have seen; but it is better still when historians and theologians no longer demonize retrojection.

9. Retrojection is better where scholars set out an *apology* for a particular value-rich conversation in a value locale. The apology must include criteria and warrants, and justification for frames and paradigms.

10. The apology must connect the *choice of methods and sources* to underpinning values.

11. The apology must set out a *rationale for rejecting options* in the research.

12. A retrojective value locale has strength when it is in correlation with leading elements of a *theology of culture*. Theologians must be alert to value conversations invited by the press of contemporary culture.

13. Retrojective value is stronger when it has been checked *against the larger history of Christian faith and practice*. Theologians need to have a working sense for what Schleiermacher names as "the principle

---

99. We will illustrate elements of this conversation with the theology of culture in second volume of this project.

of the present:[100] in other words, a contemporary expression of what Christian life has been about.

The result of these standards brings the above together into a value-laden, warranted conversation with something in the Jesus saga in which both objective and subjective poles in history writing find a place. *Roughly speaking, the theologian has before him/her the quested elements of a christology, the results of an informed culture study, and a sense of the tradition in a mutual critical correlation.*[101] At this point, with a revised notion of retrojection we are now in a position to reappraise the criticism of the anti-quest position. Its revelation of retrojected value really means anti-questers recognize when subjective elements are smothering objective elements. That is, they see the manipulative retrojection of value. We should applaud this discernment but we are no longer willing to entertain the idea that good Jesus research is or should be value-free. Rather, proper and possible retrojection is really an explicit, self-conscious, public, value dialogue with historical evidence.[102] With its interests and perspectives, it seeks out points of resistance in the evidence.[103] It listens to them; it allows them to speak; it does not wander too far from those points. It is uneasy about asserting values, where there is no resistance. But, again, where there is no resistance, a historian must and can step up and make a deliberate case for a value conversation with an item in the Jesus saga.

---

100. Schleiermacher, *A Brief Outline*, 73.

101. To use David Tracy's spin on Tillich's method of correlation.

102. See Wright's sense that Jesus research proceeds as a dialogue between the informed, self-critical student and the sources: *Jesus and the Politics*, 117.

103. Historians and theologians have to judge when points of resistance promise potential retrieval and when they do not pertain to our situation. It might be a historical point, for instance, that Jesus thinks the world is flat but we have to judge there is not much *there* there.

5

Case Study in Retrojection: The Invention of Jesus-Sage

Jesus research may be in the midst of a paradigm shift. In the last twenty years or so, it has turned more and more from focus on Jesus as an apocalyptic prophet to new attention to Jesus as a sage. As Robert Funk of the famous Jesus Seminar states simply:

> The Seminar, in contrast, came to the view that Jesus was not an apocalyptic prophet, but a sage in the tradition of Israelite wisdom. His parables and aphorisms had been overlaid with apocalyptic views at the behest of his first followers, who had come from the circle of John the Baptist. They brought John's views with them into the Jesus movement, and when Jesus was gone, those older views simply displaced Jesus' own views of the Kingdom of God.[1]

Today, many scholars are abandoning the pattern of the *thoroughgoing eschatology* of Schweitzer which had dominated the twentieth century. And they are doing so by following the pattern that Schweitzer regards as the only alternative to his position: the *thoroughgoing skepticism* of Wrede.[2] Finally, they abandon the Schweitzerian tradition for the same reason that

---

1. Funk, "The Jesus Seminar," in Meyer and Hughes, eds., *Jesus Then and Now*, 136.

2. The "skepticism" of the Sage option pertains to scholars' abandonment of the privileged position of the gospel of Mark and its apocalyptic narrative in constructing Jesus. Here many develop Wrede's insight that Mark shapes the Jesus saga theologically (not historically) by arguing that the apocalyptic has been added to the saga from apocalyptic circles like that of John. N. T. Wright employs the Wrede-Schweitzer polarity also but he cuts the issue somewhat differently. He emphasizes the continuity of the Jesus Seminar with Wrede's skepticism, of course, but puts Bultmann in the same group without crediting how dependent Bultmann is on the apocalyptic paradigm. See: Wright, *Jesus and the Victory*, 21.

Schweitzer heads for Africa, as it were: the prophet of end time fails.³ History disproves him and all apocalypticists. But we are not to worry, since Jesus himself and his message should not be tied to the fate of end time.⁴ The turn to the heritage of Wrede actually liberates Jesus from the apocalyptic frame, since, like Wrede, many contemporary Jesus researchers free themselves from the way that the narrative of Mark has dominated past quests. As Funk notes, a new slant on Jesus begins when scholars spring free from the "steady canonical bias" which relies on the synoptic gospels against other sources.⁵ It is possible, then, to see Jesus anew without the apocalyptic lens. In that light Jesus appears as a sage.

In some circles of Jesus research the apocalyptic paradigm has been dismantled. Now the question in this chapter aims to figure out *how one invents Jesus-Sage and what is at stake theologically in a shift to a sapiential paradigm for Jesus research.*⁶ Here we are not arguing the virtues of the new paradigm, nor would we presume to tell historians what they must do in their research. Rather we ask concerning the advantages for theologians if they shift modes and begin to think of Jesus as a sage? Are there risks? Ultimately we will wonder whether there can be anything christic about a sage Jesus and, if so, in what way. Of course, there is nothing categorically astonishing about viewing Jesus from within the wisdom tradition. After all, there are plenty of wisdom sayings attributed to him: depending on how one counts them, the Jesus saga contains 1,026 or 1,337 wisdom sayings.⁷ It would be easy to think of Jesus as one imbued with the wisdom of Israel or even of the wider Mediterranean world. But to view him essentially as a sage is quite a step for New Testament and theological research.⁸ What prompts it? Interestingly, to see Jesus as a *sage* represents a return to the view in certain sections of the Josephus text.⁹ The category actually appears in the text and does not match the sort of claims and terms typical among early

---

3. Funk, "The Seminar," in Meyer and Hughes, eds., *Jesus Then and Now*, 136.

4. It is difficult not to notice a deep sense in this alleged paradigm shift that Jesus must be relevant to this world.

5. Funk, "The Jesus Seminar," in Meyer and Hughes, eds., *Jesus Then and Now*, 136.

6. Recall how much theological hay grew in light of the century of the apocalyptic paradigm.

7. According to Charles E. Carlston's count: "Proverbs, Maxims," 91.

8. Notice the thrust of Mack's argument in *The Lost Gospel*: that the Jesus of Q is a Jesus without Christ, or in my language, a Jesus who is not christologically interesting, since the christic possibilities emerged later in the christianizing of the Jesus movement.

9. Admittedly, this reference is from the "Testimonium Flavianum" which may be a Christian interpolation: see the discussion in Witherington, *The Jesus Quest*, 162.

Christians, nor does it match the views of Pharisaic Judaism.[10] Consequently, by the application of the criterion of dissimilarity, one can assume that at a very early stage some people must have named Jesus as a "wise man." The view may be confirmed independently from the letter of the Syrian stoic Mara bar Sarapion.[11] The effort to recover that naming may be worthwhile historically and theologically. How does one imagine Jesus as a sage?[12]

A. Methodological Issues:
A How-To Manual for the Construction of a Sage

First, scholars must undermine the power of the apocalyptic prophet paradigm. As we have already seen, the typical move locates apocalyptic all around Jesus but spares of him apocalyptic views: instead, scholars tie Jesus' message to the sapiential tradition, despite his association with the Baptist movement.[13] Indeed, it is the followers of John who apocalypticize the Jesus saga.[14] The task, say the critics of the apocalyptic, is to risk seeing Jesus within a different paradigm: to make that skip of mind by which the duck becomes a rabbit in one's vision.

By now the critique of the apocalyptic paradigm is familiar[15] and centers on the theory that there is a tension between the world of wisdom and the world of apocalyptic, namely, that wisdom presupposes the conditions of an enduring world while apocalyptic directs attention away from this world. This tension is compounded by the fact that the Jesus saga seem-

---

10. It is the case that *sophos aner* is a rare title for Jesus within Christian sources and yet it appears in Josephus: by a criterion of dissimilarity we can possibly assume that it is a primary designation for Jesus: cf. Theissen and Merz, *The Historical Jesus*, 67.

11. This letter, from the end of the first century, names Jesus as the "wise king" of the Jews who gives his people a "new law," and, interestingly, identifies his wisdom as countercultural and dangerous in a violent world; the Jews, like others, kill their wise leader. See the discussion in Theissen and Merz, *The Historical Jesus*, 76–79. Quite evidently, the "new Law" Mara mentions is a dispensation of wisdom which he seems to endorse as something a Stoic would like.

12. For a sample of the immense critical literature on Jesus as sage, see: Carlson, "Jesus the Sage," 204–205; Hultgren, "Jesus of Nazareth," 263–273; Perkins, "Jesus before Christianity," 749–51; Scott, "Jesus as Sage," in Gammie and Purdue, *The Sage in Israel*, 399–415; Mack, "Lord of the Logia," in Goehring et al., eds., *Gospel Origins*, 3–18.

13. Most scholars continue to tie Jesus to John; the exception comes from the far left within the sage paradigm: Mack, "Lord of the Logia," in Goehring et al., eds., *Gospel Origins*, 10. Mack judges the association of Jesus with John to be an added part of the large campaign to mythicize the Jesus movement in an epic-apocalyptic frame.

14. Funk, "Seminar," 136.

15. See a summary of the critique of the apocalyptic paradigm in Goehring et al., eds., *Gospel Origins*, or Mack, *The Lost Gospel*, 38.

ingly contains both this-worldly wisdom and apocalyptic materials, as do the other sources, for instance, from Qumran. But in the critique, scholars separate Jesus from the apocalyptic by undermining the efforts of twentieth-century historians and theologians to locate the world-oriented message of Jesus within an apocalyptic frame. *In the new sage paradigm scholars intend to save the worldly message and ethic of Jesus from its association with apocalyptic eschatology.* Advocates of the sage paradigm routinely complain that the sayings of Jesus have received little attention in the apocalyptic era; they assert that the wisdom and the moral imperatives of the sayings source(s) are foundational for our knowledge of Jesus. Indeed, the new paradigm envisions a completely new reconstruction of Christian origins and may even boldly claim that Paul and the gospel of Mark are not actual apocalyptic sources.[16]

We may speculate why some historians are moving to the sapiential paradigm. Of course, we have to remember that the historical protocol requires historians to justify new paradigms via claims about method and source evidence. But beyond that, the suspicious eye of retrojection notices that the sage paradigm emerges at a time in the academy when so-called post-modern methodological considerations reign. It is fashionable to take apart reigning paradigms and to build alternative constructions, warranted finally by the coherence of their picturing. Of course, in the case of Jesus research, the mode of historical inquiry protects against the most extreme post-modern constructivism. After all, Jesus researchers commonly see themselves as historians and necessarily understand their task to interpret data which stand there waiting for the historian's eye. They debate among themselves whether a particular formulation responds adequately to the data in the sources, and in this mode of conduct, they claim to differ from each other concerning what counts as evidence.

But, as we have already seen, the actual work of these historians is much more complicated. Increasingly, what counts for evidence turns on what is a legitimate source for knowledge of Jesus, and what is a legitimate source turns on the historian's elected method, which in turn depends on the historian's meta-methodological orientations. These decisions, as we have seen, circle within a hermeneutic. This is the hermeneutical turn that characterizes the Third Quest. Contemporary historical research on Jesus explicitly recognizes the manner in which the values and orientations of the researcher shape the construction of a Jesus. But Jesus research takes the next step toward the post-modern at the point where it becomes *explicit model-building*. Because of the nature of Jesus research, it is unlikely that

---

16. I.e., Mack, "Lord of the Logia," in Goehring et al., eds., *Gospel Origins*, 7.

historians will ever do model-building without a dialogue with evidence in sources. Still, they build a Jesus, either explicitly to deconstruct dominant, unacceptable Jesuses sometimes merely to launch a plausible Jesus amid implausible or unappealing ones within the terrain of the ambiguities of historical research on an ancient, obscure figure. Nonetheless, *Jesus-Sage is the first Jesus in a post-modern style.*

The first step in the construction of Jesus-Sage is to criticize the apocalyptic prophet paradigm. Contemporary Jesus researchers will offer an array of arguments why the apocalyptic paradigm distorts good historical evidence. And they do. But it is interesting and typical of the current scene that Robert Funk rejects the apocalyptic paradigm for larger hermeneutical, not simply historical, reasons. For Funk *apocalyptic* means the entire "sacred canopy" of churchly salvation history: it is the tip of a comprehensive worldview that is passing away and no longer has currency in our culture.[17] An apocalyptic Jesus can function only in a *mythic universe* which has collapsed for us post-modern people. Further, apocalyptic fits within a boneheaded literalism about the Jesus saga and misses the rich and witty metaphorical meaning of Jesus' speech.[18] Indeed, apocalyptic is "humorless." Today we need to turn to the "witticisms of Jesus," to discover how scholars are constructing the post-modern Jesus.

Second, advocates of the sage paradigm turn to a *saying-dominated conversation with the sources of knowledge of Jesus.* They set aside the domination of the canonical sources and their narrative, emplotted framing (a la Wrede). They are unpersuaded by a deeds-oriented reconstruction of Jesus' life.[19] Instead they turn to a "sayings" gospel which they regard as earlier and less developed.[20] Unlike the actions of Jesus which are always third-hand interpretations, the sayings of Jesus give us the real Jesus in immediacy.[21] Primary is "the body of instructions that circulated in his name, what these teachings called for in terms of ideas, attitudes, and behavior, and the difference these instructions make in the lives of those who took them seriously."[22] These are sayings from the Logia tradition (found especially in Q): typically, in the sage paradigm the Logia are construed as an actual text that Matthew and Luke have at their disposal when they construct their gospels. We see

17. Funk, "The Jesus Seminar," in Meyer and Hughes, eds., *Jesus Then and Now*, 137.

18. Ibid.

19. A view pioneered by Sanders, *The Historical Figure*; see the discussion in McGaughy, "The Search for the Historical Jesus," 17–26.

20. I.e., Mack, *The Lost Gospel*, 1–2.

21. The protestant naiveté of Funk here is almost breathtaking: Funk, "The Jesus Seminar," in Meyer and Hughes, eds., *Jesus Then and Now*, 137.

22. Ibid.

here a *textualizing* of the Q source which may be enhanced when scholars begin to construe it as a *gospel*: the "Sayings Gospel of Q."[23] In this reading the narrative portions of the canonical gospels, especially those tied to the passion, are vastly different and represent developing Christian reflections, and maybe even loss.[24] We must note here that the sayings tradition appears to be both devoid of narrative and of a passion story.

Third and related to the second point above is the choice for wisdom speech, especially the aphorism and parable, as the privileged and revelatory expression for the reconstruction of Jesus' life. Notice the exact formulation: it is not that the parables and aphorisms reveal Jesus' message, an idea long recognized by questers. Rather, it is that *the sayings are the most reliable entrance into the life of Jesus*. Consequently, scholars within the sage paradigm construe the sayings of Jesus differently. The sayings no longer function to fill out the *message* of a man whose life, roughly, can be known from the synoptic outline. Rather, they are the reliable, if not the exclusive, entrance into his life. The Jesus scholar is to work backwards from the sayings to the life.

These wisdom genres can be found in all the sources for knowledge of Jesus, except John, and usually consist of riddles, parables, true aphorisms, personifications, and beatitudes. We shall abbreviate all of these subgroups under the category of *aphorisms* and note that they tend to be short, sharp, acontextual, non-narrative language forms. The decision that the sayings of Q belong to the genres of the Wisdom tradition, for instance, has been a powerful development in *the invention of the sage-paradigm*; it rests in James M. Robinson's influential early articles.[25] It is not enough to turn to the sayings in the Logia tradition; scholars must decide that these sayings arise from the pre-Easter sage, and not from later ecstatic charismatics who proclaim new words from the Risen Lord.[26] Scholars within the sage paradigm have decided that the wisdom of the sayings sources, at least substantial potions of it, goes back to the pre-Easter situation.

The fourth step in the construction of Jesus-Sage is the choice of sayings-oriented sources: scholars who think of Jesus as a sage tend to privilege Q. In this source is our earliest access to the Jesus-movement.[27] It reflects the

---

23. Keck notices the subtle ennobling of the source which, of course, scholars have reconstructed: Keck, *Who Is Jesus?*, 66.

24. Funk notes that the centrality of the words and deeds of Jesus began to diminish as the Jesus saga got wrapped up in a mythically shaped passion story: Funk, "The Jesus Seminar," in Meyer and Hughes, eds., *Jesus Then and Now*, 139.

25. Robinson, "LOGOI SOPHON," and Robinson, "Jesus—From Easter."

26. Again, the work of Robinson.

27. Helmut Koester argues that some of the wisdom sayings of Thomas can be dated to the first generation after Jesus' death, and thus they match Q in antiquity: Koester,

logoi sophon genre which implies a teacher of wisdom.[28] One of the most important transformations of our understanding happens when scholars begin to construe a sayings source in a new mode. For instance, scholars must first accept that there is distinct material in Matthew and Luke that can be isolated. Then scholars may decide that Q is not simply what Matthew and Luke hold in common (independent of Marcan material), but that it is an actual source. Indeed, it is one source. Further, they may decide that the source is a single book, with discernible coherence, and not simply a rag-tag set of scraps.[29] Then they may go even further and suggest that there is an actual community with a social milieu behind the book, whose values can be read backwards from the discreet aphoristic fragments of the source. The items in the catalogue of Q, scholars then assume, represent accurately, adequately, and representatively the views of the putative community of Q.

Once scholars are on board with all of these assumptions (filled with retrojected value!), they face a further difficulty: even the privileged source Q has apocalyptic materials in it. Consequently, in order to think of Jesus as a sage primarily, and not as a prophet of end times, scholars have to react to apocalyptic sayings in Q with a theory. After all, if the earliest source contains apocalyptic materials, how then is Jesus a sage? Their task has been complicated by the studies of Lührmann and his successors which argue that the theme of judgment is the organizing principle of the composition of Q.[30] If these studies were correct, then apocalyptic thinking would be central to the nature of Q and scholars could hardly overturn the apocalyptic paradigm for interpreting Jesus.[31]

"The Gospel of Thomas," 37. The scholars of the Jesus Seminar typically regard Thomas as early, from the middle of the first century, and they are ones who are likely to view Jesus as a sage: Funk, *The Five Gospels*, 474.

28. Robinson, "LOGOI SOPHON."

29. Here we need to note the caution of Dunn who thinks the Q people have not attended enough to the oral character of their sources and labor under a "literary paradigm" as they examine the saying sources: Dunn, "Jesus in Oral Memory," in Donnelly, ed., *Jesus*, 124, 128.

30. Judgment is dangerously close to apocalyptic concerns. See Lührmann, *Die Redaktion der Logienquelle*. We need to note the connection between apocalypse and judgment. See also: Jacobson, *Wisdom Christology in Q*; Zeller, *Kommentar zur Logienquelle*; Sellow, *Early Collections of Jesus' Words*, etc.

31. It is interesting to note that the discussion has assumed that the theme of judgment is apocalyptic while wisdom materials are non-judgmental. There is a disguised value retrojection here, of course, since scholars assume wisdom is worldly and affirming, and free of judgment; the judgment in question must be that of the end time: that associated with the coming Son of Man. See Mack, "The Lord of the Logia," in Goehring et al., eds., *Gospel Origins*, 8.

After Kloppenborg's studies, however, scholars found a way to separate the apocalyptic in Q through a theory that in the single source Q, one could find chronological strata, and thus, a history of Q development might be reconstructable. Kloppenborg's influential contribution dissociated the main body of wisdom sayings from those in Q that appear to be apocalyptic in nature, i.e., the Son of Man sayings. Today scholars frequently suggest that there are layers of development within the Q materials and theological-ideational developments within the source. In typical reconstructions, scholars *read the apocalyptic sayings in Q to be a later, even judaizing, reaction to a crisis in the Q community.* At its heart, however, Q1, as it is called, is non-apocalyptic and non-judgmental. Indeed, the earliest may not be Jewish at all or "very" Jewish.[32] The most important point for our purposes here is that the sage paradigm depends not simply on turning to Q as a primary source, but on a particular set of interpretations of Q.[33]

The next step in the invention of the Sage happens when scholars *connect their theory of development within the Q source to social history, to a real community.* They find support from the many new studies of Galilee during the period of Roman occupation and discover that the image of Galilee as a quaint, fisher-peasant, Jewish, village world is substantially inaccurate. The new Galilees are cosmopolitan, hellenized, Gentile worlds of provincial Roman culture and affairs.[34] They are exactly the kind of worlds needed to support the emergence of a sage's wisdom. Typically scholars characterize this world as a sophisticated center of Hellenistic culture. Greek-speaking Romans, Gentiles, rule the Galilean territory from great bureaucratic Hellenistic cities, like Sepphoris. In the sage's world are few Jews, and the ones there are oppressed by a brutal Roman colonial system. It is not a world in which the religious issues of being a Jew demand center stage; indeed, there is little focus on common Jewish themes, i.e., rival views on keeping Torah, of the meaning of the Kingdom of God etc., in the Galilean life of the first century CE. Rather, *it is an urbane, educated, and prosperous world in which the sage emerges like an itinerant philosopher.*[35] Of course, lifting Jesus-Sage (somewhat) out of once-typical patterns of reconstruction of Palestinian Judaism means that a scholar judges that the world of lower Galilee is substantially different from the rest of Jewish Galilee and certainly very dif-

32. As in Mack and Crossan.

33. A set of assumptions that many find ridiculous: Sanders, "Jesus in Galilee," in Donnelly, ed., *Jesus*, 6.

34. Influenced by the studies, among others, of Freyne, *Galilee, Jesus, and the Gospels*.

35. For a summary of this model of Galilee, see Sanders, "Jesus in Galilee," in Donnelly, *Jesus*, 6–19.

ferent from the culture of Judea.[36] In the dominant reading the Q source represents the cosmopolitan culture of lower Galilee. In another reading the Q source emerges from a subversive (and egalitarian) element within the Galilean situation.[37]

Here we note that scholars connect the single Q source to a real community in Galilee. The new Galilee sponsors the emergence of the wisdom of Q, they assume. Further, advocates of the sage paradigm assume that Q as a source accurately and adequately captures what was on the minds of the Q community.[38] Even further, *they assume that tensions and apparent contradictions within the source can be explained through a developmental theory* within the source. What is simply there as apparent formal and material tensions has been *emplotted into a coherent developmental theory: what is in tension represents actual changes in the thinking of a people.* Then scholars assume that development in the source reflects developments in the history of the community, and it does so accurately and adequately. Apparently formal and material tensions in the source[39] can be explained by social and intellectual-spiritual crises the community faces in the period before the Jewish War. Each step of the way is a judgment.[40] So, in the Q source—and it is a source—on the earliest layer, we find sayings that recommend charismatic itinerancy. We can assume that there is a community for which this has been a value and that, further, their lifestyle mimics that of their leader, the sage.[41]

Connecting the Q source to a putative Q community represents an imaginative leap; connecting the Q community to Galilee is wildly speculative.[42] Then we have to face the next question: which Galilee, whose Galilee?[43] We need not repeat the arguments we discussed in earlier chapters here,

36. A set of assumptions that many, including Sanders, ibid., find unfounded.

37. Schüssler Fiorenza, *Jesus and the Politics*, 166.

38. Keck names this assumption as "complete congruence": *Who Is Jesus?*, 67.

39. I.e., the Son of Man sayings or not, judgment or not.

40. In this step alone, we have about five opportunities to insert value into historical construction.

41. Theissen and Merz, *The Historical Jesus*, 19.

42. We should note here that some scholars think there is no evidence, period, for a Q community: i.e., Witherington, *The Jesus Quest*, 176.

43. See the section on Galilee above. For a recent review of the archaeological evidence which argues against the new Galilees, see Jonathan L. Reed, "Galilean Archaeology," 113–30. At every point Reed relativizes the new Galilees with counter evidence drawn from archaeological studies: Galilee was essentially a Jewish locale with substantial attachment to life in Judea and the Temple; despite the two Greek cities, it was vastly less hellenized than advocates of the sage paradigm wish; indeed, even Sepphoris and Tiberias were less hellenized and more provincial than typical Mediterranean cities: ibid., 113–121.

but simply note that *those within the sage paradigm tend to see a less-Jewish and a more hellenized Galilee,* and one often quite alienated from oppressive Judean and colonial powers. In addition, they tend to trust the signals about Galilee in the saying sources. Among reconstructions within the sage paradigm there remains an unresolved tension between portraits that emphasize more the Hellenistic theme (i.e., Mack, Batey, and Downing)[44] and those focusing more on the theme of oppression (i.e., Horsley, Hanson, Borg, Applebaum).[45] A few interpreters combine both models of Galilee (i.e., Crossan).

The decision to trust the sayings sources and their picturing of Galilee, either in the Hellenistic or the oppressive key, is hardly without controversy. Sanders, for instance, thinks that the entire Galilee construction supporting the sage paradigm is all wet[46] and he argues convincingly against most of the typical features of the sage's Galilee. On each of the central issues above, the sage-people have simply ignored too much of the evidence. More important for us is the recognition of the chicken-or-egg circumstance of Galilee reconstruction: namely, *the Galilee one reconstructs depends on the methodological decisions on sources one makes, and the sources find their confirmation in that portrait of Galilee.* Construal of evidence dominates everything in the issue of Galilee, since our knowledge of the Galilean situation is yet so lean and fragmentary.[47]

The next step in the construction of the sage points to a more specific social location within the Galilean world. *The sage speaks wisdom for the road.* That is, typically, advocates of the sage paradigm point to a *charismatic itinerant movement as the social home of the primitive Jesus movement.*[48] We have seen the itineracy theme before, of course; what we need to add here is *the coincidence of wisdom and its atomistic genres and the on-the-road social setting. Neither the language form nor the social world is firmly rooted in a richly emplotted or established reality.* The assumption centers on the notion that Jesus is a charismatic sage who creates a movement that continues his

---

44. Note that those favoring the Hellenistic model of Galilee typically prefer some form of the cynic hypothesis.

45. See the recent discussion of rival portraits of Jesus' Galilee in: Sanders, "Jesus in Galilee," in Donnelly, ed., *Jesus*, 5–8.

46. For instance, Sanders argues that the evidence shows incontrovertibly that there was no Roman colonization, properly speaking, in Palestine, nor was there an occupation of the land: *The Historical Figure*, 24. From where, then, does the liberationists' portrait of oppressed Palestine come?

47. Sanders, *The Historical Figure*, 5.

48. Theissen's famous claim: "[T]he earliest Christian itinerant charismatics continued the preaching and life-style of Jesus": Theissen and Merz, *The Historical Jesus*, 30.

itinerant lifestyle. What typifies itineracy within the sage paradigm is that it abandons the *restorative eschatology* of the apocalyptic paradigm for a more philosophic model: less the desert prophet of end time and more the traveling school master.

Next, scholars who view Jesus as a sage tend to employ a range of apocryphal sources.[49] The most important is The Gospel of Thomas.[50] Also of importance may be the Egerton Manuscript, the Secret Gospel of Mark,[51] the Gospel of the Hebrews, and the Gospel of Peter. The main line of debate centers on whether there is any material in these sources independent of the canonical gospels and whether such material is from the earliest layer of the Jesus saga.[52] Those favoring the sage model typically support the critical use of these sources and locate them surprisingly early, while those operating within the apocalyptic prophet mode reject their usefulness as primary sources. *It is a major methodological decision with powerful, shaping consequences when a scholar judges non-canonical sources to be independent of the synoptic tradition.*[53] This view, pioneered by Koester and Robinson, argues that the Gospel of Thomas, for instance, contains early and independent Jesus materials, and in Thomas is the Eastern version of the Logia materials we find in Q. Thomas, therefore, is not simply a later, gnostic re-hash of the synoptic tradition.[54] In Thomas, we can see materials as close as Q's to the figure of Jesus.

---

49. Cf. ibid., 30.

50. Scholars may depend on a re-dating of the Gospel of Thomas to the first century, a proposal that started to gain acceptance among some from the 1980s: cf. Koester, *Ancient Christian Gospels*, 21, 84. Some may be amused to note that the Jesus Seminar found more genuine Jesus material in Thomas than in the canonical gospel of Mark: cf. Keck, *Who Is Jesus?*, 14.

51. Which Crossan (with Koester) champions as an early version of what becomes the Mark of the New Testament. The contrary view sees the Secret Gospel of Mark as a later Gnostic recension of the canonical Mark.

52. Note the recent trend to drop the date of Thomas to earlier, rather than later, times in the Christian era. If the carbon dating on the Oxyrhynchus papyri pertains to materials in Thomas, then we know that Thomas does not come from the second to the fourth century CE, but at the latest, early second century. Other historical judgments may drive Thomas or Thomas materials into the first century: Theissen and Merz, *The Historical Jesus*, 38.

53. Those opposed to the use of the apocryphal sources include: Ehrman and Meier. Their point is that these sources are later and derivative of the synoptic tradition. The counter position, of course, argues that Thomas represents a gnostic condensation of materials in the synoptic tradition.

54. As in the conservative position, i.e., Meier, Schrage, Grant, Freedman, Fieger, etc.

Whether this judgment is true or not is up for discussion among the scholars. We must note, however, as in the case with Q, *the turn to Thomas is not a transparent one*. Even if scholars decide to opt for the camp which advocates the independence and antiquity of Thomas,[55] they still must work their way through Thomas with a particular, and controversial, reading of the text. Of course, even an amateur can recognize the obviously gnostic picture of Jesus in Thomas, and, following the methodology of questing, obvious elements of gnostic theology must be purged to get close to materials in Thomas useful for questing. Then scholars must look for shadows and fragments from an earlier stage that have been gnosticized in the Thomas source itself. These are elements in the Jesus saga (for instance, itineracy) that can be successfully spiritualized in gnostic fashion and therefore suggest what may have been in the Logia tradition before it gets to the hands of gnostic Christians. If all this reconstruction were not complicated enough, advocates of the value of Thomas for Jesus research must bracket these shadows in Thomas' picture which presuppose that Jesus faced an apocalyptic worldview. This move is tricky, but within the sage paradigm it typically involves *a decoding of the apocalyptic immediacy of certain sayings*. So while Jesus may have faced apocalypticized peoples and views, "In each case Jesus counters the very concern that underlies such questions, usually by means of a reapplication of apocalyptic metaphor to the moment of personal transformation, or to the situation of self-awareness in relation to a gnosis about the present constitution of the world."[56] Finally, while the social location of Thomas itself is of little concern for questing, it becomes important when scholars detect antique traces within the gnosticized materials. Inside them, not surprisingly, scholars detect the same itinerant charismatic movement they have discovered in Q.[57]

The next step in the invention of the sage requires scholars to judge which materials, which genres, are primitive. Concerning Q the question turns on whether the apocalyptic sayings are early; concerning Thomas, the question turns on the status of the parabolic material. Typically, scholars who build a Jesus within the sage paradigm discount the long, parabolic materials and value the more aphoristic materials. Significantly, they turn away from the more narrative, extended genres to the pithy one-liner sayings and short similes. While the decision to privilege aphoristic genres may seem innocent enough, it is not. *Discounting the primacy of larger language forms*

55. I.e., Blatz, Vielhauer, Koester, Robinson, Patterson, Davies, Crossan, etc.

56. Mack, "The Lord of the Logia," in Goehring et al., eds., *Gospel Origins*, 8: sounds of a good existentialist interpretation re-emerging!

57. The judgment makes sense, of course, if Thomas and Q contain two versions of the same logia tradition: Theissen and Merz, *The Historical Jesus*, 41.

means that a putative connection to the Jesus saga in the synoptic gospels cannot be made and that much of the non-aphoristic materials of the synoptic tradition must be judged as highly developed.

A further decision appears when scholars decide that the non-canonical materials are, in fact, better sources for knowledge of Jesus than those of the canonical gospels. Here I mean not only the non-canonical gospels but the Q materials pulled out of the narrative gospels of the New Testament. *If these sources are privileged, then Jesus is well on the way to sagehood.*[58] We note that these sources are essentially non-narrative.

Commonly, *scholars find bedrock where Q and Thomas, both critically sorted, presuppose a similar vision of the Jesus figure.* Stephen Patterson's work on reading Thomas remains important here, for Patterson shows that if we can view the Thomas logia outside of the usual gnostic frame (just as we must see the Q logia outside of the apocalyptic paradigm), then suddenly the sayings of Thomas look surprisingly similar to those of Q1. At this point scholars can apply a criterion of coherence and build a sturdy foundation for reconstructing the earliest picture of Jesus. Indeed, the *coherence between Q and Thomas has replaced the older criterion of coherence among the synoptic gospels as the best test for the real Jesus.* In such an application scholars find confirmation that apocalyptic is secondary.[59]

Next, scholars typically continue to build a Jesus-Sage by seeking out analogies for interpreting the wisdom of the privileged, earliest sources. However, since the wisdom of the best sources does not quite match that of typical Mediterranean and biblical sapiential materials,[60] scholars likely will turn to atypical and non-biblical parallels to illumine the sayings of Jesus. Since the sayings of Jesus are hardly the bland truisms common in so much wisdom, *the favorite analogy is with the edgier sayings of cynic philosophers,* both in content and form or with the tradition of radical wisdom as we see in Job and Ecclesiates. Further, scholars need a theory and technique to discover this particular sage among all the sages. Since wisdom often gets mixed into the lore of the ages and into popular culture, it is difficult to discover the contribution of any one sage. Therefore, scholars must search for the "distinctive voice"[61] of one sage within the wisdom of the ages. For

---

58. More than anyone else Crossan has pointed to the priority of the non-canonical sources.

59. I.e., Mack, "The Lord of the Logia," in Goehring et al., eds., *Gospel Origins*, 6.

60. A potentially damaging admission: since many scholars today routinely dissociate Jesus' core message from typical apocalyptic pronouncements by showing the difference between the genre of apocalyptic and that of wisdom; yet they also must admit that Jesus' message is not exactly like typical wisdom. See Mack, *The Lost Gospel*, 46.

61. Scott, "Jesus as Sage," in Gammie and Purdue, eds., *The Sage in Israel*, 405–9.

instance, in his early work, Crossan heard the voice of Jesus where he found materials parodying Jewish case law.[62] Finally, the most important step rests in the question: *can one regard the sayings of a sage as a gospel?* Construing wisdom sayings as gospel or a gospel presupposes that there is a christology or an implied christology in the fragments, and that they bear something of a *kerygmatic* intention. While this issue may seem obvious, it is not, since it depends on *a scholar's construction of coherence and mission from the discreet sayings, and since the construction itself works causally backward, in a Schleiermacherian spirit, from the words of a sage to the person of the sage, and then supplies a hunch about the intentionality embedded in the sage's project.*

From Schweitzer's era on, the difficulty for scholars has been to secure a christology founded mostly on the atomistic sayings of Jesus, since a gospel appears to require the actions of the savior, a narrative plotline, and, most of all, a passion. Would it be proper to say that Q is a gospel, since it (apparently) lacks these elements? How about the Gospel of Thomas: is it really a gospel? The question requires a clear sense of the meaning of gospel and of christology, of course. But the difficulty has been deepened by the methodological decisions of many in the sage camp, since they typically do not regard actions, plot, and passion as primary. Consequently, their positions are open to the challenge from theological critics, and some historical ones, who insist that the wisdom of a sage—even if the sage is Jesus—is insufficient. Without action, plot, and passion, there is by definition neither history nor kerygma. The words of Jesus are not gospel since a gospel starts logically in the passion (and resurrection) of the Christ and plays the story backward.[63] Since many scholars turn entirely to a small catalog of the earliest sayings, they have little to work with that could generate a christology.[64] So are the sayings a gospel? Do they represent gospel?

62. Crossan, *Raid on the Articulate*, 67.

63. Cf. Robinson's discussion of the exchange between Harnack and Barth. Harnack's liberal Jesus, founded on the sayings of Jesus, represents the option which today works up a picture of the meaning and message of the Sage Jesus from the earliest sayings. Barth judged this Jesus to represent the world of the Law and thus not gospel, not kerygmatic for Christian faith, since it framed a Jesus independent of the saving death. Undoubtedly, Barth and others who are critics of a sayings-founded christology norm "gospel" from Paul and the developed synoptic gospels where plot and passion define the genre. Robinson, *A New Quest*, 14.

64. Cf. Mack's position, in which the sayings source is a trajectory of development away from the Jesus-Sage which employs a salvific role for the death of Jesus: "The Lord of the Logia," in Goehring et al., eds., *Gospel Origins*, 4–5. Note that Mack does not care that there is nothing kerygmatic about a sayings-sourced sage: he thinks the kerygmatic theme comes in the later development of Christian movement, and tellingly, that it represents a mythologization of the Jesus movement.

If we define gospel in a low-flying or generic fashion, then any effort to interpret the meaning and significance of Jesus is a christology. Advocates of the sage paradigm can speak of a christology of Thomas or Q without challenge. But if by gospel we mean the kerygmatic standards of the (surviving) church of 50–100 CE, then the critics have a complaint with the sage. The best we could say is that he is pre-Christian and that there are incipient or divergent christologies in the sayings sources, but not truly Christian christologies. If, with Bultmann, we view the sage as pre-Christian and thus a function of Judaism, we posit a considerable discontinuity between the message of the sage and Christian receptions of him. Under a sage paradigm, the pressure would be considerable to account adequately for the founding of Christian religion and the departure from Second Temple Judaism. If, however, we honor the sage christologically, we have to broaden our definitions and have lost our orthodox standards for Christian christologies. But ironically, we have also opened up continuity between the project of Jesus and his earliest followers and that of the church. *Where there is continuity, we have the historic dream of every christologically interested quester: historical research on Jesus can generate christological help, support, critique, or clarification.*[65]

Can there be anything christological about Jesus the Sage? Is the sage within Judaism and thus, pre-Christian? Or is he already christic in the conduct of his wisdom? Can the Jewish sage be received christologically, and rightly so? At first these questions seem to ask if we can discover whether a sage sees himself as the definitive mouthpiece of the Divine Wisdom who rules the world. If we say yes, we indeed have a christology, albeit a low-flying one, but one nonetheless *dependent on the interpreters' coherentizing of a set of postage-stamp sayings and on their speculation about the intentionality of a (single) person who stands behind the fragments.* There are times, after all, when what we say reveals who we are and what we are about. As Robinson articulates the *intentional leap*, it is fair to assume that Jesus' message must have meant something for him, and consequently, we are safe in moving from words to intentions, from sayings to mission and identity of the sage.[66] But which things of the many things I say reveal me? And how do we know we have a representative sampling of revelatory sayings? Most of the scholars within the emerging sage paradigm proceed with a confidence that they can read the sayings in this mode with certain checks for adequacy.[67]

---

65. Whether as support for christological claims or critique of them.

66. Robinson sees the intentional leap to be rooted in Schweitzer's legacy, even when Schweitzer applied the move in a way that turned out to be mistaken: Robinson, *A New Quest*, 15.

67. I.e., Q checked against Thomas. Even Mack has confidence enough in the

We really can use Q; Q is a source; Q is a single source; Q is coherent; Q1 is recoverable; Q pictures Jesus' Galilean ministry and does so adequately; and we are able to leap backward from the sayings to the human psyche which stands behind the wisdom and reconstruct a mission and identity of a sage.

Scholars, especially those on the left wing of Jesus research, tend to test their coherentizing and intentional assumptions by checking elements of their reconstruction internally against other foundational sayings and against those in other primary sources.[68] Of course, historians typically argue for their revisionist Jesuses on evidentiary and methodic grounds: but they will claim their pictures to be more real than other Jesuses. Often the new Jesuses will be startling, inasmuch as scholars have produced them independently of the familiar action, plot, and passion of the canonical gospels. Such recommendations, therefore, have a kind of historical norming power and usually they are explicitly critical of Jesuses shaped by the narrative/canonical approach and of the developed evangelical traditions. Some of the sage Jesuses may aim the critique against churchified Jesuses. All of them will include badly needed recommendations for the Galilean world of the first century, and some scholars will even recommend certain edgy values for us today.

The question emerges, at what point do the historians enter christological waters? We would have to say that most historians of Jesus pose low-flying christological recommendations. We can easily call them christologies, if we use the term in a descriptive normative way, appropriate to historical conclusions. But when historians reject the canonical/narrative accounts and also pose a critique of certain church christologized Jesuses, they enter *a more explicit christological territory*, if only by way of the negation of some christology. The line between a descriptive-normative historical claim and a normative-normative christological judgment blurs when a historian starts to make recommendations to church and culture on the basis of a Jesus. Negating classical christological formulations sounds like an anti-christology, and recommending values on church and culture sounds like a constructive, alternative christology. The latter is close to the work of the theologian. Perhaps the theologian would term the descriptive-normative work pre-christological, that is, a christological form-in-waiting to be realized. In the proposal we are advocating here, a revisionist one, the christological promise of pre-christological forms must be actuated. These might be foundations for doctrine, for lifestyle, for the moral life, for the life of faith, and so on. But as revisionist theologians say, all the historical

---

procedure to be certain that Jesus was not like Christian receptions of him.

68. The new *criterion of coherence*.

recommendations must be drawn into a comprehensive christology.[69] As we say, a Jesuology is not a christology.

More conservative scholars within the sage paradigm follow the above steps but, additionally, bounce the sayings of the sage against developed evangelical traditions. Here, in a *new tendency criticism*, a theme in the sayings gets confirmed as scholars discover it flourishing in later synoptic tradition.[70] Such an added procedure gives scholars more to work with and accents the continuity in the developing reflections on Jesus. It may also mean that the sage is not only a sage. When is a sage a sage, and not, say, also a prophet or a teacher? One of the most difficult tasks is to determine the adequacy of modern categories, like sage, seer, and prophet. The difficulty rests not only in the ambiguity of the materials (and possibly within the figure of Jesus), but also in that scholars may recognize an overlap among categories. The sage is prophetic and something of a seer as well, but only if scholars construe the materials in the saying sources as tendencies which show up in the more developed 50–100 CE traditions.

From the liberal wing, the second procedure (bridging from the sayings of the sage to the developed tradition) seems like a tendentious effort to secure traditional christology, as if the sage could save traditional Christian claims for Jesus. These scholars stand on the earliest sayings of the sage to protect their procedure from intruding value. To those in the right wing, sticking only with the earliest-sayings sage seems capricious, almost perverse. *Why should we start with a hostility to the emerging Christian movement?* These scholars protect against a hermeneutic of suspicion by drawing the sayings into a larger christological plot. To the critics of the Third Quest, the intentional-guessing game on both sides seems speculative, and in the coherentizing of the sayings of the sage, they quickly recognize the insertion of value drawn from the historian's own world. They *play a Schweitzer* against the production of the sage and say that these scholars are finding in the sayings what they want to find.

B. Is the Sage a Jew?

As scholars construct Jesus-Sage, they face a new struggle, over the Jewish question in Jesus research. For the last couple of generations it has been an axiom of Jesus research that Jesus must be returned to the world of Second

---

69. Including the scriptural resources, the doctrinal and theological traditions, the liturgical and iconographical resources, the modern research on Bible and Jesus, studies in culture, and so on.

70. I.e., Q itineracy grows into a theory of discipleship in Mark.

Temple Judaism. Indeed, scholars have competed to out-judaize the Jesuses of their predecessors: the more Jewish the Jesus, *the more a Jesus portrait is immune to charges of Christian bias.* The Jewish Jesus has protected against church retrojections and for many generations of Jesus research the Jewish theme has helped researchers find freedom from the Christian doctrinal traditions.

In the Third Quest[71] the Jewish question plays differently, however. Jesus' Jewishness no longer needs to anchor historical integrity against Christian dogma. Indeed, christological pressures no longer choke the historical task; scholars continue to expand our knowledge of the Second Temple period; and, for the first time ever, historical work on the period has entered a post-Holocaust era. The minute one faces the new studies of Galilee, it is possible that the Greekness of Jesus, of Jesus' movement, and certainly of his environs becomes an issue. If it is the case that Jesus and his people are hellenized, if it is true that Jesus' world is substantially non-Jewish, or if he emerges in and with a subversive subset of the general culture of Galilee, we face again how he relates to his Jewish neighbors and ways. The scholarly discussion spreads across the spectrum. As we can imagine by now, the most radical view, that of Mack, has Jesus and the earliest Jesus movement as non-Jewish and living in a cosmopolitan, hellenized Galilee. More typical of scholars on the left is the impression that Jesus is Jewish but that his Jewishness is not much of a focus for his work per se (Crossan and Borg).[72] That is, here Jesus is not a figure who struggles with the meaning of Jewish identity, with interpreting Torah properly, with questions of holiness, etc. The center (Robinson) or the right (Witherington) among those who imagine Jesus as a Jewish sage tend to view his work as a program or reform within Second Temple Judaism. James M. Robinson, for instance, views the earliest mission as a critique of Israel for its lack of faith.[73] Schüssler Fiorenza's point has Jesus as a Jew allying with a subversive, prophetic tradition within Judaism against some dominant and oppressive expressions of the culture and

---

71. Theissen claims that it is typical and distinctive of the Third Quest to find Jesus within Judaism; the point is well taken, but refers more to the European side of the Quest and less to tendencies in the American conversation: Theissen and Merz, *The Historical Jesus*, 30.

72. As Keck correctly notes concerning the Jewish question, Crossan "seems unable to find Jesus affirming anything in his environment or heritage" (Keck, *Who Is Jesus?*, 29). In Keck's reading, Crossan's Jesus, while not ignorant of, separated from, or indifferent to things Jewish, finally plays the peasant class card against the Jewish religious card: ibid, 30.

73. Robinson, "The Image of Jesus in Q," in Meyer and Hughes, eds., *Jesus Then and Now*, 8.

Israelite tradition.⁷⁴ She represents Jew against Jew with a proposal to live out an alternative, egalitarian community.

The first strategy separates Jesus completely from Judaism. The second is certain that Jesus says nothing bad about Judaism. This view overlaps with a third, in which scholars find Jesus aligning with Israel's ancient prophetic tradition: Jesus can say nasty things about Jews because Amos does and because he allies himself with good Judaism against bad.⁷⁵ In other words, Jesus is a good Jew. A fourth strategy may overlap with the last two: namely, Jesus judges only certain Jews among the many of the first century. Then the guessing game is to identify his targets in relation to our knowledge of the groups. The most difficult issue here will be to determine Jesus' relationship to the Pharisees who, more or less, found the religion of Judaism.

Embedded in the de-judaizing tendency of the sage paradigm is a complex historical question. *If the sage is removed more and more from the Jewish world, do we not have more and more difficulty interpreting Jesus?* An interpretive network drawn from the "Jewish patrimony" would be no help.⁷⁶ Of course, the left wing of the sagists would be willing to interpret Jesus in (relative) isolation from the Jewish world. But, by isolating Jesus from a Jewish world, scholars have rather more difficulty explaining why Jesus evoked such opposition in such a short time (the *opposition criterion*) and why he was executed (the *execution criterion*). The only way to resolve these questions is to separate the Jews from opposition to Jesus and from his execution: undoubtedly, so to absolve the Jews fits nicely with other values that historians have (namely, *the post-Holocaust theme*).

Consequently, there may be moral reasons why so many Jesus scholars risk disrupting the rejudaizing of Jesus of the last generations of Jesus research. They face dangers, it seems, entering the rough waters of the post-Holocaust situation. We can only speculate here what they gain. But surely, we can sense the negative reason for the disruption: *a hyper-judaized Jesus no longer corrects Christian theologized Christs, since, for a hundred years under the influence of the apocalyptic paradigm, theologians have learned how to construct christologies consonant with a Jewish Jesus. Judaizing Jesus no longer serves critically to clean Christian christologies and thus it no longer has power to energize the questing protestants out there in the world of Jesus research.* For them there is more critical ammunition in turning away from the Jewish Jesus, toward a suave, cosmopolitan figure. Identifying the positive value in the turn is even more speculative, but it is not difficult to

---

74. Schüssler Fiorenza, *Jesus and the Politics*.
75. Schüssler Fiorenza's option.
76. As Keck and Wright notice; see: Keck, *Who Is Jesus?*, 67.

imagine that Jesus scholars see a judaized Jesus as tribal, exclusive, vastly too particularized to be appealing today, in a world driven by global and multicultural pressures. From this world, where toleration of difference is a minimal requirement, where the enjoyment of and cultivation of difference is the preferred expectation, a tribal Jesus is problematic.

C. Is the Sage a Cynic?

One of the liveliest discussions of the Third Quest is the proposal that the best analogue for the Sage is the cynic philosopher. The attractiveness of this analogy depends on following the steps in the invention of the Sage, outlined above. If one does not embrace the steps, the analogy seems almost ridiculous.[77] Instead, in order for the cynic theory to work, scholars must decide: to commit to one of the new Galilees, to cut Jesus (relatively) free from a Jewish world in Galilee, and to separate him (somewhat or completely) from a "religious" project, such as reforming Second Temple Judaism. Further, the cynic analogy depends on certain reconstructions of our knowledge of cynic philosophy as a movement.[78] But once we take these steps and turn back to the materials of Q1, it is quite easy to see the shape of a cynic philosopher forming before one's eyes. Indeed, properly understood, one can also see the shape of the cynic Jesus under the gnostic Jesus of Thomas.[79] Purge oneself of the passion, the familiar narrative connections, the longer connected plot; cut out the connection to John the Baptist and apocalyptic and dispel the sheep-fish-pastoral image of Galilee; then redirect the sage to a wider, maybe Greek world—and suddenly the only model that makes sense is of a roving philosopher. That sage becomes *cynic* when the themes of itineracy, begging, plain dress, and countercultural wisdom emerge as definitive.

---

77. Cf. the remarks by Reed: "Finally, it should be stressed that since Galilee lacked a substantial gentile component, had only two cities that were Jewish and in their infancy of hellenization, and lacked much evidence for interregional contacts via trade or otherwise, notions of Cynic itinerants influencing Jesus or his first followers seem improbable": Reed, "Galilean Archaeology," 122.

78. The discussion is endless, but it turns on questions such as these: do we have any evidence that cynics ever got to Galilee?; do we know if cynic philosophers ever touched lower classes in the provinces?; and can we trust knowledge of the cynic movement, since so much of the evidence comes from Stoics who caricature cynics?

79. Patterson's argument in *The Gospel of Thomas*.

D. Is the Sage Moral?

Possibly, the question itself is a strange one, since all humans have a morality and, perhaps, live in relationship to some vision of the moral life. Yet for Jesus research the morality of the Sage is very complicated. There is the general methodological issue in history writing: can one move from sayings and actions of a human to reconstruct an ethic operative in a past life? The question becomes doubly complex when the evidence is spotty and from questionable sources. For those in the sage paradigm of Jesus research, *discovering the ethic of Jesus is especially daunting,* since they rely on the cryptic aphorism and the like as the reliable access to a man and his causes. The genre of wisdom itself is extremely difficult to pin down contextually, since sages commonly save the wisdom of the people in the highest, and most bland, generalities. Of course, the radical anti-wisdom of Jesus is hardly bland, but it is cryptic and devoid of evident interpretive clues. "Let the dead bury their dead" knifes with power, but its power depends on the listener and/or the historian applying the interpretive and moral context. Even a list of knifing sayings alleged to be from a single sage may defy interpretation, unless one assumes that one saying provides the interpretive network for another or that a whole body of sayings (i.e., the whole of Q or the earliest layer of Q) provides the intelligibility for the interpretation of a single saying.

Even if one can settle on how best to supply the interpretive network for the cryptic aphorisms of a long-gone sage, one still faces further methodological issues. Does this saying, or even this body of sayings, represent a vision of the sage's vision of the moral life? Does it do so adequately? Do these sayings match a moral vision of a human, or are they random jottings, remembered for who-knows-why? Once again the interpreter or the historian must apply something to the interpretation of what comes without a narrative: in this case, a *coherence.* Do these fragments make a whole? Can we be certain someone designed the jigsaw pieces to be a picture, and one picture at that? Once scholars apply a coherence to the fragments, they face the further question: do the sayings, read morally, amount to a program, a moral campaign, or project? Thus, can we say that this sage crusades for certain causes? Does he have a mission?

At each stage of interpretation scholars make decisions based on assumptions that work to build up a sage with a mission. Even the most radical sage, that of Mack, has an anti-mission mission. Among all of the Jesus researchers who see Jesus as a sage, we find the *assumption that the sayings build collectively into a campaign,* even if it is, as in Mack, a campaign to deconstruct familiar campaigns. Thus, Jesus researchers show an extraordinary confidence that a batch of cryptic sayings can amount to a moral project, commendable to people, then and maybe now. They find support for their confidence in theories of strata, say of Q, and in bridging strata to an ideational development in a real community with a social history. The assumption here is that social crises generate new ideas which show up in strata of sayings.

Behind this common confidence rests *no agreement on the kind of mission of the sage*, however. Scholars build the moral project of the Sage in different ways. Of course, they conclude that Jesus represents this—and not that—position on a moral issue: where does he stand on the use of violence?; was he a pacifist?; did he really say, "Love your enemies"?; what is the meaning of his Temple fit?; etc. And they make judgments on an issue within the frame of *a presupposed, earnest moral project*. But more interestingly, each scholar locates the sage's positions within a framing whole that envisions comprehensively what Jesus is about as a campaigner. Is he primarily a campaigner about the narrow exclusivism of his day (Crossan, Borg)? Is he primarily a critic of colonial oppression and the effects it has on Israel (Crossan, the legacy of Horsley and others[80])? Is he primarily a critic of patriarchy (Schüssler Fiorenza)? Is he fundamentally a liberator from oppression (Patterson),[81] or a bemused critic of the way things go in the Mediterranean world (Mack)?

For instance, in a question spurred by our multicultural concerns: does Jesus represent fashionable inclusive values or is he an exclusivist? The question points scholars to Jesus' relationship as a Jew to Gentiles. We have already seen that many researchers are drawing Jesus away from Judaism: a less Jewish Jesus, or a less "religiously" Jewish Jesus, compared to the pictures of Jesus from the Bultmannian era.[82] Mack can handle this question easily: Jesus is not a Jew and he focuses entirely on Gentiles. But other researchers tiptoe through a minefield: everyone wants a Jesus to be inclusive, to be freed of narrow parochialism or immoral othering.[83]

Yet how does one loosen Jesus from Second Temple Jewish exclusivism without saying bad things about Judaism, things that Christians would not

---

80. Horsley portrays Jesus as a non-violent revolutionary set against the Roman colonial oppression of the Jewish nation: Horsley, *The Spiral of Violence*.

81. Patterson, "The End of Apocalypse," 43.

82. Recall that Bultmann assigns Jesus' ministry, his sayings and actions, entirely to the history of Judaism: Bultmann, "The Primitive Christian Kerygma," in Braaten and Harrisville, eds., *The Historical Jesus*, 15.

83. Lest one imagine that it is obvious that Jesus was an inclusivist, consult Dale Allison's argument that it was Jesus' exclusivism which offended people, not his daring openness: Allison, "Jesus and the Covenant," 72.

want to say after the Holocaust? If the sage focuses only on a Jewish world, he can be an internal critic. However, if he shames the faithlessness of Jews and replaces them at the messianic banquet with Gentiles (as Robinson puts it), does he not open the door to successionist theologies? These successionist theologies, suggesting that the church has replaced Judaism as the true Israel, have been fingered as dangerous in a post-Holocaust situation. Is Jesus an exclusivist? One of the appealing features of the sage paradigm is that it recovers the universalism of the Wisdom tradition. While it may have to close the door (somewhat) on Jewish particularity, that risk and cost is worth the price, since, for the first time in over a century, Jesus can speak easily to Gentiles.

Does the Sage Jesus tacitly endorse the colonial occupation of Palestine? The old question asked was whether Jesus was a Zealot, and mostly scholars found nothing that suggested he was a violent revolutionary; indeed, scholars were not certain there were Zealots yet in the first years of the first century. But in an era of Jesus research shaped by liberation theologies and post-colonial hermeneutics, the question takes on new urgency. After all, everyone seems to want a Jesus who stands against oppression.

Is the sage a patriarch? Does he endorse patriarchal values or lead a campaign to liberate women and men in the name of God-Sophia from the evil of patriarchy? Schüssler Fiorenza's sage emerges out of an emanipatory heritage, a minority, prophetic voice within Judaism, which we can find traces of with the proper hermeneutic. He eschews patriarchal values, encourages a congruent lifestyle, and even abandons the notion that God is Father. Jesus-Sage is not patriarchal, nor are his earliest followers, and we would see this liberative practice, were we freed of the "kyriocentric" and the repatriarchalized vision of the church. Other scholars' sages do not campaign against patriarchy as such, but do include women and those othered in their movements. James Robinson notes that the authentic materials imply that Jesus included women in a remarkable way, and his ministry disrupted gender and family roles, but, he argues, Jesus does not challenge the larger patriarchal culture.[84] Witherington argues that wisdom in Judaism is patriarchal and not liberative and that its and Jesus' view of God is thoroughly fatherly, even if he is inclusive.[85] Interestingly, however, both the enthusiastic and the critical position work with an implicit (christic) sense that a decent Jesus must be moral and would be opposed to patriarchal exclusivity, were he with us today. Undoubtedly, many researchers find the

---

84. Robinson, *A New Quest*, 8–9.
85. Witherington, *The Jesus Quest*, 178.

sage paradigm promising because of the daring way that the Wisdom tradition has used female images for divinity and for salvation.[86]

When we see the efforts of some Jesus researchers to construct Jesus as a moral crusader, when we see how strained their constructions are, when we see how little consensus there is on the sage's project, we face the nagging large question: *can we get an ethic out of Jesus?* Or can we get the ethic we want out of the sayings of a sage? What if the sayings do not touch the major ethical issues of his day? What if he does not address our issues? How do we proceed in light of these gaps? Typically, if a moral insight or demand is not *there* in the sayings—whatever that thereness would mean, it might be teased out of the contextual and holistic framing of a saying via coherence with other sayings or actions. And if a moral insight cannot be constructed at all in relation to the fragments of the sage, then it might be discovered by an analogical stretch from available sayings. Or if stretching seems tendentious, then possibly scholars can construct what Robinson calls an "ethical idealism," that is, a generalized principle or set of principles out of the wisdom of the sage which can be commended. Such an ethical idealism would pose a project for us based on the words, not actions so much, not plotline, and not the outcome, of a sage.

We may identify *three typical types of moral campaigns* among scholars within the sage paradigm: the restorative one, in which the sage crusades to reform Second Temple Judaism, possibly in the spirit of the indigenous, northern prophet Elijah;[87] the liberative campaign, aimed at colonial, patriarchal, and traditional-religious structures of oppression;[88] and the countercultural one, in which the sage brings trenchant insight that presses his pupils to see the world differently.[89] No construction of the historical Jesus can escape the Schweitzerian suspicion of retrojected values drawn from the interpreter and from his/her culture. Today we recognize that all historical research is retrojective and hermeneutically engaged, and that the drive to create a pure Jesus back there, free of our retrojected values, is itself a retrojection of value from a very particular time/place. It is fairly easy for contemporary critics to sleuth out the modern values in Jesus-Sage: many scholars, like Luke Johnson, Leander Keck, C. Stephen Evans, Keith Jenkins, etc., have launched this critique. Typically, these critics ally with the Herrmann-Kähler tradition and its Kantian-Kierkegaardian understanding of the relationship of faith and reason/history. As one of the insiders to the

---

86. Cf. ibid., 193.
87. Horsley represents this type fully: Horsley, *Whoever Hears You*, 261–63.
88. Crossan and Schüssler Fiorenza represent this type.
89. Mack comes to mind most immediately.

Third Quest, Theissen suspects, "The 'non-eschatological Jesus' seems to have more Californian than Galilean local colouring."[90] In one devastating sentence, he articulates the suspicion of all those hostile to questing: the sage Jesus could only emerge out of California, of all places.

On another level, the issue is not so simple, since *the sheer uncovering of retrojection does not solve the historical complexities*. After all, what makes the Sage Jesus rather more Californian than Bornkamm's Jesus was Germanic existentialist? The emergence of the apocalyptic Jesus was no less shocking and novel to the Victorians than is Jesus-Sage to today's apocalyptic orthodoxy. If we enter the hermeneutical room, in which retrojected values are recognized and on the table, then what privileges a certain constructed Jesus over against another? Is it that some Jesuses are free of retrojected value? Perhaps some do have less value thrown back on them and therefore they are better. Are we implying that there are safer values to retroject, ones that somehow allow more of the real Jesus to appear?

Seemingly, we return to the same three options at the end of every quest:[91] First, some version of the positivist position, which continues to claim historical objectivity and sees all value retrojection, wherever found, to be problematic in historical research. Here historical research must continue to work the evidence cleanly and free of the hand of the interpreter to produce the *realest* Jesus possible based on intelligent work with the evidence. If some scholars today step into the room of wisdom when they think of Jesus, their efforts will be judged entirely according to their presentation of the evidence. Second, some version of a fideistic type, from the faith community, which continues to have little faith interest in historical research on the figure of Jesus and which views questing to be misguided or dangerous to Christians. To view Jesus within the sage paradigm is simply the current version of a two-hundred-year mistake, since the real Jesus is the preached Christ of the church. Nothing new is to be discovered in Jesus Sage. Or, third, one of the both/and positions, which, for whatever reason, understands that there can be *a partnership of some kind between historical research and theological articulation*. Of course there are several models of how this partnership might look. The most familiar ones suggest that certain

---

90. Theissen and Merz, *The Historical Jesus*, 11.

91. Logically, of course, it is possible to redefine either the notion of history or of faith so radically that the engagement between history and a faith/theological claim avoids these three formal options. C. Stephen Evans redefines the nature of history and the conditions of historical knowing so as to make questing a support for traditional Christian claims. The Kählerians, I would argue, redefine faith away from any of its classic senses. In order to make the faith/engagement effortless, they make the ships pass silently at night.

or all christological claims might be confirmed or denied by good historical research. Witherington thinks Jesus-Sage shores up the main defenses in the christological arsenal, while Robert Funk is certain Jesus-Sage will trim away most of the outlandish claims the church has made about Jesus. Interestingly, both share the same expectation from questing: the return of the classic notion of partnership from the first quest in which historical research more or less should confirm or deny christology.[92] Behind these blunt positions is an almost unquestioned assumption among contemporary questers with theological interests: what shows up in Jesus-Sage pertains directly to the nature of Christian life and faith.

The first position risks hermeneutical naiveté and can never successfully duck the charge of retrojection. In addition, it has not faced the notion that its commitment to historical objectivity is itself a retrojected value. The second must defend itself against the perennial charge of docetism and the modern worry that Christian claims for Jesus are illusory or downright deceptive. The third, the formal position of most Third Questers with theological interests, shows the most promise but needs the most work. *Neither a simple appeal to the evidence, nor a simple discovery of retrojected value settles any issue of the partnership.* How does Jesus feel about colonial oppression? The evidence as such never simply gives an answer, and certainly not one that can be transferred to Christian life. Simply to see California in the sage does not cut it either, since that seeing of California comes from Atlanta or Heidelberg . . . or someplace else. What makes one constructive vision of Jesus preferable to another? Evidently, just as historians continue to develop the use of sources and methods, they must also *develop criteria for acceptable retrojection of value.*

While we are playing with the "California" theme, nonetheless we are not dealing with a superficial theme in Jesus research. We are not dealing with some minor application of the results of a scholar's Jesus research to, say, whether Jesus' struggle with authorities has meaning for baby boomers who still hate institutions. Rather, we are dealing with the fundamental methodological decisions a scholar makes in launching Jesus research. Why does a Crossan think that non-canonical sources get us closer to Jesus, while a Meier, just as knowledgeable a historian, sticks with the canonical gospels? Why are some scholars convinced that formal and material tensions within Q mean the developing of the Q tradition and particularly socio-historical developments in the Q community, while others see this construction as wild speculation? Why does one scholar opt to hear the evidence in an

---

92. In part, I believe, because of the disappearance of the Lutheran, existentialist, Kierkegaardian, Kantian presuppositions which dominated the periods of the no quest and the new quest.

apocalyptic key, when another has a gut hostility to that hearing? What triggers one construction and not another? What prompts one researcher to enter a new paradigm when another will not? Clearly, the answer to the question, is the sage Jesus?, depends on how a historian chooses to invent a Jesus.[93]

F. Does the Sage Die?

Of course, sages die. The question is whether there is anything interesting about the death of a sage. Here we pursue the question of whether there is any surplus of value in the death of the sage, and if so, how we should formulate this value. In their critical mode questers have often been suspicious of atonement theories: they appear to evoke the very kind of doctrinal bias good historical work unmasks. Under the apocalyptic paradigm, theologically interested scholars found ways to make peace with certain atonement themes. Most troublesome for historians have been strikingly mythic, meta-historical formulations, while low-flying, historized theories do better. Ransoms with the devil do not play well, while a self-sacrificial death at the hands of a colonial power has promise for those interested in atonement. But now with the emerging sage pattern, what role does the death of the sage play?

Three factors condition our questions. First, as scholars enter the sage paradigm, they are still not likely to be drawn to high-flying atonement constructions; indeed, some scholars, especially on the left, have no patience for any suggestion that the death of the sage begs for an interpretive thickness. What value can be found in the death of the sage must be historized. Those readings of passion which see the death of Jesus in grand salvific ways, are mythic overlays that speak to developing Christian theology, not history.[94] Second, few scholars today want to retreat from the steady gain of the generations of questing: that the death of Jesus must be seen as continuous with his life.[95] The death must be in keeping with his life, consonant with his life, inseparable in value from the course of that life. The point is that, while the death might be a historical surprise to the sage, it cannot carry

---

93. And to some extent on how one defines a sage.

94. Funk, "The Jesus Seminar," in Meyer and Hughes, eds., *Jesus Then and Now*, 139.

95. Such is a rich value retrojection onto the fragments of the Jesus saga. Or better yet, it is to construct a Jesus whose life and death are continuous in the same way that the New Testament spins the narrative. Contemporary value retrojections often continue those of the early church. We know of this connection because it is logically possible that Jesus' death was accidental and unrelated to the rest of his life.

categorically different value beyond what might be discovered in his life. It is a fundamental value of questing that the death of Jesus must be no value surprise. That is, historians know they must account for the death of Jesus and put it within a historical, not meta-historical, intelligibility. Finally, in the post-Holocaust situation of the Third Quest, no one wants to blame *the Jews* for the death of the sage. As we have seen, the Romans are convenient scapegoats in the project to absolve the Jews of the death of Jesus. This campaign usually employs a post-colonial hermeneutic in which the guilt of the death can be channeled to the favored sins of colonial oppression; less predictable, however, is the campaign to move the death of Jesus out of the world of religious explanation. *The death of Jesus cannot be a religious issue, in part, because making it a religious issue would open the messy issue of Jesus' relationship to the Judaism of his world, and possibly, the unpleasant issue of theological sadism.* The sage is not centrally a *religious* figure, not really focused on what we might think of as religion, and his death is not a religious event. It does not evoke the issue of sin, except as corporate oppression, and it does not deal with the Jews' relationship to the God of Israel.

G. Is the Sage Ironic?

The sage is indeed an ironic figure. The apocalyptic prophet rages like John the Baptist and takes his stand on a denunciation of the evils of the age. He will have no truck with civilization, denounces the city from the wilderness, and demands that the righteous separate themselves from evil. He will not compromise even if he loses his head.[96] The sage is just as critical but cooler with his critique of the way of the world; he is able to travel among the villages with quipping insight into the foibles of the day, but not with a Manichean renunciation. The critique of the sage is mellow, even when it stings, and often it is informed by a worldly affirmation. It might react *flippantly* toward social conventions, and by example of countercultural behavior and by iconoclastic zingers, it presses people toward new insight and new patterns of life. But the sage does not burn down the barn and he may not embark on any campaigns or social programs of reform.

Consequently, we face irony. The ironic sage, the one who meets experience with ironic comment, gives voice to ironies within the culture, to competing world constructions and incommensurable themes in tension within cultures. The most powerful of these arise out of a complex relationship with the critique of reigning values, mentioned above. While the sage may share elements of the prophet's critique of the world, he departs from

---

96. Such is the caricature of apocalyptic thinking within the sage paradigm.

the prophetic pattern of denouncing, abandoning, rejecting, and withdrawing. The sage comments on the world, educates, redescribes the world, and evidently works with very different techniques from that of the apocalyptic prophet.

Under the eye of suspicion, Jesus-Sage is an ironist in part because Jesus researchers are haunted by ironies of questing, among other ironies. Consider these unresolved issues in questing as they bear on the production of the sage paradigm: First, most scholars read the entire history of questing to be dominated by the sayings of Jesus. There are a variety of reasons for the focus on the message of Jesus in the different phases of questing. Yet advocates of the sage paradigm, particularly those of the Jesus Seminar, think that the sayings of Jesus have never really been understood by questers. Consequently, *to produce a new Jesus, they turn to the very sayings of Jesus that created the apocalyptic prophet.* To reverse the earlier interpretation, they proceed with different methodological decisions and spotlight their own values, even as they fight the apocalyptic paradigm over the evidence. The more they succeed at a sapiential reading of the sayings of Jesus, the more they show how fragile and value-laden is their edifice. Jesus looks this way if . . . And what would prompt one to take up that *if*? The *if* would be answered by a second *if*: if one chooses to see the issue in this way. And what would prompt one to see the issue this way rather than that way? If one held these values . . .

Consider a second irony of the research. Historical research requires locating a historical figure in the particularities of a culture, yet the more particularized the reconstruction, the less transferable value. In the case of Jesus research, the more particularly Jewish a Jesus, the more he is a problem for a world that seeks to be inclusive. Good historical sense works against the application of value, not simply because history changes, but because in this case, a particularized Jewish Jesus presents value that has to be repudiated today: exclusivism. *Generalizing of value is useless for the contemporary world and particularizing of value is deadly.* How to solve? Turn to the tradition of radical wisdom and find a feisty sage who says pointed things that are particularly . . . generic! So the sage turns emphatically against the generic establishment.

Then, the movement into a post-modern era of the academy has pressed onto Jesus research a third irony, that between historical plausibility and historical objectivity. So far as scholars have been trained in the craft of modern history writing, they know they must be fair to the objective evidence in the sources. And even the most radical of the contemporary Jesus researchers (e.g., Mack) claim to read the evidence of the primitive Jesus movement better than others. Such is the objectivism of historical research, even when it recognizes the hermeneutical turn. Yet many researchers of the Third Quest have turned the burden of proof around so that *constructions of the figure of Jesus need only be plausible within the evidence*. At times they seem to launch Jesuses that function simply to deconstruct reigning Jesuses from the apocalyptic paradigm or from church tradition. Other times they launch a putative Jesus which claims space simply in the absence of counter-evidence. These are methodologically uncharted waters, especially since, in the absence of *criteria of acceptable plausible constructions*, the more one plays the plausibility card, the more one accents the values the researcher brings to the research. Obviously, no simple appeal to the evidence can secure for good the fragile nature of this historical endeavor.

A fourth irony rests in an achievement of the history of Jesus research: the growing recognition that the historical Jesus can be found only where researchers have carefully *located Jesus in his social-historical world*. In the early years of modern questing, the impulse of this historical intuition worked primarily to prune the Christian, dogmatic debris from the Jesus figure. As Julius Wellhausen said, Jesus is a Jew and not a Christian. Indeed, research on Jesus underwent waves of re-judaizing of Jesus' ministry and of the earliest Jesus movement; indeed, Gerd Theissen speaks of locating Jesus within Judaism as a hallmark of the Third Quest.[97] Yet today, certain Jesus researchers are unconvinced by the results of the judaizing of Jesus, and, thus, we have before us one of the *great divides among contemporary Jesus researchers*. The one party favors the notion that Jesus is best understood against the life of Israel, as a figure who seeks somehow to renew Israel. The other looks to a wider Mediterranean world against which Jesus works. Two different Jesuses, two different projects, two different social worlds, two different Galilees; the irony in the Galilee point is that it may lead away from the long-standing critical judgment that Jesus' project must be seen entirely within issues facing Second Temple Judaism, and into the hazier world of a Hellenistic iconoclast-sage who does not work with what we call religion. On the one hand, an honored achievement of Jesus research seems to be disappearing; on the other, scholars have not discovered a rich social world for the sage. So far the sage seems a-social and a-historical while good historical research would instantiate Jesus in a concrete social reality.[98]

A fifth irony overlaps with the point above: *the a-social sage seems to proclaim a very individualized program*. The Kingdom of God, if at all an

---

97. Theissen and Merz, *The Historical Jesus*, 10.

98. Perkins suggests that Mack gives such an a-social reading of the Jesus figure (an "antisocial individualist") that he cannot even account for the development in the Q collection and community he presupposes for his portrait of Jesus: Perkins, "Jesus before Christianity," 749.

operative image, articulates the sage's proposal that people envision a world different from the one dictated to them by society. Wise ones stand alone and against. Non-conformity is the high value. If so, we have a vision of the "Kingdom" that lies *in tension with the sociological turn of so much of recent New Testament research*. We face the difficulty of figuring out how there could be a community of wise loners. Finally a sixth irony appears when scholars ask about what themes the sage poses a non-conformity. Against what ideas, what cultures, what themes and values do wise ones stand? Among the researchers on the left, some like Mack think that Jesus is indifferent to or untouched by the concerns of Jews in Palestine to define what Israel means in the period of the Second Temple (Mack). Perhaps wise ones oppose colonial oppression, as in Crossan? Or they may oppose patriarchal structures, as in Schüssler Fiorenza? The typical reconstruction of Jesus-Sage has him leading a group of individual itinerants away from hometown, from family, from ordinary work in the world, while they are loyal to him as the master. The independent non-conformity of the wise ones seems to pull against the schoolishness of the master-pupil relationship.

H. The Retrojection Critique: Testing an American Jesus

The pictures of Jesus-Sage emerging in some of the recent historical scholarship can be quite shocking.[99] Some of these pictures unnerve the pious in the long-standing tradition of historical research on Jesus; less evidently, but just as dramatically, some depart significantly from the apocalyptic paradigm, which dominated both New Testament research and theology in the twentieth century.[100] For a century, historians told theologians and pastors that Jesus was some kind of a prophet who preached the end of time and the imminent coming of the Kingdom of God. Meanwhile theologians got busy debating the meaning and timing of the Kingdom, and what Jesus' life, message and death did for the coming of the Kingdom. More or less, *historians identified the real Jesus with an exit strategy from life in this world*,[101] while

---

99. Though we need to be cautious not to accent only the radical themes. There are plenty of recent Jesuses which avoid the sensational.

100. There were a hundred spins on determining what it means to think of Jesus as an eschatological prophet. Here we are interested neither in charting all the varieties and nuances of meaning within the historians' apocalyptic paradigm nor enjoying the theological richness of twentieth-century theological responses; rather, we focus on the issue of change of culture as it bears on Jesus research.

101. Exit strategies can be literally apocalyptic (see Mack, *The Lost Gospel*, 134, 139; Patterson, *The God of Jesus*, 180, for a critique of Jesus as a Jewish apocalyptic prophet) or more metaphorical, as in various otherworldly, existentialist, religious, or privatized

twentieth-century theologians passionately converted the apocalyptic into livable, worldly forms for the life of faith.

Obviously, twentieth-century theology came to discover that the apocalyptic Jesus was not as threatening as Schweitzer thought. In its reaction we see the *domesticating pattern, that familiar questing rhythm of historical discovery and theological recovery* that goes back to Reimarus and the founding of the quest. Perhaps, it was the crises of Europe during the war-and-depression eras which made the apocalyptic Jesus seem familiar and full of meaning. Surely, theologians knew that, so far as they kept their eyes on the apocalyptic prophet (via the alien criterion), their imaginative transformations of the apocalyptic for faith could be warranted. That is, as they developed their translations of Schweitzer's apocalyptic Jesus, they discovered the perfect cake-and-eat-it-too: *they had the comfort of the real Jesus in front of them, yet they knew how to derive real meaning from the alien one.* Despite the worldview in which Jesus appeared, theologians knew he really meant the metaphorical, or the otherworldly, the critical, the mystical, the existentialist, the privatized, or the liberative-prophetic translations of twentieth-century apocalyptic. The historians brought to the table assurance that theology had the real stuff while the theologians worked up hermeneutically sophisticated ways to put it to use.

This arrangement represented a *happy alliance between history and theology*. History launched a Jesus with sufficient difference for him to be taken seriously in the wake of Schweitzer, and historians and theologians picked up *the different one* and brought him home in theologically viable conversion vans. To some, the arrangement looked too cozy. Hard-nosed retrojection sleuths noted that Schweitzer's alien Jesus was being tamed by the likes of Barth, Bultmann, Pannenberg, Sobrino, and a whole lot more in twentieth-century theology. They saw in the theologies of the apocalyptic paradigm either proof of the failure of questing, or worse, the unstoppable power of the retrojective imagination, in which the very tool to protect against retrojection (the alien and different criteria) had been co-opted by retrojected value.

We know, but often forget, that the retrojective imagination can domesticate. We know that theologians need to be armed with insight and standards of protection against domestication. But we have to be very careful when we identify the exact failure in the taming of Jesus. Against many views, we argue that the failure in domestication is not that scholars convert elements of his world and ministry into viable forms for life and faith; it is, rather, that *domestication can be a form of manipulation*, aimed at taking

---

pieties.

away the edginess of some feature of the Jesus saga. **(Theological) Rule 83:** *Theology needs to guard against domestication of Jesus and reads that kind of retrojection as manipulation.* A more generous reading of the theologies spawned by the apocalyptic paradigm suggests we have, not retrojective failures so much, but a fulsome array of value-rich conversations with evidence in the Jesus saga. More often than not, the conversations modeled well a successful partnership between historical research on Jesus and theological deployment of it, since these conversations so often emerged with meticulous attention to evidence, critically secured, from the saga, and hermeneutically sophisticated re-enactments of Jesus' relation to the coming of the Kingdom. They were *models of revisionist theologies.*

In the twenty-first century the earlier alliance is no longer so sturdy, as we have seen, since many Jesus historians have abandoned the apocalyptic prophet in the judgment that the paradigm would not hold the evidence any longer.[102] Historians tend to abandon paradigms by an appeal to evidence, of course, and it is conceivable the evidence really had burst apart the paradigm. *Theologians, however, need to be suspicious of any appeal to the evidence, as if it had a voice of its own:* **(Theological) Rule 84.** We know a simple appeal to evidence never solves the large interpretive issues in history writing, and certainly not in Jesus research, even though we would also insist that evidence has a role in paradigm change. Today many Jesus historians are abandoning the apocalyptic paradigm entirely. Other scholars are rethinking apocalyptic in dramatic ways,[103] even as others rally to defend

---

102. For a summary of many of the difficulties in conceiving of Jesus as an apocalyptic prophet, see Patterson, *The God of Jesus*, 164ff; Mack, The *Lost Gospel*, 124, 134–36. Patterson announces the end of theologies informed by the apocalyptic paradigm, ibid., 177. We note that historians routinely speak of the difficulty of historical paradigms through the language of choice of sources and methods, on the one hand, and of bias, on the other: such judgments we reject as only partially adequate to explain paradigm shifts.

103. Cf. Wright's view that Jesus *uses* the available apocalyptic for his ministry, since it provides "the only set of metaphors adequate to express the significance of what will happen" (*Jesus and the Victory,* 208). Interesting exceptions are: Dale Allison who aggressively defends the apocalyptic paradigm as a contemporary Schweitzerian (see his case, *Jesus of Nazareth,* 39–44) and who takes a Weiss-like move on the theological significance of Jesus' apocalypticism; and who places Jesus firmly in the "eschatological piety" of Second Temple Judaism (Vermes, *Religion of Jesus,* 117), but as a Jew has no (positive) Christian theological agenda. Two things in Vermes intrigue: 1. his notion that Jesus studies have powerful, negative significance for christology (Christian religion is essentially a mistaken reading of Jesus; see *Religion of Jesus,* 8–15). And 2. Vermes' intense effort to locate everything in Jesus within options of Second Temple Judaism ends with a very pleasant and reasonable, *protestant* Jewish Jesus. See Vermes' efforts to steer Jesus clear of the cultic-ritual-holiness side of Judaism and of the rabbinic-midrashic theme toward an intimate, ethicized trust-God charismatic Judaism: ibid.,

the apocalyptic paradigm from attack. Theologians, of course, stand outside the historical debate, though they do need to keep alert to the deeper value issues under the surface discussions of evidence and method. For our purposes we do not need to settle on a path through the current interpretive disarray, but we should think of the theological consequences of thinking of Jesus within the new paradigm, that of the sage.[104]

It is easy for theologians, and not only anti-quest ones, to suspect that we are dealing with a first-world, cultural change expressing itself as disease over the older way to think about Jesus.[105] An increasingly apocalyptically minded culture finds little surplus of meaning in an apocalyptic Jesus: he has lost his critical difference and has become too much likened. In other words, an apocalyptic Jesus would not arm us sufficiently to sustain and transform a world really falling apart.[106] Many historians and theologians seem to be saying that the real Jesus represents a different ideal, an inspiration, not an exit: perhaps we need a hero, maybe a mythic figure, who aids us as we construct a picture/policy strong enough to face a dying world.[107]

74, 114-18, 139-48. One can suspect Vermes is domesticating Jesus in a surprising way to make Judaism (!) palatable for modern consumption. The idea that Second Temple Judaism can be pinned down as the "imitability of God's loving kindness" is both astonishing and predictable (ibid., 204). In either case an apocalyptic Jesus is, apparently, bad news for modern humans: irrelevant or badly needing cleaning. This insight is important for the argument that follows.

104. Of course, it is more than ironic that the new reading of apocalyptic among some Jesus researchers emerged at a time when first world cultures faced an actual growing apocalyptic consciousness.

105. There may be generational changes among scholars also that account for new ways to think about Jesus.

106. Jesus historians of all stripes seem to have embraced the "Christ transforming culture" model of H. Richard Niebuhr and emphatically disavow the Christ-against-culture orientation of apocalyptic (as they read it), so far as that model flushes this world. See Borg, "Jesus and Eschatology," in Charlesworth and Weaver, eds., *Images of Jesus*, 142, for instance.

107. See Patterson's reading of the theological options left after Schweitzer: bland moral liberalism or a world-negating theology of the apocalypse: *God of Jesus*, 180. Cf. the typical end-of-this-world-order theme of millenarian cults and cultures in social-scientific research: Dulling, "Millennialism," in Rohrbaugh, *Social Sciences*, 198. We should note that there are species of apocalyptic and of millennial thought that *are* revolutionary of the political order: Jesus and his movement could be among those. Among those historians who remain within the apocalyptic paradigm, the positions divide between political apocalyptic and an apolitical form. While the political options are by far the most winsome for historians, Sanders, Theissen, and a few others head in an apolitical direction. Among sapiential types only Mack holds out for an apolitical message from Jesus. The point is that we have an age that craves a political Jesus and believes that an otherworldly Jesus is not the real Jesus: Schüssler Fiorenza, *Jesus and the Politics*, 113.

Whether our suspicion is accurate or not,[108] we have a warrant for including a critical theology of culture component within a quested christology. After all, dramatic cultural change puts new questions to historical research and we want to know if historians are conducting new conversations with the Jesus saga.

Critics of questing look at the new Jesuses and wonder if the historians have learned any lessons from Schweitzer. Indeed, they argue that recent Jesus historians continue to do with modern methods and questions what the liberal Jesuses did in the nineteenth century, namely, make a Jesus in the image of the cultural ideals of the era.[109] The charge is that *they have created an American Jesus*, who is a wonderful picture of leading American values but who has little to do with first-century, Mediterranean, Jewish life.[110] The critics have been all over the Jesuses of the Third Quest and find predictable values in them. What stands out among the themes and differences is the notion that Jesus is an advocate of inclusion and an enemy of exclusion. The favored word of the Third Quest is "marginalized," to identify Jesus' concern for those who have been excluded from power and dignity in his world: women, the poor and unhealthy people, those who are shamed and dehumanized. Jesus' campaign would include the marginalized in God's reign.[111]

Today's critics of questing commonly see in the Jesus of the marginalized *a figure crafted to address the American struggle with cultural difference, one who can articulate the gospel of multiculturalism*. It is hard not to agree with them, in the sense that the *inclusive Jesus* emerges at a particular time and place in the history of the quest. No one mistakes Crossan's Jesus with that of Schweitzer or Harnack. However, the values of a Jesus who enfranchises the marginalized run into difficulty when scholars conceive Jesus within the apocalyptic paradigm. As Mack writes, "How could an

---

108. With a good bit of suspicion Wright sees many Jesus scholars reacting against the apocalypticism of popular American evangelicalism; in this reading historians, as liberal academics, are participating in culture wars that have divided American society for thirty years or more and their Jesuses are deliberately countercultural: Wright, *Jesus and the Victory*, 39–43.

109. Cf. the stinging critique of the Jesuses of the Jesus Seminar people for mistakes in methods influenced by American values and culture wars: P. Jenkins, *Hidden Gospels*.

110. See John P. Meier's criticism of the liberal, American, academic values of so many Jesus researchers in: Meier, "The Present State," 460–87, and Meier's sense for the contemporary values in contemporary Jesus research, "Reflections on Jesus-of-History," in Charlesworth, ed., *Jesus' Jewishness*, 84–87. See also Gowler, *What Are They Saying*, 115.

111. Even centrist, right-wing, and non-theologized Jesuses today seem to favor a gospel of inclusion: see Meier, *A Marginal Jew*, I, 6–9, for his elaborate defense of the *marginal* category for Jesus and his people.

apocalyptic hero also have offered instruction for living in his present messy world?"[112] Consequently, Mack and others sought to overturn the apocalyptic prophet paradigm in favor of a vision of Jesus as a sage. Evidently, among many American Third-Questers *apocalyptic* means Left-Behind world-denyingness, and a world-denying Jesus cannot help generate a morality for a world in crisis.

So what about the sagey American substitutes for the apocalyptic prophet? No construction of the historical Jesus can escape the Schweitzerian suspicion of retrojected values drawn from the interpreter and from his/her culture. Today we recognize that all historical research is retrojective and hermeneutically engaged, and that the drive to create a pure Jesus back there, free of our retrojected values, is itself a retrojection of value from a very particular time/place. Students of the quest know that paradigm change commonly bespeaks a subtext of profound value change in the culture. So naturally, contemporary critics of the quest (like Luke Johnson, Leander Keck, C. Stephen Evans, Craig Evans, Philip Jenkins, etc.) have had a field day unearthing the modern values in Jesus-Sage.

Suspicion is fun. Locating hidden value is good detective fun. Revealing the real story behind the apparent is even more fun. But the historiographical issue is not so simple, since the sheer uncovering of retrojection can be as blinded as endeavor as the retrojection it reveals. And in certain cases the blindedness comes with an unbecoming arrogance that does not see the log in its own eye. In any case, revealing suspicion does not resolve the historical complexities. Even when we find manipulation and anachronism in the Californianized Jesus, we have not thereby determined whether the inclusive/exclusive conversation with the Jesus saga should be banned. That judgment would require a historical study of things that look to us as *inclusivity* in Jesus and a comparative-cultural study between those items in their world of value and ours concerning the social and ideological instantiation of exclusivity. Logically, it is possible that we could have a very Californian conversation with Jesus without it being manipulative. As we have seen, when suspicion uncovers hidden value, it does so from some value. When anti-questers ridicule trendy values in the left wing of Jesus research, they do so by participating in a pervasive, retrenching cultural defense happening in most areas of first world cultures. So there! *I have just given a retrojective critique of the retrojective critique used on the American Jesus.* Both critiques say something true about the new Jesuses; both represent the values woven into our study of the historical Jesus.

---

112. Mack, *The Lost Gospel*, 31.

If we really take seriously that there is "no Switzerland of the mind" in Jesus research (Meier), we return to the question: why is one nation of values superior to another? What makes Jesus-Sage more intolerably Californian than, say, Bornkamm's apocalyptic Jesus was Germanic existentialist? Notice that we ask the question, not expecting neutrality, but only that we recognize that value colors historical constructions. We ask the question, not seeking freedom from perspective and value, but only from manipulative anachronism. Interestingly, in the swirling winds of Jesus research those associated with more centrist or conservative positions today tend to favor the once-radical apocalyptic model for Jesus. Yet the emergence of the apocalyptic Jesus shocked the Victorians more so than Jesus-Sage does today's apocalyptic orthodoxy. If we move beyond positivism into the hermeneutical room, if we really do recognize the pervasiveness of value and put our perspectives on the table, then what privileges a certain constructed Jesus over against another? Is it that some Jesuses are free of retrojected value? Hardly. Do some have less value thrown back on them? Possibly. Are some Jesus historians more self-critical and more explicit about their values and perspectives in history writing? Definitely. Undoubtedly, some historians set in place more critical checks against manipulative value intrusions. Are we implying that some conversations with the Jesus saga are better and others essentially off limits? Are some values safer to retroject, either because they are insignificant or they somehow allow more of the real Jesus to appear?

Value is pervasive in the construction of Jesus-Sage. Therefore, there are good reasons to be skeptical of the whole business of questing after the historical Jesus. Undoubtedly, these American Jesus scholars are doing exactly what Schweitzer discovered about the lives of Jesus from the nineteenth century. They are giving us glorified self-reflections under the label of Jesus. No doubt, contemporary Jesus researchers are modernizing Jesus. They are creating a Jesus to fit the world of alienated, first-world, bourgeois, mostly American, liberal, mostly male intellectuals who are in despair over our institutions, over the state of our society, with the oppressive systems and traditions that dehumanize sizable portions of the world's underclass. They have invented a Jesus, as they are discovering Jesus, who is a giant in the moral struggles they value, one who must first deconstruct the oppressive systems of the world in order to build an agreeable, humane place.

This Jesus is perfectly made for an alienated liberal. There are other Jesuses that could be invented but this one valorizes the liberal despair about the way things are going in the world and thinks Jesus, if he is any good at all, ought to help us fix the messes. The salvation here has little to do with a never-never land, but has much to do with the murder rate in Chicago, the destruction of the rain forest, the homeless and undernourished masses:

an appealing Jesus for certain populations who do not have much faith in governments and social institutions, who see churches as essentially dead, who are busy but cut off from the gospel, who are dismayed by the growth of right-wing religion and the return of spiritless, legalistic, moralistic Christianity. This Jesus is perfectly tailored for the educated, liberal American baby boomers who are now in their mature years, who are looking up from their busy-ness, only to discover their families, their towns, their country, their world, and their planet are in disarray. This Jesus fits perfectly within the new apocalyptic consciousness which is dawning among educated and liberalized populations of the first world. Behind him is a deep despair over the future among people who are bombarded daily by the sense that everything about our world is falling apart, just as they are discovering that they, too, are falling apart.

But the new Jesus researchers know they cannot respond to the apocalyptic crisis by selling society a Left-Behind Jesus. The Jesus for an apocalyptic age cannot be a Jesus who tells people to give up on the world: back your bags, sell the farm.[113] No, the real Jesus, the Jesus we need, must energize those who live in apocalyptic paralysis. The real Jesus has to disrupt our patterns. The real Jesus must cut down our dragons and calm our panic and excite our hope that things can still be changed in this world. Many new Jesus researchers seem to be finding a christology for a world of apocalyptic dread. But first they have had to dump two other Jesuses: that Jesus of popular piety in its current therapeutic form, and the Jesus of ecclesiastical-academic authority. They seem to read the former Jesus as Freud would interpret all religion: it is Linus' security blanket. However much this Jesus makes us feel good, it still distracts us from the real christic battlefield. The Jesus of church and academic authority, of doctrine and creed, of learned paradigm implicitly is also a danger, because he participates in the slimy world of tainted institutions and powers. Instead, Jesus has been reared for the transformation of the world and all its institutions in an age of Western downward mobility.

What are the salient features of these American Jesuses? At this point we will simply itemize nine main themes:

---

113. Dale Allison's determinedly apocalyptic Jesus is the most aggressive exception to the patterns of the new Jesuses and, as such, supports the argument here. Deliberately critical of the new Jesuses, Allison, as a quester himself, offers up a Jesus fully within the Schweitzerian mold: religiously Jewish, apocalyptic, judgmental, ascetic: *Jesus of Nazareth*, 102–3, 172, 217–18. Tellingly, the same Allison can find little of meaning to retrieve in his historical Jesus. Allison's Jesus is a nightmare for the inventors of the new Jesuses, as he is emphatically otherworldly, ascetic, grumpy, apolitical, mistaken about the eschaton, and absolutely useless for fixing the world: ibid., 218.

1. It is very important for recent American historians to identify Jesus as *spiritual figure*, interested in cultivating the spiritual life of his followers. He shows relatively less interest in religion, as we know it: in cult, in ritual, in interpreting Torah and the like. Decidedly, these historians are certain he is not a midrashist and that he conducts himself either with sovereignty over Torah or relative indifference. Consequently, even as many American historians know they must imagine a Jewish Jesus, their Jesuses may relax the Law or at least spiritualize the Law into its essence. Certainly, he is no legalist but advocates humane and gentle values.

2. As a *charismatic*, he conducts himself with immediacy, swagger, and self-authoritativeness toward Law and cult and tradition and mores. His charismatic sense of mission seems to bypass institutional structures of religion, even without criticizing them. His charisma is immediate and he seems to conduct himself with an immediate relationship to God independent of temple, rabbi, priest, even scripture.[114] We are dealing with a subtle and complex issue here in Jesus research. Among scholars disposed to constructing a liberal Christ out of the Jesus who relaxes the Law, the natural move is to emphasize the critique of legalism. This Jesus holds up the essential spirit of the Law against, say, Pharisees who are formalist and wooden in their attention to detail. To accent the spiritual freedom of Jesus, however, risks setting back the achievement of recent Jesus research: namely, to put Jesus within a generously reconstructed portrait of Second Temple Judaism.[115]

---

114. Sanders, *The Historical Figure*, 238–39.

115. So we have an irony of contemporary Jesus research: scholars want a Jewish Jesus and yet, many want to locate his christological significance in his spirituality. Borg, for instance, gets a lot of mileage out of his four-stroke portrait of a spiritual giant. A spiritual Jesus commonly opposes, ignores, or transcends the trappings of *religion*: cult, law, traditional morality and the like. And while such a picture may actually emerge out of the liberties of an itinerant charismatic, it does indeed appeal to this era's hostility to *organized religion*. While we may not be able to determine whether a spiritual Jesus has a basis in history, we do have to worry that an appealing liberal christological theme may house latent, and possibly unthematized, anti-Judaic ramifications. How difficult it is to honor Jesus' freedom in relation to the law, without turning the theme into an unsavory picture of Judaism. To be blunt about it: can a *spiritual* Jesus be a Jewish Jesus? Or if he is so spiritual, can he be really Jewish? And how can one emphasize his spirituality without accenting (alleged) defects in Judaism: that it is wooden, fossilized, oriented to legalistic formalism etc.? And of course, such an accent works against the powerful achievement of contemporary research on the New Testament: treating the figure of Jesus within a living religion. It appears that a Jewish Jesus and a so-called spiritual Jesus (as defined above) are in tension; indeed, to find the so-called spiritual Jesus squarely within Judaism may inevitably set up an insidious anti-Judaic situation

3. The American Jesuses *eschew doom and gloom judgment*, whether of the apocalyptic or of an authoritarian or of an anthropological sort. Jesus has little to do with end of the world madness, with the establishment, or with grim views of human nature, education' and jurisprudence. Virtually every contemporary Jesus researcher is certain that there is no theme of judgment in Jesus. Whatever they may say about the rigor in Jesus' ethic, they do not want it to be judgmental. The God of Jesus is no Judge of sin,[116] not one fixed on repentance,[117] but one who gently reaches out to the victims of life.

4. The American Jesuses typically aim at *worldly values*. They are far from asceticism or world-denying themes.

5. The this-worldly Jesuses turn *away from privatized, individualized pieties, and therapies*.

6. They are therefore more interested in *social issues*. The Jesuses of many American historians and others represent inclusive concern for the poor and outsiders.[118] Jesus is essentially the Good Samaritan who bypasses purity codes and attends to the needs of outsiders.[119]

7. These Jesuses envision the *Kingdom of God as essentially worldly*. We can say the Kingdom stretches beyond the world, if we do not think of a crazed, apocalyptic David Koresh or of old-fashioned Christian otherworldliness.

8. According to most of the Jesus researchers Jesus is *compassionate* and he represents a compassionate God. In message and in deed he conducts himself in the mode of the Beatitudes: extending God's concern for those who are weak, failed, lowly. As Sanders says, *the God of Jesus is lenient.*[120]

---

in Jesus research: the more spirit one finds in Jesus the more bad things one says about his Jewish world, since his spirituality plays off the inert, legalistic and formalistic in Judaism. Oddly then, the danger may be: *the more Jewish is one's Jesus the more anti-Jewish is one's Christ.*

116. Sanders, *The Historical Figure*, 203. "Jesus was not given to censure but to encouragement; he was not judgmental but compassionate and lenient; he was not puritanical but joyous and celebratory. Yet he was also a perfectionist": ibid., 204.

117. Cf. Sanders' campaign to purge repentance talk from Jesus' message: *The Historical Figure*, 229–33, and Meier's critique in *A Marginal Jew*, II, 149.

118. Sanders, *The Historical Figure*, 226–33.

119. Luke Johnson notes the irony: typically, Jesus researchers want a Jesus who is a Good Samaritan, while the actual parable in Luke may not be genuine according to the standard criteria used by many Jesus researchers: *The Real Jesus*, 26.

120. Sanders, *The Historical Figure*, 202; Sanders, *Jesus and Judaism*, 119.

9. Finally, the new American Jesuses tend to be *upbeat*. The Jesus researchers want to dissociate Jesus from doom and gloom postures, for whatever reason. This motive seems to comport with a concern to flatten the apocalyptic in Jesus. Instead, Jesus is "joyous and celebratory."[121]

I. Preliminary Judgments

Now, many elements of the portrait are appealing. But it is not the picture that Witherington and Wright produce as they pitch traditionally to traditional Christians who may want assurance that what they have always believed can be confirmed by historical research. The striking American Jesus is a fully modernized Jesus. But it is hardly alone as the only modernizing picture. All Jesuses are modernized, after all. Every sermon modernizes Jesus. Popular piety modernizes Jesus. Historians modernize Jesus, even when they seek scientific objectivity. Jesus researchers modernize Jesus even when they are worried about modernizing Jesus, even when they are conscious of Schweitzer's warnings about self-reflection. Here we argue that there is only a difference of degree between what popular piety does with Jesus and what the best critical historians do with him: only a difference of degree between what faith does in picturing Jesus for an age and what reason does in determining a generous, factual portrait of Jesus. One difference is *the degree of methodological self-consciousness*: does the handling of the Jesus figure contain enough critical checks which allow the evidence about Jesus to have otherness independent from our self-interests? Another difference is in the degree to which a picturing of Jesus is conscious of and builds *checks against manipulative retrojection*.

It is possible that the above caricature of the American liberal Jesus sounds cynical and a reductive fodder for the anti-quest perspective. But in the argument we are developing it is no big deal, and certainly not shocking news, when a picturing of Jesus modernizes him. Therefore *historians and others need to get over avoiding modernizing and focus on manipulation:* **(Quest and Theological) Rule 85**. Theologians have another agenda too: *modernizing is one means by which we find, even produce, what is christic about Jesus*. Modernizing is the means by which people bring Jesus into the conversation they are living. It is one means by which a dead guy lives today.[122] By itself it is no danger, either for good history writing or for faith, *if* it is done critically, with an ear to resisting evidence and a sensitivity to ideological uses of Jesus. The danger lies where Jesus is a sheer self-reflection of the

---

121. Sanders, *The Historical Figure*, 204.
122. And essentially a spiritual activity of Easter.

inventor of this Jesus, where Jesus can have no otherness to the historian's self-project, where Jesus has been totally co-opted into the service of the inventor's self-project. There Jesus is a sheer invention when he should be inventively imagined and not a sheer fantasy. *In the ideal invention, a Jesus emerges in a dialectic of discovery and imagination.* I make this claim, knowing full well that *both the discovery side and the imaginative side are dialogues which need to be put into dialogue.* The perfect example of the *double dialectical relationship* can be found in the recent gender conversation with the Jesus saga. It is a new, illumining conversation with the saga and comes with some good news and some bad, as we know. But without both results, faith and theology and learning cannot grow. Revision is possible.

Therefore, we are not prepared to follow Luke Timothy Johnson who rips apart the American Jesuses and shows that their value rags prove the failure of all questing. His claim is that after critique there is nothing of the real Jesus in these American Jesuses.[123] We argue that Johnson's criticisms are often on track, if somewhat reductive and positivistic in their epistemology. But we can embrace his criticisms and still think questing serves faith and theology. Johnson has a point: for his ecclesial audience the real Jesus is not what the historians come up with when they are questing, not because what they come up with is unreal about Jesus so much as that historians work up only a partial Jesus, relatively cut off from the experience of faith and the worshipping life of the church. In other words, their failure (from the vantage of Christian faith and theology) is not the historical mistakes they are supposed to have made. Rather, their so-called failure is that they do not do a comprehensive christology (and many have no interest in such). A historical Jesus can contribute to a christology but it is not a christology in drag, as both Johnson and some historians seem to think. *A historical Jesus is always pre-christological, a christology in waiting, waiting to be played by an interested party:* **(Theological) Rule 86.** For christology the real Jesus is not simply the historical Jesus, and surprisingly, it is not simply what the canonical gospels picture for us, or what the creeds and the councils and the liturgies capture of Jesus either, not because they are unreal, but because they may be plural and dated modernizations of Jesus. However authoritative they may be for Christian identity, nonetheless, they must be tested today against two standards: contemporary experience and the current lived life of faith.

Today we work up the reality of Jesus in a critical conversation among all the Jesus pictures, and the leading configurations of our experience and

---

123. Here I am focusing mostly on the left-wing American Jesus and de-emphasizing now the centrist and right-wing advocates of questing.

the contemporary fabric of faith. The real Jesus is not back then in first-century Galilee, simply. The real Jesus is not frozen in the pictures of Jesus in the canonical gospels, simply. The real Jesus is not simply saved in the formulations of the creeds and councils nor in the confessional symbols or the dogmatic ideas of the great theologians. The real Jesus is not simply in the contemporary experience of the Spirit. And the real Jesus is probably not some essentialized substrate that attempts to bring unity to all these different, modernized Jesuses. *The real Jesus, we suspect, is the history of Jesuses intelligently re-enacted in light of the great Jesuses of the past, the contemporary scene, and the current experience of faith in the worshipping community:* **(Theological) Rule 87**. In that mix in which Jesus can become realized for understanding and faith, historical work on Jesus can play an important role.

J. Christological Opportunities in Sophialogies

If we assume that it makes good sense to construe the figure of Jesus within the sage paradigm, what theological issues do we face? The first one is surprisingly familiar, since it mimics formally the situation of theology when scholars decided that Jesus should be considered an apocalyptic prophet. The first issue turns on whether we can determine if Jesus self-consciousnessly understands himself as Sophia-God's definitive mouthpiece or not.[124] Historians continue to think that it is a good idea that Jesus knows what he is doing. Many imagine more christic opportunities if they can uncover a Jesus who, in the full light of consciousness, knows what he is about, who has an intentional, not accidental, mission, and who sees himself as a or the divine agent. Jesus-Sage, thus, is more theologically interesting if his wisdom includes a crafted, self-reflexive identity, a mission, and an intentional connection between identity and mission. Were these items missing in a historical reconstruction, most scholars assume, there would be less to work with theologically. So both a liberal like Schüssler Fiorenza and a conservative like Witherington hold to the very same conviction (that the evidence suggests that Jesus saw himself as embodying God's Wisdom), and the very same method (that the historian can move from sayings/actions to a self-consciousness). To be sure, for Schüssler Fiorenza it is unlikely or historically doubtful to suggest that Jesus thinks of himself as Sophia, and, indeed, it would be immoral to overlay the good-hearted message of Sophia's prophet with kyriocentric notions. Meanwhile, Witherington thinks we have evi-

124. Here we set aside the idea that the Sage presupposes a *collapse* of God into the divine agent and alter ego, Sophia.

dence that amounts to a sophic self-consciousness, and thus, christological considerations are appropriate to the historical reconstruction, and not simply the optional theological meditation on the work of the historian.

Schüssler Fiorenza makes an indirect and implicit move while Witherington employs a full-bore explicit christological application. Schüssler Fiorenza's approach is more typical of the questing style of the twentieth century, while Witherington returns to elements of the nineteenth-century quest, though in a positive voice: namely, the same method allows confirmation of Christian claims rather than destruction of them. He is certain that we can cross from actions and sayings of the historical Jesus to the self-consciousness of the Sophic One, so that Jesus can be said to have a christology. The position, dependent methodologically on Schleiermacher's christology, works causally and presupposes that there must be coherence and continuity between the external works of a person and his interiority. In this view, where we find this continuity, we have historical support for Christian claims for Jesus, and thus, one kind of continuity (say/do to a self-consciousness) anchors another kind, namely, that Christian claims for Jesus are appropriate to his history. The conservative position, then, finds in the sage paradigm exactly what christologically interested questing has always hoped for: confirmation of, or at least warrant for, christological claims.[125]

The liberal position does not wear christology on its sleeve. Indeed, it often plays its historical work as anti-christology, as in Mack's non-Christian reconstruction of the earliest Jesus group or of Schüssler Fiorenza's hostility to the church's tradition of kyriocentrism. In such positions, historical work clarifies by critique and boldly rules out some christological formulations on the basis of historical claims. Consequently, the liberal position too has (negative) christological interests, obverse ones from those of the conservative questers, and reenacts the enduring confidence of questing, that historical research on Jesus has christological significance.

Many liberals also want to have a constructive christological resolution to their questing. They go beyond their critique of possible christologies and pick up the argument from continuity *by positing a continuity between what Jesus says and does and that of his earliest people.* His followers continue his lifestyle, in the trendy language of the Third Quest. In a Mack, the continuity is of a philosophical life which the disciples share with the Sage in a pre-Judaized, pre-Christian innocence. In a Schüssler Fiorenza, the liberative, egalitarian practice of Jesus continues in that of the earliest

---

125. Or the inversion for another interpreter of the Sage: the disproof of traditional christological claims.

community. Both imagine disruptions in the continuity, but nonetheless there is *a consonance between the project of Jesus and that of his first followers*. Of course, it is central to the liberal sage argument that the continuity between Jesus and his people gets wrecked by the church, by the Christians, by the cultural forces of oppression, etc.[126] But the consonance itself places even Mack and Schüssler Fiorenza, however radical their work seems to some, on the side of traditional questers.[127] The authentic Jesus movement has a moral and uncluttered clarity to it, on the basis of which it is possible to clean house. Mack makes it clear that the christianizing of the pure Jesus is foolish; Schüssler Fiorenza sees the ugly head of patriarchy in the growth of kyriocentric christologies. *Jesus is a moral figure and his earliest people recognize his moral concern and live out his lifestyle appropriately*. Where liberals part company is over the nature of the lifestyle, whether it is a campaign and whether it should be read as a politically charged one. However one judges that issue, Jesus-Sage is a moral leader and evokes a life pattern from his people who continue his ways.

J.1. The Novelty of the Sage

The most suggestive christological opportunity about the new Jesus is his novelty, the novelty of a break with an established paradigm, in this case, that of the apocalyptic prophet. New paradigms for the historical Jesus generate new christologies, of course, just as new needs and values generate new historical Jesuses. The emergence of a new Jesus routinely appears with a critique of an old Jesus, deemed unacceptable any longer. Thus, *the christological opportunity of a new Jesus brings with it critique of old Jesuses and the christologies they foster*. Once again we see the protestant character of Jesus research, even when it is conducted by Roman Catholics and secular scholars: namely, it proceeds by critique of the established and finds a purer possibility in overturning what had been accepted and in discovering an earlier Jesus. *This earlier Jesus is cleaner and has the normative capacity to undermine cluttered christologies*. For instance, Jesus-Sage may vault over Christian receptions of Jesus (Mack), or patriarchal constructions (Schüssler Fiorenza), or fossilized, organized religion (Borg). In each case the sage figures in a myth-of-Christian-beginnings construction.[128]

---

126. The disruption of continuity points to the protestant character of questing.

127. Vs. Reimarus' effort to drive a wedge between Jesus and his disciples.

128. In Robert Wilkin's phrase. Ironically, *the-myth-of-Christian-beginnings* logic works most powerfully in Mack who uses the pure Jesus-Sage to undermine Christian receptions of Jesus: Wilkin, *The Myth of Christian Beginnings*.

What is new about the Sage is protestant iconoclasm: Jesus the iconoclast.[129] Interestingly, it is not just that sophialogical questers tear down the Christs of faith (a task long completed) but that they feed off the work of earlier historians. It is not just that some current questers deconstruct the apocalyptic orthodoxy, it is that they picture *Jesus as an iconoclast himself. An iconoclastic use of an iconoclast!* Jesus' wisdom deconstructs the world as people live it; it is countercultural and presents new options for value and meaning. It is a radical wisdom or even an anti-wisdom,[130] and thereby takes its stand against the status quo valuing of popular wisdom. Tellingly, it deconstructs the apocalyptic perspective for historical studies on Jesus at a time when theologians had learned to make peace with the apocalyptic paradigm, the established catholic position of the twentieth century. Today on the liberal extreme we have a Sage, formally similar to that of the nineteenth century,[131] whose message of radical wisdom does not imply a connectedness to divine Wisdom: this Jesus-Sage is his own man and is no self-conscious agent of God or a founder of religion, least of all Christian religion. Typically, the moderate liberal position moves cautiously about connecting the wisdom of a sage to claims about his self-consciousness. An implicit connection instead is all that can be discovered. Meanwhile on the conservative pole the Jesus-Sage represents, even embodies God's Wisdom (i.e., Patterson, Witherington) and even the effort at collecting the sayings of the sage is an exercise in christology.[132] The conservative position typically moves from the message of the Sage to his self-consciousness. These are explicit sophialogies.[133]

Of course, sheer novelty has virtue, as people may see missed historical nuance and christological opportunities for the first time. But the newness factor is more complicated than it seems. Repeatedly, scholars express surprise at the new Jesus they find in their researches. The Jesus that emerges in the new paradigm surprises them. They are reassured by their surprise, again, because being surprised by the shape of the new Jesus is to be protected against the retrojection critique. So powerful has been the Schweitzerian critique of retrojection that contemporary Jesus researchers scramble to insulate themselves: by *discovering* Jesus, by being surprised by what they find, they have proof that they are doing real history, real historical research

129. Funk, "The Jesus Seminar," in Meyer and Hughes, eds., *Jesus Then and Now*, 139.

130. Patterson, "Pensive Provocation," 10.

131. Where, in old liberal style, the teaching of Jesus stands opposed to the emergence of the church: cf. Perkins, "Jesus before Christianity," 749.

132. Patterson, *The God of Jesus*, 10.

133. Witherington, *Jesus the Sage*, 381.

and not theological musings. Passing the *surprise criterion*, then, is essential for the integrity of the historian's research. And every new Jesus is a surprise to those who leap into the new paradigm, and every critic of every new Jesus bets a lifetime of scholarship that there are no reasons to be surprised by the new Jesus. *The surprise is exactly what the Jesus people want, exactly the surprise already dimly anticipated in the emerging worldview of the Jesus researcher.*

J.2. The Egalitarianism of the Sage

In most reconstructions, the Sage is a figure who stands against oppression. The motif is hardly new, inasmuch as the apocalyptic prophet could be a critic of oppression also. But the moral edge of the Sage's message directs us to *democratic values*: "Jesus' Kingdom of nobodies and undesirables in the here and now of this world was surely a radical egalitarian one, and, as such, it rendered sexual and social, political and religious distinctions completely irrelevant and anachronistic."[134] Indeed, Jesus' actions, such as his healings, symbolic acts, exorcisms, and certainly his itinerary, strike against the religious and cultural establishment. We can discover the distinctive critical edge of the new sage by focusing on the objects of critique. One object presents itself immediately: *Jesus-Sage is a critic of patriarchy*. We have seen Schüssler Fiorenza's well known reconstruction, where Jesus-Sage takes on the patriarchal structures of Mediterranean and Jewish societies. What is interesting here is not simply that Jesus is of eqalitarian sensibilities, or that such values may be modern retrojections onto Jesus;[135] rather, it is the fascinating issue of *added value*. Why must the critique of patriarchy be added to all the critiques of the apocalyptic prophet? Why does it deserve a place of honor among the critical guests? More centrally, why does the gender-egalitarian Jesus press the switch into a new reconstructive paradigm, that of the sage, instead of the prophet? Evidently, there are more values afoot than hostility to patriarchy.

Scholars who launch an anti-patriarchal sage must be careful not to play the critique of patriarchy against Judaism. According to the ethos of contemporary Jesus research, it is *unacceptable for Jesus to be hostile to Judaism*. Jesus-Sage can be separated from Judaism or rather indifferent to Judaism, but he cannot be hostile: according to the research expectations of

---

134. Crossan, *The Historical Jesus*, 298.

135. Cf. Witherington's critique of Schüssler Fiorenza's Jesus in the language of Judith Plaskow: "My essential criticism of her work is that she modernizes Jesus, making him an advocate of a politically correct egalitarianism": *The Jesus Quest*, 165.

decades of re-judaizing of the earliest Jesus movement and the moral canon of post-Holocaust historiography. Consequently, a Jesus-Sage must be virtually removed from Jewish life, or become a Jewish critic from within and represent an "inner-Jewish renewal movement."[136] The fascinating thing about this renewal movement is that it should not look like religion, like a religious crusade, like organized religion, in our language. *It can be neither hostile to Judaism nor too religious to satisfy the values of the day.*

The egalitarian point then can play against Second Temple Judaism but not if it plays on the *religious* turf so as to undermine the integrity of Judaism. Jesus-Sage can attack the patriarch of Jewish life as a good Jew (Schüssler Fiorenza); he can go after the Judean aristocrats who are driving the Galilean peasants into poverty and who side with the Roman colonists (Crossan). He can hint that ritual-sacrificial-Jerusalem-centered life of holiness is undemocratic (Crossan, Borg) or that the Second Temple Judaism got constrained by colonial life to narrow its borders too much. *But he cannot say or imply that Judaism is dead or that Torah has been abrogated.*

J.3. The Flight from Judgment

Clearly, the sage must be non-violent and eschew the violence of end time, as we have seen in the critique of apocalyptic.[137] On a more worldly stage, the sage also opposes colonial oppression: here we have a theme given prominence in the work of Crossan. We have seen the critique of the apocalyptic paradigm and have noted the widespread discontent with the notion that Jesus is a prophet of the end times. Interestingly, it is the theme of judgment tied to the coming of the Kingdom of God which many within the sage paradigm find absent in the earliest materials. True, there is plenty of judgment in the synoptic tradition, but if one turns to Q and to the earliest layer of Q, one does not find the theme of judgment. Indeed, according to Kloppenborg's influential reconstruction of the life history of Q, the earliest layer contains no judgment: none of the grim apocalyptic message of John, no threat, no exclusion, not even a decent battle with the Pharisees.[138] All these themes appear in Q2. For the sage enthusiasts, *apocalyptic* means the grim judgment of a wrathful God who will destroy the world to bring the Kingdom of God.[139] That is, in apocalyptic they think of John the Baptist

---

136. Witherington, *The Jesus Quest*, 165.

137. Crossan, "Eschatology, Apocalypticism, and the Historical Jesus," in Meyer and Hughes, eds., *Jesus Then and Now*, 110; Patterson, "End of Apocalyse," 43.

138. Mack, *The Lost Gospels*, 37–47.

139. Schüssler Fiorenza thinks the judgment theme enters the Jesus saga at the

roaring about repentance in the wilderness and they want nothing to do with this kind of religion.¹⁴⁰ While liberal interpreters abandon this apocalypticism entirely, conservative interpreters tend to emphasize that the real sage brings, not judgment, but a soothing word of grace.

More subtly, sage enthusiasts frequently redefine the apocalyptic. It indeed sounds like doom and gloom, but the real meaning lies in a metaphorical intensification of badly needed judgment of a social or communal sort. Central to this reconstruction of apocalyptic is Kloppenborg's theory that Q1 is devoid of apocalyptic and that Q2 materials represent a later position of Q community after it encounters opposition in Galilee. As Mack spins it, the Q community reacts with anger and judges those who have not joined them. And importantly, they use the form of apocalyptic thinking to level their judgment. Here we have a novel interpretation of apocalyptic and one, significantly, that explains apocalyptic by decoding it out of its familiar meaning: divine culmination of history. That is, *apocalyptic is not fundamentally a religious event, and certainly not an act of divine anger.* According to Mack, people resort to apocalyptic forms in a crisis, to "justify a social program in trouble." As he puts it, "Apocalyptic language was entertained at points where social formations and programs were in need of additional mythic or fictional rationale."¹⁴¹ So, not only does the explanation move apocalyptic away from its religious significance, it naturalizes the theme of judgment into *the shunning of the group*. Here Mack reads apocalyptic as an ideological thickening for social cohesion or revenge, at a time when social niceties like conversation had ended: "mythic rationalization for their rejection."¹⁴² With such a view of apocalyptic, that apocalyptic is a mythic-rationalizing-attack ideology of defensive people, it is no wonder that scholars spare Jesus-Sage from having to pronounce a word of judgment. In this reconstruction people were not attracted to Jesus because he preached apocalyptic judgment, but because he envisioned for them a better way to be in the world.

Within the liberal wing of the sage paradigm, where liberationist sensibilities have been internalized, scholars suspect that a judgmental God would sponsor an oppressive world construction. It could be the oppression of a colonial sort, as if God were playing the game of the emperors, or that of patriarchy, where the suspicion is that *God is the chief architect of a system*

---

point of the patriarchalizing of the movement: *Jesus and the Politics*, 170.

140. See Mack, *The Lost Gospel*, 134–36, on the left and Witherington on the right: *Sage*, 170.

141. Mack, "Lord of the Logia," in Goehring et al., ed., *Gospel Origins*, 7–8. It is difficult not to hear a portrait of our own apocalyptic era in this characterization.

142. Ibid., 8.

that oppresses people and especially women. It is patriarchal and imperial religion which is into judgment and the hardness of heart. Schüssler Fiorenza, for instance, separates Jesus from the message of wrath and judgment of John the Baptist[143] and performs exegetical marvels to achieve the egalitarian message of Sophia-God. Patterson, further, sees a warrant for the sage in that the apocalyptic paradigm is wedded to the violence of end time.[144]

Why is it that this sage opposes judgment? Because judgment opposes wholeness in this reading, and wholeness is a high value inherited from liberationist and feminist sensibilities.[145] It is evident that the liberal wing of the sage paradigm understands apocalyptic judgment to foster doom and gloom and an unhealthy otherworldliness. Were the sage to be a critic of the way of the world, he would have to be a "positive" one who affirms as much of the world as possible.[146] After all, a judging Jesus would be too grim to celebrate the goodness of life. From the eye of suspicion it is evident that the sage paradigm has been constructed by a generation of scholars who viscerally react against the doom and gloom of the apocalyptic prophet and who recoil from popular apocalypticism in our culture. They want a playful, but world-useful, Jesus who celebrates life in the world. He is to be a witty and urbane ironist, who knows how to throw a good party: "It is difficult to crack a joke if you think the world is about to end."[147]

J.4. The Flight from the Establishment

The new Jesus is apt to crack a joke. More exactly, he may make an ironic quip designed to bring to consciousness an awkward reality or a witty challenge to an accepted way. Typically, *according to the sage paradigm, Jesus uses an array of wisdom forms for iconoclastic purposes. The Jesuses of the Third Quest must be countercultural or subversive.* As Robert Funk says it, the Jesus-Sage is "a powerful critic of sedimented institutions and orthodoxies."[148] Interestingly, the sage stands against things that have become fossilized and doctrinaire. Of course, Schweitzer's apocalyptic prophet once stood against the

---

143. Schüssler Fiorenza, *In Memory of Her*, 119. Cf. Witherington, *The Jesus Quest*, 168: "Like Crossan, Fiorenza dismisses all material that might suggest that Jesus spoke of God's judgment or wrath or the need for atonement for sins."

144. Patterson, "The End of Apocalypse" 43.

145. Witherington, *The Jesus Quest*, 168.

146. Crossan, "Eschatology, Apocalypticism," in Meyer and Hughes, eds., *Jesus Then and Now*, 110.

147. Cf. Funk, "The Jesus Seminar," in Hughes and Meyer, eds., *Jesus Then and Now*, 137.

148. Ibid., 139.

way of the world, against European Victorian culture, and against reigning church theologies. But now, as we have seen, this prophet appears to many Jesus researchers to be one more sedimented orthodoxy. Consequently, they turn away from the domesticated prophet of the End. The iconoclastic sage, instead, appears to offer critical insight against stultifying structures.[149] Note how central is the use of *subversion language* in the sage paradigm.[150]

When scholars decide that behind both the primary texts (Thomas and Q) is an antique, itinerant charismatic movement, they have set in place a Jesus who is firmly and permanently anti-establishment. Jesus is an itinerant charismatic and his followers mimic his lifestyle. Whether or not one reads the movement as Christian is not so important as the sense that he and his people represent a radical social movement that pushes against the grain.[151] *Jesus is countercultural.*[152]

J.5. The Turn to Difference

If one trims away the remnants of the apocalyptic construction of Jesus, what is left? We have a sage who is breaking new ground for us in his attention to violence and oppression, one who stands against the powers that be in the world. One important value clusters with the flight from the establishment: it is the notion that *Jesus-Sage invites his people faithfully to be different*. The concern not to conform to the reigning patterns, to be countercultural, need not take only the form of opposition to oppression. It can be a more gracious, philosophical permission to be out of step with typical values of the people. Undoubtedly, this permission arises from the opportunities of the cynic hypothesis, but also from the contemporary attention to multiculturalism.

---

149. "Even a partial recovery of Jesus of Nazareth will serve to purge the clogged arteries of the institutional churches, arteries blocked with self-perpetuating bureaucracies and theological litmus tests designed to maintain the status quo. His voice will redefine the nature and parameters of the Christian life. The recovery of the historical figure of Jesus may well serve as the catalyst of a new beginning for the Christian movement as it enters the third millennium": Funk, "The Jesus Seminar," in Hughes and Meyer, eds., *Jesus Then and Now*, 139.

150. For instance, Crossan, *The Historical Jesus*, 263, etc.

151. Theissen and Merz, *The Historical Jesus*, 41.

152. Keck, for instance, notices how much Crossan privileges countercultural values in his interpretation of Jesus: *Who Is Jesus?*, 29.

J.6. The Turn to the World

The overwhelming theme of the sage is his this-worldly orientation and message.[153] The sage says no to transhistorical doom and gloom. He rejects the futurism of apocalyptic thinking, with its devaluing of immediacy. He does not think in the dualisms that periodize history. And he certainly does not advocate sitting on one's hands, waiting for God to do the dirty work in the world. No fatalism here; no apocalyptic paralysis allowed.

Behind the turn to this world is a discontent with the otherworldly eschatology of the apocalyptic paradigm.[154] More than anything, *it is the theme of a cataclysmic end to history that disappears when scholars turn to the sage paradigm*. Indeed, their choices of primary sources (i.e., Q and Thomas) guarantee the "presenting" of all eschatology: as Theissen says of Thomas, "Therefore the kingdom of heaven is both within human beings and outside them, and equally present at all times."[155] Crossan, for instance, makes it clear that eschatology in Schweitzer's sense (e.g., apocalyptic eschatology) means world-negation.[156] *Apocalyptic eschatology* means a negation so thorough that a prophet judges the world cannot be fixed, changed, or improved; only a divine coup will clear the decks. If we think within the apocalyptic frame and are horrified by a God who destroys the cosmos, then our only option is to retreat to Africa with Schweitzer. Why? Because the Jesus who proclaims a God who would wipe out the world and bring history to an end is historically wrong and immoral, and we cannot get value out of such a monumental mistake. But in Crossan's famous phrase, how is it possible "that the wronger they [the early Christians] were, the stronger they were?"[157] *The apocalyptic paradigm then makes the emerging Christian movement unintelligible.* It would make much more sense, Crossan argues, if we abandon thinking of Jesus within the apocalyptic paradigm.

But the rejection of an apocalyptic frame for salvation is complex. First historians need to employ a social-historical orientation in their history writing. They turn away from ideas and the world of so-called religious ideas[158] and favor concrete social conditions. Then scholars must embrace

---

153. Patterson notes that the pessimism of the apocalyptic paradigm was a Euro-invention that never fit into the American consciousness: "The End of Apocalypse," 32.

154. Ingolfsland, "An Evaluation of Bart Ehrman's," 183; cf. Keck, *Who Is Jesus?*, 78.

155. Theissen and Merz, The *Historical Jesus*, 40.

156. Crossan, "Eschatology, Apocalypticism," in Meyer and Hughes, *Jesus Then and Now*, 110.

157. Crossan, "Eschatology, Apocalypticism," in Meyer and Hughes, eds., *Jesus Then and Now*, 110.

158. In an interesting twist, the sagist Borg charges the judaizer Sanders with

the worldly theology of creation of the Wisdom Tradition and find in it world-affirming opportunities for Jesus. They notice that Wisdom lives in a world far from the doom-and-gloom world of John the Baptist. Its home is in the happy issues of health and wealth, of beauty and fortune, of eating and working together, and of marriages and families that work well.[159] The world is ordered and moral for Wisdom. *The great advantage of the sage paradigm is that it can honor well elements in the Jesus saga which have been left orphaned by the apocalyptic paradigm.* Compared to the dark and grumpy proclamation of John the Baptist, Jesus' message is remarkably worldly. It affirms nature, beauty, human enjoyment and celebration, and the primal orders of creation. Jesus-Sage can even be the gentle Physician when healing is needed.[160] Unquestionably, *accenting the worldly aspects of the Jesus saga is refreshing.*

Of course, the actual world is not as well-oiled and cheery as it appears in Proverbs. Scholars within the sage paradigm cannot imagine a Jesus who would simply affirm the values of this world to which they turn. There are too many things wrong with his world, wrong with our world. Consequently, they must turn to the radical tradition within Wisdom and suppose that Jesus-Sage must find his identity in the heritage of a Job or Qoheleth or the Wisdom of Solomon. The world is broken; the moral order upset. The tradition of radical Wisdom teaches Jesus-Sage to expect an inversion of the upset world, a righting of the wrongs, based on the moral expectations of the Creator. Indeed, this is the meaning of the image, "Kingdom of God," for Jesus-Sage. Within this reconstruction, scholars separate Jesus from cheery, popular wisdom and turn the critical edge of his work, hitherto founded on the recognition of the divine end of the age, to Wisdom's restoration of the created order. In the spirit of a sapiential theology of creation the brokenness in the world can be repudiated and opposed, because of the Sage's insight into the goodness of creation. Here is a this-worldly critique of elements of this world that aims at transforming, not destroying the world.[161] Consequently, the world-denying elements assumed to be central to the

---

abstraction from the real Jewish world, since Sanders tends to focus on ideas, not social realities. That is, what counts for a Jewish work is up for grabs, and Borg, under the influence of Vermes here, favors social realities as more real than ideas. Similarly, he thinks Mack's extreme vision of the Sage is abstract and without a real context: Borg, "Portraits of Jesus," 5, 8.

159. The eye of suspicion sees the values of mega-churches of suburban America.

160. Witherington, *The Jesus Quest*, 192.

161. Crossan, "Eschatology, Apocalypticism," in Meyer and Hughes, eds., *Jesus Then and Now*, 110.

apocalyptic paradigm are channeled into social critique in a different, affirming sort of renunciation of the world.

The move to draw upon the radical Wisdom tradition is brilliant, for it achieves two badly needed results: first, it completes the victory over the apocalyptic paradigm. By appealing to the radical Wisdom tradition scholars have before them sources that integrate apocalyptic into a sapiential frame: i.e., Daniel, Wisdom of Solomon, Parables of Enoch, etc. The pattern of integration then inspires contemporary Jesus researchers with an interpretive caveat for any apocalyptic residue that remains in the earliest Jesus materials. We have already seen that scholars in the sage paradigm set most apocalyptic elements to the later Caligula or Jewish War periods. And we have seen that they often assign a metaphorical reading to apocalyptic themes that cannot be tied to later dates. Now we notice that anything apocalyptic that sneaks into Jesus-Sage's message (i.e., possibly the Son of Man theme) can be interpreted as the typical blending of themes in radical Wisdom tradition. Jesus-Sage learns the ropes from this tradition where royal, prophetic, and sapiential themes are commingled.[162]

Second, the move to radical Wisdom roughs in the plotline for the *salvation* offered by the Sage: *discerning and living the new life of spirit*. Within this world the wise one discerns who walks in the way of the Spirit and who does not. Therefore, the sage paradigm presses with it a subtle sectarian-protestant and gnostic orientation.[163] Whether this cast of thought is logical only or causally historical remains to be seen. James Robinson argues that there is a typical trajectory of development within the unfolding Jesus saga: that sapiential thinking tends to move toward gnostic thinking.[164] That is, there is a universalizing tendency in the saving of the wisdom of the sage that supports the gnostic potential of wisdom. In any case, the movement leaves behind historical-end time specificity, and trudges beyond the first application of the wisdom of the sage. But to what *telos*, we might ask? To discernment itself, possibly. At one point Mack suggests "self-awareness" as the alternate concretion for the message of the sage, and possibly toward "personal transformation."[165] Even more comprehensively the goal may be toward envisioning a world ruled in a transformed way, a world without

---

162. Witherington, *The Jesus Quest*, 185. Note that no single category system seems to work to capture the figure in the Jesus saga. Note also that moderate sage enthusiasts and centrist apocalyptic types believe that the sage vs. apocalyptic prophet set up of this discussion is defective. They argue that by Jesus' time apocalyptic and wisdom were blended together.

163. Even if it tends to seek out the sect of those who are not exclusive!

164. Robinson, "LOGOI SOPHON," 104.

165. Mack, "The Lord of the Logia," in Goehring, *Gospel Origins*, 8.

the Caesars in charge.[166] Those who are saved discern and act according to another way of being in the world: they live in the spirit. Jesus-Sage works as a gnostic Jesus for a spiritual age.

As we have seen, behind the turn to the sage paradigm stands a discontent with the particularity of the Jewish prophet of end time. The particular, especially as it is rooted in a historicality tied to the fate of Israel, appears to be exclusive of others and too tied to an established religion. Having a Jesus rooted in organized religion, with its ritual and legality, in the scandalous particularity of the Chosen People—having such a Jesus hardly appeals to a spiritual age. Instead, it is the cosmopolitan, rather universalized message of a secular sage which resonates. When Koester and Robinson note that the wisdom tradition in the ancient Mediterranean world contains an inherent tendency toward gnosticism, unknowingly they offer a clue why the sage paradigm seems to be winning the day.[167] *The sage can offer de-particularized, de-historized wisdom for an age that wants to be generically spiritual but not religious, for a (liberal) culture that is deeply troubled by tribalism.* But the sage may have to gather a secular tribe of followers who stand against tribalism. This tribe is that of the discerning, ones who bring to Jesus a laundry list of complaints. The sage valorizes what they have seen in their fits of complaint. At times he seems to energize the spiritual ones to make a difference in the world; at other times he seems only to permit them to live out private, countercultural ironies. At times the sage presses for level-headed critique and rebuilding of the social order; at other times, the sage only can console those who feel helpless about the bigger picture of life.

In this worldly picture of Jesus as a sage, many will hunt for a little old-fashioned religion. They, like Leander Keck, may complain that the sage paradigm is so wedded to its social-historical and cross-cultural methods that the Jesuses under this paradigm show little interest in piety, in religious ideas and rituals, in being a Jew, indeed, even in the action of God.[168] Keck judges Jesus-Sage as a secularized reduction of Jesus' message and mission. Keck's position makes some sense, but in defense of the sagists, we have to say that the sage paradigm can sponsor some very needed, worldly notions of religion.[169] Crossan's Jesus criticizes ritual purity in several parables,[170]

---

166. Crossan, *The Historical Jesus*, 283–92.

167. Robinson, "LOGOI SOPHON," 104.

168. Keck, "The Second Coming," 786–88.

169. Ibid., 788. Luke Johnson, one who rejects questing entirely, also recognizes how little religion and Jewish religion figure in the sagey Jesuses.

170. Crossan, *The Historical Jesus*, 280.

opens the door of the family to non-believers,[171] collapses the difference between magic and religion,[172] attacks the sacred place of the Temple in lifestyle and in aggressive act,[173] and substitutes a ritual meal independent from Jewish ritual practice.[174] We end with a powerful quote from Witherington:

> A sapiential approach to Jesus and his ministry can explain things as diverse as Jesus' word of healing, including his exorcism, why he never uses the prophetic phrase, 'thus says the Lord,' why he spoke in aphorisms and parables and beatitudes, why he gathered disciples, why he spoke as one with independent authority, why he used the language of Father for God, why he does not spend much of his time quoting or exegeting the Pentateuch and engaging in halakic discussions, why his message has a more universal flavor to it, why he goes back and appeals to the creation order in his discussions of marriage and its purpose, why he said there was something greater than Solomon present when he came on the scene, why the phrase 'Son of David' seems to be associated with Jesus when he performed miracles and why his message seemed so positive in comparison to John the Baptist's.[175]

---

171. Ibid., 300.
172. Ibid., 309.
173. Ibid., 355.
174. Ibid., 367.
175. Witherington, *The Jesus Quest*, 185.

APPENDIX

Rules and Warrants Summary

Chapter 1: Orientation

- (Quest) Rule 1: History as history cannot pose normative christological views (whether negative or positive) without falling into a category error.
- (Theological) Rule 2: Theology needs to be extremely suspicious of sweeping claims, both in defense of and in attack on christological claims, in the name of history.
- (Theological) Rule 3: To apply the results of historical research directly to a theological issue is a category error.
- (Quest) Rule 4: Historical research by itself can never *yield* a christology or christological application.
- (Theological) Rule 5: Theologians and others must reject the historian's fundamentalism that would apply a fact about Jesus directly to theology or the life of faith.
- (Theological) Rule 6: Theology must hold to a *relative* interest in questing and deploy the results of the quest in a *critical* and *relative* way.
- (Theological) Rule 7: Historical results, even those which promise *recommendations* to theology, need to be *refounded* within a christological environment for them to be christic.
- (Theological) Rule 8: Nothing the historian gives theology is directly christic.
- (Theological) Rule 9: Theology should never seek a direct continuity between Jesus and the Christ.

Chapter 2: Terms

- (Theological) Rule 10: Theologians have to live with bias, with prejudice, with speculation along subjective lines; in short, they have to live with *the historicity of historical work.*

- (Historical and Theological) Rule 11: The Jesus of history cannot be categorically, but only relatively, different from the value-rich Christ of faith.

- (Meta-Historical) Rule 12: In Jesus research the whole must be in place before the part.

- (Meta-Historical) Rule 13: Every Jesus that historians' craft must be mediated through the history of Jesuses.

- (Meta-Historical) Rule 14: The constructive approach realizes a historical Jesus, an invention, within a circled conversation of resisting evidence and the values, perspectives, and concerns of the researcher. The intelligibility of a historian's Jesus depends on how well it picks up the duck-rabbit fragments and performs a *coherentizing* of the saga.

- (Theological) Rule 15: Theology requires that a (partially) realized historical Jesus must be completely realized in the resonances of the culture in question and of the experiences of the faith community.

- (Theological) Rule 16: A christological opportunity must be *there* in the evidence for it to become a recommendation. A christology, of course, can go a number of ways independent of a historical Jesus, but so far as it wishes to be a *quested christology*, it must respond to evidentiary opportunities.

- (Theological) Rule 17: Theologians have to conduct a *genealogy of value* in all historical Jesuses, whether in old portraits of Jesus that hide value under objectivist presuppositions or in sophisticated, hermeneutical constructions.

- (Theological) Rule 18: Theologians need to keep historians from acting as christologists even as they honor and support value-rich history writing.

- (Theological) Rule 19: Theology need not get all of its christology out of Jesus, but the quested moment of christology must be in dialogue with actual features from the Jesuses of the historians.

Historical Rules and Theological Supports

- 20. Historians must be self-critical and public about their values and perspectives; theologians must honor and encourage the effort;
- 21. Historians must be aware of the questions and interests they bring to historical work; theologians must help bring to light these interests and make critical judgments about them;
- 22. Historians must be willing to change their positions and revise their minds in the dialogue with resisting evidence; theologians must respond when the guild poses new ideas and yet must check against historical orthodoxies;
- 23. Historians must honor beliefs, worldviews, and values both within casual explanations and among potential points of resistance; theologians must guard that a *Geisteswissenschaft* not degenerate into the story of "fleas and ticks";
- 24. Historians must explicitly set out their criteria and make public methods for selection and valuing sources; theologians must evaluate those choices from a meta point of view and compare what is at issue in other choices;
- 25. Historians must proceed according to public standards for better paradigm choice and better synthetic judgments and must respect limits to reasonable synthesis; theologians must judge what is at stake in comprehensive historical judgments and in rival paradigms;
- 26. Historians must hone these major judgments in the fray of public and scholarly debate; theologians must press historians to make all arguments in the light of day and with public rationales;
- 27. Historians must strain judgments through the history of the research; theologians must guard the history of the quest and nag historians concerning the lessons and mistakes of the past;
- 28. Historians must learn to trust relatively consensus among informed researchers; theologians must meet every historical revision with immediate skepticism and press the new for defensible rationales.
- 29. Historians must learn to be enriched by many different interpretations of the same thing; theologians must offer historians their typical tolerance of ambiguity and plurality.

- (Theological) Rule 30: When theologians elect to draw questing into a christological project, they necessarily enhance and make explicit the correlative activity already operative in the historian's questing.
- (Theological) Rule 31: The theologian's critique of the historical conversation aims to make judgments on the value conversation embedded in the historians' Jesuses.
- (Theological) Rule 32: Theology judges the descriptive-analytical adequacy of the cultural portrait implied in historical Jesuses.
- (Theological) Rule 33: Revisionist theologies need carefully crafted, critical checks for theology to find the balance between being culturally sensitive and boarding a cultural bandwagon.
- (Theological) Rule 34: Theology must resist the notion that retrojection of value is simply a fixable, historical mistake.
- (Theological) Rule 35: At some point theologians have an interest in insisting that retrojected value can actually be a legitimate conversation with historical evidence.
- (Quest) Rule 36: A proper Jesus must be mediated today through the study of the historians who study Jesus.
- (Historical and Quest) Rule 37: Questing requires a hermeneutical turn today.
- (Theological) Rule 38: The theological study of Jesus aims to identify the way of being in the world posed by the produced Jesus, even if that way is only implicit in the historical figuration or inchoate in the mind of the historian. Theologians take apart the Jesus analytically, in the genealogical step, to discern the values the figure intends. At this point, the theologian effects a value conversion and turns to consider the values, midwife to the historical production of a Jesus, as candidates, putative proposals that aim to launch a way of viewing the world and living in it.
- (Theological) Rule 39: Theologians should welcome the turn to method in Jesus research but not celebrate it as a resolution of the issue of retrojection.
- (Theological) Rule 40: Theologians must keep a critical eye on method in historical research and guard against the ideological use of method in history writing.
- (Theological) Rule 41: The sociological turn in history should be welcomed by theology.

- (Theological) Rule 42: Theologians must remain critical of any effort to import sociological results (as with historical results) whole-hog into christology, as if these results were theological insights.
- (Theological) Rule 43: Theologians need to be suspicious of the subtle hostility to ideas and textual evidence in certain of the sociological turns.
- (Theological) Rule 44: Theologians must guard the use of the alien criterion and check that the criterion does not blind historical research to the same, the similar, and the continuous.
- (Theological) Rule 45: Theologians must check that the historians' use of the alien criterion not create a faulty assumption that a historical Jesus is free of value.
- (Theological) Rule 46: Theologians must discover the values operative in what surprises the historians about their historical Jesuses.
- (Theological) Rule 47: The theologian must interpret the balancing of the shock of the new/alien with the domesticating power of a familiarizing imagination.
- (Theological) Rule 48: Theologians need to be alert to the points where the use of the alien criterion presses an interest to sacrilize a point of otherness.
- (Theological) Rule 49: Theologians must be suspicious of the use of the alien criterion.
- (Theological) Rule 50: The most useful, quested Jesuses for christological employment are ones that are crafted within a heightened sense for the history of questing.
- (Quest) Rule 51: Historians and theologians should not be trapped by the periodizing of the history of the quest or by individual divisions and labels of methods/styles/goals/eras.
- (Theological) Rule 52: The most useful, quested Jesuses for christological purposes will have internalized changing senses of the historical.
- (Theological) Rule 53: The best Jesuses for christological purposes have been honed by the public academic discussion of the historians and theologians.
- (Theological) Rule 54: Questing for a Jesus cannot simply be left to the historians.

- (Quest) Rule 55: An application of the *alien criterion*: be suspicious if one's invented Jesus matches closely *the needs of the day*.
- (Quest) Rule 56: Be suspicious of any certain claims for the *real Jesus*.
- (Quest) Rule 57: Be suspicious of the suspicion of questing.
- (Quest) Rule 58: Avoid an artificial separation of historical and theological themes on the turf of Jesus studies.
- (Theological) Rule 59: Theologians need to learn from the critique of the quest but must criticize it too.

Chapter 3: Warrants

- (Factual) Warrant 1: Our first warrant, then, is a meta-warrant, the need for warrants.
- (Factual) Warrant 2: Theology must respond to the persistent impulse of continued questing by historians.
- (Theological) Warrant 3: Faith Seeking Understanding: Theology can employ continued research in history to help the faithful understand their beliefs.
- (Factual) Warrant 4: Historical research on Jesus is a possible human activity of inquiry and the warrant is a simple appeal to curiosity and honesty.
- (Theological) Rule 60: Theology's affirmation of historical research includes honoring the self-correcting stance of history writing.
    - (Theological) Corollary 60a: Theology endorses a history-of-the-research criterion central to revisionist history-writing.
    - (Theological) Corollary 60b: Theology must reject the sweeping claim that there is nothing new in Jesus research, that questing is, in fact, a narrative of ever-repeating errors.
    - (Theological) Corollary 60c: Theology endorses the hermeneutically self-consciousness criterion of recent historical work.
- (Historical) Rule 61: Good Jesus researchers must know how to avoid the pitfalls of the history of the quest, and must, upon hermeneutical self-reflection, turn possible lessons onto their own images of Jesus.
    - (Historical) Corollary 61a: Historians and theologians no longer should expect neutral portraits of Jesus.

RULES AND WARRANTS SUMMARY

- (Theological) Rule 62: Revisionist theologians suspect that it is impossible and undesirable for historians to exclude their perspectives and stances from historical research.
- (Theological) Rule 63: Theologians must trust the scholarly consensus within the historical guild.
  - (Theological) Corollary 63a: Theologians honor a spectrum of views from the historical guild.
  - (Theological) Corollary 63b: the plurality rule: Theologians may have to honor a plurality of historically responsible constructions of Jesus at a given time.
  - (Theological) Corollary 63c: Theologians support the genealogical effort to uncover those values operative in the construction of historical Jesuses.
  - (Theological) Corollary 63d: Theologians also honor consensus methodological choices from the guild, but support the criticism of method from within the guild.
  - (Theological) Corollary 63e: Theologians must support internal historians' critique of the conduct of questing every bit as much as trusting the scholarly consensus.
  - (Theological) Corollary 63f: Theologians must remain open to paradigm change.
- (Theological) Warrant 5, the fundamental warrant: Theologians feel pressed to determine whether the Christ of faith somehow matches what Jesus of Nazareth was about historically.
- (Theological) Warrant 6, the kergymatic warrant: The early Christian kerygma makes historical claims for Jesus.
- (Theological) Warrant 7, the soteriological warrant: Christians claim that salvation is possible because of events that happen in the history of Jesus of Nazareth.
- (Theological) Warrant 8, the anti-docetic warrant: Questing can be a powerful, modern means to guard against the heresy of docetism.
- (Theological) Warrant 9, the incarnational warrant: The logic of incarnation involves faith and theology in historical claims.
- (Philosophical) Warrant 10: A full human nature must be actual in a history, and must be found, located, identified, and emphasized, so far as possible.

- (Theological) Warrant 10a, the Chalcedonian warrant: A full human nature must be actual in a history, and must be found, located, identified, emphasized, so far as possible.
- (Theological) Warrant 11, the christological warrant: Historical Jesus study is one the best ways to proceed with a *from-below* approach to christology because of the concrete and complex way it can picture human life.
- (Theological) Warrant 12, the theological warrant: Contemporary Christian theologians often feel the need to criticize classical notions of God and to reconceive God from the vantage of the history of Jesus in order to construct a genuinely Christian doctrine of God. Jesus Research can be an aid in this reconception.
  - (Theological) Corollary Warrant 12a, the theo-propos critique: A historical Jesus can inform what is appropriate in a God and can press for a purging of incredible and reprehensible elements in the doctrine of God.
- (Meta-Theological) Warrant 13: The study of the study of Jesus, converting the skepticism about modernizing into a self-critical modesty, reminds theology to be humble and circumspect about any imaging of Jesus.
- (Meta-Theological) Warrant 14, the plurality issue: Careful questing can deliver potential historical configurations that anticipate judgments among the many Christs.
- (Meta-Theological) Warrant 15, the dialogical warrant: Historical work on the figure of Jesus may be a useful mediator in interreligious dialogue.
- (Meta-Theological) Warrant 16: Questing for Jesus can clarify what is at stake in each way within a typology of ways of being Christian, each anchored in a rather different imaging of Jesus.
- (Meta-Theological) Warrant 17, the iconoclastic warrant: A new Jesus can work as an iconoclastic force to break apart religious and theological orthodoxies.
  - (Meta-Theological) Corollary Warrant 17a, the limits of language one: Jesus research makes christology face the limits of language because of the spotty sources of knowledge and of the inadequacies of any category to capture the elusive figure.

RULES AND WARRANTS SUMMARY 269

- (Meta-Theological) Corollary Warrant 17b, the issue of modernizing: Questing for the historical Jesus can remind both historians and the faithful about the dangers of uncritical modernizing of Jesus.
- (Meta-Theological) Corollary Warrant 17c: The historical study of Jesus can force theology to sharpen the focus of christology onto essential christic matters.
- (Meta-Theological) Warrant 18, the Christian renewal one: The historical study of Jesus can be a means for Christian renewal.
- (Philosophical) Corroborative Warrant 19: Philosophical reflection can support theology in clarifying key categories entailed in the theological use of the quest in order to avoid category errors.
- (Philosophical) Corroborative Warrant 20, the anti-idealist one: Biblical religion is worldly and the metaphysical bias of Christian religion points away from an abstract idealism, if by idealism we mean an otherworldly or essentialist devaluing of history and material life.
- (Philosophical) Corroborative Warrant 21, the anti-myth version: The incarnational logic of Christian religion takes it to real time and real history and not to the eternal time/place of myth.
- (Philosophical) Corroborative Warrant 22, the critique of religion one: Questing can present a healthy lesson in the critique of religion.
- (Philosophical) Corroborative Warrant 23, the defense warrant: The historical study of Jesus can support the apologetic defense of Christianity against the modern criticism of religion as illusory.
- (Philosophical) Corroborative Warrant 24, the apologetic warrant: Questing can be a component of theology under its apologetic mode.
- (Historical) Warrant 25, the anti-gnostic one: The Anti-Gnostic Warrant restates the theological warrants and the anti-myth point.
- (Historical) Warrant 26, the concretion point: Historical research on Jesus can return the experience of faith to the world.
  - (Theological) Corollary Rule 26a, the anti-heroic one: A theology interested in the historical Jesus should check itself against making Jesus the heroic individual.
- (Historical and Theological) Warrant 27: Jesus research can participate in the effort to enrich and concretize the notion of salvation.

- (Cultural Historical) Warrant 28, cultural criticism: Jesus research can contribute to the critique of culture.
- (Historical and Theological) Warrant 29, the Jewish Jesus warrant: Both history writing and theology must establish Jesus as a Jew and reestablish him in his Jewishness.
  - (Theological) Corollary Warrant 29a, the anti-Marcion one: Historical research on Jesus is an efficient and reliable means of reclaiming Hebrew Scripture and Israelite religion for Christian theology.

Chapter 4: Retrojection

- (Theological) Rule 63: Theologians need to be skeptical of both left wing and right wing optimism about the theological use of the Jesuses.
- (Theological) Rule 64: Revisionist theologies must find their way between undue historical skepticism (vs. the Wredean impulse) and yet be mindful of retrojected value coloring Jesus histories (with Schweitzer).
- (Theological) Rule 65: Revisionist theologians are suspicious that better method fixes retrojection and that it can yield a Jesus of direct (positive or negative) christological significance, yet they favor continuing to refine method and making explicit the values and orientations of historical researchers.
- (Theological) Rule 66: Revisionist theologians reject a historical-fundamentalistic application of historical results to christology, while still holding to their interest to discover if historical results can support christological possibility.
- (Theological) Rule 67: Revisionist theologians elect to rethink what happens in retrojection.
- (Quest) Rule 68: A complete theory of retrojection must include a critique of itself that recognizes its own limitations to order to account how it is possible, given the ubiquity of retrojection, that *real* light from the past can emerge.
- (Quest) Rule 69: Historians and sympathetic theologians must establish standards of good and bad retrojection.
  - Standard 69a. All things equal, better retrojection is the opposite of manipulative retrojection.

RULES AND WARRANTS SUMMARY 271

- Standard 69b. Better retrojection does not avoid what we call retrojection but is self critical about the value issues in the production of any Jesus.

- Standard 69c. Better retrojection makes explicit the choices of methods and sources and spells out the stance and aim of the production so that all can see and judge.

- Standard 69d. It respects the research of the guild and especially consensus views but not in a doctrinaire way.

- Standard 69e. Better retrojection locates a Jesus in relation to the spectrum of classic Jesuses and filters a Jesus through the history of Jesuses.

- Standard 69f. It identifies how a researcher enters the hermeneutical circle. Of particular importance, scholars must make explicit how they are reading contemporary culture and how that reading plays away in the streets of Galilee of the first century.

- Standard 69g. At each step on the way better retrojection sets out warrants and publicly argued criteria of adequacy for every decision.

- (Quest) Rule 70: Jesus research must be especially careful to justify when a Jesus departs radically from the chorus of Jesuses.

- (Theological) Rule 71: Theologians locate the sameness criterion by identifying the ways in which a Jesus continues known ways of imaging Jesus.

- (Theological) Rule 72: Theology's use of the difference criterion begins when theologians turn a critical eye on difference and thematize difference as an issue in the historical construction of a Jesus.

- (Theological) Rule 73: Theologians also need to sift critically the locales of difference pictured in historical Jesuses.

- (Theological) Rule 74: Given that persistent evidence of difference is intense, clear, distinct, long-lasting, and widely honored in the guild of historians, and that more persisting evidence gives more reliable difference for theological reflection, theologians have relative confidence that such difference resists the power of domesticating imagination as a strong feature of Jesus' relationship to his world.

- (Historical and Theological) Rule 75: If there is an imbalance between interest in difference in a historical Jesus and the power of the resisting evidence, we know we are putting much value into the conversation with the item of difference.

- (Theological) Rule 76: Theology must sustain the suspicion of retrojection throughout the entire process by which it puts quested materials to use christologically.
- (Theological) Rule 77: Theologians (and historians) must distinguish perspective from bias and anachronism which must now be identified as ignorant and manipulative retrojection of value.
- (Theological) Rule 78: Theologians (and historians too) must rethink bias as perspective, to use an innocuous word for explicit, self-critical engagements with historical evidence.
- (Quest) Rule 79: Properly reconstructed, the retrojection theory must be an enduring ideological critique within Jesus research.
- (Quest) Rule 80: Better value conversations in the production of a Jesus happen when people, schooled in the retrojection theory, are aware of the issue of retrojection of value.
- (Theological and Quest) Rule 81: Careful and critical use of the history of the quest can be a guide by which we can anticipate value locales.
- (Quest and Theological) Rule 82: Historians and theologians need to move beyond the issue of uncovering the modernizing of Jesus and begin to focus on manipulation of the past.

Chapter 5: Sage

- (Theological) Rule 83: Theology needs to guard against domestication of Jesus and reads that kind of retrojection as manipulation.
- (Theological) Rule 84: Theologians need to be suspicious of any appeal to the evidence, as if it had a voice of its own.
- (Quest and Theological) Rule 85: Theologians have another agenda too: modernizing is one means by which we find, even produce, what is christic about Jesus.
- (Theological) Rule 86: A historical Jesus is always pre-christological, a christology in waiting, waiting to be played by an interested party.
- (Theological) Rule 87: The real Jesus is the history of Jesuses intelligently re-enacted in light of the great Jesuses of the past, the contemporary scene, and the current experience of faith in the worshipping community.

Bibliography

Akenson, Donald H. *Saint Saul: A Skeleton Key to the Historical Jesus*. Oxford: Oxford University Press, 2000.
Allison, Dale C., Jr. *Constructing Jesus: Memory, Imagination, and History*. Grand Rapids: Baker Academic, 2010.
———. *The Historical Christ and the Theological Jesus*. Grand Rapids: Eerdmans, 2009.
———. "Jesus and the Covenant." *Journal for the Study of the New Testament* 29 (1987) 72.
———. *Jesus of Nazareth: Millenarian Prophet*. Minneapolis: Fortress, 1998.
———. "A Plea for Thoroughgoing Eschatology." *Journal of Biblical Literature* 113 (1994) 651–68.
Appleby, Joyce, et al. *Telling the Truth about History*. New York: Norton, 1994.
Arnal, William E. *Jesus and the Village Scribes: Galilean Conflicts and the Setting of Q*. Minneapolis: Fortress, 2001.
———. *The Symbolic Jesus*. London: Routledge, 2014.
Arnal, William E., and Michel Desjardins, eds. *Whose Historical Jesus?* Studies in Christianity and Judaism 7. Waterloo, ON: Wilfrid Laurier University Press, 1997.
Aslan, Reza. *Zealot: The Life and Times of Jesus of Nazareth*. New York: Random House, 2013.
Avis, Paul. *God and the Creative Imagination*. London: Routledge, 1999.
Barker, Gregory A., and Stephen E. Gregg, eds. *Jesus Beyond Christianity*. Oxford: Oxford University Press, 2010.
Barnett, Paul W. *Finding the Historical Christ*. Grand Rapids: Eerdmans, 2009.
———. *Jesus and the Logic of History*. Grand Rapids: Eerdmans, 2001.
———. *Jesus and the Rise of Early Christianity*. Downer's Grove: IPV Academic, 2002.
Barr, James. "Abba Isn't 'Daddy.'" *Journal of Theological Studies* 39 (1988) 28–47.
Bartlett, David L. "The Historical Jesus and the Life of Faith." *Christian Century* 109/16 (1992) 489–93.
Barton, Bruce. *The Man Nobody Knows*. New York: Bobbs Merrill, 1925.
Batstone, David B. "Jesus, Apocalyptic, and World Transformation." *Theology Today* 49 (October 1992) 383–97.
Benedict XVI, Pope. *Jesus of Nazareth: From the Baptism in the Jordan to the Transfiguration*. Translated by Adrian J. Walker. New York: Doubleday, 2007.
Berger, Peter L., and Thomas Luckmann. *The Social Construction of Reality*. Garden City: Anchor, 1966.
Bock, Darrell L. *Studying the Historical Jesus: A Guide to Sources and Methods*. Grand Rapids: Baker, 2002.

Borg, Marcus J. *Conflict, Holiness, and Politics in the Teaching of Jesus*. Rev. ed. Valley Forge: Trinity, 2008.

———. *Jesus: A New Vision*. San Francisco: Harper & Row, 1987.

———. *Jesus in Contemporary Scholarship*. Valley Forge: Trinity, 1994.

———. "Portraits of Jesus in Contemporary North American Scholarship." *Harvard Theological Review* 84 (1991) 1–22.

———. "A Renaissance in Jesus Studies." *Theology Today* 45/3 (October 1988) 280–92.

———. "A Temperate Cast for a Non-Eschatological Jesus." *Foundations & Facets Forum* 2/3 (1986) 81–102.

Boring, M. Eugene. "The 'Third Quest' and the Apostolic Faith." *Interpretation* 50 (1996) 341–354.

Bornkamm, Günther. *Jesus of Nazareth*. Translated by Irene and Fraser McLuckey with James M. Robinson. New York: Harper, 1960.

Braaten, Carl E., and Roy E. Harrisville, eds. *The Historical Jesus and the Kerygmatic Christ*. Nashville: Abingdon, 1964.

Brandon, S. G. F. *Jesus and the Zealots: A Study of the Political Factor in Primitive Christianity*. New York: Scribner, 1967.

Brock, Rita Nakashima. *Journeys by Heart: A Christology of Erotic Power*. New York: Crossroad, 1988.

Brodie, Thomas L. *Beyond the Quest for the Historical Jesus: Memoir of a Discovery*. Sheffield: Sheffield Phoenix, 2012.

Brundage, Anthony. *Going to the Sources*. Wheeling: Harlan Davidson, 1997.

Bultmann, Rudolf. *Jesus and the Word*. Translated by Louise Pettibone Smith and Erminie Huntress Lantero. New York: Scribner, 1958.

Bunzl, Martin. *Real History*. London: Routledge, 1997.

Cadbury, Henry J. *The Peril of Modernizing Jesus*. New York: Macmillan, 1937.

Caird, George B. *Jesus and the Jewish Nation*. London: Athlone, 1965.

Carlson, Jeffrey, and Robert A. Ludwig, eds. *Jesus and Faith: A Conversation on the Work of John Dominic Crossan*. Maryknoll: Orbis, 1994.

Carrier, Richard C. *On the Historicity of Jesus: Why We Might Have Reason for Doubt*. Sheffield: Sheffield Phoenix, 2014.

———. *Proving History: Bayes's Theorem and the Quest for the Historical Jesus*. Amherst, NY: Prometheus, 2012.

Casey, Maurice. *Jesus: Evidence and Argument or Mythicist Myths?* London: Bloomsbury Academic, 2014.

———. *Jesus of Nazareth: An Independent Historian's Account of His Life and Teaching*. London: T. & T. Clark, 2010.

Catchpole, David. *Jesus People: The Historical Jesus and the Beginnings of Community*. Grand Rapids: Baker Academic, 2006.

Charlesworth, James H. "From Barren Mazes to Gentle Rappings: The Emergence of Jesus Research." *Princeton Seminary Bulletin* 7/3 (1986) 220–30.

———, ed. *Jesus' Jewishness: Exploring the Place of Jesus in Early Judaism*. New York: Crossroad, 1995.

———. "Jesus Research: A Paradigm Shift for New Testament Scholars." *Australian Biblical Review* 38 (1990) 18–32.

Charlesworth, James H., and Loren H. Johns, eds. *Hillel and Jesus: Comparative Studies of Two Major Religious Leaders*. Minneapolis: Fortress, 1997.

Charlesworth, James H., and Petr Pokorný, eds. *Jesus Research: An International Perspective*. Grand Rapids: Eerdmans, 2005.

Charlesworth, James H., and Walter P. Weaver, eds. *Images of Jesus Today*. Valley Forge, PA: Trinity, 1994.

———, eds. *Jesus Two Thousand Years Later: Faith and Scholarship Colloquies*. Harrisburg, PA: Trinity, 2000.

Carlston, Charles E. "Proverbs, Maxims, and the Historical Jesus." *Journal of Biblical Literature* 99 (1980) 87–105.

———. Review of *Jesus the Sage: the Pilgrimage of Wisdom*, by Ben Witherington III. *Horizons in Biblical Theology* 17 (December 1995) 204–205.

Childs, Hal. *The Myth of the Historical Jesus and the Evolution of Consciousness*. Society of Biblical Literature Dissertation Series 179. Atlanta: SBL, 2000.

Chilton, Bruce A. *The Galilean Rabbi and His Bible: Jesus' Use of the Interpreted Scripture of His Time*. Good News Studies 8. Wilmington, DE: Glazier, 1994.

Chilton, Bruce A., and Craig A. Evans, eds. *Authenticating the Activities of Jesus*. New Testament Tools and Studies 28/2. Leiden: Brill, 1999.

———, eds. *Studying the Historical Jesus: Evaluations of the State of Current Research*. New Testament Tools and Studies 19. Leiden: Brill, 1994.

Collingwood, R. G. *Essays in the Philosophy of History*. New York: McGraw-Hill, 1965.

———. *The Idea of History*. Oxford: Oxford University Press, 1961.

Craffert, Pieter F. *The Life of a Galilean Shaman: Jesus of Nazareth in Anthropological-Historical Perspective*. Matrix: The Bible in Mediterranean Context 3. Eugene: Cascade Books, 2008.

Crossan, John Dominic. *The Birth of Christianity: Discovering What Happened in the Years Immediately after the Execution of Jesus*. New York: HarperOne, 1999.

———. *The Essential Jesus: Original Sayings and Earliest Images*. San Francisco: Harper, 1994.

———. *The Historical Jesus: The Life of a Mediterranean Jewish Peasant*. San Francisco: HarperSanFrancisco, 1991.

———. *In Parables: The Challenge of the Historical Jesus*. Sonoma, CA: Polebridge, 1992.

———. *A Long Way from Tipparary*. New York: HarperOne, 2000.

———. *Raid on the Articulate: Comic Eschatology in Jesus and Borges*. 1976. Reprint, Eugene, OR: Wipf & Stock, 2008.

———. "Some Theological Conclusions from My Historical Jesus Research." *The Living Pulpit* (January–March 1994) 18–19.

———. *Who Killed Jesus? Exposing the Roots of Anti-Semitism in the Gospel Story of the Death of Jesus*. San Francisco: HarperSanFrancisco, 1995.

Crossan, John Dominic, et al., eds. *The Jesus Controversy: Perspectives in Conflict*. Harrisburg, PA: Trinity, 1999.

Cunningham, Adrian, ed. *The Theory of Myth: Six Studies*. London: Sheed & Ward, 1973.

Dahl, Nils. *The Crucified Messiah and Other Essays*. Minneapolis: Fortress, 1974.

Dawes, Gregory W., ed. *The Historical Jesus Quest: A Foundational Anthology*. Leiden: Deo, 1999.

De Jonge, Marinus. *God's Final Envoy: Early Christology and Jesus' Own View of His Mission*. Grand Rapids: Eerdmans, 1998.

———. *Jesus, The Servant-Messiah*. New Haven: Yale University Press, 1991.

den Heyer, C. J. *Jesus Matters: 150 Years of Research*. Valley Forge, PA: Trinity, 1997.

Denton, Donald L., Jr. *Historiography and Hermeneutics in Jesus Studies: An Examination of the Work of John Dominic Crossan and Ben F. Meyer*. London: T. & T. Clark, 2004.

———. *Historiography and Hermeneutics in Jesus Studies: An Examination of the Work of John Dominic Crossan and Ben F. Meyer*. Journal for the Study of the New Testament Supplement Series 262. London: T. & T. Clark, 2000.

Derrida, Jacques. *Of Grammatology*. Corrected ed. Translated by Gayatri Chakravorty Spivak. Baltimore: Johns Hopkins University Press, 1998.

d'Holbach, Baron Paul Tiry. *Ecce Homo!: An Eighteenth-Century Life of Jesus*. Edited by Andre Hunwick. The Hague: Mouton de Gruyter, 1995.

Dick, Philip R. "Reality_is_that_which_when_you_stop_believing." *How to Build a Universe That Doesn't Fall Apart Two Days Later*. http://deoxy.org/pkd_how2build.htm.

Dilthey, Wilhelm. *Einleitung in die Geisteswissenschaften*. Detroit: Wayne State University Press, 1988.

Dimont, Max I. *Appointment in Jerusalem: A Search for the Historical Jesus*. New York: St. Martin's, 1991.

Dolgin, Janet L., et al., eds. *Symbolic Anthropology: A Reader in the Study of Symbols and Meanings*. New York: Columbia University Press, 1977.

Donnelly, Doris, ed. *Jesus: A Colloquium in the Holy Land*. New York: Continuum, 2001.

Doty, William G. *Mythography: The Study of Myths and Rituals*. Tuscaloosa: University of Alabama Press, 1986.

Downing, F. Gerald. *Cynics and Christian Origins*. London: T. & T. Clark, 2000.

Dray, William H. *Philosophy of History*. Englewood Cliffs, NJ: Prentice-Hall, 1964.

Dunn, James D. G. *The Evidence for Jesus*. Philadelphia: Westminster, 1985.

———. *Jesus Remembered*. Grand Rapids: Eerdmans, 2003.

———. *A New Perspective on Jesus: What the Quest for the Historical Jesus Missed*. Grand Rapids: Baker Academic, 2005.

Ebner, Martin. *Jesus von Nazaret in seiner Zeit: Sozialgeschichtliche Zugänge*. Stuttgarter Bibelstudien 196. Stuttgart: Katholisches Bibelwerk, 2003.

Edwards, Richard A. *A Theology of Q: Eschatology, Prophesy, and Wisdom*. Philadelphia: Fortress, 1978.

Ebeling, Gerhard. *The Problem of Historicity in the Church and Its Proclamation*. Translated by Grover Foley. Philadelphia: Fortress, 1967.

Ehrman, Bart D. *Did Jesus Exist? The Historical Argument for Jesus of Nazareth*. New York: HarperOne, 2012.

———. *Jesus: Apocalyptic Prophet of the New Millennium*. New York: Oxford, 1999.

Eliade, Mircea. *Cosmos and History: The Myth of the Eternal Return*. New York: Harper and Brothers, 1954.

Ellegård, Alvor. *Jesus—One Hundred Years before Christ: A Study in Creative Mythology*. Woodstock, NY: Overlook, 1999.

Evans, C. Stephen. *The Historical Christ & The Jesus of Faith: The Incarnation Narrative as History*. Oxford: Oxford University Press, 1996.

Evans, Craig A. "Authenticity Criteria in the Life of Jesus Research." *Christian Scholar's Review* 19 (1989) 6–31.

———, ed. *Encyclopedia of the Historical Jesus*. New York: Routledge, 2008.

———. *Fabricating Jesus: How Modern Scholars Distort the Gospels*. Downers Grove, IL: Inter-Varsity, 2007.

———. "Life-of-Jesus Research and the Eclipse of Mythology." *Theological Studies* 54 (1993) 3–36.

Falk, Harvey. *Jesus the Pharisee: A New Look at the Jewishness of Jesus*. New York: Paulist, 1985.

Farmer, William R., ed. *Crisis in Christology: Essays in Quest of Resolution.* Livonia, MO: Dove, 1995.

———. *The Gospel of Jesus: The Pastoral Relevance of the Synoptic Problem.* Louisville: Westminster John Knox, 1994.

Fiensy, David A. *Jesus the Galilean: Soundings in a First Century Life.* Piscataway, NJ: Gorgias, 2007.

Flusser, David. *Jesus.* New York: Herder & Herder, 1969.

———. *The Sage from Galilee: Rediscovering Jesus' Genius.* With R. Steven Notley. Grand Rapids: Eerdmans, 2007.

Foucault, Michel. *Language, Counter-Memory, and* Practice. Edited by Donald F. Bouchard. Translated by Donald F. Bouchard and Sherry Simon. Ithaca, NY: Cornell University Press, 1977.

Frei, Hans W. *The Eclipse of Biblical Narrative: A Study in Eighteenth and Nineteenth Century Hermeneutics.* New Haven: Yale University Press, 1974.

Freyne, Sean. *Jesus, Galilee, and the Gospels: Literary Approaches and Historical Investigations.* Philadelphia: Fortress, 1988.

Fredriksen, Paula. *From Jesus to Christ: The Origins of the New Testament Images of Jesus.* New Haven: Yale University Press, 2000.

Fuchs, Ernst. *Studies of the Historical Jesus.* Translated by Andrew Scobie. Studies in Biblical Theology 1/42. London: SCM, 1964.

Funk, Robert W. *Honest to Jesus: Jesus for a New Millennium.* San Francisco: HarperSanFrancisco, 1996.

———. "The Issue of Jesus." *Foundations & Facets Forum* 1/1 (1985) 7–12.

Funk, Robert, et al. *The Five Gospels: The Search for the Authentic Words of Jesus: New Translation and Commentary.* New York: Macmillan, 1993.

Gaiser, Frederick J. *The Quest for Jesus and the Christian Faith.* St. Paul. MN: Luther Seminary, 1997.

Galvin, John P. "'I Believe . . . in Jesus Christ, His Only Son, Our Lord': The Earthly Jesus and the Christ of Faith." *Interpretation* 50 (2004) 341–75.

Gammie, John G., and Leo G. Perdue. *The Sage in Israel and the Ancient Near East.* Winona Lake, IN: Eisenbrauns, 1990.

Gaventa, Beverly Roberts, and Richard B. Hayes, eds. *Seeking the Identity of Jesus: A Pilgrimage.* Grand Rapids: Eerdmans, 2008.

Giorgi, Dieter. "The Interest in Life of Jesus Theology as a Paradigm for the Social History of Biblical Criticism." *Harvard Theological Review* 85 (1992) 51–83.

Girzone, Joseph F. *Jesus: A New Understanding of God's Son.* New York: Doubleday, 2009.

Goehring, James E. et al, eds. *Gospel Origins and Christian Beginnings.* Forum Fascicles 1. Sonoma, CA: Polebridge, 1990.

Gowler, David B. *What Are They Saying About the Historical Jesus?* New York: Paulist, 2007.

Gris, Robert. *Life of Christ.* Lanham, MD: University Press of America, 2013.

Harvey, A. E., ed. *God Incarnate: Story and Belief.* London: SPCK, 1981.

———. *Jesus and the Constraints of History.* Philadelphia: Fortress, 1982.

Harvey, Van. *The Historian and The Believer: The Morality of Historical Knowledge and Christian Belief.* New York: Macmillan, 1966.

Hays, Richard B. "Faith and History." Review of *The Jesus Quest*, by Ben Witherington III and *The Real Jesus*, by Luke Timothy Johnson. *First Things* 64 (2001) 44–46.

Hegel, G. W. F. *The Phenomenology of Spirit*. Translated by A. V. Miller. Oxford: Oxford University Press, 1977.
Hendrickx, Herman. *The Sermon on the Mount*. London: Chapman, 1984.
Hermann, Wilhelm. *The Communion of the Christian with God*. Edited by Robert T. Voelkel. Translated by J. S. Stanyon. Philadelphia: Fortress, 1971.
Herzog, William R., II. *Prophet and Teacher: An Introduction to the Historical Jesus*. Louisville: Westminster John Knox, 2005.
Hoffmann, R. Joseph. *Sources of the Jesus Tradition: Separating History from Myth*. Amherst, NY: Prometheus, 2010.
Hollenbach, Paul W. "The Historical Jesus Today." *Biblical Theology Bulletin* 19 (1989) 11–21.
———."What's the Good News? Competing Visions of Jesus." *Perspectives* 8/10 (1993) 13–16.
Holmen, Tom, ed. *Jesus from Judaism to Christianity: Continuum Approaches to the Historical Jesus*. Library of New Testament Studies 352. London: T. & T. Clark, 2007.
———. "A Theologically Disinterested Quest?" *Studia Theologica* 55 (2001) 175–97.
Hooke, S. H. *The Labyrinth*. London: SPCK, 1935.
Horsley, Richard A. *Jesus and the Spiral of Violence: Popular Jewish Resistance in Roman Palestine*. 1987. Reprint, Minneapolis: Fortress, 1993.
———. *The Prophet Jesus and the Renewal of Israel: Moving beyond a Diversionary Debate*. Grand Rapids: Eerdmans, 2012.
———, with Jonathan A. Draper. *Whoever Hears You Hears Me: Prophets, Performance, and Tradition in Q*. Harrisburg, PA: Trinity, 1999.
Horsley, Richard A., and John S. Hanson. *Bandits, Prophets, and Messiahs: Popular Resistance in the Time of Jesus*. 1985. Reprint, Harrisburg, PA: Trinity, 1999.
Howell, Martha, and Walter Prevenier. *From Reliable Sources: An Introduction to Historical Methods*. Ithaca, NY: Cornell University Press, 2003.
Hultgren, Arland J. "Jesus of Nazareth: Prophet, Visionary, Sage, or What?" *Dialog* 33 (1994) 263–73.
Hurst, L. D., and N. T. Wright, eds. *The Glory of Christ in the New Testament: Studies in Christology in Memory of George Bradford Caird*. Oxford: Clarendon, 1998.
Hurtado, Larry W. *How on Earth Did Jesus Become a God? Historical Questions about Earliest Devotion to Jesus*. Grand Rapids: Eerdmans, 2005.
Ingolfsland, Dennis. "An Evaluation of Bart Ehrman's Historical Jesus." *Bibliotheca Sacra* (158/630) 182–83.
Jacobson, Arland Dean. "Wisdom Christology in Q." PhD diss., Claremont Graduate School, 1978.
Jaroš, Karl. *Jesus von Nazareth: Ein Leben*. Cologne: Boehlau, 2011.
Jenkins, Keith. *Re-Thinking History*. London: Routledge, 1991.
Jenkins, Philip. *Hidden Gospels: How the Search for Jesus Lost Its Way*. Oxford: Oxford University Press, 2002.
Jeremias, Joachim. *The Problem of the Historical Jesus*. Translated by Norman Perrin. Facet Books: Biblical Series 13. Philadelphia: Fortress, 1964. Reprinted as "The Search for the Historical Jesus," in Jeremias, *Jesus and the Message of the New Testament*, edited by K. C. Hanson, 1–17. Fortress Classics in Biblical Studies. Minneapolis: Fortress, 2002.
Johnson, Luke Timothy. *The Living Jesus: Learning the Heart of the Gospel*. San Francisco: HarperSanFrancisco, 1999.

———. *The Real Jesus: The Misguided Quest for the Historical Jesus and the Truth of the Traditional Gospels*. San Francisco: HarperSanFrancisco, 1996.
Joseph, Simon J. *The Nonviolent Messiah: Jesus, Q, and the Enochic Tradition*. Minneapolis: Fortress, 2014.
Kähler, Martin. *The So-Called Historical Jesus and the Historic, Biblical Christ*. Translated and edited by Carl E. Braaten. Seminar Editions. Philadelphia: Fortress, 1964.
Käsemann, Ernst. *Essays on New Testament Themes*. Translated by W. J. Montague. 1964. Reprinted, Philadelphia: Fortress, 1964.
Kaylor, R. David. *Jesus the Prophet: His Vision of the Kingdom on Earth*. Louisville: Westminster John Knox, 1994.
Keck, Leander E. *A Future for the Historical Jesus: The Place of Jesus in Preaching and Theology*. Nashville: Abingdon, 1971.
———. "The Second Coming of the Liberal Jesus?" *Christian Century* 111/ 21 (1994) 784–87.
———. *Who Is Jesus? History in the Perfect Tense*. Studies on Personalities of the New Testament. Columbia: University of South Carolina Press, 2000.
Keener, Craig S. *The Historical Jesus of the Gospels*. Grand Rapids: Eerdmans, 2009.
Keith, Chris, and Anthony Le Donne, eds. *Jesus, Criteria, and the Demise of Authenticity*. New York: T. & T. Clark, 2012.
Kloppenborg, John S. "Symbolic Eschatology and the Apocalypticism of Q." *Harvard Theological Review* 80 (1987) 287–306.
Kloppenborg, John S., and John W. Marshall, eds. *Apocalypticism, Anti-Semitism, and the Historical Jesus: Subtexts in Criticism*. Journal for the Study of the New Testament. Supplement Series 275. London: T. & T. Clark, 2005.
Koester, Helmut. *Ancient Christian Gospels: Their History and Development*. Philadelphia: Trinity, 1990.
———. "The Gospel of Thomas: Does It Contain Authentic Sayings of Jesus?" *Bible Review* 6/2 (1990) 37.
———. "Jesus the Victim." *Journal of Biblical Literature* 111 (1992) 3–15.
Kugel, James L. *Studies in Ancient Midrash*. Cambridge: Harvard University Press, 2001.
Kuhn, Thomas. *The Structure of Scientific Revolutions*. Chicago: University of Chicago Press, 1962.
Le Beau, Brian F., et al., eds. *The Historical Jesus through Catholic and Jewish Eyes*. Harrisburg, PA: Trinity, 2000.
Le Donne, Anthony. *The Historiographical Jesus: Memory, Typology, and the Son of David*. Waco, TX: Baylor University Press, 2009.
Lee, Bernard J. *Jesus and the Metaphors of God: The Christs of the New Testament*. Conversations on the Road Not Taken 2. Mahwah, NJ: Paulist, 1993.
Lessing, Gotthold Ephraim. *Lessing's Theological Writings*. Translated by Henry Chadwick. Stanford: Sanford University Press, 1967.
Levine, Amy-Jill, et al., eds. *The Historical Jesus in Context*. Princeton: Princeton University Press, 2006.
Lindbeck, George. *The Nature of Doctrine*. Philadelphia: Westminster, 1984.
Loader, William. *Jesus and the Fundamentalism of His Day*. Grand Rapids: Eerdmans, 2001.
Long, Didier. *Jésus de Nazareth, juif de Galilée*. Paris: Presses de la Renaissance, 2011.
Long, Thomas G. "Stand Up, Stand Up for (the Historical) Jesus." *Theology Today* 52 (1995) 1–6.

Lührmann, Dieter. *Die Redaktion der Logienquelle: Anhang: Zur weiteren Überlieferung der Logienquelle.* Wissenschaftliche Monographien zum Alten und Neuen Testament 33. Neukirchen-Vluyn: Neukirchener, 1969.
Mack, Burton L. *The Lost Gospel: The Book of Q and Christian Origins.* San Francisco: HarperSanFrancisco, 1993.
Malherbe, Abraham J., and Wayne A. Meeks, eds. *The Future of Christology: Essays in Honor of Leander E. Keck.* Minneapolis: Fortress, 1993.
Malina, Bruce J. *The Social Gospel of Jesus: The Kingdom of God in Mediterranean Perspective.* Minneapolis: Fortress, 2000.
Marsak, Leonard M., ed. *The Nature of Historical Inquiry.* New York: Holt, Rinehart & Winston, 1970.
McCullagh, C. Behan. *The Truth of History.* London: Routledge, 1998.
McEvenue, Sean E., and Ben F. Meyer, eds. *Lonergan's Hermeneutics: Its Development and Application.* Washington, DC: Catholic University of America, 1989.
McGaughy, Lane C. "The Search of the Historical Jesus: Why Start with the Sayings?" *The Fourth R* 5–6 (Sept.–Dec. 1996) 17–26.
McGill, Arthur C. *Death and Life: An American Theology.* Edited by Charles A. Wilson and Per M. Anderson. 1987. Reprinted, Eugene, OR: Wipf & Stock, 2003.
Meier, John P. "Dividing Lines in Jesus Research Today." *Interpretation* 50 (2004) 341–75.
———. *A Marginal Jew: Rethinking the Historical Jesus.* 5 vols. Anchor Yale Bible Reference Library. New York: Doubleday, 1991–2016.
———. "The Present State of the 'Third Quest' for the Historical Jesus: Loss and Gain." *Biblica* 80 (1999) 460–87.
Melanchthon, Philip. *The Loci Communes of Philip Melanchthon.* Translated by Charles Leander Hill. Boston: Meador, 1944.
Meyer, Ben F. *The Aims of Jesus.* London: SPCK, 1979.
Meyer, Marvin, and Charles Hughes, eds. *Jesus Then and Now.* Harrisburg, PA: Trinity, 2001.
Miller, Robert J., ed. *The Apocalyptic Jesus: A Debate.* Santa Rosa, CA: Polebridge, 2001.
Miranda, José Porfirio. *Being and the Messiah: The Message of St. John.* Translated by John Eagleson. 1987. Reprinted, Eugene: Wipf & Stock, 2006.
Morgan, David. "Would Jesus Have Sat for a Portrait? The Likeness of Christ in the Popular Reception of Warner Sallman's Art." *Criterion* 33/1 (Winter 1994) 11–17.
Morgan, Robert. "The Historical Jesus and the Theology of the New Testament." In *Studies in Christology in Memory of George Bradford Caird,* edited by L. D. Hurst and N. T. Wright, 187–206. Oxford: Clarendon, 1987.
Moser, Paul K., ed. *Jesus and Philosophy: New Essays.* Cambridge: Cambridge University Press, 2009.
Moxnes, Halvor. *Putting Jesus in His Place: A Radical Vision of Household and Kingdom.* Louisville: Westminster John Knox, 2003.
———. "The Theological Importance of the 'Third Quest' for the Historical Jesus." In *Whose Historical Jesus?,* edited by William E. Arnal and Michel Desjardins, 132–42. Studies in Christianity and Judaism 7. Waterloo, ON: Wilfrid Laurier University Press, 1997.
Moxnes, Halvor, et al., eds. *Jesus beyond Nationalism: Constructing the Historical Jesus in a Period of Cultural Complexity.* London: Equinox, 2009.
Neil, Stephen, and N. T. Wright. *The Interpretation of the New Testament.* 2nd ed. New York: Oxford University Press, 1988.

Neusner, Jacob. "Mr. Sanders's Pharisees and Mine." *Bulletin for Biblical Research* 2 (1992) 143–69.

———. *A Rabbi Talks with Jesus*. Montreal: McGill-Queen's University Press, 2000.

Newman, Carey C., ed. *Jesus and the Restoration of Israel: A Critical Assessment of N. T. Wright's "Jesus and the Victory of God."* Downer's Grove: InterVarsity, 1999.

Nodet, Etienne, OP. *The Historical Jesus? Necessity and Limits of an Inquiry*. Translated by J. Edward Crowley. Jewish and Christian Texts in Contexts and Related Studies 3. New York: T. & T. Clark, 2008.

Novick, Peter. *That Noble Dream: The "Objective Question" and the American Historical Profession*. Ideas in Context. Cambridge: Cambridge University Press, 1988.

O'Collins, Gerald. *Christology: A Biblical, Historical, and Systematic Study of Jesus*. Oxford: Oxford University Press, 1995.

Ogden, Schubert M. *The Point of Christology*. San Francisco: Harper & Row, 1982.

Olson, Alan M., ed. *Myth, Symbol, and Reality*. Notre Dame: University of Notre Dame Press, 1980.

Overduin, Nick. Review of *The Jesus Quest*, by Ben Witherington, III. *Calvin Theological Journal* 33 (1998) 200–205.

Pannenberg, Wolfhart. *Basic Questions in Theology*. Vol. 1. Translated by George H. Kehm. Philadelphia: Westminster, 1970.

———. *Jesus—God and Man*. Translated by Lewis L. Wilkins and Duane A. Priebe. Philadelphia: Westminster, 1968.

Patterson, Stephen J. "The End of Apocalypse." *Theology Today* 52 (1995) 29–58.

———. *The God of Jesus: The Historical Jesus and the Search for Meaning*. Harrisburg, PA: Trinity, 1998.

———. *The Gospel of Thomas and Jesus*. Foundations & Facets: Reference Series. Sonoma, CA: Polebridge, 1993.

———. "Pensive Provocation." *Living Pulpit* 9/3 (July–Sept 2000) 10–11.

Patterson, Stephen J., et al., eds. *The Search for Jesus: Modern Scholarship Looks at the Gospels*. Washington DC: Biblical Archaeology Society, 1994.

Pearson, Birger A. "The Gospel according to the Jesus Seminar." *Religion* 25 (1995) 334.

Perkins, Pheme. "Jesus before Christianity: Cynic and Sage?" *Christian Century* (1993) 749–51.

Porter, Stanley E. *The Criteria for Authenticity in Historical-Jesus Research: Previous Discussion and New Proposals*. Journal for the Study of the New Testament Supplement Series 191. Sheffield: Sheffield Academic, 2004.

Powell, Mark Allan. *Jesus as a Figure in History: How Modern Historians View the Man from Galilee*. Louisville: Westminster John Knox, 1998.

Price, David W. *History Made, History Imagined: Contemporary Literature, Poiesis, and the Past*. Urbana: University of Illinois Press, 1999.

Rau, Eckhard. *Jesu—Freund von Zöllnern und Sündern: Eine methodenkristische Untersuchung*. Kohlhammer Theologie. Stuttgart: Kohlhammer, 2000.

———. *Perspektiven des Lebens Jesu: Plädoyer für die Anknüpfung an eine schwierige Forschungstradition*. Beiträge zur Wissenschaft vom Alten und Neuen Testament 203. Stuttgart: Kohlhammer, 2013.

Reagan, Charles E., ed. *Studies in the Philosophy of Paul Ricoeur*. Athens: Ohio University Press, 1979.

Reed, Jonathan L. "Galilean Archaeology and the Historical Jesus." In *SBL Seminar Papers* 33. Edited by Eugene H. Lovering, Jr. Atlanta: Scholars, 1994.

Reimarus, Hermann Samuel. *Reimarus, Fragments*. Translated by Ralph S. Fraser. Lives of Jesus Series. Philadelphia: Fortress, 1970.

Reiser, Marius. *Kritische Geschichte der Jesusforschung: Von Kelsos und Origenes bis heute*. Stuttgarter Bibelstudien 235. Stuttgart: Katholisches Bibelwerk, 2015.

———. *Der unbequeme Jesus*. Biblisch-theologische Studien 122. Neukirchen-Vluyn: Neukirchener, 2011.

Riches, John K. *Jesus and the Transformation of Judaism*. New York: Seabury, 1982.

———. "The Social World of Jesus." *Interpretation* 5 (2004) 376–93.

Ricoeur, Paul. *Essays on Biblical Interpretation*. Edited by Lewis S. Mudge. Philadelphia: Fortress, 1980.

———. *Fallible Man*. Translated by Charles Kelbley. Chicago: Regnery, 1995.

———. *Interpretation Theory: Discourse and the Surplus of Meaning*. Fort Worth: Texas Christian University Press, 1976.

Robinson, James M. "Jesus—From Easter to Valentinus (or to the Apostles' Creed)." *Journal of Biblical Literature* 101 (1982) 5–37.

———. *A New Quest of the Historical Jesus*. Studies in Biblical Theology 1/25. Naperville: Allenson, 1959.

Robinson, James M., and Helmut Koester. *Trajectories through Early Christianity*. 1971. Reprint, Eugene, OR: Wipf & Stock, 2006.

Rohrbach, Richard L., ed. *Social Sciences and New Testament Interpretation*. Peabody, MA: Hendrickson, 1996.

Rousseau, John J., and Rami Arav. *Jesus and His World: An Archaeological and Cultural Dictionary*. Minneapolis: Fortress, 1994.

Sanders, E. P. *The Historical Figure of Jesus*. London: Penguin, 1993.

———. *Jesus and Judaism*. Philadelphia: Fortress, 1985.

Schaberg, Jane. *The Illegitimacy of Jesus: A Feminist Theological Interpretation of the Infancy Narratives*. San Francisco: Harper & Row, 1987.

Schleiermacher Friedrich. *A Brief Outline of Theology*. Translated by Terrence N. Tice. Atlanta: John Knox, 1977.

Scholl, Norbert. *Jesus von Nazaret: Was wir wissen, was wir glauben können*. Feldafing: Schneider, 2012.

Schröter, Jens. *Jesus von Nazaret: Jude aus Galiläa—Retter der Welt*. Leipzig: Evangelische Verlangsanstalt, 2006.

Schüssler Fiorenza, Elisabeth. *In Memory of Her: A Feminist Theological Reconstruction of Christian Origins*. New York: Crossroads, 1983.

———. *Jesus and the Politics of Interpretation*. New York: Continuum, 2000.

———, ed. *Searching the Scriptures*. New York: Crossroad, 1993.

Schweiker, William. *Mimetic Reflections: A Study in Hermeneutics, Theology, and Ethics*. New York: Fordham University Press, 1990.

Schweitzer, Albert. *The Quest of the Historical Jesus*. 1st complete edition. Edited by John Bowden. Fortress Classics in Biblical Studies. Minneapolis: Fortress, 2001.

———. *The Quest of the Historical Jesus: A Critical Study of Its Progress from Reimarus to Wrede*. Translated by W. Montgomery. New York: Macmillan, 1968.

Sebeok, Thomas A., ed. *Myth: A Symposium*. Bloomington: Indiana University Press, 1974.

Segal, Robert A. *Myth*. New York: Oxford University Press, 2004.

Segovia, Fernando F., and Mary Ann Tolbert, eds. *Teaching the Bible: The Discourses and Politics of Biblical Pedagogy*. Maryknoll, NY: Orbis, 1998.

Sellow, Philip E. "Early Collections of Jesus' Words: The Development of Dominical Discourses." PhD diss., Harvard Divinity School, 1986.
Simpson, Benjamin I. *Recent Research on the Historical Jesus*. Recent Research in Biblical Studies 6. Sheffield: Sheffield Phoenix, 2014.
Smith, Jonathan Z. *Drudgery Divine: On the Comparison of Early Christianities and the Religions of Late Antiquity*. Chicago Studies in the History of Judaism. Chicago: University of Chicago Press, 1990.
Smith, Morton. *Jesus the Magician*. San Francisco: Harper & Row, 1978.
Spangenberg, Volker, and André Heinze, eds. *Der historische Jesus im Spannungsfeld von Glaube und Geschichte*. Leipzig: Evangelische Verlagsanstalt, 2010.
Stegemann, Ekkehard W., and Wolfgang Stegemann. *The Jesus Movement: A Social History of Its First Century*. Translated by O. C. Dean Jr. Minneapolis: Fortress, 2001.
Stein, Robert H. *The Method and Message of Jesus' Teachings*. Louisville: Westminster John Knox, 1994.
Stewart, Robert B. *Memories of Jesus: A Critical Appraisal of James D. G. Dunn's "Jesus Remembered."* Nashville: B&H Academic, 2010.
———, ed. *The Message of Jesus: John Dominic Crossan and Ben Witherington III in Dialogue*. Minneapolis: Fortress, 2013.
———. *The Quest of the Hermeneutical Jesus: The Impact of Hermeneutics on the Jesus Research of John Dominic Crossan and N. T. Wright*. Lanham, MD: University Press of America, 2008.
Strauss, David Friedrich. *The Life of Jesus Critically Examined*. Translated by George Eliot. Edited and with an introduction by Peter C. Hodgson. Lives of Jesus Series. Philadelphia: Fortress, 1972.
Taylor, Vincent. *The Life and Ministry of Jesus*. New York: Abingdon, 1955.
Theissen, Gerd. *Jesus als historische Gestalt: Beiträge zur Jesusforschung. Zum 60. Geburtstag von Gerd Theissen*. Edited by Annette Merz. Forschungen zur Religion und Literatur des Alten und Neuen Testaments 202. Göttingen: Vandenhoeck & Ruprecht, 2003.
———. *Sociology of Early Palestinian Christianity*. Translated by John Bowden. Philadelphia: Fortress, 1978.
Theissen, Gerd, and Annette Merz. *The Historical Jesus: A Comprehensive Guide*. Translated by John Bowden. Minneapolis: Fortress, 1998.
Thiede, Carsten Peter. *Jesus und Tiberius: Zwei Söhne Gottes*. Munich: Luchterhand, 2004.
Thompson, Thomas L. *The Messiah Myth: The Near Eastern Roots of Jesus and David*. New York: Basic Books, 2005.
Thompson, Thomas L., and Thomas S. Verenna, eds. *"Is This Not the Carpenter?" The Question of the Historicity of the Figure of Jesus*. Copenhagen International Seminar. Sheffield: Equinox, 2012.
Tolbert, Mary Ann. *Sowing the Gospel: Mark's Work in Literary Historical Perspective*. Minneapolis: Fortress, 1996.
Troeltsch, Ernst. *Die Bedeutung der Geschichtlichkeit Jesus für den Glauben*. Tübingen: Mohr/Siebeck, 1929.
Twelftree, Graham H. *Jesus the Exorcist: A Contribution to the Study of the Historical Jesus*. Peabody, MA: Hendrickson, 1994.
Tyrrell, George. *Christianity at the Crossroads*. London: Longmans, Green, 1909.

Van Ness, Peter H. *Spirituality and the Secular Quest*. New York: Crossroad, 1996.
Vermes, Geza. *The Authentic Gospel of Jesus*. London: Penguin, 2004.
———. *The Changing Face of Jesus*. London: Lane, 2000.
———. *Jesus the Jew: A Historian's Reading of the Gospels*. 1973. Reprint, Philadelphia: Fortress, 1981.
———. *The Religion of Jesus the Jew*. Minneapolis: Fortress, 1993.
Voigt, Emilio. *Die Jesusbewegung: Hintergründe ihrer Entstehung und Ausbreitung—eine historische-exegetische Undersuchung über die Motive der Jesusnachfolge*. Beiträge zur Wissenschaft vom Alten und Neuen Testament 169. Stuttgart: Kohlhammer, 2008.
Walsh, W. H. *Philosophy of History: An Introduction*. Harper Torchbooks. New York: Harper, 1960.
Weaver, Walter P. *The Historical Jesus in the Twentieth Century: 1900–1950*. Harrisburg, PA: Trinity, 1999.
Weiss, Johannes. *Jesus' Proclamation of the Kingdom of God*. Translated by Richard Hyde Hiers and David Larrimore Holland. Lives of Jesus Series. Philadelphia: Fortress, 1971.
Wells, G. A. *The Historical Evidence for Jesus*. Buffalo: Prometheus, 1982.
———. *The Jesus Myth*. Chicago: Open Court, 1998.
Wengst, Klaus. *Der wirkliche Jesus? Eine Streitschrift über die historisch wenig ergiebige und theologisch sinnlose Suche nach dem "historischen" Jesus*. Stuttgart: Kohlhammer, 2013.
White, Morton. *Foundations of Historical Knowledge*. Beijing: Rainbow-Bridge, 1965.
Wilken, Robert L. *The Myth of Christian Beginnings: History's Impact on Belief*. 1971. Reprint, Notre Dame, IN: University of Notre Dame Press, 1980.
Windschuttle, Keith. *The Killing of History: How Literary Critics Are Murdering Our Past*. Pittsburgh: Encounter, 1994.
Witherington, Ben, III. *The Christology of Jesus*. Minneapolis: Fortress, 1990.
———. *The Jesus Quest: The Third Search for the Jew of Nazareth*. Downers Grove, IL: InterVarsity, 1997.
———. *Jesus the Sage: The Pilgrimage of Wisdom*. Minneapolis: Fortress, 1994.
———. *What Have They Done with Jesus? Beyond Strange Theories and Bad History—Why We Can Trust the Bible*. San Francisco: HarperSanFrancisco, 2006.
Wrede, William. *The Messianic Secret*. Translated by J. C. G. Greig. Library of Theological Translations. Cambridge: James Clarke, 1971.
Wright, N. T. *Jesus and the Victory of God*. Christian Origins and the Question of God 2. Minneapolis: Fortress, 1996.
———. "The New, Unimproved Jesuses." *Christianity Today* 37/10 (Sept. 13, 1993) 22–26.
———. "Quest for the Historical Jesus." In *Abingdon Dictionary of the Bible* 3 (1992) 796–802.
Zannoni, Arthur E., ed. *Jews & Christians Speak of Jesus*. Minneapolis: Fortress, 1994.
Zeller, Dieter. *Kommentar zur Logienquelle*. Stuttgarter kleiner Kommentar: Neues Testament 21. Stuttgart: Katholisches Bibelwerk, 1984.

www.ingramcontent.com/pod-product-compliance
Lightning Source LLC
Chambersburg PA
CBHW021654230426
43668CB00008B/623